W9-CBK-208

275

POPULAR
LITURGI-
CAL
LIBRARY

The Church's

YEAR OF GRACE

by

DR. PIUS PARSCH

TRANSLATED BY
Reverend William G. Heidt, O.S.B.

Volume 5
September, October, November

THE LITURGICAL PRESS
ST. JOHN'S ABBEY   COLLEGEVILLE, MINNESOTA

Nihil obstat: John Eidenschink, O.S.B., J.C.D., *Censor deputatus. Imprimi potest*: ✠ Baldwin Dworschak, O.S.B., Abbot of St. John's Abbey. *Imprimatur*: ✠ Peter W. Bartholome, D.D., Bishop of St. Cloud, August 22, 1958. Copyright 1958 by The Order of St. Benedict, Inc., Collegeville, Minnesota.

Printed by The North Central Publishing Company, St. Paul.

The Proper of the Season

TWELFTH SUNDAY AFTER PENTECOST

Christ, the merciful Samaritan

During the coming week the picture of Christ as merciful Samaritan who nurses and heals the wounds of holy Church will be uppermost in our thoughts; and the commandment to which we will give zealous attention will be the first and greatest — that of love toward God and neighbor. So may it be a week framed by love and mercy.

1. **Content Structure.** A similarity that is quickly evident exists between the present Mass text and last Sunday's, even though today's formulary lacks a festive and joyous spirit. Thought unity too is hardly present, for neither the Readings nor the chants chime well together. The only perceivable sequence arises from the reference to Moses as a type in the Epistle and Offertory verse, and from the contrast between the old and the new Covenants (*Epist.* and *Gosp.*). Still the whole glistens like a colorful mosaic.

2. **Holy Mass** (Deus, in adjutorium). Today's Mass is far from being charged with that triumphant Easter joy proper to last

Sunday's text; rather we see mankind hastening to God's sanctuary sorrily in need of redemption. For centuries the *Introit* has been man's cry in distress; its first verses are used at the beginning of each hour of Divine Office, and the whole psalm is prayed in connection with the Litany of the Saints. (We will pray the entire psalm both for ourselves and in the name of unredeemed humanity.) In the *Collect* Mother Church teaches us to extend our hands in prayer "that we may run without stumbling towards the divine promises."

The Readings and the Offertory have this in common that they compare the new Covenant with the old and place the former high above the latter. Taken historically the *Epistle* is somewhat difficult to apply, but understood liturgically it describes not only the glory of the new Moses, Jesus Christ, who now in the holy Sacrifice steps before us in all the brightness of His splendor, but also the excellence of God's kingdom which the Holy Spirit is giving us through the instrumentality of Mother Church. Of ourselves we are helpless creatures because "our sufficiency comes from God," from Christ, from the *pneuma*, from the Holy Spirit "who bestows life." After our Sunday Mass we should be able to face daily life fearlessly, fortified, as we are, by the grace and glory granted to God's children.

The *Gradual* expresses heartfelt thanks for the glory that has been given to us. A rare combination is that had in the *Alleluia* verse: sorrow and distress in an Alleluia setting (pray the entire psalm, it is the saddest in the psalter). We may think of the Church in her present sufferings awaiting future resurrection; perhaps your own soul must sing in a similar key. Gradual and Alleluia have again exchanged their proper places today.

A *Gospel* extraordinarily rich in thought nuances compensates for the somewhat abstruse Epistle; more fortunate than the prophets and kings of old are we, for today in the Sacrifice we may again behold Redemption's work accomplished; we are "they who see and hear" (recall last Sunday's *Ephpheta*). The parable became clothed with reality through Christ's work on Calvary, a reality that takes place again today at the altar, for while we are gathered together in this true πανδοχειον or "inn,"

Jesus pours oil and wine (i.e., the sacraments, holy Eucharist) into our wounds. In today's holy Mass we see our Redeemer, Jesus the good Samaritan, paying our ransom, paying the price of our health upon the Cross.

The *Offertory* singles out a figure from the Old Testament, Moses, the mediator and reconciler between Yahweh and the Israelites, a telling figure of our cross-laden Savior. The *Secret* and *Postcommunion* touch upon the expiatory character of the Mass and implore forgiveness. Again the *Communion* is a beautiful Eucharistic hymn, with a timely allusion to the harvest now in progress in field and countryside. The three principal parts of this Mass, Epistle, Gospel, Offertory, underscore its three major functions; like Moses, the great mediator, Christ, the merciful Samaritan, pleads for sinful men; He heals us from the wounds of sin, and He fills us with the brightness of His glory.

3. Divine Office. Since the thoughts of man's heart form the theme of his songs, Mother Church prompts her children to sing portions from the Gospel as the day's greater antiphons. In the morning eternal Truth answers our question with: "You must love the Lord your God with your whole heart, alleluia." In the evening the beginning of the parable is sung: "A certain man went down from Jerusalem to Jericho and fell among robbers; having stripped and wounded him, they went away, leaving him half dead." The homily on the Gospel is from the quill of St. Bede the Venerable (d. 735).

4. The Offertory. The text of today's Offertory, consisting of a single verse, forms but a tiny relic of the chant which the Roman Church once sang during the Offertory procession. Since the movement of an entire congregation would take considerable time, the greater part of an entire psalm was frequently employed. Gradually, however, the Offertory procession lost favor, with the result that less text was needed; some of these intermediate Offertories are preserved for us in ancient antiphonaries. Finally a single verse remained, that in our present missals. Nevertheless, for a full understanding of the Mass the more complete text is often necessary. Of special importance is the so-called *repetenda*, the refrain or verse repeated after each strophe, which often betrays the theme. Both from a literary and a musical viewpoint today's Offertory belongs to the more significant chants in the missal. In its original form it reads:

Moses prayed in the sight of the Lord his God, and said:
Why, Lord, is your wrath blazing up against your people?
Do turn from the fierce anger within you.
Remember Abraham, Isaac, and Jacob;
to them you swore to give a land flowing with milk and honey.

And the Lord was appeased from doing the evil
he had threatened to inflict upon his people.

Then the Lord said to Moses:
You have found favor before my eyes
and for no one have I greater esteem.
In haste Moses flung himself upon the earth and prayed, saying:
I know that you are merciful
and that you blot out sins and injustices a thousand times.

And the Lord was appeased from doing the evil
he had threatened to inflict upon his people.

Moses and Aaron spoke to the whole gathering of the sons of Israel:
Draw near to God. The majesty of the Lord appeared in the clouds;
he has heard your murmurings in due time.

And the Lord was appeased from doing the evil
he had threatened to inflict upon his people.

It is easily seen how dramatic the chant becomes when arranged in this manner, and how its message of Moses as type of Christ in His sacrifice of propitiation is brought into sharp relief.

5. **Sunday Meditation.** A. What the holy Sacrifice means and what it effects can best be learned from the Mass text itself, for in it Mother Church has placed her most profound reflections. And certainly you know that it is her most earnest wish that

you understand the Mass well and co-offer it with her to the best of your ability. In the Mass the river of redemption's graces flows unobstructed into your soul, perfecting the sanctification begun by baptism. Therefore, do not think that you have already plumbed the depths, that through baptism you have become a perfect Christian. At baptism the sprout was ingrafted; but its growth, its foliage, its flowers and its fruit are due to the holy Eucharist. Baptism and Eucharist are the two great fountains of divine life which assure your salvation. What today's holy Mass brings you specially is given in three pictures.

First picture. The Gospel recounts the immortal parable of the merciful Samaritan. By this parable Jesus wished to teach a lesson concerning the love of neighbor, but the Church uses it to illustrate His own activity at holy Mass. The man who fell among robbers is poor human nature robbed of its supernatural endowments, weakened in its natural powers, lying prostrate in utter misery. The Jewish Law passes by, for it can effect no healing. The humble God-Man, Jesus, the good and merciful Samaritan, comes and picks up the poor, wounded man. He pours oil and wine into his wounds, takes him to an inn, and cares for him. This is the work of salvation. It is also the work of the Mass.

Now let us see lying there not mankind but our own selves, myself, yourself. In baptism, at every Mass the good Samaritan comes to you, picks you up. Your nature is still inclined to evil, you still bleed from many wounds, you are still weak and helpless and of yourself cannot "hasten to the divine promises" (*Coll.*). In the holy Eucharist, however, Jesus pours oil and wine into your wounds — oil, the sweet, and wine, the bitter tenets of Christian teaching. He dresses your wounds and cares for you as a father. Be convinced that at Mass your soul's wounds are healed. Doesn't this beautiful parable of the good Samaritan excellently sketch the fruit of today's sacred liturgy?

Second picture. The Gospel depicts the effects of the holy Sacrifice somewhat negatively; the Epistle presents its fruits more positively. The Epistle compares the old and the new Covenant. In the old Law the letter was paramount; in the new, spirit or πνεῦμα. St. Paul says: The countenance of Moses became so radiant from his interview with God that the children of Israel could not behold his face. But if the new Law is more perfect than the old, how indescribably more radiant must the face of a Christian be, since at each Mass he beholds the God-Man's face; incomparably more resplendent must the faces of God's children be after their meeting with Jesus at the holy Banquet. Yes, this is the fruit of holy Communion, that it transfigures us. Of course, as long as we are upon earth that glory is hidden, veiled; nevertheless it is present, and no one could face the sight of a soul in the brightness of that glory. Feel convinced that you depart from Mass into the workaday world with a face radiant, beaming, and a soul transfigured.

Third picture. The Offertory, heralding Moses as the mediator for the sons of Israel, forms the third tableau. While Moses was upon Mount Sinai speaking with God, the Israelites fashioned for themselves a gold-plated bull and worshipped before it. It was sufficient reason for Yahweh to break His covenant with them, but Moses pleaded in behalf of his unfaithful fellow men and the divine wrath abated. The message for us? Moses was the forerunner of Christ, the true and eternal Mediator and Peacemaker. Through every Mass (which is Christ's atoning sacrifice on Calvary made present here and now) "the Lord is appeased from doing the evil He had threatened to inflict upon His people."

Thus with startling clarity the effects and fruits of holy Mass are shown in three memorable scenes: the good Samaritan heals the wounds of our souls; we gaze upon Christ's glorified face and retain the radiance of that glory with us for daily life; and lastly, God wills to be appeased through the mediation of Christ, the divine Moses.

B. Christ and Christians. To the question, "About what does the liturgy speak most?," the reply could quickly be given: The liturgy loves most to speak of the bridegroom Christ and of His bride, the faithful; for the lips must tell that of which the heart is full. In the first half of the Church year the liturgical texts are constantly treating of and glorifying Christ. During

Advent it is "He is coming"; at Christmas, "He is here, He has appeared"; at Easter, "He has died for us and has risen again; He has ascended into heaven and is sending the Holy Spirit." During the time after Pentecost, however, greater attention is accorded to His Bride, to His Church. It should be profitable to consider briefly what today's liturgy has to say about us Christians and about Christ.

1) Christians. Again today the soul is pictured as she really is: on the one hand poor, pursued, sin-stained; on the other, a fortunate, transfigured child of God. With many petitions and with manifold needs we approach the house of God; the wicked enemy is following in hot pursuit. "O God, hasten to my aid. . . . I am needy and poor, Lord, stand by me." Too well do we know this aspect of human life. Of himself and by himself man is nothing, always afflicted and destitute; but the Collect already points to a brighter side: "with Thy grace are we able to serve Thee worthily." If we use God's gifts, a sublime destiny awaits us, an end called *promises* by the liturgy. We know what these promises are: grace here and glory hereafter.

In substance the very same point is made in the Epistle. True, of ourselves we are nothing, incapable to think or do anything; but with the grace of God we are strong. "Our sufficiency is from God." Then follows a comparison: as the face of Moses beamed radiantly after communicating with Yahweh on the mount, so the spiritual appearance of God's children is changed by communion with Christ Jesus their Lord. How the countenances of the just will shine in heaven when that glory becomes fully manifest! These are the promises after which we ought hasten! Every Sunday, every Mass leads us closer to that glory.

The twofold nature in the child of God is well shown in the Alleluia chant, for it is a song of sorrow in a joyous Alleluia setting: "Alleluia, alleluia. In Your presence, O Lord, my God and Savior, I cry day and night. Alleluia." Such is Christian life upon earth — pain and suffering transfigured by Easter Alleluias!

In the Gospel too the Church tells her children many things. She praises them as blessed because they partake of the Eucharistic mystery, because they are permitted to see and to hear their Lord. She places in their hearts the twofold commandment of love. She teaches them who their neighbor is, be he friend or enemy in need of assistance. Note too that the man who fell wounded among robbers represents mankind, mankind without Christ; yet he is given a Physician and Savior who is deeply concerned, who takes him to the inn of the Church and cares for him.

Let us summarize what today's Mass says of the individual Christian. Of himself poor, he goes through life subject to many needs and much suffering; yet in his soul he bears the beginnings of beatitude and hastens onward toward its perfect attainment. Of this the Alleluia is a fine expression: deep earthly suffering suffused and transfigured by Easter joy.

2) *Christ.* Now let us consider what the liturgy says about Christ. It places Him before us in two scenes, as Moses and as the good Samaritan.

It is in the Epistle that Christ is first compared to Moses. The comparison is an ancient one for Yahweh Himself used it when speaking to Moses: "I will raise up for them a prophet resembling you." And Christ spoke in similar terms: "Moses did not give you bread from heaven, but My Father gives us the true bread from heaven."

Between these two prophets there are many points of similarity. Moses fed the Chosen People with manna, he struck the rock with a rod, he led Israel through the Red Sea and through the wilderness into the Promised Land; he gave them the Law, he ordered the immolation of the paschal lamb. All these acts are readily applicable to Christ. But the Epistle employs a different approach. The radiant face of Moses prefigured our glorified Savior who in majesty is enthroned at God's right hand, who appears during Mass in all the splendor of His glory.

Another picture of Moses is given in the Offertory verse. It tells a whole story. When the Chosen People became unfaithful and worshipped before the golden calf, God determined to reject them; but Moses besought forgiveness and appeased the divine wrath. Here Moses prefigured Christ, who through His death upon the Cross became the great Mediator and Intercessor, and who at every Mass utters the perfect prayer of expiation.

Today's Mass presents Christ to us in still another picture, an exceptionally beautiful one, the parable of the good Samaritan. Who was the unfortunate victim of robbers? Mankind. And the priests of Levi and all the precepts of the old Law could provide no effective aid. Then Jesus, the divine Samaritan, appeared in the form of a humble servant, poured oil and wine in his wounds and carried him to an inn. Christ could not have portrayed His work more poignantly.

Whatever the liturgy wishes to tell us about Christ and about ourselves is excellently summed up in this parable. The souls of men, despoiled by robbers, are the objects of His special solicitude. Like the good and merciful Samaritan, He takes them to shelter and cares for them. Jesus is actually doing this now at holy Mass. The inn is the Church, the medicine is the holy Eucharist. Only permit Him to heal you!

THIRTEENTH SUNDAY AFTER PENTECOST

From Easter Eve to Sunday Mass

Two contrary moods dominate today's liturgy, the one grave, earnest, pleading, sad; the other joyous, thankful. Of special importance in understanding the Mass in its present form are the three chants taken from Psalm 73 (*Intr., Grad., Comm.*), which give the day its sombre, sober spirit; while the Gospel's drama-miracle is best understood as a vivid visualization of the sacrifice-mystery being enacted at the altar.

1. Content Structure. This Mass is the third in that trilogy which has the Church's life as its object, viz., baptism, sacramental living, holy Eucharist (see eleventh Sunday after Pentecost). Perhaps it is the antithesis between the old Law and the new, between Jew and Gentile found in the two Readings which

gives today's formulary a certain inner unity and a semblance to last Sunday's. Again today the Gospel gives the Samaritans precedence over the Jews. The formulary's leit-motif is Psalm 73, a psalm lamenting a national disaster; some joyous strains, however, may be detected.

2. Holy Mass (Respice, Domine). Let us begin with the *Gospel*. We see ten lepers healed by Christ, nine of whom simply vanish after their cure, while the tenth, a Samaritan, returns singing his gratitude to the Lord. What does the Church wish to convey by the narrative? Here again we have a good example of "mystery" in liturgy, for it is not the Church's primary intention to inculcate a lesson on gratitude; she wishes rather to unravel the meaning of Sunday Mass and its sanctifying efficacy. Sunday is Easter, the day of baptism; and its Mass effects the renewal of baptismal graces. In the ten healed lepers we must see a figure of the baptized. Recall that in the ancient Church adults were baptized on Easter eve, and that ever since, the baptized in the eyes of the Church are considered men cleansed in the baptismal font from the leprosy of original sin. Moreover, every Sunday witnesses the renewal of the graces of baptism, for the Eucharistic banquet reinforces the substructure of baptism, completing and perfecting it.

The Eucharist too is subtly portrayed in today's Gospel. Of the ten who were healed one returned "with a loud voice glorifying God, and he fell on his face before His feet, *thanking* Him (εὐχαριστῶν αὐτῷ); "Eucharist" means giving thanks. Sunday Mass is a thanksgiving liturgy celebrated by the fortunate few who have been healed from the leprosy of sin. Let us sum up the significance of Sunday. It is the day on which we should praise God with loud voices, a day of thanksgiving for the grace of baptism, a harvest day for the soul, a day on which it receives an "increase of faith, of hope, and of charity" (*Coll.*), an "increase of eternal redemption" (*Postc.*). So much for a better understanding of the Gospel.

In the person of the grateful leper have we been prefigured who now come to the holy Sacrifice. For this morning "the Lord enters a certain town," His Church. We "go to meet

Him" and He heals us from the leprosy of sin, He seeks to give us freshening graces during the Sacrifice and its Banquet. This is the joyous and lightsome feature of the Gospel. There also is a sad, dark side — Jesus complaining over the ingratitude of "the other nine." These represent lukewarm Christians who, though baptized, no longer practice their faith, no longer offer Sunday Mass (in some countries nine out of ten might not be too high an estimate). This, our Savior's complaint, links the Gospel to the melancholy chant of Psalm 73.

A well-phrased *Collect* pleads for basic Christian virtues; "growth in faith, hope, and love" constitutes that renewal and deepening in the graces of baptism of which mention has been made. We plead not merely to be enabled to fulfill God's will but to *love* His commands. The *Epistle* (perhaps the most vexing passage in the whole missal) teaches that we have become God's children through grace alone without any merit on our part. At the *Offertory* procession we place in God's hands, together with the usual Offertory gift, our whole life's fortune: "My times are in Your hands."

At the consecration Jesus appears and heals us sinners from leprosy, while in the sacrificial Banquet He gives "increase in eternal redemption — *redemptionis aeternae augmentum*." And at the *Ite missa est* He sends us away as other Samaritans to act out a true Christian life: "Arise and go. . . ." But do take time to notice the excellent *Communion* verse which extols the holy Eucharist as the Manna full of sweetness. — This Mass could well be entitled "From Easter Eve to Sunday Mass," for its texts point up the intimate relation of Sunday Mass to holy baptism. Sundays are links in the chain binding the two great days of life, the day of baptism and the day of death — our two birthdays, that unto grace and that unto glory.

Certainly it is not the mind of the Church that we should touch upon the Gospel merely during the Mass; rather we ought use it as inspiration for the entire day. Therefore, as the sun rises at Lauds Jesus enters a certain town, i.e., the Church, and we, the lepers, go to meet Him: "As Jesus entered a certain town, there met Him ten men who were lepers. They stood afar off and lifted up their voice, saying: Jesus, Master, have mercy on us!" (*Ben. Ant.*). Our evening song voices our gratitude for being healed: "And one of them, when he saw that he was made clean, went back with a loud voice glorifying God, alleluia." There follows a thanksgiving canticle, the Magnificat.

3. Sunday Meditation. A. Psalm 73. To appreciate fully today's holy Mass it is necessary to know Psalm 73. It reads:

I. *Stricken by misfortunes*

Why, O God, have you rejected us so completely?
  Why does your wrath flare up against the lambs
    in your own pasture?
Give some thought at least to your people,
    your own possession from the beginning,
      one which you redeemed as a personal inheritance.
Think of Mount Sion,
    which you made your dwelling-place.
Raise up your hand against their insolence,
    see how the enemy has desecrated the sanctuary.

How they who hate you swagger about,
  on the very sites of your sacred feasts!
Their standards they have erected as trophies;
  with axes they hacked down the gates as in a woods,
  with hatchet and ax they smashed their way in.
Your sanctuary they set on fire,
  desecrating to the dust the dwelling-place of your name.
Together they agreed, that hellish brood:
  "We will abolish God's feasts throughout this land."
No longer do we witness wonders as once we did;
  no prophet arises, and no one knows what still will come.

II. *Confident of divine assistance*

How long will the enemy continue to scoff?
  how long will he continue to blaspheme your name?
Why do you hold back your hand?
  and hide your right hand in your bosom?
Surely you, O God, have been our king for ages;
  marvels you have wrought in this land.
The sea, you have cloven it by your power,
  dragon heads, you crushed them on the waters.
You smote Leviathan,
  made him food for beasts in the wilderness.
You caused streams to flow,
  and dried up the ever-flowing rivers.
To you belongs the day, and to you the night,
  you fashioned the dawn and the sun.
You fixed the boundaries of the earth,
  summer and spring are your creation.

III. *The sufferer pleads*

Should, then, the enemy scoff at you,
  a godless people revile your name?
Do not abandon to wild beasts the souls of your
      faithful ones,
  or be utterly unmindful of your poor.

Your covenant, honor it;
    and do not permit the oppressed to be put to shame.
    Make the poor and the needy praise your Name.
Bestir yourself, O God, and safeguard your interests,
    note the insults sinners are constantly heaping
        upon you.
Do not disregard the haughty yelling of your foes,
    insolence that grows continually bolder.

This psalm, one of the gloomiest in the psalter, describes a sad phase in Israelitic history. Enemies had penetrated into the temple precincts, demolishing, destroying, desecrating. The psalmist sought to console himself by recalling past marvels. God had once freed His people from Egypt and had annihilated their enemies. A meditation upon nature follows; the beauty of the dawn, the sun, spring and its splendor are the works of God. Strengthened by these considerations, he pours forth to heaven a heartfelt plea for help.

We may ask, what are the Church's intentions in employing this psalm? The desecrated temple represents God's holy kingdom, Christ's mystical Body, pursued by enemies, defiled through sin. Mother Church is thinking of those children who no longer fulfill their duty of thanksgiving on Sunday; and for these, our lukewarm fellow Christians, we will pray this psalm. Three times during the Mass we will link our hearts to its public recitation: upon entering the Lord's house, at the Gospel, and at the Communion. Our spirit of gratitude will help smoothen the lines of grief on the brow of Mother Church.

B. The Gospel story. Our Savior completed His mission in Galilee about four months before His death, not long after the transfiguration. Then He left that country, not to appear there again till after His resurrection. On His way to Jerusalem Jesus entered a town in whose neighborhood was a leper colony. The victims of that dreadful disease, still common in the Orient, literally rot away as member after member falls off. Because of its contagious character, Mosaic Law had decreed that lepers live apart and avoid all contact with the clean. When they wished to speak with someone, they were obliged to remain at a distance and give notice of their miserable lot. Ten such outcasts, all of whom belonged to the same colony, met Jesus as He journeyed along. "Standing afar off" they called upon Him to help: "Jesus, Master, have mercy on us" (the Greek original, *eleison*, is the same as in our *Kyrie, eleison* — Lord, have mercy). Without further ado Jesus sent them to the priests whose office it was to declare lepers clean. For it was prescribed in the Law of Moses that anyone seemingly cured of leprosy must appear before the priests; it was their duty to make a thorough examination and to decide whether such was actually the case. After the examination the one-time leper was shorn and subjected to a thorough washing; then he presented an offering of two sparrows, three lambs and a food-offering according to the Law, and the priest declared him clean; only upon the completion of such ritual was he again allowed to associate freely with others.

But Jesus sent the ten to the priests unhealed. It was to try their faith, for He demanded some evidence of faith in connection with most any favor. All ten withstood the test and were healed upon the way. Of these, nine were Jews, and one a Samaritan. Upon realizing the miracle, the Samaritan returned to Jesus even before reporting to the priests; he thanked his Benefactor sincerely, falling down on his face before Him and praising God with a loud voice. This Samaritan, this stranger, this half-Jew put the other nine Jews to shame; for they did not consider it worth the trouble to return and show thanks. In sorrow Jesus noted their conduct and saw in it a type of the ingratitude and fickleness of the Jewish people, who cast away from themselves His mercy and grace, while strangers, pagans joyfully accepted the good news of the kingdom.

The miracle occurred soon after their departure from Jesus; they could easily have returned if they had wanted to pay their debt of gratitude. Reflect at some length upon Jesus' sorrowful complaint over the ingratitude of "the other nine." For this certainly is the key verse in the whole account. Jesus is seeking the gratitude of men, not for Himself, but for God. And He asks it especially from His own.

C. On gratitude. Gratitude is one of the more important virtues that should adorn a child of God. It is a sign of a noble soul, for only a good man will be grateful. There is a proverb about ingratitude being the world's reward. An egotistic, selfish society ignores this virtue. Thankfulness is related to faithfulness. Therefore let us be grateful to everyone who has benefited us, especially our parents. The evil others have inflicted upon us we will write in sand, but the good with which they have blessed us we will carve in marble!

In the first place we will be thankful to God not by way of some few isolated acts but with a constant spirit of gratitude. How beautifully it is put in the preface of the Mass: "It is truly fitting and right . . . that we at all times and in all places give thanks. . . ."

Think of the many blessings which have been accorded you. First, your natural faculties; your life is a chain of gifts, for without God you could not continue existing a split second. Every member of your body, eyes, ears, hands, are His gift to you. And visible nature in all its loveliness. Every flower, every blade of grass is calling: "I am God's gift to you." The splendor of nature God created for your enjoyment. In fact, nature is a picture book given you by your heavenly Father that in it you may see a wholly different world. And still greater blessings are yours, for you are God's own child, called by Him to heavenly joys, to a divine kingdom. Church, sacraments, ecclesiastical year, sacred liturgy, the Redeemer are all for you, given to you that through them you may be eternally blessed. And so soon you do cease your song of thanks?

So far you have been grateful from motives of self-interest; proceed a step further now. You have reason and faith, and through reason and faith God permits you to gaze upon His glory, His love, His greatness, or at least to surmise His infinite attributes. Therefore you ought pray in the spirit of the *Gloria* at Mass: "We thank Thee for Thy own great glory," that is, "for Thy own great glory" as you now know it and as you shall learn to know it when once you shall see Him face to face.

A song of gratitude should be on our lips even in sufferings, even when we do not understand the ways of God, for we know that all that God wills is to our good. To be grateful when one's heart is bleeding is truly heroic!

Now we can more easily see why the sacred liturgy, the prayer of the Church, radiates gratitude. Each succeeding day of salvation is replete with prayers of thanksgiving. The Church's morning prayer (Lauds) and her evening prayer (Vespers) are *the* prayers of praise and thanks. Especially in the evening is she grateful when in that grand hymn of God's own Mother she sings her gratitude for all the blessings of salvation: "My soul magnifies the Lord!" Before the Son of God makes His appearance upon the altar at the consecration, the Church chants a hymn of thanks, the preface: "It is truly fitting and right, reasonable and salutary that *we give thanks* at all times and in all places. . . ." Every Mass is concluded with the response: *Deo gratias*, Thanks be to God! And the etymology of the word *Eucharist* is "good thanks." Never forget that the nobility proper to a Christian demands a spirit of gratitude toward God and men.

FOURTEENTH SUNDAY AFTER PENTECOST

Seek first the kingdom of God

Because of its Gospel this Sunday is sometimes called "Divine Providence Sunday." Its Readings for the last time highlight the differences between the two kingdoms, an antithesis today between the kingdom of the flesh and of mammon and the kingdom of the spirit, of God (*Epist.* and *Gosp.*). From the contrast the moral lesson is evident: cling to God with your whole soul! The Communion verse would serve well as the spiritual motto for the week: "Seek first the kingdom of God, and all other things shall be given you besides." This text is also used as the Magnificat antiphon at the close of the day's Office. At sunrise we hear Christ's consoling words: "Do not be anxious, wonder-

ing: What are we to eat? or, What are we to drink? Your
Father knows that you need all these things, alleluia" (*Ben.
Ant.*).

1. **Content Structure.** It seems that a new group of three
Sundays is beginning (indicated by the Introit psalms, 83, 85,
85), even though continuity in content is lacking. There is an
obvious parallelism between the two Scripture Readings, viz.,
works of the flesh — fruits of the spirit; God — Mammon. The
Collect's content betrays a similar structure: preservation from
that which is harmful and assistance toward that which is good.
The same pattern is noticeable in the Gradual: Lord — man,
God — princes.

2. **Holy Mass (Protector noster).** Another inspirational, joyous Mass! This morning the soul is filled with bridal happiness
after longing ardently to pass the "Lord's day" in the "courts of
the Lord," in His "dwelling-place." Now she enters her "home,"
calling down God's blessings upon His "anointed" (individual
souls; the members of the parish; the mystical Christ) in Psalm
83, one of the more glowing and fervent of entrance chants.
Yes, today's *Introit* would be a most appropriate prayer for any
visit to church: "How lovely is Your dwelling-place. . . . for
Your courts my spirit burns within me. . . ."

In full accord with the thought content of the Readings and
the child-like trust characteristic of the entire Mass we pray the
Collect: Preserve Thy Church by Thy constant mercy, for without Thee we are weak, ever prone toward the spirit of the world.
Man's soul is like a child learning to walk; without aid at every
step, it tumbles to the ground. Your assisting grace, Lord, must
effect two things: it must deter us from evil, as the angel de-
terred Lot from Sodom; and it must direct us to the good, as a
shepherd guides his sheep. In a word, grace upon grace is required to make us lead a saintly life (another thought-packed
Oration).

Now the apostle Paul rises to instruct us, and today he tells
us bluntly what is good and what is evil. He speaks of two kingdoms, the kingdom of the spirit and that of the flesh, the
kingdom of grace founded and grounded in the soul by the Holy

Spirit, and Satan's realm of sin. Within man's soul these two forces are battling, their trenches scarring the very core of every human heart. The apostle lists "the works of the flesh" as also the "fruits of the spirit," for every Christian is a tree planted by the Holy Spirit and destined to bear His priceless fruit. Life in Christ, it must be remembered, is no gay fling, rather a continuing struggle: "They who belong to Christ have crucified their flesh with its vices and its lusts!" Trust and confidence in God provide the "ultimate weapon."

Likewise in the *Gradual* may be seen two opposing principles, trust in God aligned against trust in princes. With the *Alleluia*, however, Easter jubilation floods in upon us, for in Easter's great Warrior our battle against the flesh is won. The Christian can make no compromises with the world, serving God to a degree while pilfering from Satan's dainties; for Christ demands utter reliance upon his Father's gracious providence in today's *Gospel*, certainly one of the loveliest passages in Holy Writ. What endless consolation this Gospel narrative of the birds God feeds and the lilies He clothes so gloriously has brought to needy men! Oh how the virtue of trust rings through the entire Mass!

If only we were conscious of being a holy people faithfully guarded by God's angels against whom the world and all its cohorts cannot prevail! Of this the *Offertory* verse seeks to remind us. Christian hosts are encamped about their King (viz., the altar), God's angels are constructing defences against the enemy, the faithful receive strength and nourishment for the conflict from the altar. As the birds of the air and the lilies of the field we are clothed and fed by the Lord in the Communion Banquet; our response is a carefree: "Seek first the kingdom of God, and all these other things shall be given you besides" (*Comm.*). We rely on the Eucharist's power to cleanse and strengthen as the means to reach our goal (*Postc.*). Yes, today's is one of the most beautiful Masses in the Pentecostal cycle.

3. Divine Office. In the morning we hear from the lips of our Savior the consoling words: "Do not be anxious, wondering: What are we to eat? or, What are we to drink? Your Father knows you need all these things, alleluia" (*Ben. Ant.*).

The day's leit-motif has been selected as the Magnificat antiphon (and also as the Communion): "Seek first the kingdom of God and the holiness it implies; then all other things will be given you besides, alleluia." The Gospel is explained by St. Augustine:

"No man can serve two masters. To clarify this statement our blessed Lord continued: For he will detest the first and love the second, or bear with the first and resent the second. The words must be applied correctly. Who the two masters are Jesus immediately indicated: You cannot serve God and mammon. The Jews called money mammon. The Phoenicians used practically the same idiom, since in their language mammon is equivalent to net profit. Now if one serves mammon, he actually worships as his god the one placed over earthly things because of his perversity, the one whom our Lord called the Prince of this world. Now man has no alternative but to hate that one and love the other, namely, God; or he will bear with the one and resent the Other's wishes. He who works for mammon must suffer under a cruel and killing master; enchained by his own lusts, he subjects himself to the devil, whom he cannot love. For how could anyone love the devil? Still there are those who serve him."

22

4. Sunday Meditation. A. Psalm 83, the Introit psalm of this Sunday's Mass, must be numbered among the finest in the psalter. Without changing any of its phrases it is well suited for use as a daily prayer:

Yearning for God, vv. 2–5

How lovely is your dwelling-place,
    Yahweh Sabaoth!
With longing for the courts of Yahweh,
    my spirit burns within me.
My heart and flesh
    shout for joy to the living God.
The sparrow finds a house,
    the swallow a nest where she may put her
        young —
Your altars, Yahweh Sabaoth,
    my King and my God!
How fortunate are they who dwell in your house —
    ceaselessly they praise you.

The pilgrimage, vv. 6–8

How fortunate the man who looks to you for
    assistance,
    whose mind is set
    to cross the arid valley
    and reach the sought-for goal.
God gave the command,
    he will also give his blessing.
Step by step they go, their strength increasing,
    until they see in Sion
        the God of gods.

Consoled by God's presence, vv. 9–13

Yahweh Sabaoth, hear my prayer,
    give heed, O God of Jacob.
Look kindly upon our Shield, O God;
    with mercy, upon your Anointed.

Truly, one day in your courts
    is better than a thousand elsewhere.
Much rather would I stand at the portals
    of the house of my God,
    than live in the tents of sinners.
For Yahweh, God, is a sun and a shield,
    a Lord who confers grace and glory;
No favor does Yahweh withhold
    from those who live virtuously.
O Yahweh Sabaoth,
    how fortunate is he who relies on you.

Originally this psalm was one of the songs pilgrims sang on their journey to Jerusalem. For us "Jerusalem" is our parish church with its altar as the site of sacrifice. Jerusalem, too, for us is heaven. The psalm needs no further explanatory comment; some of its verses are so soul-satisfying that we ought learn them by heart. Pray it daily until you have become thoroughly familiar with it. It will be a new jewel in your prayer treasury.

B. The Christian army about its King. If some artist wished to express the principal thoughts of today's liturgy in a single scene, the Offertory hymn could serve admirably well for inspiration. It reads: "The angel of the Lord encamps round about those who fear Him and rescues them. Oh, taste and see that the Lord is sweet!"

Let us first note the highlights in the picture. It is the Offertory. The assembled faithful are offering the holy Sacrifice; they want to unite themselves with the offering of Christ, and for that purpose they march to the altar and place their oblation gifts there. Linked to these externals there is another area of truths. The altar is Christ, the King of God's kingdom; here He is enthroned, and about His throne are encamped His soldiery, the Christian hosts; and encircling the whole ensemble there maneuvers an army of angels who ward off the attacks of Satan's hordes; wholesome nourishment is furnished by the King Himself. Or we may arrange the lesson in this way: Christ upon the altar is the head of God's family; about Him

His children are gathered; guardian angels watch over the group, protecting them from evil; the children receive the Bread of Life from their Father.

Now various details in the picture deserve consideration.

The Place. The rallying place for God's children is about the altar. God is their Father, Christ their King and good Shepherd. Holy Church is their Mother, the church building is their Father's house, their home upon earth. Oh, if only this would become abundantly clear that the church is our home! It is so beautifully worded in Psalm 83: "How lovely is Your dwelling-place, Yahweh Sabaoth! With longing for the courts of Yahweh, my spirit burns within me. . . . The sparrow finds a house, and the swallow a nest where she may put her young — Your altars, Yahweh Sabaoth. . . ." How we should want to hasten to church each Sunday to behold the face of our God after the week's turmoil and labors! There our aching hearts should find the peace and solace so desperately sought after. For what St. Augustine observed after years of sad experience still holds true: "Our hearts are restless until they find rest in Thee."

The Father. A second point for consideration is the trust and confidence stressed in the Mass formulary. Our relationship to God is likened to that of a child to its father. Especially is this true of the Gospel, in which Jesus encourages us to trust lovingly in divine Providence. He speaks of the birds, of the lilies which, though they neither sow nor spin, are nourished and dressed by His heavenly Father. Clothed in the resplendent beauty of divine childhood, are we not fairer than the lilies of the field or nobler than the birds of the air? Should we not then feel ourselves secure in God's hand, carefree and happy, knowing well that we have a Father who loves us, who cares for us? As an immediate proof of His love we have the Mass; in it at this very hour He is giving His Son for us.

Protection. God's family, God's army is surrounded, besieged by enemies, the battalions of hell. Here again the Church employs the familiar contrast of the two kingdoms. As long as we are upon earth, the conflict will rage within us. Which, however, will dominate, flesh or spirit? Gazing into the human heart St.

Paul speaks of the works of the flesh and of the fruits of the spirit; and in the Gospel too mention is made of two masters, both of whom cannot be served. The Collect acknowledges that man is frail, weak, and consequently God must keep away all harmful things, must guide him toward that which is good. In this conflict, however, we need never rely upon our own strength for guardian angels are ever present to protect us.

The Bread. Angels are not the only ones aiding us in this spiritual battle; a mightier One than any angel enters the field, Christ Jesus our King. Long ago He vanquished mankind's primeval foe, "I have overcome the world," and His victory is our victory. He gives Himself as Bread for our nourishment: "Oh, taste and see for yourselves that the Lord is sweet." Here lies the key to the heart of each Mass. The Church brings to our mind the two rival kingdoms, not that we may choose between them, but to show that in this conflict our side possesses the only weapon which is invincible, the sacrifice of Mass, the Bread from heaven. With It we can be victorious over any enemy. How well St. Paul phrases it in today's Epistle: "They who belong to Christ have crucified their flesh with its vices and lusts." This happens at holy Mass, for in that sacred act, not only is Christ's death upon the Cross made present, but we too are affixed to the Cross to the degree of our union with Him.

The message of the Mass is also summarized in the day's spiritual motto: "Seek first the kingdom of God, and all other things will be given you besides" (*Comm.*). Stay close to Christ; let your primary concern be His kingdom. Then you will be strong, courageous, victorious; neither will your heavenly Father forsake you in your needs, be they of the body or of the soul.

C. The Epistle. It is St. Paul who addresses us. With the light of truth focused upon our hearts, he points out the two forces aligned against each other for battle. We may recall descriptions of the War with its foxholes, tanks, embankments, machine gun nests. We may imagine our souls having a somewhat like appearance, a great battlefield, two hostile armies, runways and launching platforms. The Apostle calls one side *the flesh*, the other *the spirit*. What does he mean by "flesh"? Human nature inclined to evil, the sad legacy of our original parents, a marred personality that is ours to contend with throughout life, even after baptism. It is this nature bent toward vice and sin that is constantly misleading us. By "spirit" the Apostle means the whole ensemble of gifts and privileges given us in baptism, e.g., habitual grace; indwelling of the Holy Trinity; divine sonship; gifts of the Holy Spirit; faith, hope, charity; membership in the Mystical Body; forgiveness of sin, etc.

Doubtlessly these two must ever be in mortal conflict, with ourselves in the midst. It is a condition that never ceases from early morning to evening, although usually it resembles a cold war with only an occasional sally. Now and then, however, there occurs a general offensive, a day on which both sides fight to the finish. All reserves must then be called out, every muscle and nerve strained. It should be easy to see why God's kingdom on earth is called the Church Militant.

Two examples of a general offensive. First we will discuss an attack made by the forces of evil, then an offensive under God's initiative.

The holy hermit Antony had often been tempted and tortured by the devil. Once however when the attack was exceptionally violent, Antony called out loudly: "Here am I, Antony, and I will not flee your assaults, for no matter how long you continue your onslaughts, nothing will separate me from the love of Christ." Then he began singing: "If armies in camp should stand together against me, my heart will not fear." Satan redoubled his attacks. Antony remained firm. The Lord, however, would not forget His servant in the hour of crisis. The saint glanced upwards and saw the roof open and a beam of light descending upon him. Instantly the demons departed, his bodily afflictions ceased, and his cell took on its customary appearance.

Realizing that aid had come from heaven, Antony breathed more freely, regained composure, and then addressed the beam of light: "Where were you all the while? Why did you not appear to me sooner to quiet my pains?" A voice replied: "I was always with you, Antony, yet I waited to observe you fighting. Since you remained firm and did not waver, I will always be your helper and I will spread your glory far and wide." As the saint heard this he arose to pray; and a greater strength of body came to him than he had known previously.

Sometime during this season is celebrated the feast of St. Augustine. Till his thirtieth year he remained an unbeliever leading a scandalous life. His good and pious mother Monica was indeed praying constantly for him but with little more consolation than the words of a bishop: "A son of so many tears cannot go lost." And Augustine continued enmeshed in the world's sinful pleasures to her intensest sorrow. During a stay at Milan, however, the grace of God began its offensive, employing the sermons of St. Ambrose to soften the hard terrain. The life of the above-mentioned Antony also had an influence. It made him soliloquize: "If this man was able to live so virtuously, why cannot I, I Augustine!" And holy Scritpure, too, especially the letters of St. Paul, was prompting him back to God. In the other camp strutted the prince of this world furiously defending his position. The lustful joys of the world beckoned to him in the persons of lewd women: "How can you live without us? If you serve God, you must forego us." So the battle raged, and Augustine knew not which side to favor.

One day while sitting in a garden he suddenly heard a boy's frail voice saying repeatedly: "Take, read." He regarded it as a sign from God. In his hands were the letters of St. Paul; the passage upon which his eyes first would alight would decide the future. He opened the book and read: "Know that it is now the hour for us to rise from sleep . . . the night is passed, and the day is at hand. Let us therefore cast off the works of darkness and put on the armor of light. . . ." The struggle was won. Augustine asked for baptism and became a fervent, saintly Christian.

It is true that Augustine's story is not ours in every detail; yet on a smaller scale a similar conflict rages day by day in every heart.

The battlefield. St. Paul enumerates the "works of the flesh," the sins into which our lower nature tends to lead us. They need not be repeated here, those vices which are the tools of Satan. It

LORD, LOOK KINDLY UPON YOUR CHURCH.
PROTECT HER FROM ALL MISFORTUNES,
AND PERFECT HER IN YOUR LOVE.

is obvious that we must be alert against even their subtlest intrusions.

Then the Apostle begins considering the brighter side and lists the works of the spirit. But note he uses a different word, *fruits* of the spirit. He has in mind a tree planted by our good God, a tree watered and nourished by our Savior, a tree whose foliage and fruit have been kissed and ripened by the blazing rays of the Holy Spirit. He sees this tree as present before him laden with fruit, the good fruits of "charity, joy, peace, patience, kindness, goodness, faith, modesty, continency." Doesn't your heart thrill as you read this inspiring passage? Note especially the first triad: charity, joy, peace! These are the sweetest and the finest fruits on the tree of Christian life.

Tell me, beloved Paul, how can I overcome my lower self and make my own such priceless fruit? "They who belong to Christ have crucified their flesh with its vices and lusts." But how can I nail my flesh to the Cross of my Savior, O Paul? "It has already been done. In baptism you were crucified with Christ unto death; moreover, you do it again every time you co-offer holy Mass, for this sacred act is nothing else than Jesus' death on the Cross repeated in your presence. Only permit yourself to be affixed."

FIFTEENTH SUNDAY AFTER PENTECOST

I am the Resurrection and the Life

A wonderful Sunday Mass! It could be entitled: "Easter and the Parousia." In two ways Christ raises men from death to life: spiritually through grace at baptism, bodily through glory at the parousia. Every Sunday brings Easter and the parousia together in the Eucharistic sacrifice (a) by renewing the graces of baptism; (b) by effecting beforehand the meeting with Christ proper to the Second Advent; and (c) by bestowing through the Bread

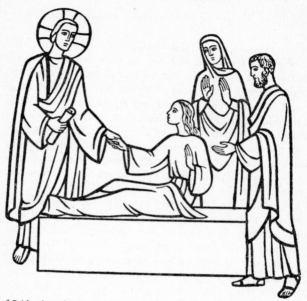

of Life the pledge of bodily resurrection. These various truths receive excellent attention in today's holy Mass.

1. **Transition to "The Church's Harvest Time."** Since Pentecost Sunday our spiritual sights have been fixed upon two principal areas, Easter, namely, and our present circumstances of life. The memory of Easter kept us busy renewing and perfecting our baptismal graces, while the impact of the moment called for continual struggle against the forces of hell. Therefore the subject matter typical of past Sundays was either a miracle cure presented as a sign of spiritual renewal, or an account concerning the two kingdoms, God's kingdom versus Satan's. As has often been observed, Mother Church did not leave us choose our line of action, for that choice was already made at baptism; rather she sought to conduct a spiritual analysis by shining her light into our hearts to show that contrary wills are still operative. With today's liturgy a new turn in the post-Pentecostal liturgy may be noted, with emphasis on the parousia, Christ's

Second Advent. We are entering the final phase of the Church's year of grace, the period devoted to preparation for the Lord's return. It may be named "the Church's Harvest Time."

2. Structure Analysis. Does our Mass formulary today possess a unifying theme? Definitely. It is that of *death and life*. The key texts are the following: "If we *live* by the spirit, by the spirit let us also walk" (*Epist.*). "Young man, I say to thee, *arise*" (*Gosp.*). "The Bread that I will give is My flesh for the *life* of the world" (*Comm.*). Applying these passages to ourselves, we may say: The divine life of grace we received from Christ at baptism; through the Eucharist it is maintained and brought to maturity. Our external activity must bear witness to our internal transformation. This spiritual reality is dramatically visualized in the Gospel episode (see page 35 for a point-by-point development). At the Entrance Chant and Collect our prayer rises as if from the bier of the dead youth of Naim; but the Epistle, Gradual and Alleluia presuppose the resurrection loudly proclaimed in the Gospel and effected in the Sacrifice proper. The Offertory antiphon comes from hearts grateful for spiritual resurrection.

The relation of the Gospel to the Epistle is analogous to that between dogma and moral. Accordingly the Epistle takes second place from the viewpoint of content; you have been raised up from death to life; if now you live by the spirit (i.e., possess sanctifying grace), you must act accordingly (i.e., show the fruits of the spirit). It is a categorical imperative that finds an echo in the Secret and Postcommunion. Try to discover further applications of this unifying theme.

3. Holy Mass (Inclina, Domine). Today the child of God enters the sanctuary not with a face beaming and transfigured, but rather as an exile, care-worn, struggling, oppressed by the week's heavy burdens. Here in the sanctuary he seeks "joy," here he "lifts up his soul" to God (pray the entire psalm, for by employing the first verse of a psalm as the antiphon, the liturgy wishes to include the whole psalm in the thought pattern). Men stand in continual need of God's great mercy to "cleanse and defend" them, otherwise no one would be saved (*Coll.*).

In the *Epistle*, which has links to that of last Sunday, St. Paul discourses on life in the spirit in opposition to actions of the flesh. He gives practical advice summarized succinctly in the words: "Let us also walk in the spirit." The Epistle represents a fine synthesis of excellent norms for daily life and instils in our hearts certain lessons on community spirit: no vainglory, no envy among Christians; meekness and compassion toward those who fail; "bear one another's burdens in order to fulfill the law of Christ"; "do good to all men but especially to those who have the faith." Mother Church is ever keeping before our eyes the ideal: a parish community united in the love of God!

With the *Gradual*, and more so with the *Alleluia*, Easter sunshine breaks through the clouds; and presently Christ, "the great Lord and great King over all the earth," Christ who raises men from the dead, stands before us in the *Gospel*. We may note a definite climactic development in the texts from the "Lord, have mercy" of the Introit, to the Church's anxious and solicitous pastoral prayer for her children in peril (*Coll.*), to the sincere pleas of St. Paul (*Epist.*). In the Gradual the clouds part, permitting the sun to cast its bright Easter light in the Gospel. Finally in the Sacrifice proper, Christ implants the divine seed wheat in our souls to bear the fruit of eternal life.

Again today He is raising the dead to life; again today He "wills to visit His people" and to give them "the Bread that is life for the world" (*Comm.*). I tell my thanks for this awakening in the *Offertory*, which is a beautiful hymn of thanks — a "new canticle" of praise placed in my mouth by God Himself. Summed up in the *Secret* are the effects of the Eucharist, defense and protection. The *Communion* is a Eucharistic hymn and easily related to the Gospel; through the Eucharist Christ is continuing His work of raising men to life. In the *Postcommunion* echo thoughts of the two kingdoms; may Eucharistic grace ever control and direct my soul and body.

4. **Divine Office.** It is the mind of the Church that throughout the day we relive the Gospel story. While the morning sun is rising I see Christ approaching: "Jesus went to a town called Naim; and behold a dead man was being carried out, the only

son of his mother" (*Ben. Ant.*). With the conviction that *I* am this dead man, I go to Mass; and in the evening I sing my thanks for having been spiritually awakened: "A great prophet is risen up among us! God has visited His people!" We know in what that "visitation" consists; for the "Orient from on High" met us at Mass. An edifying homily on the Gospel comes from the lips of St. Augustine:

"When the young man was raised to life, his mother, a widow, was filled with joy. When day after day persons are raised to life supernaturally, Mother Church rejoices; for in the first instance the young man was dead physically, but these latter were dead before God. The one was dead visibly, and there were visible tears; but about the invisible death of these other ones no one bothered, and no tears were shed. Christ, however, knew their condition, and went forth to seek them. Their death was known only to Him who had the power to make them live again. For if He had not come to revive those spiritually dead, the Apostle would not have said: Awake, you who sleep. Rise up from death and Christ will flood you with light.

"As far as we know, Christ brought back to life only three persons in a visible way — but thousands invisibly. Yet does anyone really know how many Christ actually raised to life physically? His every deed is certainly not recorded. John says so explicitly: Many other things too did Jesus do; if every action were recorded, the world itself would not hold, it seems to me, the books that need be written. Many others, then, may have been brought back to life, but that only these three are described is no mere accident. For Christ Jesus our Lord would have all His visible activity understood in a supernatural light. The miracles He performed were not wrought as ends in themselves; to the casual observer they may have seemed wonderful, but to the wise they were meant to manifest truth.

"For example, a person may recognize and praise the very artistic script in which a scroll is written, but if he cannot read it, it will be impossible for him to know its contents; he praises what he sees but does not understand what he praises. Another person will be able to appreciate and praise both the scroll's artistic merits and its message; such a one sees not only the script—as anyone can—but he can also read, a skill one does not acquire without effort. Here we have a parallel applicable to those who witnessed the miracles of Christ but did not recognize their purpose or the message they conveyed to the wise. Such individuals marveled over the apparent wonder; others, however, were amazed not merely at the marvel but attained to an understanding of what it signified. We should resemble these latter in the school of Christ."

5. Sunday Meditations. A. Bridge-building. The pagan high priest in ancient Rome was called *pontifex*, a word which, literally translated, means *bridge-builder*. Perhaps this was due to the custom of offering sacrifice near a bridge. The Roman Church adopted the word in her liturgical language and employs it to denote popes and bishops. In the term there is a beautiful significance, for a priest is indeed a bridge-builder when he spans heaven and earth as the mediator between God and man. Moreover, it would be most fitting to apply this title to the Church, for she in the highest sense is *the* Bridge-builder, spanning a mighty arch over each person's life from the cradle to the grave. The one abutment of this cosmic bridge is baptism, the other is the parousia, and the arch between, the holy Eucharist. As we have mentioned, the way of ancient piety led from baptism to the parousia by way of the sacrament of Love.

Already at birth I carried within myself the germ of death. Already on that first day I was burdened by the curse: *Dust thou art and to dust thou shalt return.* My earthly life, then, may be likened to a funeral procession; my passions and vices, like pall-bearers, were hastening the march in order to bed me sooner in the dust. But Christ intervened and uttered death-defying words: "Young man, I say to thee, arise." That was my baptism. I then received new life, eternal life. Still it remained necessary to preserve this life, to develop and to perfect it. Through baptism my soul became like a newborn child, and growth was all-important. Enemies were not lacking to rob me of this life, but Christ again was present extending to me each Sunday, perhaps even daily, the "Bread for the life of the world." Day by day, then, will I labor upon that wonderful bridge until the glorious dawn heralding the return of Christ Jesus my Lord.

The Church's Harvest Time is upon us, and already the harvesting has begun (Assumption of Mary). The wise virgins are awaiting their Bridegroom with burning lamps, and the vigilant servant goes to meet his Lord with girt loins and burning light. Already the great golden Cross, the sign of the Son of Man, appears resplendently in the heavens (Exaltation of the Holy Cross). The time is short; let us hasten to complete the work on our bridge that we may merit a joyful and blessed crossing.

B. The young man of Naim. Our miracle occurred during the first half of the Galilean ministry. Our blessed Savior was going from town to town preaching and working miracles. Picture His little caravan realistically — Jesus accompanied by His twelve apostles and a number of disciples; at some distance pious women are following, Mary His Mother, Mary Magdalen, some of the other apostles' mothers. To this group people from far and wide attach themselves to hear His teachings and to witness His miracles. Jesus is journeying to the south from His native Nazareth and is approaching a town called Naim (literally, "beautiful meadow").

Let us review a few points concerning the locality. It is sacred ground. Close by is Mount Tabor, the scene of the transfiguration. Not far away is the place called Endor whither in the last days of his unhappy kingship Saul came in distress to seek counsel from its far-famed witch. At his request she conjured the spirit of the prophet Samuel; by God's permission he actually appeared and announced to Saul the rejection and defeat of his army and his own death. On the following day the armies met in battle on the hills of Gelboe (also in the neighborhood) and thousands of the doomed army fell victim to Philistine swords; and Saul resorted to a self-inflicted death. That day Israel's throne passed to David. Today David's Son, Jesus of Nazareth, passes Endor. In the same neighborhood might likewise be seen the town of Sunam where the prophet Eliseus raised to life the son of the hospitable widow. Did our Savior perhaps refer to these incidents as He journeyed along?

Already the sun was declining when Jesus approached Naim. Before the gates lay an ample open space, the scene of all community affairs. The market was there, the court of law, the meetings of the people. Now as Jesus was about to enter the village with His band, a funeral procession was filing out. What a meeting! How gripping for those who have eyes of faith! Two processions, two trains meet each other. Death is faced by Life!

Leading the funeral cortege are the professional wailing women accompanied by flute and cymbal players. The bier follows; it is no coffin, the corpse wrapped to the face in linen is simply carried upon a litter. Four or five men act as pall-bearers; after them follows a mother bowed down by grief, attended perhaps by two other women. Relatives and sympathetic acquaintances come next, of whom there are many in this case, as the Evangelist notes. The young man's premature death had caused a stir in the city and a multitude wanted to be present for the burial rites. Great numbers too gathered before the city's gates; and a large crowd was accompanying Jesus. Truly Jesus did not perform His works in secret.

And the dead person? He was the only son of his mother, a youth in the bloom of life. His mother, moreover, was a widow. An only child always enjoys a special predilection, it is the object of all the love that God has placed in a mother's heart. And now he lay lifeless before her. Certainly her sorrow was a great sorrow, a sorrow deep and righteous as life itself.

Furthermore, she was a widow. After the death of her spouse she refrained from further marriage, an action considered honorable and pleasing to God in Jewish piety. Her whole joy and fortune had been her child — and now God had taken him from her.

But see, at the moment of her greatest anguish and abandonment this sorrowing woman meets her Savior. Jesus' response? Could we imagine otherwise of His deeply sympathetic soul? Luke says: "He was moved with pity towards her." The woman's desolation strikes Him to the quick; compassion was a special characteristic of our Redeemer. St. Paul later wrote: "We have a High Priest who can have compassion upon us." Perhaps Jesus thought of His own dear Mother somewhere in the entourage. In a not too distant future she too would be following a bier in tears.

He would not content Himself with a mere demonstration of sympathy, positive assistance was in order. Stepping apart from His immediate attendants and approaching the weeping mother, He said softly: "Do not weep." Note the common suspense that ensued. What is about to happen? What will He do? were questions on everyone's lips. "Do not weep." Had not others spoken those very words to her already? Yet theirs was an empty solace. But Jesus' words were truly consoling, He was the "consolation of Israel" (as the aged Simeon had said). And some recalled His words during the sermon upon the Mount: "Blessed are they that mourn, for they shall be comforted."

Jesus steps toward the bier, and the bearers halt. Life is standing before death. All is silent, scarce anyone dare breathe. Then Jesus speaks in a loud voice: "Young man, I say to thee, arise!" And he that was dead, he that was bound in winding sheets, sits up and begins to speak as if awakened from a heavy sleep. His first glance falls upon his benefactor, Jesus.

And his mother? All eyes and ears she had watched the proceedings; speechless she observed how her son wrested himself from death. As yet she dared not believe her eyes. Mystified she stands there in anxious waiting. Presently Jesus perfects His work of mercy. He will keep to Himself the joy of restoring this son to his mother. Another beautiful human trait. He respects the joy of a mother even as He displayed sincerest regard for her sorrow! He loosens the linen sheets binding the youth and conducts him to the arms of his mother. The Gospel tells us nothing of that meeting. Surely they embraced each other silently, with tears; and then falling upon their knees before the Wonder-worker they thanked Him from the depths of their hearts. Nothing further is heard of them in the Scriptures, but it may piously be believed that they were numbered among the first Christians.

A final remark about the miracle's effect upon the multitude present is added by the evangelist St. Luke. It was over-powering. Fear seized them, the holy fear of God which always shook the Jew when he witnessed the intervention of God. But soon fear burst into praise and they cried aloud: "A great Prophet is risen among us," and "God has visited His people." It seemed as if the Messianic era had come.

C. The Gospel *mysterium*. The account of the raising to life of the young man at Naim is part of Mother Church's message to us today. Let us ask ourselves now what really prompted her to choose this passage? But first, why does she select any passage from the life of Christ as, for instance, the miracle at Naim for today's Gospel? True, she intends to edify us; it shows us the Lord in His compassion and mercy, His human heart, His respect for the sufferings and joys of motherhood. And a sure proof is afforded of His divine mission. For He speaks with sovereign authority: "Young man, I say to thee, arise." Accordingly, instruction and edification are certainly among her motives; still such considerations are not primary. For if the Church should want to teach and edify her children, she surely could have chosen more suitable passages, for instance, some appealing parable of doctrinal discourse. Mother Church, therefore, must have in mind another reason.

She recounts a past event, still she sees and treats it as a present reality. She wants to say: Those things that happened so many years ago are happening sacramentally in our own lives, yes, now, this morning during this holy Mass. Christ's activity was not limited to raising a youth from the dead some nineteen hundred years ago, He is repeating the same in His Church today in a spiritual manner.

We may even go so far as to say that our Redeemer performed miracles not as something unique in themselves but with reference to the future. For all the wonders in Christ's life serve merely to show His wonderful work in the Church. The purpose of His earthly life was not to heal or to raise to life a few isolated individuals, rather the salvation of mankind through His holy Church. Therefore it may rightly be said that today's miracle of restoring life foreshadowed that which He accom-

plishes now in His Church, that which He achieves presently
through the holy Sacrifice, viz., the bestowal of divine life, spiritual resurrection. On one occasion He even referred to Himself
as the Giver of life in a twofold way: by raising the soul from
spiritual death to supernatural life in the present, and in the
future by raising both body and soul from physical death to a
life transfigured in glory.

Therefore we must apply to our own individual selves this
miracle of the awakening of the young man at Naim. I must
regard my own soul as the dead youth whom the Lord wills to
awaken to spiritual life. It would be tragic to see no more than
the historical episode, the symbol; the full reality lies in the
realm of grace, access to which Christ today makes so easy and
inviting.

The raising to life of the widow's son is the burden of the
Gospel, which we now know is not intended to be a mere repeti-
tion of a portion of holy Writ. The lights, incense, Alleluia
chant, and other sacred adjuncts are pointed witnesses to the
truth that at the Gospel Christ Jesus Himself appears and speaks
to us. In mystery the historical becomes present, Jesus is living
and speaking in our midst. It often happens that a phrase from
the Gospel re-echoes as the Communion verse; such is not the
case today. Why? To show that the event has already become
real, actual, through the Eucharist.

The entire Mass text bears witness to its *mysterium* character.
In the Introit we feel ourselves under the pall of death. All that
is dead, all that requires redemption both in ourselves and in the
Church pleads for resurrection: "Save Your servant, O my God,
who trusts in You. Have mercy on me, O Lord." In the Collect
Mother Church petitions the gift of life for her children. The
Epistle is the Church's motherly admonition to *live* in the spirit.
In the Gospel the Wonder-worker appears in our midst. And
finally in the Sacrifice proper the spiritual awakening is effected, for at the sacrificial Banquet the Lord bends down and
says: Go in peace. Holy Communion has given the strength "to
live and walk in the spirit," as also a claim to future, bodily
resurrection. Because of the Mass, the day falls into two parts:

before Mass I had been spiritually inanimate; after Mass I return home re-enlivened.

Yet the Church, not satisfied to limit this sacred mystery drama to the Mass alone, extends it through the whole day in the hours of Divine Office. Yes, the breviary is the Mass extended, prolonged; the divine Sun, Christ in the holy Eucharist, casts its golden rays over the entire day. Each day is granted a glorious setting, sunrise and sunset, at which moments the Church voices her profoundest thoughts. It is a sacred moment when at sunrise she hails the "Orient from on high — *Oriens ex alto*" — and when at sunset she sings the Magnificat of the humble Virgin in thanksgiving for the day's redeeming graces. At these sacred moments she begins and ends the day's *mysterium*. For at sunrise and at sunset she chants key passages from the Gospel. Take today's, for example; plainly and simply the Church prays at sunrise: "Jesus went into a city called Naim; and behold a dead man was carried out, the only son of his mother." At sunset the curtain falls upon the mystery while the Church recounts the fruit of the miracle: "A great Prophet is risen up among us; God has visited His people!" A similar grace came to me this day, for this day I was awakened from spiritual death.

SIXTEENTH SUNDAY AFTER PENTECOST

He who humbles himself will be exalted

Transitional from summer to autumn are the three Sundays, the fifteenth, sixteenth, and seventeenth after Pentecost. In addition to the themes found heretofore, there appears that of hope and preparation for Christ's Second Advent — it is harvest time in the Church's year of grace. Of this new turn last Sunday's Gospel mystery of the resurrection of the young man at Naim may be taken as introductory. This new spirit in the liturgy is not quite as evident today, but a sensitive ear will not fail to perceive certain strains — the afflictions of the final days are struck in various keys. Paul in chains foreshadows and discourses on the end of the world. The chants petition aid and forgiveness. Autumn is nature in old age (*Comm.*). Humility is the virtue desperately needed.

1. Text Analysis. It is always easier to participate intelligently and profitably in a Mass if we know its central theme. Between the meal described in today's Gospel and the holy Banquet of Mass there is indeed an evident analogy (and the use of such "banquet narratives" as figures of the Mass are common in the missal), but it would seem forced to fit the other texts into any given pattern. It would be preferable to use another approach, viz., to single out the formulary's teaching on the parousia. Three headings could be made: (a) cries of suffering due to oppression and earthly evils; (b) a spirit of hope in things to come; (c) concern over personal salvation. A bit of commentary on each.

a) The increasing darkness in the world of nature about us is a sign and symbol of the suffering and affliction that will usher in the final era, as well as the last moments of each person's life. With this in mind we have the proper background for the tearful tone of the chants from the Introit to the Communion; only once is there a gladsome strain, at the thought of the hereafter in the Gradual. Today's texts show us how the Mass can be true solace in the sufferings of life.

b) Into the darkness of present afflictions the star of heavenly hope does cast its bright beams. Before our eyes the Gradual momentarily places the dazzling scene of the heavenly Jerusalem (prompted by the final lines of the Epistle): "The Lord makes His kingdom resplendent. He now appears in grandeur!" What a singularly apt introduction to the Alleluia, heaven's hymn; it is indeed the "new song" that only the saved can sing when they behold the marvels of God in all their transcendent beauty.

c) Our certain hope of beatitude must not engender spiritual idleness. Quite the contrary. The expectation of the Lord's return is a challenge to ready ourselves, to strive heroically for personal perfection. Here we touch upon the formulary's principal message, and one easily detectable in the Lessons and other prayer texts. Three prerequisites to holiness are underscored, i.e., actuating grace, prayer, humility. In the whole missal there can be found no more incisive statement on God's grace which "precedes and accompanies us, ever inciting us to the performance of virtuous deeds." Such actuating grace is given in response to persevering prayer. Our formulary offers numerous apt forms in which to cast our pleas, e.g., Psalm 85; the Offertory and Communion verses; and St. Paul's magnificent Epistle on prayer. Without prayer, no actuating grace; without actuating grace, no good act; without good acts, no holiness. Presupposed, moreover, in all efforts toward holiness is the spirit of humility (*Gosp.*).

The characteristics of true holiness are not absent from Paul's thought-packed Epistle: first, Christ's abiding presence within us; secondly, a charity, firm and solidly established; thirdly, an ever-expanding comprehension of the mystery of faith. Thereby we may become "filled with all the fullness of God." Could any class period on holiness be more helpful and enlightening than our Mass today?

2. Holy Mass (Miserere mihi). The skies are clouded over; persecution, spiritual trials and conflicts weigh heavily upon the mystical Christ. Last Sunday the sun soon shone through, but today the storm clouds stay until the end, with the light penetrating but once (*Grad., Allel.*). In nature too the approach of winter is evident; the days are becoming shorter, the nights longer — a symbol of the "dark night of the soul" and persecution. With today's holy Mass there begins a series of Epistles culled from the letters St. Paul wrote in prison, letters containing profound theology. In the Gradual are heard the parousia bugles, and their call will swell louder and louder on coming Sundays.

The Mass begins with a gripping *Miserere*; the members of Christ's Mystical Body are imploring mercy for needy souls; they rest their plea on three counts: (a) because as the Mystical Body they pray throughout the day (hours of Divine Office);

(b) because God is "sweet and mild and plenteous in mercy"; (c) because souls are so "needy and poor." Much grace is necessary, grace that will act as a guide (even as a star guided the Magi), and as a companion (as Raphael accompanied Tobias) upon the way of life (*Coll.*), or souls cannot yield "good fruits."

In the words of St. Paul and after his example, Mother Church with a heart deeply moved urges us on to perfection in a *Lesson* aglow with unusual warmth. It is her plea (a) that we too may ever grow unto the perfection of the "inward man" (i.e., in sanctity); (b) that Christ may live by faith in our hearts; and (c) that we may be rooted and founded in charity (what roots are to a tree, love is to the spiritual structure). The heart of Mother Church (St. Paul's too) is so moved that she struggles for words to express more adequately God's goodness and love — "That you also may understand Christ's love, a love which transcends all human experience, enabling you to be filled with all the fullness of God." A life superabundantly rich in grace is the Church's concern for all her children.

Hardly has the Reading concluded with the doxology "to God be the glory through the Church, and through Christ Jesus," when the *Gradual* discloses the vision of the parousia when all things will be perfected, when Christ at His Second Coming will gather all earth's kings about Himself, when the "heavenly Sion," the Church, which is now so severely persecuted, will be newly built, and the Lord will be seen shining in majesty. Then will the fullest, boundless Easter joy reign, then will the Church sing the "new canticle" of redemption, the eternal *Alleluia*.

The *Gospel*, one of the so-called banquet-parables, opens two major thought areas: (a) Jesus, the Savior, is the Physician of man's sick soul (especially on Sundays); (b) His medicine is humility. Here you have the reason why the virtue of humility is inculcated so often in the liturgy. It is the foundation virtue of Christianity, a panacea for many ills. The Sabbath-day meal to which Jesus came symbolizes the Sunday Eucharistic banquet; here Christ heals us from the dropsy of worldly spirit by giving us instruction in the Mass of the Catechumens and by nourishing us with divine Food in the Mass of the Faithful.

With the *Offertory* tears flow again as we recognize our miserable lot in the midst of enemies; with growing vehemence the opening cry for aid is repeated. Imagine how powerful this Offertory was in its former extended form with the antiphon, "Hasten, Lord, to help me," repeated three times. The *Secret* is cast in a somewhat negative mold; may the Sacrifice effect a greater purification of our souls. No Eucharistic hymn is sung at the *Communion*, rather a thanksgiving prayer for God's gracious guidance during youth and an anxious glance toward old age; may He accompany me then also — thus making holy Communion a true *Viaticum* upon the way. My whole life's story is covered in this Communion chant; God is my Savior during childhood, youth, middle and old age. Purification and spiritual renewal by means of the Eucharist constitute the burden of the *Postcommunion* prayer; as a special turn it petitions help for the body. The Eucharist is a fountain of life for one's body too.

3. Divine Office. The two greater antiphons cull out the Gospel's main message: "When Jesus entered the house of a leading pharisee on the Sabbath day to have a meal, a certain man appeared before Him who had dropsy. Taking hold of him, Jesus healed him and sent him away." (Keep in mind the *mysterium*, i.e., the re-actualizing of past events at the present time in a sacramental, mystical manner through the liturgy.) "When you are invited to a wedding dinner, go and sit at the far end of the table. Then when your host comes he can say to you: My friend, take a place higher up. In that case it will be to your honor before all the other guests, alleluia." Opportunities for practicing humility are never hard to find.

4. Sunday Meditation. The Gospel. A "leading pharisee," that is, a pharisee enjoying an influential position in the Synagogue, once invited a number of other pharisees and Jesus to dinner. But his real motive was not to entertain his Messianic Guest or to gain a better understanding of His teaching; rather, as the Gospel says, it was "to watch Him closely," that is, to gather incriminating evidence against Jesus. The desired opportunity soon presented itself, for a man afflicted with dropsy

slipped into the dining room unnoticed (not an extraordinary occurrence in the East) and placed himself before Jesus, undoubtedly with the silent plea to be healed. It was the Sabbath. Jesus Himself placed the question whether it was lawful to heal on the Sabbath. No answer. The pharisees maintained an icy silence. The Savior made answer by action. He healed the sick man by His touch and dismissed him.

Since the pharisees remained silent still, Jesus proceeded to prove that the cure was no violation of God's Law. He said: If your ox or ass would happen to fall into a pit on the Sabbath, would you hesitate as much as an instant before drawing the poor animal out? Now why should a sick man be treated worse than an ox? The logic was overpowering, and the pharisees could not retort. Those sticklers on the letter of the Law had again condemned themselves. Now the lesson we must learn is that love of neighbor cannot be divorced from love of God. The Lord's day is indeed holy; it can never, however, be desecrated through deeds of love done toward one's fellow man. For every good act toward one's neighbor is likewise a good act toward God.

Upon what, then, were the thoughts and aspirations of these much-to-be-pitied pharisees centered? Their own ego. Beneath attractive turbans and pompous festal robes were hidden hearts chuck-full of pride and self-love. Jesus had observed this in the way they had chosen the first places at table before the meal. Now He would comment upon that. He said: Even human tactfulness should prompt you to choose the lower seats at a banquet and not the highest. Otherwise it may happen that if the guestmaster has invited a person of nobler rank, you will have to step down, to your own humiliation. How it would re- dound to your honor if you had seated yourself at the end of the table and then were advanced by the guestmaster!

Now what is the point our Lord wished to make by that observation? Surely it was not a lesson in etiquette. He wished to teach a fundamental virtue of our religion, holy humility. Christ was not speaking of mere human prudence, as if man could merit and obtain an exaltation through fictitious self-abase- ment. Such would be a calculating humility, yes, it would be pride concealed. In this instance Jesus is speaking of true hu- mility which is infinitely removed from that species of pride which exteriorly selects a humble place yet interiorly covets the higher. Our Master wishes that *even in our hearts* we feel at home when in the lowest place. The Christian especially should be humble, for he knows that he is a poor sinner; he knows that the good he has is wholly due to the grace of God, not to himself. The great lesson which Christ teaches today is humility. Add to your spiritual stature by absorbing its spirit somewhat more perfectly.

SEVENTEENTH SUNDAY AFTER PENTECOST

Be enthroned at My right hand

As has already been pointed out, the past two Sundays to- gether with the present seventeenth Sunday after Pentecost are

transitional from summer to autumn; and therefore they exhibit characteristics of both seasons. Beginning with the seventh Sunday after Pentecost, the major and most frequently recurring theme consisted in the antithesis between the flesh and the spirit, between the world and God. During the approaching fall and winter phase of the Church year, emphasis will lie on preparation and expectation for the Lord's Second Advent. Let us analyze these strains more closely.

1. **Text Analysis.** The Summer Theme. Ever since Adam's sin, disorder and conflict have wearied the soul of man. Original sin takes its toll — and this is what St. Paul refers to by the term *flesh*. Christ endowed us with another principle of action, and Paul calls this *spirit*. "Spirit" consists primarily in the manifold supernatural gifts granted us by God. It was not part of the divine plan to restore paradise to us as such. Earth would continue to be the battleground between good and evil, the stage for the holy war of which Christ said: "I did not come to bring peace, but the sword." The Christian, therefore, must be

a soldier — this line of thought was developed in the liturgy on summer Sundays. His struggle continues all during life, with light and darkness, spirit and flesh constantly at odds. God's side will not always emerge with flying banners, and there will be some major disasters. But final victory will be ours. Today's Mass gives a preview of the aftermath, when it no longer will be a matter of opposing parties but of peaceful unity.

The peculiar beauty of our formulary is its clear picture of the compelling unity of our holy religion: unity in faith, unity in morals, unity in grace and worship. One Christ, one Church, one Love. The wonderful sevenfold oneness of the Church is seen through the prism light of the Epistle; one Body, it is enlivened by one Spirit and strives for a single goal, heaven. That Body has a single head, Christ; one faith enlightens us, and but one sacramental order sanctifies us from baptism to our last anointing. While above all reigns God, our only Father! With bowed heads we stand in reverential fear before this awesome unity, a oneness into which we have been immersed and by which we have been assimilated. Are we then to continue vacillating between spirit and flesh? The Gradual, perfectly fulfilling its function of echoing the Epistle, places the proper words on our lips: "How fortunate is the nation for whom Yahweh is God, how fortunate the people whom He has chosen as His inheritance." The Collect outlines the way to attain the good fortune of such blessed unity: avoid all contact with the devil and practice perfect obedience to the only God.

From another approach, that of the Gospel, the oneness of our holy religion is due to Christ and to supernatural charity. Christ stands at the center of our faith. One of the objectives of the liturgical apostolate is to restore a Christocentric outlook. "I am the Way, the Truth, and the Life." Both the Epistle and Gospel contain memorable words on the virtue of charity. "Bear with one another in love, anxious to preserve the unity of the spirit by means of the bond of peace." "You must love Yahweh, your God, with your whole heart. . . . You must love your neighbor as yourself." It was toward the realization of such earth-transcending unity through the Church, through Christ, through love that the liturgy of the summer Sundays was oriented.

The Church's Harvest Time. The Christ-picture unfolded before us in today's liturgy is set against the background of harvest time in the year of grace: "Christ enthroned at God's right hand until He makes His enemies His footstool." It is a fearsome scene, embracing the whole of world history and the Last Judgment. Serene and calm Christ sits as King and abides the time till He may place His foot upon the neck of every foe. Unto the proud and stubborn He "stands in dreadful magnificence; He breaks the obstinacy of princes and strikes down with fear all the kings of the earth" (*Comm.*). Upon the docile "beams the light of His countenance from the sanctuary; and He turns mercifully toward the people upon whom His Name is invoked" (*Off.*). How well this passage pinpoints the purpose and nature of holy Mass.

2. Holy Mass (Justus es). Today's liturgical mood is not quite as heavy and depressing as last Sunday's; there is a greater sense of calm and composure arising from the knowledge that all human suffering forms part of God's just judgment; and the Church pleads for mercy (*Intr.*). As her obedient children, our great endeavor is to walk "undefiled in the way of the Lord," to "follow God alone with a pure mind" and to "avoid the diabolical contagion" of sin (*Coll.*). (Note the words, *via, ambulant, sectari, ambuletis* — life is a pilgrimage.)

The Apostle of the Gentiles stands before us "in his chains" and entreats us "to walk worthy of our Christian vocation in humility and meekness, in patience and charity, ever anxious to maintain the bond of unity and peace" (*Epist.*). Mother Church is greatly concerned over keeping these ideals alive in her children's hearts; for this end she seeks to impress us by unveiling before our spiritual eyes the profound sevenfold oneness that is hers: (1) one body, Head and members, (2) enlivened by one Holy Spirit, (3) having one common goal, heaven, (4) one Lord, Christ Jesus, (5) one common faith, (6) unified by the same sacraments (baptism, Eucharist), and (7) governed by one common Father in heaven. What mighty motives for peace and harmony in one's own soul and among all mankind! Every Christian should reflect this unity, should strive constantly to exemplify it, because it alone can transform us into the "blessed nation that He has chosen as His inheritance" (*Grad.*), a people whose strength is the Triune God.

From this thought of the earthly Church united in Christ, it is but a small step to the heavenly Sion; therefore the *Alleluia* verse is a *maranatha*, a longing cry to be at home with Christ (the whole of Psalm 101 could be interpreted as the outburst of a homesick soul in exile). The Master Himself speaks of the great law of love of God and neighbor in the *Gospel*. But we must limit ourselves to its principal feature, the 109th psalm, which is prayed so often in the liturgy. This psalm adumbrated the Messiah as God's eternal Son sharing the royal throne with the Almighty on High; furthermore, it has afforded the liturgy a Christ-picture which may still be seen portrayed in richest colors in the apses of ancient basilicas. The liturgical thought-content of the Gospel may be summed up thus: in the midst of persecutions, in the soul's dark night, the Church (individual members too) glances longingly upward toward her glorified Lord at the Father's right, waiting for Him to subdue all enemies.

Since our glorified Lord is very near during the holy Sacrifice, we keep in mind this Gospel scene, and during the *Offertory* procession we petition Him to "look favorably upon His sanctuary and upon His people" at His Second Coming and also now during the holy Sacrifice because holy Mass is the parousia anticipated. In the *Communion* too the Lord appears in glory, annihilating all enemies (the entire psalm would fit wonderfully well here). *Secret* and *Postcommunion* plead for the remission of sin.

A discerning eye would quickly perceive references to "The Returning King" throughout the Mass. *Introit*: the just and merciful Judge; *Collect*: following in His train; *Gradual*: Creator, King; *Alleluia*: parousia prayer; *Gospel*: at the Father's right hand; *Offertory*: let Your face shine upon us; *Communion*: awe-inspiring, glorious One!

3. Divine Office. The two principal thought areas in the

Gospel — charity, Christ — are found summarized in the day's greater antiphons. "Master, which is the great commandment in the Law? Jesus answered: You must love Yahweh, your God, with your whole heart. Alleluia." Charity is *the* great commandment! "What is your position regarding the Messiah? Whose son is he? They said to Him: David's. Jesus asked them: If so, how then can David, being inspired, call him Lord, saying: Yahweh said to my Lord: Sit at My right hand"? Jesus Christ is equal to almighty God! St. John Chrysostom comments on the law of love:

"Why did He say: *And the second is like unto this*? Because the second commandment prepares the way for the first, and itself in turn is supported and aided by it. For, as it is written, *Everyone who does evil hates the Light and never attains to the Light.* Or, according to another passage: *The fool says in his heart: God does not exist.* This passage then continues: *They have become corrupt, their deeds abominable.* Another text tells us: *The root of all evil is avarice, and its victims have strayed far from the truth.* While in the Gospel we read: *If anyone loves Me, he will keep My commandments.*

"Now for all of these quotations the basis is: *You must love the Lord your God, and your neighbor as yourself.* If, then, to love God implies love of neighbor (according to Christ's words: *If you love Me, Peter, feed My sheep*), and if love of neighbor results in the observance of God's commandments, it is indeed quite right for the Lord to say that on these two commandments the whole Law and the prophets depend. Once, when questioned on the subject of the resurrection, Jesus replied at greater length than they had anticipated; now again, although questioned only with regard to the first commandment, does He add the second gratis, a commandment not too distantly related to it at all; for although it is second, it is like unto the first. Thus very unobstrusively He brings home to them that it had been out of hatred that they had questioned Him."

4. **Sunday Meditation.** A. Psalm 109. For a better understanding of the Gospel it would help immensely to study this important psalm in detail:

I. *The King*

An oracle of Yahweh to my Lord (the Messiah):
  Be seated at my right;
    your enemies, I will make them your footstool.
The sceptre of your power Yahweh extends from
    Sion (saying):
  Rule in your enemy's midst,
    for the triumph is yours.
  On the day of your might
    you will proceed in holy splendor.
  I have begotten you from the womb
    before the morning-star.

II. *High Priest and Judge*

Yahweh has sworn an oath, never will he retract it:
  You are a priest forever,
    after the model of Melchisedech.
At your right hand
  Yahweh destroys kings on the day of his wrath.
A judgment day he holds against the nations,
  makes corpses lie in heaps.
Heads he shatters
  over the plains.
From a brooklet on the wayside he drinks,
  then nobly lifts up his head.

Psalm 109 is directly Messianic; and Jesus Himself used it as such. In boldest pictures it depicts the Messiah's victory and triumph. Divided into two strophes, it first considers the Redeemer as co-Regent with His eternal Father (according to Oriental etiquette a co-regent assumed the place at the ruler's right). In due time He will vindicate His regency by triumphing over all enemies and on the day of His Second Advent He will appear in the full glory of His majesty.

In the second strophe the Messiah appears as a Priest resembling Melchisedech and remains such even though a portion of

mankind rejects and despises His priestly work. The final verses
show Him as Judge. On the day of retribution, the great judgment day, He deals with His enemies like the conquerors of old;
He heaps corpse upon corpse, crushes the skulls of adversaries,
fills the land with ruins — a very realistic picture indeed. Even
though in the original and in translations the psalm suffers from
obscure phrases, for purposes of prayer the text remains sufficiently clear; we need simply to keep our gaze fixed upon the
Messiah as King, as Priest, and as Judge.

This venerable psalm, so deserving of prayerful meditation,
will, if permitted, exercise a beneficent influence upon one's
daily life. For in it we children of the light are privileged to
behold in clearest sunlight the One for whom the psalmist so
ardently awaited, Christ our King. What new insights fulfillment throws upon the oracle! He does not make His enemies
into a footstool through force, but through grace brings them to
their knees. Recall St. Paul's reflections. The sceptre which He
stretches forth from Sion is the Cross; on it He truly reigns in
the midst of enemies. Then the psalm raises the curtain hiding
eternity and we behold our King "proceeding in holy splendor"
in the glory and brightness of His saints. Shall I also be numbered among them?

And now I see Him as the eternal High Priest upon the altar
of the Cross (Priest and Victim simultaneously); I see this Sacrifice offered daily upon the altar, myself standing in His place.
I am a star, illumined by Him the Sun — a priest, too, after the
model of Melchisedech. And now I behold Him in a still different
role, as Judge, as Victor. The story of the Church has indeed
been that of world-judgment under the hand of the Messiah-
King. Julian the Apostate was not the only one forced to the
final acknowledgment: "O Galilean, Thou hast conquered!"
Such vindication of divine justice, however, is but a weak
shadow of that last *dies irae*. Psalm 109 should be prayed with
sentiments of deepest homage, awe, and adoration.

B. The King, His kingdom, and His law. Under these three
headings let us consider the doctrine contained in today's holy
Mass. (1) The King. No doubt most diverse answers would be

received in reply to a questionnaire concerning the Christ-picture present-day Christians preferred. For some it would be the Child in the crib, for others the Man of sorrows upon the Cross, still others the Good Shepherd, while others would choose the Sacred Heart. But if we ask how Christians in olden times or how the liturgy pictures Christ, the answer could only be that every page of the liturgy represents Christ as *King*.

Proof is easily forthcoming. The first greeting to Christ in the Mass at early morn, the *Gloria*, praises the majesty of Him "who is enthroned at the right hand of the Father." Every liturgical prayer ends with the royal dedication: "Through our Lord Jesus Christ who lives and *reigns*. . . ." In the Divine Office the Church is constantly praying to Christ the King. The altar serves as His throne. In today's Gospel Christ speaks of His royal dignity, referring to the well-known Psalm 109; according to the flesh He is from David's family, but in His divine nature He is God's eternal Son in whom the words of the psalm have been fulfilled: "Be seated at my right; your enemies, I will make them your footstool."

How long will Christ continue enthroned at the right hand of the Most High? The psalmist says: till the final judgment. The picture of the judgment has two aspects, one terrifying, one consoling. Against His enemies the divine Judge, as today's Communion indicates, "stands in dreadful magnificence; He breaks the obstinacy of princes and strikes down with fear all the kings of the earth." But He is full of loving kindness toward His faithful ones: "Blessed is the nation for whom Yahweh is God, the people whom He has chosen as His inheritance" (*Grad.*). To this King we must tender loyal adherence; this is the King whose Second Advent we will anxiously await.

2) The kingdom. The realm established by our King is the Catholic Church. To His kingdom He has given the perfection of unity described in the Epistle. We are one body and one spirit in Christ, i.e., we are blended into His Mystical Body; we have been destined unto one hope, namely, heavenly beatitude where the consummate beauty of this unity will be fully manifest; one Lord, one faith, and one baptism (to which could well be

added, one heavenly Bread); one God and Father who alone
rules. To this only kingdom we must belong, into its unity we
must be homogenized; and our lifelong efforts must be ex-
pended to ward off its one great solvent, sin.

3) The law. The royal law that our King promulgates today
we will embrace with devotion and obedience; it is the law of
love. We are thrilled to hear from His lips the glorious command: "You must love Yahweh, your God, with your whole
heart and with your whole soul, and with your whole mind . . .
you must love your neighbor as yourself." With understanding,
with will, with heart, in short, with all the powers of soul and
body we will accept this commandment to love God, and its
companion precept, to love our neighbor.

4) But what is most appealing in the liturgy is that the Mass
is not a mere study hour in which we hear about our King
and about His kingdom and law. No, what is told and taught
in the Mass of the Catechumens becomes actuality, reality, during the very hour; for it is sacramentally, mystically re-enacted
when the King appears in the Mass of the Faithful. He ascends
His throne, the altar; He is surrounded by His followers; "in
the sight of His saints" He comes to us. See, here He "stands in
dreadful magnificence, He who breaks the obstinacy of princes,"
even though it seems that He lies upon the altar immolated
like a helpless lamb. It is He who shatters the enemies of His
kingdom within my soul, your soul, till He has made of them
His footstool. But to His subjects He wills to be indulgent; therefore, again today He invites them to a royal banquet, with Himself as Food. He gives us not only a law but also the grace and
strength needed to keep and love that law.

Yes, we could say: "How fortunate is the nation for whom
Yahweh is God, how fortunate the people whom He has chosen
as His inheritance." For we are that nation and heirs of heaven.
But we must remain docile as we await His Second Advent.

C. The Gospel presents two questions which strike to the very
depths of our spirituality (or lack of it): (a) What does Christ
mean to us? (b) When are we true Christians?

1) We believe that Christ is God and Man. Both points in

this profession are very important, Christ's divinity *and* His humanity. To our inmost depths we must be convinced of this sacred mystery. It must become part of our very flesh. If in these days, as at no other time, threatening fists are raised against Christ; if hatred against Christ is preached, then must we place ourselves close to Him, then must we remain faithful to Him, living for Him and, if needs be, dying for Him. The Apostle is able to tell what this profession of faith in Christ implies. "To me living means Christ; and death, gain." It means: "With Christ I am nailed to the cross. It is now not I who lives, it is Christ who lives in me."

Paul radiated a love for Christ that knew no bounds. If Christ is God, then I belong to Him wholly, body and soul, flesh and blood; then too He is my Judge, my King, and my All. If Christ is Man, then He is my Savior, my Redeemer, my Way, and my Guide. If He is the God-Man, then He will lift me out from the helplessness of puny human nature to the glory of the divine. O Christ Jesus, do Thou fill me to the depths!

2) The liturgy shows and teaches us how to become perfect Christians. Without doubt hatred against Christ and Christianity is being stirred up by the hosts of hell, yet are not we Christians also somewhat the cause of the anti-Christian spirit in the world today? Our lukewarmness, our perversity, our pharisaism have shown to the enemies of Christ a caricature of Christianity. Straining at gnats and swallowing camels is particularly noisome. Such is the case when Catholics insist strenuously upon periphery minutiae and disregard essentials.

We are true Christians only through love. Love is the magic word that can make the world Christian, love is the Orpheus that can tame the wild animal instincts within us. We must perfect ourselves in love. And love of God must impel us to the love of neighbor. If we have charity, we can beautify the earth, dry tears, offer sympathy, disarm and conquer a hostile world. "We are reviled, and we bless!" "Be not overcome by evil, but overcome evil by good!" "If someone strikes you on your right cheek, turn to him also the other!" Such is true Christianity, such are the means by which the world can be redeemed.

THE CHURCH'S HARVEST TIME

EIGHTEENTH SUNDAY AFTER PENTECOST

Arise and enter your heavenly home

1. **Text Analysis.** Today's formulary becomes more intelligible if we keep in mind that it does not belong to the sequence of Sunday Masses proper to the Pentecostal cycle. For in ancient times the Sunday following the Ember days was aliturgical; the Ember service lasted throughout the night into early Sunday morning. Only later when the vigil celebration was anticipated and observed on Saturday morning was the present formulary introduced. It seems certain that a Church-Dedication Mass was chosen, at least for the various chants. Note the psalm (121) at the Introit and Gradual: "How my heart joyed at the good news: We are going to the house of Yahweh." In the Offertory there is reference to the construction of an altar; and to "the courts of God" in the Communion.

Whether the two Readings are to be related to the church structure is not too clear. Still it is not difficult to see "Dedication" implications. That would give the formulary unity. In the church we receive the greatest of gifts, i.e., faith (see Epistle), pardon (see Gospel), and grace (see Offertory). The word *peace* (see Introit) would include all three. Notice the strong accent placed on preparation for the parousia in the Epistle and Alleluia verse. The Epistle, culled from First Corinthians instead of the Captivity letters, is another indication of the extraneous character of today's Mass. One might note that from now until the first Sunday of Advent the Introit antiphon (with one exception) is never taken from the psalter.

2. **Holy Mass (Da pacem).** Since the parish church in a very special way symbolizes the heavenly Jerusalem today, the theme

song of the Mass very appropriately is the "song of Sion," Psalm 121: "How my heart joyed at the good news: We are going to the house of Yahweh!" Leaving the world of conflict, of unrest, and of persecution, we enter the peaceful sanctuary chanting: "Give peace, Lord, to those who hope in You." What do these words mean? O God, give us that eternal beatitude for which we yearn in order that Your prophets who have painted Your return in such glorious colors may be proven truthful. The entrance of priest and servers portrays our journey to heaven — joyfully we go to the mansions prepared for us on high (pray the whole psalm). *Collect*: conscious of our own helplessness we implore "divine grace to direct our hearts," for such is the nature of the Mass.

In the *Epistle* (which breaks the *lectio continua* as already noted), Mother Church stands before us. The end of the Church year is approaching; therefore, she glances back and thanks God for His many gifts and graces. Oh, how rich are we, God's children! Were we not flooded with every needed grace? Even at this very moment Christ "will confirm you unto the end" (in the Mass). The Church tells us to "await the appearance (Second Advent) of our Lord Jesus Christ," and that it must be our greatest concern to appear "without sin in the day of His coming." She would have us look back in gratitude and forward in desire for the return of Christ Jesus. Meditation on His "Advent" takes us in spirit to the heavenly "house of the Lord" where "peace and abundance" reign (*Grad.*). The *Alleluia* verse conjures up a vision of the final judgment when the Redeemer, surrounded by kings and Gentiles, will appear in "glory."

Then a cripple comes before Christ and by a miracle He proves His "power on earth to forgive sins." That man sick of the palsy represents us Christians, for we too are beneficiaries of a similar healing. Even as that sick man, you once were sick in soul; and the Lord healed you. That was your baptism. Every Sunday, this Sunday included, perfects the graces you then received. There still remain paralyzed areas in your soul; the world, self, lower nature, like leaden weights cramp it to the earth, obstructing every movement toward the things of God.

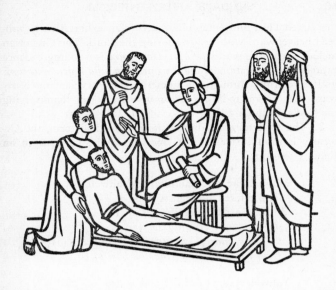

To remedy this Christ instituted the holy Eucharist; by it He supplies you with added strength and ready vigor, and thus counteracts your spiritual inertia. The holy Eucharist equips you well for your journey heavenward. In this way the *Gospel* brings together the past (baptism), the present (Eucharist) and the future (Second Advent). On the last day the word of Christ will be realized perfectly in you: "He arose (*surrexit*) and entered his (heavenly) home."

The *Offertory* will be covered in detail later. There is profound theology in the *Secret*: through the sacred "exchange" effected by the holy Sacrifice, God makes us sharers of His divinity (the exchange consists in this that God becomes man in order that man may become God-like); we pray not only to preserve the gift of faith but also that we may "put its truths worthily into practice." The *Communion* is an open invitation to participate in the sacred Banquet: "Bring your offerings and assemble round the altar." More probably, however, the ancient Church took the Latin words literally; *Tollite hostias*, receive the sacred Host and enter His courts — an exhortation to proceed heavenward with hearts adoring the Lord. The Gregorian melody set to the words *adorate Dominum* is a falling cadence expressive of adoration, while the phrase *in aula sancta eius* loses itself in eternity through an indeterminate Phrygian finale. By way of exception today's *Postcommunion* voices thanksgiving for God's "holy Gift."

3. The Offertory. Studied in its full original form, the Offertory is most impressive; its message is the parousia in an Exodus setting.

> Moses consecrated an altar to Yahweh
>   and offered holocausts upon it.
> With animals of sacrifice,
>   *he made an evening sacrifice*
>   *as an odor of sweetness to Yahweh, God,*
>   *in the presence of the children of Israel.*

> Yahweh spoke to Moses and said:
>   Come now into my presence
>   by ascending the mount unto its very peak.
> Moses rose and climbed the mount
>   designated by his God.
> And in the clouds Yahweh appeared
>   and stood before his face.
> When Moses saw him,
>   he fell upon the earth and prayed:
>   Yahweh, I entreat you,
>   forgive your people their sins.
> And Yahweh replied:
>   I will do as you petition.

> *Then Moses offered an evening sacrifice.* . . .

> Moses addressed Yahweh and said:
>   If I have found favor in your sight,
>   show me your face, that I may know you.

And Yahweh answered:
> No man can gaze upon me and live.
> But if you stand upon yon high rock,
>> my right hand will cover you as I pass by.
> But having passed, I will take my hand away
>> and you shall see my glory.
> But my face shall not be yours to see
>> for I am God, who acts in mystery upon the earth.

Then Moses offered an evening sacrifice. . . .

Moses' evening sacrifice for the sins of his people prefigured the sacrifice of atonement offered by Jesus Christ on the Cross and in the holy Mass. Thereupon Moses asked to behold the divine face, but Yahweh refused his request, remarking that no living person was able to gaze upon His countenance. However, since Moses did not cease asking, God granted him a look with covered eyes and from behind. In these words the liturgy insinuates how the Mass is Christ's Second Advent anticipated, for at Mass Christ "appears" as He will appear on the last day, now of course "veiled." His Coming then will mean "eternal enjoyment of His divinity," while now His Coming consists in a rapid "passing," with His hand placed mystically upon me. I may look upon His "back," His face remains hidden.

4. **Divine Office.** The liturgy invites us to dramatize as mystery the episode of the man sick with palsy. In the morning we hear how "The Lord said to the paralytic: Don't worry, My son; your sins are forgiven." In the evening I sing thanks for my cure: "The paralyzed man took up the bed upon which he had been lying and praised God. Upon seeing it, the whole multitude glorified God." And all present join me in chanting the Magnificat. The homily is from the lips of St. Peter Chrysologus, Bishop of Ravenna (d. 450):

"Today's Reading brings us another instance of how Christ in His ordinary acts was performing divine deeds and through visible media manifested invisible mysteries. *He boarded a boat*, the text reads, *crossed over and came to His own town.* Was that indeed necessary? Is He not the One who at an earlier date stemmed the waves and laid bare the ground beneath so that dry of foot Israel could pass between the rigid waters as through a cleft in sheer rock? Is He not the One who checked the sea's swell at Peter's feet, making the watery surface into a solid path to walk upon? Why does He now deny Himself such services from the sea and seek a ship to make the narrow crossing?

"He boarded a boat, it reads, *and crossed over.* Still, why should such an action astonish us, brothers? Christ came to take our weakness upon Himself and to share with us His strength; He came to assume what is human, to bestow what is divine; to take away shame and to confer honor; to suffer physically while healing others; for a physician who never is sick cannot qualify himself for the art of healing; nor can one who will not condescend to the weak be able to comfort the sorrowing. Even so, if Christ had not divested Himself of His infinite power, He would not have had anything in common with us mortals; and if He had not submitted to the demands of the body, it would have been futile for Him to have become incarnate.

"He boarded a boat, we read, *crossed over and came to His own town.* The Creator and Lord of the universe, after having restricted Himself to the limitations of flesh for our benefit, became a resident in a Jewish town, a citizen of a country on this earth. The Father of all parents began to have parents Himself in order that whatever had been banished by tyrants, scattered by fear, or exiled by imperious edict would be invited back through love, drawn to Himself through kindness, won through sympathy, and retained through a genuinely sincere friendship."

5. **Sunday Meditations.** A. The Church's Harvest. As has already been observed, there occurs a break in the sequence of Sundays between the seventeenth and nineteenth of the Pentecostal cycle because of the fall Ember days. This is of significance since the Church thereby would indicate that we are now beginning the final phase of the ecclesiastical year, a phase that we may call "The Church's Harvest Time." In the present calendar the Ember days are no longer kept between these two Sundays because the date would vary too greatly in successive years; in-

stead, they always occur during the third week of September (Wednesday after the Exaltation of the Holy Cross). Although the last three Sundays (15–17) already contained marked parousia overtones, expectation and desire for the Lord's Advent will ring high and clear during the remaining weeks. The subject merits further consideration.

Now during the days when nature is donning her autumnal garment, when the leaves are turning colors and are falling from the trees, when the nights are becoming longer, the cold increasing and the autumn mists spreading their veil over the landscape, the Church too is keeping harvest. It is the last phase in the ecclesiastical year with a very definite and clearly marked spirit and purpose. It is a season that should prepare us for the end, or, in the terms of the ancient Church, for Christ's Second Advent (Christ's Second Advent at the death of each individual and His Second Advent on the day of the last Judgment are identical in liturgical parlance).

It must always be kept in mind that classic liturgy is not as much concerned with the consideration of the last Judgment with all its terror as with the parousia, the Lord's glorious return with redemption. It is not the negative emotion of fear but rather a positive spirit of longing for Christ, of feeling ill at ease upon earth, and of zeal for virtue that the Church wishes to awaken in us. It is the theological virtue of hope that the liturgy is striving to make us practice and cherish during these autumn weeks. To Christians of an earlier era hope meant awaiting the Second Advent of Christ (parousia), it was an incentive to holiness, to martyrdom, to contempt for the world.

The early Christian lived not only by faith in Jesus and through His love; he yearned deeply for his Savior's return, and his hope had a twofold influence: (a) negatively, it made him estrange himself from the profits and pleasures of the world, it made him a stranger upon earth who would attach his heart to none of its enticements; (b) positively, it filled him with longing for heaven and yearning for his Savior, and drove him to the practice of virtue so as to become perfect "in the day of Christ." Nevertheless, the Church never wished to make idle daydreamers of her children, she would not have us live in the future but while here on earth to work and live in the light of the Second Advent.

The liturgical texts of this season continue rich in theology — dogmatic, moral, and mystical. A series of magnificent word-pictures is used to convey the message. First we are led into a brilliantly illumined wedding hall (the Church), where, clothed in the white garment of baptism, we eagerly await the arrival of the King who is coming to see His guests (parousia); no parable is more expressive of the season's spirit (19th Sunday). Then Mother Church shows us how closely earthly life resembles the Babylonian exile and tells us to bear the sufferings of exile in the spirit of penance and sing: "Upon the rivers of Babylon, there do we sit and weep . . ." (20th Sunday). Then she arms us for spiritual battle and prepares us to fight "on the evil day"; or, in another picture, takes us before the seat of the eternal Judge (21st Sunday). She reminds us of "the body of our lowness" and permits us to scan the approaches to our heavenly father-land (23rd Sunday). We see the heavenly Reaper as He gathers the ripened sheaves into the heavenly granaries, and Satan too, as he burns the bundles of weeds with torches lit in hell (see the 5th Sunday after Epiphany). Then on the 24th and last Sunday after Pentecost it is the fearsome scene of the last Judgment.

It is characteristic of Sunday Masses to portray the spirit and mood of a given season; such is true, too, in the present instance. Each Sunday, therefore, we will attune our ears to the theme of the Church's Harvest, although we may find numerous passages on other subjects. In the second place we will devote thoughtful attention to special feasts since they easily lend themselves to the development of the principal theme. First among these feasts ranks that of Mary's Assumption into heaven, August 15, a true "harvest solemnity." She is the most excellent fruit in the Church's garden. To the parousia cycle, moreover, belongs the feast of the Exaltation of the Holy Cross, September 14; the Cross is raised defiantly against autumnal darkness, the symbol of the power of hell. Already we see the "sign of the Son of Man" which will appear in the heavens at His Coming. The feast of the Archangel Michael, leader of the heavenly hosts in the battle against Lucifer and his adherents, soon follows; for at the end of time will this battle reach its climax. The feast of Christ the King also has a very strong eschatological ring.

During November there occur the feasts of All Saints and of All Souls; on the former the liturgy draws back the curtain of heaven and shows us the Church Triumphant, while on All Souls' she places us at the grave and reminds us of the souls suffering in purgatory. During November come two "Church Dedication" feasts in which we see the Church portrayed as the royal Bride adorning herself for her Bridegroom, and as a City — the new Jerusalem in all its glory. And lastly, to the parousia cycle belong the feasts of four virgins, one falling in each of the winter months, viz., Cecilia, "the blind" (Nov.); Lucia, "the light-bearer" (Dec.); Agnes, "the pure" (Jan.); Agatha, "the good" (Feb.).

The Scripture Readings are in harmony with the spirit of the Church's Harvest. As is well known, the Church has established a special allocation of readings to suit the ecclesiastical year broadly interpreted. September is the first of the autumn months. The darkness which now is on the increase symbolizes the battle of darkness that will rage during the last days with unprecedented ferocity. During this month, therefore, the Church introduces certain personalities; Job, Tobias, Judith, Esther, types of Christians (and the Church) who must endure unto the end to gain the crown. During the month of October we are to read the astonishing annals of the heroic warriors, the Machabees; their deeds, as it were, illustrate the Epistle of the 21st Sunday, which describes the armor needed in the spiritual conflict. The month of November is reserved for the prophets; this again is most fitting, for they tell of the consummation of Christ's kingdom, of the last days, of the transition from God's kingdom upon earth to the kingdom of God in heaven.

The last source from which the liturgy draws during the Church's Harvest is the Masses in the Common of Saints. It is in full accord with liturgical method that these formularies, which always remain the same, be influenced by the spirit of the season at which they are used. Viewed in the light of Christmas they appear differently than in the glory of Easter or in the darkness of the final weeks. Nevertheless, we may make the surprising statement that most of the Masses in the Common are cast in a parousia mold and treat of the Second Coming of the Lord. The saint commemorated experienced at death Christ's Second Coming, and we re-enact that experience with him in Mass.

Such is the underlying meaning of Masses honoring saints. It may therefore be easier to appreciate such a Mass better now during the Church's Harvest than at other times. Daily the saints are preparing us for the parousia. At one time we may be acting the part of the vigilant servant who with girt loins goes to meet his Lord, at another we may be the man who with five talents gains an additional five, or we may belong to the choir of virgins who meet their approaching Bridegroom with lamps well oiled and burning.

Thus the Christian who lives with the Church has rich fields to exploit during the Church's Harvest Time. It will occasion special pleasure to observe how the Church, the Bride of Christ, lifts her eyes and heart to her Spouse.

B. The Secret is a prayer deserving our very special attention: "O God, by means of the holy exchange proper to this sacrifice You have made us sharers in Your divine life; now we plead for the grace to show forth the divine truths we know in activities that will do You honor." First of all, we find fittingly grouped together the three greatest blessings of Christianity, *grace, faith, the virtues.* What does the Secret say concerning each? Concerning *grace*. It is a participation in the "divine life." The same doctrine we find expressed in the prayer at the mingling of the water with the wine during the Offertory — *eius divinitatis esse consortes.* The words are taken from St. Peter's Second Epistle, 1:4: "That by these (promises) you may be made partakers of the divine nature (*divinae consortes naturae*)." At Athens St. Paul spoke in a similar vein: "Being therefore the offspring of God . . ." (Acts 17:29).

Grace, consequently, is a participation in the divine nature, in the highest Godhead, in the divine life. Therefore we are accustomed to call grace *life*, eternal life, divine life. And it can best be understood in context with the mystery of the Mystical Body. As my hand partakes in the life of my body, so the Christian as a member of the Mystical Body partakes in the life of the Head, that is, of Christ. We may even say: Christ accomplishes a new incarnation in His faithful through grace. Our participation in divinity according to the Secret results from "the holy exchange proper to the holy Sacrifice." This is a new and rich idea, but among the Fathers a common one.

Where in the Sacrifice occurs this exchange? Just recall a few truths from Christology. God became man that men might become like God. Christ, the Life, underwent death to bestow upon us, the dead, life. Exactly in this does the exchange consist. And it is being realized now during holy Mass. We bring *our* bread and receive *God's* Bread; we come with our poor humanity and receive "the highest divinity." Every sacrifice is an exchange, a trade between God and man, a taking and a receiving; how absolutely true is this of Christ's sacrifice actualized now at Mass. The prayer under consideration explicitly states the sublime fruit of the exchange: through it we become "sharers in God's own life."

And now briefly concerning the other two blessings, *faith* and *virtue*. Note the Biblical expression, divine truth. Truth is the revelation God gives and which concerns God. It is faith. The "truth" is the ever-recurring theme of St. John's Gospel — to know the truth and also to *do* the truth (John 3:21). This Johannine approach is reflected in our prayer; faith and virtue go hand in hand. Faith must flower into the fruit of virtue. By God's grace we know the truth, but our cooperation is necessary to render this truth operative in our daily activity.

C. The Symbol of the "Furnished Throne." Certain mosaics from ancient Christian times portray a very striking and noteworthy symbol, i.e., a throne upon which no one is sitting but upon which several insignia are lying, evidently a throne ready for its occupant. This representation, called *hetoimasia* (etym.: "furnished throne" — later corrupted into *etimasia*), symbol-

ized Christ's Second Advent, the parousia, and gave pictorial expression to the expectation and desire of primitive Christians for the return of their God-King. In their eagerness they had, as it were, already prepared the throne upon which He was to sit at His Coming, and upon it they had already placed the insignia of His sovereignty.

The single instance extant from ancient times in which all of Christ's four insignia are found upon the throne is the mosaic of Sixtus III (432–440) in the basilica of St. Mary Major in Rome. (The words *insignia Christi* are found on an inscription in St. Crisogono's in Rome, dating from about the fourth century). These insignia are: a triumphal cross upon the throne, a scroll of Holy Writ, a crown, and a purple royal mantle spread over the seat of the throne. Their significance is self-evident. Great divergence is to be found in the choice and arrangement of these royal insignia, but the mosaic at St. Mary Major is the only one possessing the full ensemble; otherwise one or the other is always missing. Of special beauty and interest are the mosaics of furnished thrones in the two fifth-century baptisteries at Ravenna.

And there are some variations on the theme. The throne at times is embellished by a dove (the Holy Spirit) and a book (the holy Bible). The book, a symbol for Christ, is shown to be the word of God through the presence of the Sacred Dove. Sometimes a lamb is standing upon the throne, a nuance that may have been inspired by the fifth chapter of the Apocalypse. A final type, of which we will only make mention, no longer symbolizes joyous awaiting for the parousia but fear of Judgment; the royal insignia are replaced by instruments of torture. At a later date this became a common way of representing the Last Judgment in the East. The only example of it in Rome is to be found in the Church of St. Paul Outside the Walls.

NINETEENTH SUNDAY AFTER PENTECOST

Guests at God's marriage feast

This Sunday marks the beginning of a series of three featuring the virtue of Christian hope. Playing his role in the liturgical mystery, the Christian appears first as a guest at God's marriage feast, then as an alien on earth, and thirdly as a soldier in his Father's army. Life on earth is staged in the light of the parousia.

O Christian, you are a wedding guest in the Church's
    wedding halls — keep your nuptial robe of grace immaculate.
O Christian, earth is not your country; in it you are
    an enemy alien — do not forget your true fatherland.
O Christian, you are a soldier and you must win
    the conflict so that you may receive the crown of life.

The liturgy presents to us this Sunday a splendid picture of the Church during her time of harvest. In the brilliantly illumined apartments of a wedding celebration, we see seated numerous guests clothed in white. Expectant glances are cast toward the door, which at any moment may open that the king may enter to greet his guests. The wedding room is the Church; we Christians are the guests, the white garment is the baptismal robe denoting our divine filiation, the awaited king is the Lord about to return for the parousia. The great concern of our life ought to be our white wedding garment; it is symbolic of the new man whom we must put on in justice and holiness of truth (*Epist.*); it is the realization of God's will in our regard (*Coll.*).

1. Text Analysis. Today's formulary lends itself to analysis from two different approaches, (a) that of the station saints; (b) that of the wedding garment.

a) There is a relationship of dependence between today's holy Mass and the Mass of the physician-saints Cosmas and Damian, whose feast is celebrated about this time. In past centuries their titular church was also the station for today's liturgy. This titular relationship accounts for the frequent use of terms such as *healing, medicine*. The transition from our saints as physicians to Christ's healing work is not difficult. Note the very first word of the Mass, *Salus*. Christ stands at the head as *the* Healer of the souls *par excellence*. The antiphon at the Offertory originally was *salvum faciet*, "Your right hand will heal me." The Oration treats of the needs of body and soul, the Secret of health-procuring (*salutaria*) gifts, the Postcommunion of the healing efficacy (*medicinalis*) of the holy Eucharist. The Lessons make no allusions to the healing theme, but an enthusiast could easily see the cure accomplished in the wedding garment of grace and the "new man created in justice and holiness."

b) The Lessons give another key to the message of the various prayer texts. There is a wedding, and we are present in the role of both bride and guest. The Epistle is linked to the Gospel in that the wedding garment is equivalent to "putting on the new man." Clothed in the garment of grace we sit in the Church's banquet hall about her Eucharistic table. The Bridegroom Christ is present both as Host and as Food. No work is more important than to keep one's apparel immaculate (*Intr.*, *Comm.*). At our first appearance the Bridegroom greets us with *Salus*, "I am your salvation," and requests cooperation, obedience. The joyous, festive chants are wedding songs. The nuptial

theme, so deeply imbedded in Sacred Scripture, aids no little in making this Mass instructive and edifying.

2. Holy Mass (Salus populi). In this Mass it is easy to sense the spirit of the early Church; in apparent tears and sorrow, though clothed in the white robe of purity, holy Church expectantly awaits the Second Advent of the Lord. The *Introit* antiphon arranges a quite extraordinary setting; on entering the church, Christ comes to meet us and speaks to us words of comfort and of counsel: Do not be sad if now you have much to suffer; I am with you, I am your God and very soon I Myself will be your greatest joy. Presently, however, He lifts His hand in warning: Be mindful of this one thing, keep My commandments. The *Collect* is a pilgrim's prayer. Joyfully we are hastening toward our heavenly home; nevertheless, the devil and our own lower nature hang as leaden weights on body and soul; we pray for the removal of these hindrances that "with freed hearts we may fulfill the will of God."

The *Epistle* assigns to us the most serious task of our lives: "To put on the new man which God has created according to His image in true justice and holiness." It is the wedding garment of the Gospel. We must put off the dress of sin, the old man, before the setting of the sun (before the sun of life has set); we must show love to one another "for we are members" of Christ's Body. The incense which ascends at the Gospel together with our hands lifted up toward heaven in the *Gradual* attest our homesickness for heaven.

The *Alleluia* verse resounds with paschal praise to our divine King who enters at the *Gospel*. Now Christ is speaking. The parable of the wedding garment is, in the first place, an admonition; it does not suffice to belong to the Church through faith alone (to sit at the marriage feast); we must also live in accordance with the will of God, wearing the required spiritual attire. The nuptials denote the work of salvation; Christ is the Bridegroom, the Church the Bride, we Christians the guests. The Second Advent of Christ is signified by the king's entrance; sanctifying grace is the wedding garment. Hardly any other picture could better represent Christian life.

The Gospel parable also pictures Sunday Mass. The illumined wedding suite is the house of God in which a congregation of divinely chosen guests are gathered; the wedding banquet is that of the holy Eucharist, which at the same time is a symbol and pledge of the heavenly nuptials. Here too the King appears to meet His guests as a figure of His future visit. Thus is the parable fulfilled in our Sunday Mass. You need but have one anxiety, one great worry — not to be the guest indecently clothed.

Today's *Offertory* depicts life's dark pilgrimage, "If I should walk in the midst of tribulation. . . ." Such words the early Church could truly pray in the midst of persecutions and her Offering would be accepted; therefrom she drew all strength. Insisting that our ways be directed according to the commandments of God, the *Communion* teaches abstractly what the Epistle and Gospel taught by the figures of "putting on the new man" and the "wedding garment." The holy Eucharist was our spiritual medicine; may it effect a lasting cure from sin and a healthy obedience to God's holy precepts (*Postc.*).

A beautiful Mass! Note how many times the observance of the commandments is repeated (*Intr., Coll., Comm., Postc.*). It is a challenge to you. Only by obedience may you hope to meet the approaching King with the white garment of grace.

3. Divine Office. The two greater antiphons (*Magn.* and *Ben.*) linger meditatively upon the text of the parable: "Tell them who were invited: See, I have prepared my dinner, come to the marriage, alleluia." "The king went in to see the guests; and he saw there a man who was not wearing wedding apparel. He said to him: Friend, how did you get in here without wearing wedding apparel?" — The homily in explanation of the Gospel is from St. Gregory the Great. A type of allegorical syllogism is used that does not seem too convincing.

4. Meditations upon the Sunday. A. Today's Parable and the Church Year. We will better understand today's holy Mass if we consider its story of the marriage feast in relation to the liturgical life of Christians and in relation to the ecclesiastical year. The parable spans a mystic arch over the Church's year of grace, uniting Christmas, Easter, and Pentecost.

1) The parable describes a marriage feast that a king arranged for his son. Now to what was Christ referring? Primarily the work of redemption. Why the comparison to a marriage? It was an ancient figure of speech, in use already by the prophets. In the New Covenant it was adopted by St. John the Baptist (he called himself the herald of the Bridegroom), by St. John the Evangelist (in the apocalyptic symbol of the Lamb and Bride), and by St. Paul (matrimony, a great mystery portraying Christ and the Church). Yes, our Lord even called Himself the Bridegroom of the Church (Matt. 9:15). Now just where is the point of semblance? Sin separated man from God, the redemption ought again unite man to God. That union should be the most intimate imaginable, not a relationship between servant and lord, or between friend and friend, but as close and as intimate as bridegroom and bride.

We may distinguish three stages in the espousal of Christ with men. The first was the incarnation. Through His conception and birth, divinity and humanity were joined in the person of the divine Word. The second stage was that of the passion and death upon the Cross by which Christ redeemed men and reunited them to God objectively; subjectively, however, redemption is accomplished in the baptism and sanctification of individual souls. The final degree is the ultimate union of the Church (and souls) with the divine Bridegroom in heaven, a consummation St. John paints so magnificently in his apocalyptic vision: "I saw the holy city, the new Jerusalem, coming down out of heaven from God, prepared as a bride adorned for her husband" (Apoc. 21:2).

Aided by the liturgy we may compare the Christmas cycle, which has as its object the incarnation and birth of Christ, to a marriage feast. During Advent we hear the longing cries of the bride for the divine Bridegroom; she is preparing herself for His arrival. At Christmas we see the Bridegroom step forth from His bridal chamber (Ps. 18), but not until Epiphany does the Church celebrate the wedding feast. We need only recall that famous antiphon: "This day the Church is joined to her heavenly Spouse, for Christ has cleansed away her crimes in the Jordan; with gifts the Magi hasten to the royal nuptials, and the guests are gladdened with wine made from water. Alleluia." Here we have the most ideal application of the parable. Again at the final feast of the Christmas cycle, the Presentation, we sing: "Adorn your bridal chamber, O Sion, and receive Christ, your King!" In this manner the Christmas cycle exemplifies the sacred nuptials between Christ and the Church.

2) After the citizens of that city had so insolently refused the invitation extended them, the king ordered his servants to bring in from the highways both the bad and the good; and his table was filled with guests. We know that by this Jesus indicated the rejection of the Jews and the call of the Gentiles.

After the Christmas cycle is completed the Church becomes more grave in demeanor, more serious, more earnest. Her messengers and attendants are standing on the highways and at the crossroads inviting all to the marriage feast. Such is the spirit of the three Sundays preceding Lent (the workers in the vineyard). The Church is gathering her neophytes; she is insisting on penitential practices; the great fast, directed exclusively to the care of the wedding garment, is beginning. Each guest requires special attention; for one the wedding garment must be newly woven (baptism), for another it must be laundered (penance). How highly important this season is in the mind of the Church may be judged from the serious mood which has come upon her, from her fastings, and even from her feasts. In tears and penance, by fastings, by almsgiving, and by prayer the wedding garment is washed and woven. Then come two days of exceptional importance in her life, Holy Thursday and Holy Saturday. On Holy Thursday we put away the garb of penance to receive again the wedding garment; on Easter eve the catechumens are clothed with resplendent robes, and we together with them. The priest says: "Receive this white garment and bring it unsullied to the judgment seat of God." On Easter day the marriage feast is full, all the guests are seated, clothed in immaculately resplendent wedding garments.

3) "And the king went in to see the guests." By this the liturgy means the Second Advent of the Lord for each individual at death, and for all mankind at the Last Judgment. Only they will then be found acceptable who are clothed in the nuptial robes of sanctifying grace; they who are not so attired will hear from the heavenly Judge the sentence of eternal damnation. From Easter to Pentecost is the most blessed season for the children of God, for during that period their wedding garments are clean and nicely tailored. But on Pentecost the newly-baptized are declared of age and sent out into a contrary world.

The last period of the Church year, the time after Pentecost, is about to begin. This season may be characterized in these words: *With deep anxiety holy Church endeavors to preserve her children's wedding robes immaculate.* Sunday after Sunday she purifies the holy garment by the *Asperges;* Sunday after Sunday she prepares a Eucharistic banquet to preserve and cleanse the baptismal robes (*mundet et muniat*). Untiringly she pleads and counsels her children to put off the old man and put on the new man exemplifying true justice and holiness. From the seventeenth Sunday after Pentecost, however, Mother Church gazes longingly and expectantly toward her approaching Lord. In pilgrim's garb she travels as a stranger through the world, anxiously awaiting her King; her one and deepest concern is that her children will be present without blame or guilt on the day of the Lord's Advent.

B. The Epistle. We ought always appraise the Sunday Epistles as letters truly from God. Since they are rich in golden kernels of early Christian doctrine, we ought every week dedicate one day to a deeper understanding and fuller application of their contents. Today's Epistle begins with the counsel that we renew our spirit and put on the new man. Its relation to the parable of the Gospel has already been noted. We know that this renewal, this donning of the new man has already been accomplished in baptism, while at Easter each year it is publicly re-enacted. But since we earth-men are repeatedly falling from our high aims, a more frequent regeneration becomes necessary. Each Sunday, therefore, is Easter in miniature, each Sunday calls to us in the first words of today's Epistle: "Get a new heart, become a new (spiritual) personality!" The rite of the *Asperges* contains the same admonition. Wearing of Sunday clothes and the use of freshly laundered apparel may very appropriately be considered symbolic of this regeneration.

St. Paul cites three examples of spiritual renewal which may be summed up thus: love of truth, love of neighbor, love of justice. Certainly these are three fundamental virtues of our moral lives. Let us try meditating upon them in a positive manner.

1) Love of truth. Of course, we may not be addicted to the habit of direct lying, but God's command is by far not fulfilled in that alone. We want to be men so sincerely given to the ideal of truth as never to show ourselves other than we truly are. Nothing two-faced, nothing hypocritical. Sincerity is a Christian virtue. Therefore, all exaggeration, all belittling, all that is not genuine, all that is false or "diplomatic" should be equally foreign. A final consideration. The motive St. Paul gives for

being truthful is that "we are members of one another," that is, members of the Mystical Body. The Apostle is teaching us how to make the doctrine of Christ's Body practical. The hand never lies to the foot.

2) Love of neighbor. Life in action is the Apostle's concern. He sees Christians living together in family and community groups, and as a result there arise occasions for friction. This of course may happen, the Apostle admits, but love need not suffer thereby. To prevent the continuance of ill-feeling, he lays down a sound and very practical piece of legislation: "Do not let the sun go down upon your anger." Oh, if only married persons, monks in monasteries, and members of convents, and all who associate with their fellow men would make this a fast rule of conduct! I know a wedded couple who have a beautifully inscribed copy of this text hanging in their bedroom.

3) Love of justice. Perhaps one may be tempted to say: "But, Paul, how you do think of us! We aren't thieves!" Exactly. Just in this crude fashion we keep the seventh commandment. St. Paul wants us to see a positive side to this precept, *social justice*. In moving words he exhorts us to work in order that we may earn something for a poor neighbor. Poverty-stricken neighbors do still exist, in Basutoland and the Bahamas, for example. And there are other sins against social justice — race discrimination, immigration rulings, unfair exemptions, tariffs. In a democracy all are responsible for the course of legislation. When have you last criticized laws putting your South American or Asiatic neighbor at an economic disadvantage? or helped vote their supporters out of office?

TWENTIETH SUNDAY AFTER PENTECOST

By the rivers of Babylon, there did we sit and weep

The virtue of hope is the theme of today's liturgy. The negative aspect of the virtue, however, receives greater consideration because the setting of the liturgical drama is the Babylonian exile. Since life on earth is a life of exile from the heavenly fatherland, man ought feel himself a foreigner in this world (*Off.*); he ought bear his earthly exile in the spirit of penance (*Intr.*) and put each moment of time to good advantage ("redeeming the time" — *Epist.*) by atoning for sin (*Coll., Secr.*) and by living virtuously (*Intr., Epist., Comm.*). Especially ought he cherish a sacred longing for his eternal home (*Grad., Off., Comm.*). The key text is the Offertory; in it we give full vent to our homesickness for heaven: "By the rivers of Babylon, there did we sit and weep as we remembered Sion."

1. Holy Mass (Omnia quae). No Sunday Mass throughout the whole of the Church's Harvest Season is so overflowing with deep sentiments of longing for heaven welling up from the hearts of those suffering in exile. As a forlorn child the soul enters into the house of God; she recognizes, as did the three young men in Babylon's fiery furnace, that she has merited her sufferings through sin (let us bear all the misfortunes of life in the spirit of penance); yet she dedicates herself unreservedly to her heavenly country, which she sees symbolized in the sanctuary. The entrance of the priestly ministers clothed in stainless vestments is to her a symbol of life immaculately lived: "Blessed are the undefiled in the way" (*Intr.*).

Similar thoughts are expressed in the *Collect*; we pray for pardon and peace, but on this particular occasion it is a prayer especially for earthly peace in order that God "may be served with a tranquil mind." The *Epistle* depicts the reticent spirit of the virtuous Christian toward things of the world. As a stranger he "walks circumspectly," making good use of his time for it is precious; with it he is enabled to buy eternity. Our days are filled with so many spiritual possibilities, and we utilize them so badly! It is not a question of multiplying works, but rather of being permeated with the transforming energy of grace. Our days should be filled with life and action flowing from the fullness of God.

"The days are evil." This is true perhaps now more than ever.

St. Paul speaks of a twofold "intoxication." We are not to permit
ourselves to be overcome by wine or other earthly pleasures, but
we are to be inebriated with the Holy Spirit. Of this intoxication he continues: "Let psalms and hymns and spiritual canticles
resound at your gatherings, let the song of thanksgiving fill your
heart." The Apostle is thinking of a community blessed charis-
matically. "Be subject one to another in the fear of Christ." Well
does St. Paul know how to tear us loose from the worldly, to
make us feel as strangers in its environment.

The *Gradual* is a moving song of longing for our heavenly
fatherland and its pledge, the holy Eucharist. Particularly beautiful is the *Alleluia* verse. My heart is ready to receive the Lord
at His Second Coming; already I am striking at the strings,
eager to sing the eternal Easter hymn, *Alleluia*! Against the

exile background the *Gospel* story brings a fuller message. Our principal duty is to regain health for our sick soul; we should beg it from our Savior with as much confidence as did the royal official in the Gospel. "O come down before my soul has died! Now in the holy Sacrifice I call unto Thee, O Lord, come down to me that my soul may be healed; at Thy Second Advent (my death) come down into this valley of tears that my soul and body may be healed and quickened!" At the sacred time of consecration, Christ truly comes down, bringing anew to my soul the graces of redemption. It is He, the very One who some day will come down "to judge the living and the dead."

Today's *Offertory* pictures life's way of exile, as we sing one of the most tensely emotional of the psalms (pray it entirely). The *Secret*: holy Eucharist is the proper medicine for diseases attacking the soul. Sin must be atoned for before our exile comes to an end. During the exile of earthly life we have one great solace, hope for heaven. In our miseries the holy Eucharist is our comfort; it is a constant *viaticum* for us during life's pilgrimage; it is the bread of exiles (*Comm.*). But the preliminary condition for all this is "obedience to the commandments of God" (*Postc.*).

2. Text Analysis. There is no difficulty in determining the principal theme in today's Mass formulary, viz., the Christian is an exile alien while on earth. Four passages contribute significantly to this message, the Introit (a *lectio* from the prophets), the Epistle, the Gospel, and the Offertory.

a) A relic from the *Reading* from the prophetical books (the first of the three Readings in ancient liturgy) occurs as the Introit; it is a fine expression of the "exile theme." The passage is part of the prayer of Azarias, one of the three young men thrown into the fiery furnace: "Because of our sins we have been humiliated throughout the world. For the present we have lost all, we have no princes, no prophets, no temple, no sacrifice. We are not able to appease God by holocausts. With contrite hearts and humble spirit may we merit Your favor. As a sacrifice of goats and a thousand fattened lambs, so may our offering rise today before Your presence, pleasing and acceptable to You." The three youths were offering their sufferings in exile as a

spiritual sacrifice to God, and in the name of the people promised obedience to His prophets. Do not overlook the wonderful
community spirit of the three young men; they were innocent
of sin, and yet regarded themselves as guilty because they belonged to the Jewish race; and they were ready to make atonement for them. We could well bear the sufferings of life as
atonement for the sins of men.

b) How earth-exiles ought live is the burden of the Epistle.
Christians of an earlier era would have experienced a special
thrill. The citizens of earth become drunk with wine, but we
with the spirit of God. The Alleluia provides an immediate
example.

c) The Gospel too contributes to the development of the
exile theme. Christ can work miracles, even *in absentia*. While
on earth we cannot see Him physically. But He does heal us,
invisibly. We must believe without seeing. The Church prays:
"Lord, come down before my children die!" He does come,
even though our eyes see nothing. Faith is absolutely necessary.
By means of the holy Eucharist He heals us, though we see no
person present. He remains veiled in two ways, viz., in the words
of Sacred Scripture and in the bread of the Eucharist. In both
He comes to us, our "solace in misery" (*Comm.*).

d) An ideal climax and one in which can be placed the full
pathos of an alien's distress comes at that portion of the Mass to
which man can contribute most, the Offertory. That is the moment when man can give, at other times he mostly receives.
What do we bring to the altar today? Our suffering as exiles.
And to it is given expression in finest poetic form: "By the rivers
of Babylon, there do we sit and weep, thinking of you, O Sion.
There upon the willows do we hang our harps. . . ." This
brings today's "Exile Mass" to its dramatic climax. Few formularies in the missal are so well integrated thematically.

3. Divine Office. It is the wish of the Church that throughout the day we should be completely absorbed by the Gospel
account, reliving it again in word and action. Here we have the
reason for the choice of the greater antiphons: "There was a
certain ruler whose son was sick at Capharnaum. When he heard

that Jesus was come into Galilee, he requested Him to heal his
son" (*Ben. Ant.*). "The father therefore knew that it was at the
same hour that Jesus had said to him: Your son will live. And
he believed, and his whole house" (*Magn. Ant.*). The whole day
should be dedicated to this action-mysterium. Therefore at its
two extremities, morning and evening, Mother Church chants
the story of the miraculous recovery.

4. **Sunday Meditations.** A. Psalm 136. Few psalms in the
entire psalter make a deeper impression upon one at first reading
than Psalm 136. It is a soul-stirring elegy:

> By the rivers of Babylon
>   there did we sit and weep
>   as we remembered you, O Sion.
> There upon the willows
>   we hung our harps.
> Our captors there
>   demanded songs of mirth;
> Those who deported us enjoined:
>   "Sing for us some Sion songs."
>
> How could we sing
>   a Yahweh song
>   in foreign land!
>
> Should I forget you, Jerusalem,
>   may my right hand wither.
> May my tongue cleave to its palate
>   should I fail remembering you —
>   should Jerusalem cease
>   to be my perfect joy.
>
> Yahweh, do not forget how Edom's sons
>   cried on Jerusalem's evil day:
> "Demolish it, demolish it,
>   to its very foundations!"

> But first you, O daughter Babylon, you devastator —
>   fortune to him who pays you back
>   the treatment meted us;
>   fortune to him who takes your babes
>   to smash them on the rocks.

In spirit I go to Babylon. On the banks of the river Euphrates I see bands of Jews assembled for prayer. I also see chanters who once in Jerusalem's temple sang festal songs at the divine services; in tears they seat themselves on the banks of the river. See, now they are beginning the service with a song, a song of Sion, as they were accustomed to call them. But no, they seem unable to proceed. In silent sorrow, with cheeks moistened with tears, they think of the temple, of Mount Sion and Jerusalem; and they hang their harps upon the willow branches.

The Jewish psalmody was famous far and wide; therefore the natives could demand: "Sing for us some Sion songs!" No, no, a Jew could never comply with that. "How could we sing a Yahweh song in foreign land?" Then one of them with uplifted hand cries in oath: "Should I forget you, Jerusalem, may my right hand wither." Look, that Jew is clenching his fist against the friends of his foes, the Edomites, his own kinsmen who had goaded the Babylonians on to fresh atrocities: "O daughter Babylon, you devastator — fortune to him who pays you back the treatment meted us!" And now with two fists tightly clenched he screams a frightful curse against Babylon: "Fortune to him who takes your babes to smash them on the rocks!"

Such is the tone of the psalm which the Church wishes us to pray during today's holy Mass. How can we use such a song in our prayers? Our life, too, is an exile. Heaven is our fatherland, earth an exile. Especially now during her Harvest Season holy Church admonishes us to direct all our desires toward heaven. Our Jerusalem is the heavenly Sion where we will be eternally united with Christ and all His saints. Therefore we should experience in our hearts that same intense longing of which the exiled Jews sang on the banks of Babylon's rivers. Psalm 136 is the song of a soul homesick for its heavenly fatherland.

B. The Babylonian Captivity. The three liturgical processions of this Sunday's holy Mass have as background the Babylonian captivity (*Intr., Off., Comm.*). At the Offertory we even sing the original Jewish exile elegy. The Babylonian captivity prefigured our earthly life. Let us consider the points of similarity. (1) Sin. The cause of the exile was sin, the infidelity of the Chosen People toward God. Through the mouths of prophets Yahweh, the God of Israel's Covenant, had admonished His people for centuries. Again and again He showed mercy and patience. Finally the day of punishment. Yet divine punishments are not merely vindictive, they are at the same time medicinal. Accordingly the Captivity was destined for the betterment of the Jewish people.

Now how does our own lot resemble that Captivity? Earth is a vale of tears. Man begins his life with weeping, and with groans he ends it. Do we ask the wherefore of this sorrow? Only faith can give the answer. Sin. Even though Christ did redeem us from sin, He did not will to restore paradise to us; we must stay in exile. Life on earth with all its sorrows serves, in the first place, as punishment and expiation. Nevertheless, it likewise is a time of cleansing and schooling in preparation for the heavenly fatherland. This is the sense in which we are to understand the Introit; with our lives we will pay our debt; we will not wrangle over our lot. "Lord, it is good that I am poor, and ill, and burdened with suffering!"

2) Aliens. It was very bitter and humiliating for the Jews to pass their days in captivity. They were pushed about, scoffed at, trodden upon. They felt themselves strangers, and were looked upon as such. And we? Are we not also strangers upon earth? We Christians are the world's step-children. The world laughs at us, considers us queer. Somewhere there is always a persecution raging. And so it should be. If we should nestle ourselves complacently in the world's bosom, if we should build ourselves a secure and quiet dwelling, we would be traitors to our heavenly heritage. Here is the reason for patience and suffering. We may never feel ourselves too fortunate upon earth. Now we see why so few of the rich and influential are found in our ranks.

3) Homesickness. The Captivity had a very sobering effect upon the Chosen People. Previously they had trodden the Law under foot, had esteemed as naught both temple and sacrifice. But now in the Captivity they learned to appreciate these things anew. And what was more, a deep longing and a sacred homesickness for the temple and for the holy City seized their hearts. Of these emotions Psalm 136 is a good expression. It must be the same with us. While on earth we are not to forget our true fatherland. Our home, our Jerusalem, is heaven toward which all our desire and longing must be directed. This is the fruit of the virtue of hope, that great driving force in the early Church. Her whole concern was to be in readiness for her Lord's Second Coming. Such likewise is the central thought of this and other Sundays during the Church's Harvest Time. How are we responding?

St. Cyprian speaks very beautifully of this holy longing for heaven:

"We must take heed, beloved brethren, and repeatedly call to mind that we have renounced the world and that we are simply traveling here as guests and strangers. Eagerly should we embrace the day that will give to each of us his true dwelling, that will deliver us from the confines of earth and lead us back to paradise and to the kingdom of heaven. Who is there who when in a strange land would not employ every means in order to return to his native country? Who is there who when setting sail for his dear ones would not desire a favorable wind in order soon to have the pleasure of embracing his beloved ones? Why then do we not anxiously hasten toward our heavenly abode, there to be enabled to greet our fathers, brothers, children? Our presence is passionately desired by an immense host who in their immortality are without care and worry but still are deeply interested in our salvation.

"Oh what great happiness, oh what mutual joy to see and to embrace the citizens of heaven! What bliss to live without the fear of death eternally in the heavenly kingdom! Forever blessed! The glorious choir of apostles is there, the rejoicing host of prophets is there, numberless martyrs adorned with crowns because of victory in battle and in death! Virgins are there in triumph, virgins who trod under the concupiscence of flesh and body by the power of purity. There the merciful have received their reward, they who by giving alms and nourishing the poor performed works of justice; in obedience to the will of the Lord they laid up earthly possessions in the heavenly treasury. With burning desire we ought hasten there, beloved brethren, wishing to be with them soon that it may be our fortune to be united with Christ."

4) Solace. The only consolation which remained to the Chosen People during the Captivity was the Torah, the Law. It had to take the place of temple, sacrifices, Jerusalem. Therefore with all their might they stressed the Law, learned to observe it again, learned to esteem and to love it. Psalm 118, which the Church prays so often during the Little Hours, gives evidence of the love which post-exilic Jews had toward the Law.

We too have a solace in exile; it is the Church with her myriad means of sanctification. For us in exile the Church of God is a piece of our heavenly fatherland. The greatest solace, however, is the holy Eucharist. It is not only the promise but the pledge of eternal salvation. May it be "my solace in misery" (*Comm.*).

C. The Epistle. Christian life and the duties of one's vocation. The Epistle can easily be made into a program for the week. Now what does the Church wish to teach this week? She teaches that we should live as wise men and not as fools. Life for fools is without aim, without purpose. They live for the day, squander the time, gorge themselves with liquor, give vent to every passion and are ever babbling dribble. They run after the world's false fortunes, are ungrateful toward those who do them good, and with eyes bent solely upon personal aggrandisement, tyrannize, oppress, and enslave their fellow men. They are egoists, centering all their aspirations upon themselves. Such the life of fools.

We Christians, on the other hand, wish to be classified among the just and the wise. We have a definite aim and a well-marked way leading thereto. The goal and the way is Christ and His doctrine. Can we describe the appearance of this "way of the wise" in greater detail ? (1) The wise man utilizes every moment. What an appropriate phrase, "redeeming the time"! It means to buy it up entirely, completely. Just as the entire stock of a business enterprise can be purchased, so also ought every possibility that time offers be put to good advantage. The saints did. Time is a talent entrusted to us; it is to be used as a means unto spiritual enrichment. How many, many days and hours have we wasted! Is someone saying: In what way can I make better use of time? Simply ask yourself: *What does God want me to do now?* You could not imagine a better way of "redeeming the time."

2) The wise man is not the slave of unruly passions. It is quite possible to be intoxicated with other potions than alcohol. We are warned against the excessive use of liquor because it excites and stimulates the passions (Bacchus and Venus *are* friends). "Intoxication" for Christians results from being filled with the fullness of the Holy Spirit. Just call to mind the charismata of the early Church, the gift of tongues or of prophecy.

3) The wise and prudent man guards his tongue and employs it in the service of God and the salvation of souls. It is just in this that the wicked may easily be distinguished from the virtuous.

4) Above all, for all, and always are we to show a spirit of gratitude. Each and every thing in life is an added reason to be thankful, even suffering and disappointments, for all things are from God and are for our good.

5) Finally, our subordination to one another belongs to the Christian outlook on life. Such subordination is rooted in humility and love of neighbor. It sees Christ in one's fellow man; for every Christian is a member of the Body of Christ, and He once said: "The Son of man is not come to be served but to serve, and to give His life as redemption for many" (Matt. 20:28). Make today's Epistle your coming program of action.

TWENTY-FIRST SUNDAY AFTER PENTECOST

Forgive us our trespasses as we forgive those who trespass
against us

Now during holy Church's Harvest Season the liturgy manifests the most unlike moods, motives, and admonitions. Last Sunday's Mass was lyrical in character; holy longing and deep desire for our heavenly fatherland filled our hearts; life on earth was but the Exile repeated. Today, however, action receives the principal emphasis; warfare against the foes of salvation, patience in daily life, loving forgiveness are the demands laid upon us. Out of last Sunday's homesickness for heaven there has developed a sense of fear and anxiety concerning our state of soul on the day of judgment. Again this Sunday we see Christ in His Second Advent, but today He comes as King, merciful and generous in His forgiveness, yet strict and impartial in His judgments. If we would want to formulate a theme for today's Mass, it would be: Christian life in the light of the Second Advent.

1. **Text Analysis**. The formulary is a mosaic of rich and glowing colors if viewed in its totality; how the various units harmonize is less clear. The two Readings may be related to the theme of the parousia, and in fact are so understood by the liturgy. From another point of view both Lessons place emphasis on life and action, conflict and loving forgiveness. Neither do the chants possess the unifying theme or scheme which we so often find, viz., from a cry for succour in the Introit to a thanksgiving prayer for redemption in the Postcommunion. The tone, to be sure, is serious rather than joyous. The Orations are not of one mold. Whether the three pictures, that of the armored soldier, the generous and just king, and patient Job have been grouped together intentionally can neither be proven nor disproven. References to God as King (*Intr., Grad., Gosp.*) and to human activity (*Epist., Allel., Gosp., Off.*) are found throughout the Mass.

With true Christian courage today's Mass confronts life and meets death face to face. As a result we are given instructions on

how to live and directions on how to prepare for a holy death. No, we are not to flee life or escape its harsh realities; rather to utilize life's every potentiality, for death will make its appearance soon enough. Such teaching is really no new revelation to the children of God, e.g., that life is a violent struggle, that we must be fully equipped at the divine arsenal, that we must practice loving forgiveness, that patience and resignation to God's holy will is the supreme sacrifice to be made.

The points regarding death stressed in the present formulary are the following. Perfect resignation to God is the best preparation for death (*Intr.*); God is the Lord of life, and the thread of life is snapped only according to His good designs. The Epistle takes cognizance of the evil day (death) and would have us ready. The opening lines of Psalm 89, used at the Gradual, strike the awesome contrast between the eternal God and mortal man. With the Alleluia we joyously make our exodus from the Egypt of earthly life to the promised land of heaven. The Gospel summons us to the Last Judgment when God exacts a strict accounting; we look about for an able defendant and can find such in our acts of mercy and pardon while on earth. Patient Job directs our eyes toward death a last time, Job, whom Satan tested and whom God proved faithful. In the face of death the "food of immortality" becomes doubly precious. Had you suspected that a Mass formulary could serve so excellently as a meditation on death?

2. Holy Mass (In voluntate). An air of unusual seriousness envelops the Mass. Surrounded by manifold enemies, facing the harvest time of imminent judgment, the soul approaches the sanctuary. In the apse of the church it sees enthroned the all-wise Judge, Christ the King of the world; all creation is assembled before Him. He is the Creator of all, has full title to obedience and fidelity. In this setting we raise our voices in the well-known psalm, "Blessed are the undefiled in the way" (118). The *Collect* implores God's help: "Protect Your household, Lord; may it be freed from all adversities and through good works devoted to Your Name." Already allusion is made to the two ideas prominent in the Readings, conflict and acts of brotherly love.

The *Epistle* takes us to the final day of the Church on earth, "the evil day," the day of death and of the Second Coming. The Church shows us the foe, the devil, and equips us with a complete set of armor, i.e., sash (truth), breastplate (justice), shoes (preparedness), shield (faith), helmet (salvation), sword (the word of God). She shows us Christian life as a battle, especially with reference to the "evil day." The *Gradual* re-echoes the Epistle, for the eternal God is our refuge in battle. The *Alleluia* verse is parousia-centered; at home in the promised land of heaven, far distant from the servitude of earthly life, resounds an eternal *alleluia*.

According to the *Gospel* (Matt. 18:24–35), the Second Advent of Christ is the great day when all accounts must be balanced. God is kingly in forgiving; He is prepared to pardon sin here on earth, yet under the one condition that we also show

love and merciful forgiveness. Loving-forgiveness on our part
is the only title to a merciful judgment; on the other hand, severe
punishment awaits him who lacks these traits. Those generous
words of pardon which Jesus, my King, once uttered when
dying upon the Cross are being repeated today in the holy
sacraments. He forgives me my colossal debt — my return gift
must be love of neighbor.

An exceptional *Offertory* tells the story of Job's patience as
an illustration of the Epistle. Job the patient, a type of the
Church (and of me as an individual Christian), epitomizes the
battle of life; the child of God is a stepchild upon earth "whom
Satan seeks that he may tempt." No good fortunes are in store
for earth's aliens; suffering, one of God's great graces, keeps us
strangers to the world. May this life so full of bitterness be our
offering at the holy Sacrifice today. The *Secret* gives expression
to the two aims of sacrifice, propitiation and sanctification. The
formulary comes to its gloomiest mood in the *Communion*
chant; seemingly we ask God to hasten judgment upon our
persecutors; it is not easy to see why such a text was chosen here.
The closing *Prayer* embodies a petition common after holy Communion; in part it has found its way into the Ordinary of the
Mass.

3. **Divine Office.** Again the two greater antiphons repeat
salient ideas from the parable: "The lord said to his servant: Pay
your debt. But his fellow servant fell down and pleaded: Give
me an extension of time, and I will make full payment to you."
What a tremendous debt we owe God! "You wicked servant,
I canceled your complete debt because you pleaded with me;
should you not have shown leniency to your partner, even as I
showed pity to you? Alleluia." Our "gift in exchange" is love
of neighbor. In his usual sober style St. Jerome (d. 420) comments upon the parable:

"The Syrians and especially the inhabitants of Palestine are
accustomed to clothe their speech with parables in order that what
cannot be remembered by one hearing will be more easily retained by means of pictures and concrete representations. Accordingly our Lord gave His commandment to Peter in the

story of a king and of a servant who, owing his sovereign ten thousand talents, pleaded for cancelation of the debt; the first among the apostles should thereby learn to forgive his fellow servants their lesser indebtedness. For if that king and lord so easily canceled a debt of ten thousand talents for a servant, should not they who are debtors themselves much more readily remit the lesser grievances of their fellow debtors?

"To clarify this, here is an example. If one of us committed adultery, homicide, or sacrilege — which would be a greater debt than ten thousand talents — it would be forgiven if he implored pardon, provided that he also forgave the lesser faults of his associates. But if we should show ourselves irreconcilable over an insult or continued to live in a spirit of discord because of some bitter word, would we not in all justice deserve to be cast into prison? And according to the precedent set by our action, would it not be just that our crime should not be pardoned? *'So also My heavenly Father will do to you if you do not each forgive your brothers from your hearts.'*

"What a fearsome sentence! God's judgment is bent and shaped according to human dispositions! If we do not forgive our neighbors their petty offenses, neither will our great offenses be forgiven by God. And because persons say: I have nothing against him; he has God as judge; it does not concern me what he does; I simply will ignore him — the Lord put point to His words by declaring the emptiness of all feigned forgiveness: 'If you do not each forgive your brothers *from your hearts.*'"

4. Three Meditations upon the Sunday. A. The King, the Soldier, and Job. One could illustrate today's holy Mass by a three-paneled picture or triptych; in its center stands the divine Judge at His Second Advent (Gospel), on the one side the Christian soldier armed for the evil day (Epistle), and on the other patient Job (Offertory). Christian life is analyzed in the light of the Second Coming with special reference to (1) forgiveness of one's neighbor; (2) conflict in temptation; (3) patience in suffering.

1) Before us in the middle panel we see the eternal Judge. An impressive parable gives the details. Our Judge is all-merciful,

he shall be magnified
even to the ends of the earth,
and this man shall be our peace.

though at the same time all-just. At a word He pardons the immense debt of our sins, while we are reluctant to pardon the small offenses of our fellow men! Upon hearing the parable you become indignant and consider it proper that the unmerciful servant be duly punished. Yet that servant is none other than you! The moral: I must show loving forgiveness if I wish to be treated leniently when I am judged. Christ has anchored this lesson in the Lord's Prayer, "Forgive us our trespasses as we forgive those who trespass against us." (Every Mass is a fulfillment of this parable; in the holy Sacrifice God pardons our colossal debt of sin, while in the kiss of peace we forgive the insignificant offenses of our fellow men.)

2) Life is a battle. Such was the theme of several Sundays after Pentecost (the two kingdoms), but today it has reference to the end of time. It is the will of God that we battle our way to heaven ("I did not come to bring peace but the sword"). We are members of the Church Militant and have as enemies the devil, the world, the flesh, the ego. Nevertheless, we do not go unarmed to the front. The Church fits us out with all the tools of warfare as listed in the Epistle. Briefing for the week's offensive takes place at Sunday Mass. The word of God in the Mass of the Catechumens is shield and sword, while the sacrifice oblation and banquet give strength and vitality. The sacrificial death of Christ is an actual re-presentation of the epic conflict of our divine Field-Marshal on the battlefield of Golgotha.

3) Why the text about Job? Because the Church is underscoring a virtue very necessary in battle. It is patience, lifelong, patient perseverance. Job upon the ash heap of his dwelling is a picture of your life and its duties, its lot and its sufferings. What, after all, do you have to offer to the eternal Judge? Your patient, persevering devotedness.

Briefly then, holy Church gives three directions that will make our future trial an easy one — to love and to forgive; to fight the good fight; to suffer patiently until the end.

B. Christ the King and our Gospel. The feast of Christ the King occurs about this time, some years on this very Sunday. Let us touch upon the links between Christ's kingship and today's Gospel. Described in the parable is a king who resembles our blessed Savior; he acts kingly in giving, in forgiving, and in punishing. He gives a precedent that men must follow. (1) Generosity. Could anyone find a ruler so big-hearted as to condone a million-dollar debt with a wave of the hand? Christ, therefore, was revealing His own most generous and forgiving heart. He is indeed more than kingly both in giving and in forgiving. For by sinning, humanity had contracted an infinite debt, one which it would never have been able to liquidate; but God in His unbounded mercy forgave not only the debt but did much more. The work of salvation is so stupendous as to leave us gasping. In behalf of His debtors God, the royal Father, delivered His Son over to death. "O incomprehensible love divine! To free slaves You have delivered over Your only Son!" Christ's death upon the Cross and its continuation in holy Mass is a royal act. Cross and altar are the throne of Christ our King; from His throne He governs by giving and forgiving.

2) The royal precept. In return for His generosity our King expects a spirit of loving forgiveness. "Forgive us our trespasses as we forgive those who trespass against us." Let us observe the prime commandment of the Christian covenant. All talk about liturgical renewal or religious deepening is pointless if we Christians do not love our fellow men. By this shall all men know you are My disciples, if you have love one for another. "If I should speak with the tongues of men and of angels and have not charity, I am become as sounding brass or a tinkling cymbal. . . ."

3) Punishment. Christ our King is no weakling, in punishing too He shows all the strength of royalty. He will give and forgive unto the extremes of generosity, but nonetheless He remains a king and insists upon absolute equity. Whoever repays His generosity with indifference, hate, or hardness of heart is not worthy of Him and will fall victim to His punishing hand. His just censures are no less plentiful, He teaches, than His forgiveness. "Depart, ye cursed. . . ." We, however, will gather respectfully about His throne of Cross and altar. There the fire of His love is ever blazing, ready to inflame our hearts

with His royal law of love and of generosity, of forgiveness and of mercy.

C. The Armor of God. This Sunday's Epistle suggests a comparison that was very common in early times, viz., the Christian equipped as a Roman soldier. In his fallen state man is ever at war against the powers of hell. The mighty wrestling with the mightier, such is our lot after baptism. St. Paul pinpoints the enemy and specifies the needed military equipment. The adversary is cunning and strong; the struggle is not between man and man, for the opponent is a mighty spirit, the lord and ruler of the world, who when tempting Jesus said: "To You I will give all this power and their glory; for to me it has been delivered, and to whom I will, I give it" (Luke 4:6). The author of the Apocalypse paints the adversary as a mighty dragon in lurid colors. The devil, therefore, is not to be slighted. Christ never considered him of little account, neither may we.

St. Paul describes the divine armor with which Christians are equipped; accordingly it is not human strength by which we fight, but God's. It is important to have a correct understanding of the six implements of war cited by the Apostle. (1) The sash. St. Paul says: "Be girt with the sash of truth." What did he mean? Christ said something similar: "Let your loins be girt . . . and you yourselves resembling men who are awaiting their master." Truth is an incomparable good. Christ is *the Truth*, and He promised that the truth would make us free. Consequently the consciousness of possessing Christian truth is a source of tremendous strength. (2) The breastplate. Justice and holiness may be regarded as equivalent terms. In another passage St. Paul says: "Let us cast off the works of darkness and put on the armor of light." The texts about putting on the new man (Christ) belong here.

(3) The shoes. "Have your feet shod with the readiness which the Gospel of peace brings." By these words the Apostle refers to the instant cooperation with which we are to respond to the good news as new opportunities present themselves. (4) The shield of faith. The expression is easily understood. Faith, the foundation of supernatural life, is likewise the best protection

against the enemy. Faith makes one invulnerable, fearless. (5) The helmet of salvation. The helmet is the holiness a Christian receives through justification; it is his right to hope for eternal blessedness. (6) The sword of the spirit. As stated in the Epistle, the phrase refers to the inspired word of God. For from Scripture flows sacramental strength. In the account of Christ's temptation, we see how the word of God can be used against the devil. Three times Jesus said: "It is written." After the Apostle had passed in review the two adversaries, he spoke of the conflict and called it "the evil day." Which are your "evil days"? The days of temptation, especially the final day of life. We must prove victorious on the field of battle! We must be true soldiers of God!

TWENTY-SECOND SUNDAY AFTER PENTECOST

Render to God the things that are God's

Calmly, serenely the Church beholds the approaching "day of Christ" and entreats us to view our earthly life in the light of the parousia. The best preparation for that day of judgment (*Epist.*) is the perfect accomplishment of the duties of one's state of life, "Render to Caesar the things that are Caesar's, and to God the things that are God's." On the day of Christ we must appear holy and without offense, heavily laden with the ripened fruit of a virtuous life. To this end the Mass of the Catechumens presents in fine progression a wide range of practical moral principles: fatherly solicitude toward inferiors (according to the example of St. Paul; Epistle); brotherly love toward equals (Gradual); obedience to the commandments, and a full oblation of one's entire soul to God (Gospel).

1. **Text Analysis.** As on previous Sundays, the Mass structure lacks logical unity; nevertheless a spirit of preparation for the last days may very easily be sensed throughout. It would be difficult to harmonize the two Readings as to thought content,

neither do the chants possess a unifying theme; from a spirit of deep seriousness they rise to a happier mood but the finale again is one of earnest petition. Thus the formulary is another mosaic which offers the faithful scope for thought and meditation; yet it is sufficiently clearly indicated that the principal stress is on preparation for the parousia.

I would like to cull out three Biblical texts that seem to link the whole formulary together. "Render to Caesar the things that are Caesar's, and to God the things that are God's. . . . The good work that He has begun God will continue to perfect until the day of Jesus Christ. . . . Behold, how good and how lovely it is when brothers live harmoniously together." These quotations proffer very practical guidance on community life and the duties of one's state; about them one senses the aurora of the parousia as they approach earthly problems *sub specie aeternitatis*.

Thus today's liturgy accomplishes a double purpose: it readies us for death while capitalizing on life. "I die daily — I live daily." With eyes directed toward the Last Judgment we pray: If You would keep our sins in mind, Lord, who would be saved? With a similar outlook Mother Church tells us: He who has begun the good work (of sanctification in baptism) in you will bring it to perfection in the day of Jesus Christ. And then, without changing her gaze, she warns: We must be pure and immaculate on the day of Christ, filled with the fruit of justice.

With eyes directed toward life here on earth the Church seeks to make our charity grow richer and richer in knowledge and spiritual sensitivity. With eyes directed toward life here on earth the Church desires that we live together in harmony as brothers. With direct reference toward life here on earth Christ gives us a basic moral principle: Render to Caesar the things that are Caesar's, and to God the things that are God's. Thus Mother Church educates her children how to die and how to live. Recall the example of St. Martin "who neither feared death nor did he hesitate to live on and work for his brethren."

2. Holy Mass (Si iniquitates). With souls sincerely contrite and penitent we enter the sanctuary in anticipation of the Last Judgment. Loaded down by sin, from the depths of our earthly exile we cry to the Lord for forgiveness (*Intr.*). (Let us begin praying Psalm 129 in its entirety; it expresses well the soul's deepest emotions, particularly those of repentance and longing for the Second Advent.) Rising from trusting and devout hearts the *Collect* does not petition a definite or particular good but is like a golden paten upon which we place our needs for the day and for the ensuing week; on this occasion it is the faithful performance of the duties of our state of life and progress in holiness.

In the *Epistle* (the letter to the Philippians is St. Paul's most personal and intimate) the great Apostle of souls speaks to the community nearest his heart; we easily sense his sympathy, love, and tenderness. His primary concern is that the good works of his spiritual children be perfected before the "day of Christ." Even as they, we should resemble fruit-laden trees, abounding in acts of charity. Remember, it is the Church, a solicitous and tender Mother, who is speaking these words to us. In battle with the world and the powers of hell, the Christian finds true solace in the communion of saints. The *Gradual* sings of this blessed lot. Through the Sunday Sacrifice I see a parish united, a happy family, a religious community. The *Alleluia* verse is redolent with Christian hope, a virtue rare in our days.

The *Gospel* treats of the coin of tribute. Perhaps no other scene so well shows our Lord's divine majesty before cunning adversaries. And what does Christ wish to tell us by those memorable words concerning the tribute, "Render to Caesar the things that are Caesar's, and to God the things that are God's"? The same lesson as taught by the Epistle: Christian, fulfill your duties upon earth! Those duties are twofold, duties toward God and duties toward men. Such is the import of the two tables of the Law. Just as Christ's commandment of love embraces love of God and love of neighbor, and just as it does not contradict but perfects the Mosaic Law, so also this declaration further clarifies man's twofold duty. God conceals Himself behind your superior and sanctions his commands. In this manner the two Readings present one course of conduct; in face of the day of Christ be active, faithful to all obligations.

The *Offertory*, the prayer of Queen Esther in dire need, implores a "well-ordered speech" in the presence of the king. We may pray for fitting words in the presence of our King, Christ Jesus. Mother Church teaches us these words in the liturgy. Expressing the serious character of the Mass, the *Secret* pleads for forgiveness of sin and for protection against all evils. Likewise the *Communion* chant is a piercing cry of a soul in need; the holy Eucharist is a type of judgment, *now* Christ comes as Friend, *then* He will come as Judge. The *Postcommunion* witnesses to the truth that holy Mass is celebrated in memory of the Lord. Thus do two thought-threads run through the Mass text; one is negative: "I will fear the day of judgment because of personal sin"; the other positive: "I will lead an upright Christian life in order to be numbered among the just."

3. **Divine Office.** The greater antiphons place us in the midst

of the Gospel scene: "Master, we know that You speak the truth and teach the way of God in all sincerity, alleluia" (*Ben. Ant.*). In the Gospel the pharisees had spoken these words hypocritically, but we use them sincerely in professing our faith in Jesus our Teacher. It is another instance of how the words of holy Scripture take on a different meaning in the liturgy. "Render to Caesar the things that are Caesar's, and to God the things that are God's" (*Magn. Ant.*). This memorable passage will serve us during the coming week as an ejaculatory prayer.

4. Meditation upon the Sunday. A. The Gospel. Let us broaden our understanding of the Gospel. The incident occurred during the last days of our Savior's earthly life. He was standing in the temple. The Jews pressed about Him on every side, asking ensnaring questions in order to obtain grounds for indicting Him; of these the most malicious and dangerous was that recorded in today's Gospel. First they flatter Him: "Master, we know You speak and teach truth; we know, too, that You never regard the person of men or seek the friendship of men, even though they be ever so influential and wealthy. Tell us now, what do You think: May we Jews pay taxes to a Gentile emperor?"

We may ask, where in so simple a question does the malice lie? To answer this we must consider the political conditions of the Jewish people at the time. Centuries earlier the Israelites were under the direct rule of God. Yahweh was their King. Later on they chose a king who, nevertheless, held office only through God's favor. At no time, however, were they happy when under the domination of a foreign king or emperor. They would consider such a situation an insult to God Himself. But now at the time of Christ, Caesar had extended Rome's mighty sway over all Syria, including Judea; taxes and tribute were exacted from the Jews in spite of bitter resentment. Moreover, the political context became more complicated as it absorbed and distorted Messianic hopes. The Messiah whom the Jews were awaiting was a mighty king destined to shake off the yoke of foreign rule and make their own nation supreme. See the malice in the question?

The pharisees had wanted to say: You call Yourself the Messiah. How then can You justify it that we, God's own free people, have to pay taxes to the Gentiles? The Romans too were on the alert; they knew that the Jews were bearing their yoke with gnashing teeth. Accordingly they crushed with blood every attempt at defiance. The question asked by the pharisees was a two-edged sword. If Jesus replied, "Certainly you must pay tribute," He would have lost all standing with the people. And if He said, "Of course you need not pay; the Messiah will make you free," it likewise would have been very pleasing to the pharisees, for they had awaited such an answer. Immediately they would have accused Him before Pilate, and Jesus would have been put to death for high treason. The whole affair was so subtly planned, so wrought with danger.

Let us admire Jesus in His divine composure. The flattery of His enemies makes no impression upon Him; He sees through all their intrigues and deceits. Then He utters words so weighty that their depths can never be sounded. Having no money in His sash, He asks to be shown a current Roman coin. Upon it was the image of Emperor Tiberius and a Latin inscription. Jesus says: "Look at the stamp; whose profile is it?" They replied: "Caesar's." With that they had answered their own question. *They* had accepted the coin from Caesar. The image and the inscription testified that Caesar was the *true ruler* in the locality. Whoever would take Caesar's coins was also obliged to give Caesar tribute. So Christ concluded very pointedly: "Pay to Caesar the obligations you have toward Caesar."

What did Jesus wish to imply further by these words? All men are to render to accepted authority what is theirs by right, that is, obedience to their decrees. Such authority may be vested in a dictator or in a president, his title makes little difference. It must not be forgotten, however, that God too has rights and those rights must be respected. Our Savior's opponents withdrew in dismay upon hearing this answer so incomprehensible in its depths, so overpowering in its simplicity.

Much lies hidden in these few words of Christ. In the first place, Jesus says: Man is the child of two worlds, one is of earth,

visible; the other is of heaven, invisible. He must adapt himself
to both. As child of God and citizen of God's kingdom his first
duties are to his highest Lord. May one then conclude that
Christians need not bother about worldly affairs, since they are
exalted so highly? No! Just because you are a citizen of God's
kingdom, you also have duties to fulfill toward your earthly
superiors. You are a member of a family, of a parish, of a body
politic, and therefore God has laid upon you obligations toward
parents and toward civil authority.

These obligations are not at variance with each other. The
Christian must also be an upright citizen, an upright adminis-
trator, an upright employee in a factory or business. Obedience
to human authority is not service toward mere men, it is true
service toward God. The Christian says: You are substituting
for God. God has given you power and authority; because of
that and only because of that do I respect you; I honor in you
the ruling power of God but only to that degree in which it has
been given you. If you order anything against the divine will,
you no longer are God's delegate; then do I listen to God.

Our Savior included all this, even though it is not explicitly
stated. You should be good citizens of the state and you must
be good citizens of the kingdom of God. "Render to God the
things that are God's." What are "the things of God"? All, all
that you have and are; yes, everything is from God and for God.
Retain nothing, therefore, for yourself. Body and soul, intellect
and will, heart and mind belong to Him; dedicate all to His
service. Again we are face to face with the primary commandment of God's kingdom, "Thy will be done on earth as it is in
heaven!"

B. The Epistle. The Lessons from Sunday Mass should be
our guide for the entire week. The Epistle ordinarily instructs
us in practical Christian living, while the Gospel confers sacramental grace. Today's Epistle expresses perfectly the spirit of
the Church's Harvest Season; twice there is mention of the "day
of Christ" (viz., the day of death and the day of the Lord's Second Advent). First a few observations on the writer and on the
recipients of the letter. The pericope, as imbedded in the liturgy,

no longer is a paragraph written to the community at Philippi; they are words of exhortation addressed by Mother Church *to us* her beloved children. Accordingly it is important that we over-look all historical allusions and consider only what is absolute and objective. If we wish, we may see in the love of the Apostle toward his cherished community a type of the love which the Church has toward us, but it is not at all necessary. In applying texts from holy Scripture one should be fond of restraint. The passage contains sufficient doctrine objective in character.

What are these leading ideas? Life in Christ, "the good work," was begun in baptism; but now all depends upon a happy ending. At death, "the day of Christ," all work should be completed. God Himself is the Masterbuilder, but we are work-ers and must cooperate. A much needed virtue, perseverance, we may obtain by glancing constantly toward that final day. And if we ask how this "good work" can be perfected, the Church will answer: "Let your charity grow richer and richer in knowl-edge and in spiritual sensitivity that you may approve the better things." In short, the substance of "good works" is charity, that charity of which St. Paul says: "If I should speak with the tongues of men and of angels and have not charity, I am become as sounding brass or a tinkling cymbal." Love of God and love of neighbor is meant, a love embracing the whole of Christian life.

Such love brings with it a clearer insight into the needs of neighbors and makes us more concerned about the counsels and commands of God. Such love will transform us into perfect men. Toward the end of the passage the use of the word *fruit* brings to mind a picture very common in ancient Christian art, the fruit tree. On the day of Christ may we resemble a tree heavily laden with ripened fruit! What fruit? The fruit of justice, that is, of a pure and virtuous life. This "justice," how-ever, is due ultimately not to our own merits or labor, but comes "through Jesus Christ" who bought it by the Blood of the Cross. And the final goal? God's praise and glory.

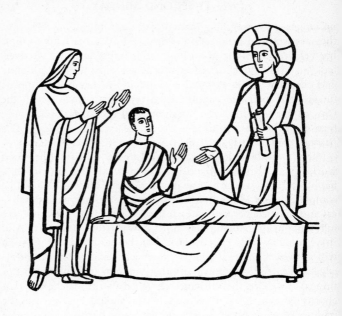

TWENTY-THIRD SUNDAY AFTER PENTECOST

Our citizenship is in heaven

The end is approaching nearer and nearer. Like an artist the Church is dramatically unfolding the mystery of the parousia. Since the eighteenth Sunday after Pentecost she has been presenting to us a whole scale of parousia moods, ranging from that of intense homesickness for heaven to that of salutary fear of judgment. The present Sunday may be characterized in the phrase "a blessed return home," words which at the same time suggest the unifying thought: I believe in the resurrection of the body. Our true home is heaven; Christ will glorify our bodies; our names are recorded in the book of life (Epistle). Christ's Second Advent will effect deliverance from sickness and the resurrection of the body, points prefigured by the Gospel account describing the healing of the sick woman and the awakening of the daughter of Jairus. We implore liberation from the chains of sin in the Collect and with hearts yearning for God we cry out from the depths of our earthly frame in the Gradual and Offertory.

1. **Text Analysis.** In the Sunday liturgies of autumn time it is not too difficult to detect a progression in three stages. The first stage consists in the Sundays transitional from summer to fall (15th to 17th after Pentecost); the second stage embraces the four finest formularies in the Church's Harvest Time (19—21); the last stage begins today and brings the season to its conclusion (23—24). Nevertheless, the liturgy is at all times concerned primarily with the present situation, even when her sights are directed momentarily to the end of things. It is no different today.

There are three areas of thought proper to today's liturgy. Return to our heavenly fatherland is the first. Note the Introit. Psalm 84 heralds the end of earthly exile while the entrance procession typifies the heavenward journey. A remnant of an obsolete third Reading from the prophets remains as the Introit antiphon (Jer. 29:10-14), taken from a letter of the prophet Jeremias to the exiles in Babylon; the prophet was announcing the exile's duration as seventy years, after which Israel would return home. Reading the original in full would, I feel convinced, greatly enrich one's appreciation of today's liturgy.

The second area for meditation would include the two Lessons (Epistle and Gospel). The principal truth is the resurrection and transformation of our mortal bodies at the end of time. One pericope complements the other in treating the topic.

The third subject comes as a surprise. For the Alleluia, Offertory, and Communion we pray the *De Profundis*, a penitential psalm (129). It brings us back face to face with harsh reality. The view we had of paradise was nothing more than a passing glimpse; but it strengthened us to take up the cross of life and carry it in procession at the Offertory, at the Communion, and out into the workaday world.

It should not be hard to retain the three lessons from a Mass formulary so well coordinated.

2. Holy Mass (*Dicit Dominus*). The chants today are more joyous and consoling than last Sunday. Most of them are permeated with thoughts of our journey home (*Intr., Allel., Off.*). Entering the sanctuary we are surprised by the enthroned Lord with His message of joy — the exile is at an end! He wills not to judge but to bestow peace (the word *peace* here denotes eternal blessedness). The last day should not be a *dies irae* (day of wrath) but a glorious arrival home to our eternal fatherland. How beautifully Psalm 84 fits the occasion; the priestly ministers entering the sanctuary clothed in festal robes symbolize God's children returning home. The time of exile has come to an end; our homeward journey to the heavenly Jerusalem is in progress. "Justice and peace have embraced each other" (familiarize yourself with this entire psalm before going to Mass).

Away, away with the chains of enslavement to sin, we pray in the *Collect*; like St. Paul we will glory in bearing chains made by men, but never in the chains of sin. Again holy Church is standing before her children as a loving and imploring Mother (St. Paul's *Letter to the Philippians*). She beholds them on their homeward march and in moving words begs them not to become "enemies of the Cross of Christ, having their belly as god, concentrating entirely on earthly things." To the faithful "whose names are in the book of life," her joy and her crown, she speaks tender words of encouragement. Of course, they feel themselves strangers upon earth and long ardently after their fatherland; *already their citizenship is in heaven*; already they are leading a heavenly life; their home is heaven, "from whence they look for their Lord Jesus Christ, who will refashion the body of their lowliness and conform it to His own glorious body."

Such is the principal import of the Epistle, which is at the same time a commentary on the Gospel; for what the Epistle states in abstract terms, the *Gospel* makes concrete. At present Christ refashions the soul through grace and the holy Eucharist; He awakens it from spiritual death and heals it from all diseases. Hereafter He will also awake and heal our bodies. Then we will know that what we call death was but a sleep. Mother Church wishes us to make this happy return home so much a part of ourselves that thinking it as already accomplished, we may jubilantly cry out with her, "We are freed," freed from this vale of tears, freed from all affliction (*Grad.*). The *Alleluia* verse, the well-known *De Profundis*, hymns our longing for the Lord's return. The Offertory and Communion also tell of our homeward journey to the heavenly fatherland, the one expressing homesickness (*Off.*), the other joyous faith (*Comm.*).

Psalm 129 may be used to lengthen the Communion chant. This penitential psalm, so expressive of live desire, is particularly efficacious when linked to Christ's promise to hear our prayers. What the Epistle and Gospel describe becomes actual in today's Sacrifice; for the holy Eucharist is in the fullest sense the pledge of future glory. From the holy Eucharist as from a seed will spring our bodily transfiguration; touching the sacred Bread gives health and virtue, not only to the soul, but to the body also. The *Secret*: May the holy Sacrifice perfect in us that which God has conferred upon us without any merit of our own (i.e, the life of grace). The final *Oration*, too, tells a startling truth; through the holy Eucharist we have become sharers in divinity. May we carry this precious Gift in the frail vessel of our body and never, never lose it.

3. **Divine Office.** For the greater antiphons texts about the woman troubled with an issue of blood are culled from the Gospel; the awakening of the daughter of Jairus is not alluded to. "The woman said within herself: I need only to touch His garment and I will be healed." "Upon turning and seeing her, Jesus said: Cheer up, daughter; your faith has made you healthy again. Alleluia." In the homily St. Jerome touches upon the woman's cure; usually his commentaries are less allegorical.

4. **Meditations on the Sunday Liturgy.** A. The Resurrection of the Body. Holy Church presents for meditation today the second last article of the Apostles' Creed: I believe in the resurrection of the body. In a clear and concrete manner she places this dogma before our eyes, adding practical applications and precepts for life.

1) Mother Church begins her presentation of the dogma of

the resurrection of the body by employing two figures, that of the woman with the issue of blood and that of the restoration to life of Jairus' daughter. By this she wishes to say: Look, just as the Lord healed the sick woman the instant she touched His garment, so will it be on the last day when all diseases and suffering will suddenly disappear. And as the maiden was awakened from death by the mighty word of Christ, so will the dead rise up from out their graves and shine with the freshness of youth. When we visit a cemetery, we could well say in the words of the Savior: They who lie here in their graves only sleep. What till now we have called death is but a sleep. Yes, let us believe firmly in the resurrection of the body.

2) The Church not only inculcates the consoling truth of the resurrection but also teaches the manner in which it will take place. In the Epistle St. Paul rises and speaks: We Christians do not belong to earth, we are a colony of heavenly citizens and our real home is heaven. Even though our feet stand upon earth, our hearts are in heaven. Certainly, we are still carrying about with us a poor, weak body subject to sickness, subject to sin, subject to death; but there will be a change. We are awaiting the Second Advent of our Savior Christ Jesus who will transform "the body of our lowliness" and make it resemble His own. These words are genuinely consoling. We know, further, how we shall rise on the last day. Soul will be united to body, yet the body will be transformed and will be similar to Christ's glorious body after His resurrection. How did the glorified body of the risen Redeemer appear? It was subject neither to suffering, nor to growth, nor to decay; it was spiritual, immortal, resplendent with the fullness of beauty. In this same way, dear Christians, our bodies will also be glorified. Let us intensify this hope within us.

3) Our work begins now. The transformation and glorification of the body at the end of time must be preceded by a spiritual transformation. We must first become spiritualized here on earth before we are sufficiently ripe to be glorified in heaven. Today's holy Mass shows the way to accomplish this. (a) In tears St. Paul complains about all those Christians who live as enemies

of the Cross, whose end is destruction, whose god is their belly. (b) In the Collect we petition God to loose us from the bonds of sin into which we have fallen through frailty. (c) Twice we break forth in unison with the Church in that heart-rending plea: "Out of the depths I cry to You, O Lord." It is a call to loose oneself from earthly attachments. (d) The attributes of a spiritual or a glorified body must have corresponding qualities in the soul. If we are to be spiritual above, we must surmount the trials and difficulties of life here below; if we are to be spiritual above, we must keep ourselves from the allurements of sin, the enticements of the eyes, and the lusts of the flesh here below; if we are to be freed from the limitations of matter in heaven, then we must be detached from material goods on earth; finally, if the body is to shine with the radiant beauty and freshness of youth in heaven, then must we be anxious after beauty of soul while still in the flesh.

We have the means by which we may prepare for the resurrection of the body and its glorification. The holy Eucharist is the sacrament of transfiguration, the sacrament by which we become "sharers in the divinity." Contact with Christ's sacramental Body will have transforming effects on our physical bodies. As the sick woman in today's Gospel became healthy by touching His garment, so we by touching His Body in holy Communion are made spiritually healthy, ready for the glorification of both body and soul in God's own good time.

B. A message, a precept, and grace. Under these three headings come three blessings which the liturgy presents to us this Sunday (as well as on all other Sundays). The day's special message enlarges our faith, while acceptance of the precept joins our will more closely to God's. Grace, besides elevating our actions to the supernatural order, gives the needed strength to believe the message and to fulfill the precept. The spirit of the liturgy for a given day may be deduced from a consideration of these three points. Let us see how it holds true today.

(1) The *message* of the twenty-third Sunday after Pentecost is the mystery of the resurrection from the dead. This truth seems hardly credible to worldly men. Will the body of man,

which ceases to exist at death and rots so quickly, live again and become immortal, youthful, handsome? A new earth and a new heaven! Christ's teaching is clear and definite. And St. Paul heralds it with joyous enthusiasm: "We are awaiting our Lord Jesus Christ who will refashion our lowly body to resemble His glorious Body. . . ." The Gospel gives the same consoling message from our Savior; He is the One who raises to life those who sleep.

(2) The message is always bound up with one of God's *precepts*; today the Epistle is a strong imperative against our sinful, earthy nature. We may not be men of the flesh. We must be men of the spirit, men with minds centered in heaven. In other words, spiritual regeneration must precede bodily transfiguration.

(3) The message and the precept are contained in the Mass of the Catechumens, while the Mass of the Faithful confers the *grace*. What is this Sunday's special grace? The special fruit of today's holy Sacrifice is faith in the message of the resurrection; the special fruit of today's holy Sacrifice is strength and courage to subdue the man of sin and to confer primacy on the spiritual man; and finally, the special fruit of today's holy Sacrifice is the preservation and perfection of the germ of immortality which we carry in ourselves already now on earth.

(On other Sundays and feasts try to determine clearly and definitely what is the message, the precept, and the special grace; that should eliminate much of the usual obscurity in liturgical explanations.)

C. The Gospel. Jesus was teaching in Galilee. He wanted to lead all into the kingdom of God He had founded on earth. And it would have been quite possible to convince the simple people that He was the Messiah had not evil-minded pharisees and doctors of the Law pursued Him day and night, raising objection after objection. The Gospels contain many instances of this nature. Once, for example, our Lord was teaching in Capharnaum at Peter's house, and while there He healed a possessed person who was deaf and dumb. The people were struck with amazement at the miracle. But the pharisees said

to those present: Do not believe that He is sent by God, rather
is He in league with the devil. He is expelling devils with the
cooperation of the prince of devils. This was a little too much.
Our Lord replied with a lengthy apology in which He showed
how absurd such an explanation was. Then He added: the
Jewish nation is possessed by seven devils whom it is most difficult to exorcize (i.e., the Jewish people could only be converted
to the faith through the most trying labors).

After this incident Jesus began to modify His method of teaching and became more recessive. Of course, He still preached to
the crowds but in a more reserved manner. He spoke in parables so that the perverse would find it difficult to get the point.
However, to the apostles whom He had just chosen He explained
the parables in detail, for after His departure from this world,
they would be bound to promote His work and carry His teaching to the Gentiles. Therefore they themselves must become
firmly rooted in the faith. Accordingly He performed in their
presence three great miracles in which He showed Himself Lord
over all that appears invincible on earth, i.e., Lord over the elements of nature, Lord over hell, and Lord over death.

The calming of the storm at sea was the first miracle. The
apostles, who were skilled fishermen, had weathered many a
nasty storm; if they would call, "Lord, save us, we perish!,"
their condition assuredly must have been desperate. Jesus spoke
but a word and the gale-tossed waves obeyed like a patted dog.
Then when He had entered the land of the pagan Gadarenes,
He met a giant who was possessed, not by one devil, but by a
whole regiment of them. These He immediately drove out. And
to enable His apostles to see those wicked spirits in all their
multitude and mania, Jesus permitted them to enter a nearby
herd of swine. The swine became so wild that in blind fury they
cast themselves headlong into the Sea of Gennesareth. By this
action our Savior proved Himself Lord over hell.

Leaving the Gentile territory, Jesus again crossed the sea and
arrived at Capharnaum, where He performed the two miracles
narrated in today's Gospel. Quickly the news spread through
the whole neighborhood. The people came in crowds bringing

with them their sick; He had hardly come to shore before He was surrounded by an immense multitude. A prominent Jew named Jairus stepped to the fore. He enjoyed a high position in the community, that of master of ceremonies in the synagogue. He was not a disciple of Jesus, yet his plight led him to the great Wonder-worker; for his only daughter lay critically ill. He fell down at the Savior's feet and earnestly begged Him to come immediately to his house: "My daughter is now at the point of death, but come, lay Your hand upon her and she will live." Let us compare the attitude of the Roman centurion with this Jewish ruler of the synagogue. The Roman had said: "I am not worthy that You should enter my roof — say only the word." A few days later the Jew Jairus asked Jesus to come personally to his house and impose hands.

Nevertheless, our Lord was ready to comply with the petition of the distraught father. Immediately He set out, but an episode happened which caused some delay. Because of the throng Jesus was obliged to proceed slowly; the people pressed about Him so closely that He was almost crushed. In this crowd a woman succeeded in approaching from behind.

Who was that woman? A poor pagan who for twelve years had suffered from a serious disease. She had sought relief from various doctors, but in vain; her condition only became worse. Then she heard of the Miracle-worker in the land of Israel and determined to seek Him out. Today as He returned from across the sea, she stood unnoticed in the multitude. Now she sees Him. Jairus is kneeling at His feet. She notices how ready Jesus is to help. Her trust grows. Yet she is a Gentile and does not dare to meet Him openly; she says to herself: I need but touch the hem of His garment to be healed. Wholly unobserved she presses forward and touches one of the tufts of His outer garment. The evangelist Mark recounts: "Forthwith the fountain of her blood was dried up, and she felt in her body that she was healed of the evil."

At the same instant Jesus perceived that healing strength had emanated from Himself. He stands still, turns about and asks: "Who touched My garments?" Denials from the bystanders.

The apostles, principally Peter, reply unsympathetically: "You see the multitude thronging against You, and You say: Who touched Me!" Jesus repeated His question in earnest and glanced around. No longer can the woman conceal herself. Trembling she comes forward, falls down before Jesus and acknowledges before all the people why she had touched Him and how she felt instantly cured. Lovingly Jesus allays her fears and praises her extraordinary faith: "Daughter, your faith has healed you! Go in peace."

(According to tradition this non-Jewish woman was named Bernice and hailed from Caesarea-Philippi. In thanksgiving for her recovery she erected before her house a bronze statue of a kneeling woman and Jesus wearing a double mantle. The Church historian Eusebius (5th cent.) claimed that he had seen the memorial.)

The Savior was on the point of dismissing the woman when a messenger approached Jairus with the report: "Your daughter is dead; no need to trouble the Master any further." A direct and heavy blow; the man's faith in the power of the Wonder-worker wavers. But Jesus is merciful, compassionate; the bruised reed He will not break. He speaks words of courage to the stricken father: "Do not be afraid; have faith and she will become well." Jairus braces himself in hope and trust. And so they come to the house.

There the Savior commanded the crowd to halt; even among the apostles He made a choice, taking only three along, Peter, James, and John. Why just three? Principally in deference to the stricken family. A house of mourning is not the proper place for a dozen strangers. Yet why does He choose these three? Here for the first time we find Peter and James and John enjoying a privilege which is later repeated at the transfiguration and in the garden of Gethsemane. These three were to be His most trustworthy representatives, and He wished to confirm them exceptionally well in the faith.

Jesus enters the house of death. If we did not know it as yet, the very appearance of the house would tell us that death had entered its portals. From the porch comes the lamentation of weeping women mixed with the playing of flutes. That was customary at Jewish funerals. Jesus steps into the midst of those cries and moans and says abruptly: "Why all this commotion, and weeping too? The girl is not dead, only sleeping." Anyone else who would have dared to speak in such a way would rightly have deserved ridicule. But Christ was no idle talker, no wag. When He spoke He spoke with dignity. Nevertheless, the common crowd, as the evangelists say, "did laugh Him to scorn."

One might ask: How could Jesus have said that the maiden was simply sleeping and that she had not died? On other occasions Jesus called death a sleep. By these words He therefore wished to say: The maiden has not died to remain dead and to be buried, as you may believe; rather, she resembles a sleeping person who is about to be awakened.

The crowd, unworthy to witness so holy a deed, were told to leave. Then Jesus took the father, mother, and three apostles and entered the room where the child was lying like a rosebud broken by the wind. Twelve years of age, an only child! Jesus approaches and takes her by the hand and cries aloud, *Talitha kumi*, "Little girl, arise!" Immediately she got up and walked about the room perfectly healthy. Jesus suggested that something to eat be given her. Picture her parents. They are quite beside themselves with amazement. How they would have thanked Him! But He charged them strictly to tell the event to no one.

What an impact this miracle must have made upon the three apostles and then upon all others present! It was God's third intervention, perhaps in a single day. It was the first time their Master had raised the dead to life. He had proven Himself Lord over the elements of nature, Lord over hell, and Lord over death. Truly He was God, the Son of God.

FEAST OF CHRIST THE KING

LAST SUNDAY IN OCTOBER

Tu Rex gloriae, Christe!

1. "The feast of our Lord Jesus Christ, the King" — in these words the Roman Martyrology announces today's solemnity. Instituted by Pope Pius XI on December 11, 1925, it is the most recent of feasts in honor of our Lord. The purpose of the feast is to renew in the minds and hearts of the faithful the ancient concept of Christ as divine King who, enthroned at the right hand of the Father, will return at the end of time in might and majesty. It is true that in the liturgy's sacred sanctuary this concept of Christ and His kingship has never lost lustre. It accompanies us throughout the Church's year of grace; daily we are brought face to face with it in missal and breviary; but the faithful to a great extent have forgotten it. The stern truth of divine kingship will give something meaty and strengthening to popular piety so strongly inclined toward sentimentalism. Furthermore, the faithful will be led to visualize Christ as He is presented in the liturgy. Therefore we lovers of liturgy see in this feast a wonderful help to our efforts in behalf of objective or sacramental piety.

2. Because translations of the texts proper to this feast are easily found in missals and English breviaries, everyone can celebrate the festivity in its entirety along with and in the spirit of the Church. Already on days previous we will acquaint ourselves with the jubilant prayers of first Vespers. Well-chosen antiphons put before us the picture of Christ, the King of peace, whose kingdom is eternal, to whom all rulers pay homage. During the leisure of the evening hours we will pray the feast's prayer-drama, Matins, in spiritual union with the universal

Church. The psalms, selected because of their rich allusions to royalty and kingship, are adorned by antiphons which clearly and beautifully set forth the mystery of the feast. The Lessons are appropriate. Those of the first nocturn (as also the Epistle) are culled from St. Paul's Christological letter to the Colossians; in a masterly way they describe Christ's royal sway over the Church and the world.

Taken from Pius the Eleventh's encyclical, the Lessons of the second nocturn in direct and solemn words authentically teach the import and meaning of our feast. The most important Lesson of the third nocturn, the Gospel pericope, is excellently commented upon by that great Father of the Church, St. Augustine. Since the texts of all these Readings can so easily be had, we will give them no further consideration here. The responsories to the Lessons are a blossoming orchard of inspirational Biblical quotations dealing with the kingship of Christ (the first four from the Old Testament, the last four from the New Testament). In the rising sun (a type of Christ) on the morning of the feast, we greet the divine King over all suns, "who delivered us from the power of darkness and made us worthy to be partakers of the lot of the saints in light" (Col. 1:12–13). Thus prepared, we go to Mass.

3. Holy Mass (Dignus est Agnus). The words of the *Introit* antiphon, taken from the apocalyptic vision of the apostle John, place us in the presence of our King's heavenly throne; as the immolated Lamb of God He stands resplendent with royal majesty even in these our times, and therefore is worthy to receive royal homage from all. With lively enthusiasm Christ's kingdom of peace is appraised in the Introit psalm (71). After a *Prayer* of thanksgiving for our incorporation into the family and kingdom of God, the Apostle of the Gentiles describes the exalted, all-powerful Head of this family and of this kingdom (*Epistle*). Christ is "the image of the invisible God; in Him were all things created; He is before all and in Him all things consist; He is the head of the Church, that in all things He may hold the primacy." What a magnificent portrayal of our God-Man King!

In spirit and in content the chant that follows is consonant with the Lessons — an echo to the Epistle, a harbinger of the Gospel. The *Gradual* is an act of royal homage (Ps. 71); the *Alleluia* verse is culled from Daniel's prophecies concerning the Messianic kingdom. In the *Gospel* we see Christ standing as a prisoner before Pilate. The official representative of Caesar, seated in judgment, asks: "Are You a king?" "I am a king." A more clear, precise and absolutely true reply could not have been given. It came from the lips of One soon to be crowned with thorns, of One soon to be exposed to the greatest ignominy in royal mantle and sceptre, but One who ever rules as King of time and eternity on heaven's high throne. Prior to the institution of our feast, this passage from the Gospel of the beloved apostle John was read only during the Passion on Good Friday. Throughout the Catholic world it now is sung as the Gospel on the great feast of the kingship of our Lord Jesus Christ. It serves well as a towering climax to the day's liturgy. The two remaining processions are graced with psalms of kingly content, Psalm 2 (*Off.*) and Psalm 28 (*Comm.*). During the holy Sacrifice Christ appears in our midst: "The Lord will sit enthroned forever; the Lord will bless His people with peace" (*Comm.*). The sacrificial Banquet is a royal banquet today.

4. Meditation. (a) Christ as represented during past centuries. We may ask, how did Christians picture Christ to themselves in times past? Of course, there has never been any substantial change in truths regarding the personality of Christ, but there have been accidental modifications in consequence of greater emphasis being placed either upon His divinity or upon His humanity. This was true already in apostolic times. The synoptic Gospels (Matthew, Mark, Luke) stress Christ's human nature and depict Him as the Son of Man journeying through Judea preaching and doing good. St. John, however, sees Christ in a more divine light; and in his mystical apocalypse on Patmos the divinely radiant King of the heavens stood before him as "the King over all the kings of earth."

This majestic conception of Christ the infant Church adopted for use in her cemeteries and churches. From the apses of ancient Christian basilicas mosaics of the *majestas Domini* shone in rich and golden colors. It was the artistic expression of their belief in the truth that the glorified God-King appeared on the throne of the altar during Mass, a sign of His Second Advent. This conception of Christ remained in the minds of the faithful until the Middle Ages. Crucifixes were royal ensigns before which the Conqueror was enthroned.

At the peak of the Middle Ages, however, the prevailing Christ-picture underwent a great change. The Crusades served to remind men of the earthly life of Jesus, especially His bitter sufferings; and the faithful wished to meditate in greater detail upon the humanity of their Savior. A great artist then arose who created two pictures of Jesus which have dominated the centuries following, even to our day. St. Francis of Assisi gave to the world the lovely Infant of Bethlehem and the "Man of Sorrows" upon the Cross of Calvary. Pictures of Christ as King in the golden background of the apse lost favor; in particular the Germanic nations with their sympathetic and compassionate hearts centered their thoughts with love and enthusiasm upon the human aspects of their Lord, especially upon His sufferings. Popular devotions, the best expression of the religious sentiments of a people, flourished along these lines. Thus till the present day. In very recent times the Christ-picture has undergone a further, though slight, modification through the cult of the Sacred Heart. Already known in the Middle Ages, this devotion has as object the sacred humanity of Christ as the source of the goodness and love proven by the Passion and the holy Eucharist.

b) Christ as represented in the liturgy. Such was the popular conception of Christ. Does it differ from the manner in which Christ is presented to us by the liturgy? Most certainly the liturgy, the official service of God by the Church, is affected by and reflects the religious trends of the centuries. The liturgy is an album in which every epoch of Church history immortalizes itself. Therein, accordingly, can be found the various pictures of Christ beloved during succeeding centuries. In its pages we see pictures of Jesus suffering and in agony; we see pictures of His Sacred Heart; yet these pictures are not proper to the nature of the liturgy as such; they resemble baroque altars in a gothic church. Classic liturgy knows but one Christ: the King, radiant, majestic, divine.

It would be an interesting and stimulating meditation to observe how this royal picture presented by the liturgy varies through the course of the ecclesiastical year and in the texts of the missal and breviary. However, we will be selective. With an ever-growing desire, all Advent awaits the "coming King"; in the chants of the breviary we find repeated again and again the two expressions "King" and "is coming." On Christmas the Church would greet, not the Child of Bethlehem, but rather the *Rex pacificus* — "the King of peace gloriously reigning." Within a fortnight there follows a feast which belongs to the greatest of the feasts of the Church year, Epiphany. As in ancient times oriental monarchs visited their principalities (theophany), so the divine King appears in His city, the Church; from its sacred precincts He casts His glance over all the world. With classic clarity and reticence the variable chants on the Sundays after Epiphany play upon the kingship theme. On the final feast of the Christmas cycle, the Presentation of the Blessed Virgin Mary, holy Church meets her royal Bridegroom with virginal love: "Adorn your bridal chamber, O Sion, and receive Christ your King!" The burden of the Christmas cycle may be summed up in these words: *Christ the King establishes His Kingdom of light upon earth!*

If we now consider the Easter cycle, the lustre of Christ's royal dignity is indeed somewhat veiled by His sufferings; nevertheless, it is not the suffering Jesus who is present to the eyes of the Church as much as Christ the royal Hero and Warrior who upon the battlefield of Golgotha struggles with the mighty and dies in triumph. Even during Lent and Passiontide the Church acclaims her King. The act of homage on Palm Sunday is intensely stirring; singing psalms in festal procession we accompany our Savior singing: *Gloria, laus et honor tibi sit, Rex Christe*, "Glory, praise and honor be to Thee, Christ, O King!" It is true that on Good Friday the Church meditates upon the Man of Sorrows in agony upon the Cross, but at the same time, and perhaps more so, she beholds Him as King upon a royal throne. The hymn *Vexilla Regis*, "The royal banners forward go," is the more perfect expression of the spirit from which the Good Friday liturgy has arisen. Also characteristic is the verse from Psalm 95, *Dicite in gentibus quia Dominus regnavit*, to which the early Christians always added, *a ligno*, "Proclaim among the Gentiles: the Lord reigns from upon the tree of the Cross!" During Paschal time the Church is so occupied with her glorified Savior and Conqueror that kingship references become rarer; nevertheless, toward the end of the season we celebrate our King's triumph after completing the work of redemption, His royal enthronement on Ascension Thursday.

Neither in the time after Pentecost is the picture of Christ as King wholly absent from the liturgy. Corpus Christi is a royal festival: "Christ the King who rules the nations, come, let us adore" (*Invit.*). In the Greek Church the feast of the Transfiguration is the principal solemnity in honor of Christ's kingship, *Summum Regem gloriae Christum adoremus* (*Invit.*). Finally at the sunset of the ecclesiastical year, the Church awaits with burning desire the return of the King of majesty.

We will overlook further considerations in favor of a glance at the daily Offices. How often do we not begin Matins with an act of royal homage: "The King of apostles, of martyrs, of confessors, of virgins — come, let us adore" (*Invit.*). Lauds is often introduced with *Dominus regnavit*, "The Lord is King" (the first psalm at Lauds on ferial days has been specifically chosen for its kingship content). Christ as King is also a first consideration at the threshold of each day; for morning after morning we renew our oath of fidelity at Prime: "To the King of ages be honor and glory." Every oration is concluded through our Mediator Christ Jesus "who lives and reigns forever." Yes, age-old liturgy beholds Christ reigning as King in His basilica (*etym.*: "the king's house"), upon the altar as His throne.

c) Christ as presented in the Bible. Most Messianic prophecies of the Old Testament were cast in terms of kingship. David beheld the Messiah as King of peace (Ps. 71), or as Priest and King enthroned at God's right and making foes into a footstool (Ps. 109). In the second psalm we listen to the announcement of the Messiah's installation and enthronement: "I have been set up by Him as King upon Sion, His holy hill." In the nuptial psalm we see the resplendent and victorious Messiah-King beside His Queen, the Church (Ps. 44). In well-known phrases the prophet Isaias described the Messiah as sovereign over the kings of earth; the same is true of other prophets.

At the annunciation the angel's message reflected the prophetic phrases: "The Lord God shall give unto Him the *throne* of David His father, and He shall *reign* in the house of Jacob for ever, and of His *kingdom* there shall be no end." Even though He lived in lowliness and humility, Jesus remained conscious of His royal dignity. This became strikingly clear at the trial during the Passion, the incident reported in today's Gospel. In the face of death He declared before Pilate: "I am a king." And surely it was divinely willed that the inscription upon the Cross should read: "Jesus of Nazareth, King of the Jews." In glory and majesty Christ entered His kingdom on Ascension day. In the Creed we pray: "He sitteth at the right hand of God, the almighty Father." Christ remains King of the world unto the end of time. Then will He return with great power and majesty "to judge the living and the dead." Only after the Last Judgment will He deliver the kingdom into the hands of the Father "that God may be all in all" (1 Cor. 15:28).

THE SUNDAYS TRANSFERRED FROM AFTER EPIPHANY

Since the feast of Easter, due to its dependence upon the date of the spring full moon, may occur early or late in the season, it often happens that some of the six Sundays after Epiphany must be omitted, while the twenty-four Sundays after Pentecost are insufficient to complete the Pentecostal cycle. Accordingly the Sundays omitted after Epiphany are transferred and inserted between the twenty-third and the twenty-fourth or last Sunday after Pentecost. However, only the Readings and Orations are thus transferred, not the chants, which are retained from the twenty-third Sunday. Though it is possible that this change may affect four Sundays (3rd to the 6th), yet practically speaking, the first of these (3rd after Epiphany) will always be omitted, as it would fall on the feast of Christ the King. Therefore we here will limit ourselves to a brief consideration of the fourth, fifth, and sixth Sundays. A fuller treatment of them may be found in the first volume of this work.

FOURTH SUNDAY FROM AFTER EPIPHANY

Christ in His power

From the fact that only the Readings and Orations are retained from the Masses after Epiphany, and not the chants, this important conclusion regarding the structure of liturgical formularies may be drawn: the chants of the proper express the spirit or mood of a particular season, while the same Lessons may be applied to different seasons. As an example let us take this Sunday's liturgy. What was the burden of the Gospel of the storm upon the sea in the liturgy during the Epiphany season? Primarily, a tremendous "epiphany," i.e., a "manifestation" of the Son of God to the world; then too it served as a fitting transition from the Christmas to the Easter cycle. In the Christmas season Christ appeared in majesty to establish Sion, His Church, yet He did not come "to bring peace but the sword." The ship buried beneath the angry waves symbolized the City of God in the midst of the powers of darkness.

Quite different, however, is the burden of the Gospel now at the year's ending. Again the storm-tossed ship is the Church coursing her way through the ages, yet there is very special reference to the final days when the calming of the storm will be the aftermath of the parousia, the Second Coming of the Lord in glory. Yes, in an instant the storms of hell will then be quieted, and the Lord who now seems to sleep will arise in His Church, and there will be "a great calm."

Of course, the themes of both Sundays meet in the great mystery of Easter, since every Sunday is a little Easter. The account of the storm upon the sea is a type of Christ's battle and victory at Easter. Every Sunday we celebrate Christ's death and resurrection, also His death and resurrection in our own selves. And though we had been tossed to and fro by the winds and by the waves throughout the week, during Mass on Sunday our Lord boards the little ship of our soul, masters the storm, and perfects the victory of His resurrection. Thus every Sunday is a link in the great chain which stretches from baptism to the last battle, to final triumph.

Holy Mass (Dicit Dominus). The chants of the proper are taken from the twenty-third Sunday. It would be worth the effort to become thoroughly familiar with these various texts, for they embody the spirit and give us the mood of these last weeks of the ecclesiastical year. Upon entering the sanctuary today, the joyous greeting from our enthroned Lord comes as a surprise: Your exile is at an end. I do not want to be your Judge; rather

I want to bless you, to give you peace. How lovely Psalm 84 sounds while the priestly ministers, clothed in festal garments, enter the sanctuary, a symbol of God's children returning home! The contrast comes with the Gospel account of the storm upon the sea. Nevertheless, such is human life, and such the life of the Church upon earth, ever "threatened by so great dangers" (*Coll.*). How sincere the cry *De profundis* as it rises from the ship buried by the waves — "*Out of the depths I cry unto Thee!*" (*Allel., Off.*).

Assuredly today, if ever, the Church attains her objective of instilling into our hearts a holy longing for heaven, and of making us realize that life on earth is an exile, an exile, as she says, in the sea's stormy depths. Between these two emotional crests of holy homesickness for heaven and sorrow over our earthly exile, Mother Church places two lessons for present conduct: love of neighbor (*Epist.*) and trustful prayer (*Comm.*). — For further comment see Volume I, p. 337.

FIFTH SUNDAY FROM AFTER EPIPHANY

Gather the cockle into bundles to burn, but the wheat bring into my barn

At the end of the ecclesiastical year, this Sunday, because of its Gospel, offers some very excellent food for thought. First, however, upon what was attention focused in the season after Epiphany? The answer is easier if we divide the Gospel parable into three parts: (1) the sowing of the wheat and the sowing of the weeds; (2) the decision of the owner that both wheat and weeds be permitted to grow; (3) the harvest. In the time after Epiphany attention was centered upon the second consideration. We then beheld Christ as the wise, long-suffering Judge and King who permits the good and bad to grow and prosper; but now in the Church's Harvest Time we gaze fixedly upon the end of life, upon the end of the world, upon heaven and

upon hell. Today the Church parts the curtain screening the future and permits us to gaze upon the smoking abyss of hell, though likewise upon the lot of the blessed in heaven. Furthermore, she teaches us to understand the mystery of malice, for during those last times wickedness will raise its head with unprecedented fury. Finally, let us recall that in holy Mass today Christ wills to sow in our hearts the good seed, the divine seed which we must let sprout into a life of virtue.

We are familiar with the chants of the proper since they are taken from the twenty-third Sunday after Pentecost. In them a sympathetic soul may perceive every mood in harmony with the Church's Harvest Time, from that of fear to that of heavenly homesickness. The Lessons present two contrasting pictures of the Church, one of these is very appealing, the other is rather disheartening — the ideal parish and the parish in reality. In the Epistle St. Paul sketches the ideal; we see a community of saints adorned with every virtue; love is enthroned as queen and in her train follows the peace of Christ. The Apostle then permits us to observe their sacred services and their private lives. We hear them singing psalms and spiritual canticles and see them at home doing all things in the Name of Jesus. The word of God has found its kingdom.

Quite different is the scene presented by the Gospel. Again we see a community of Christians, but one in which human weaknesses, sin, scandal, indifference, lukewarmness, jealousy still remain. And we are grieved. Our blessed Redeemer, however, shows us how to meet and solve the mystery of evil operative in the Church and in individual souls. My program during the coming week will be to strive zealously to realize St. Paul's ideal, no matter what happens to me; I will not be scandalized at what others do, but will try to imitate the patience of God toward the wicked. Moreover, I will give serious thought to the reality of hell.

Holy Mass (Dicit Dominus). Both Church and soul are awaiting the "day of Christ." Already we hear the kind invitation of our gentle King, already we see earth's exiles entering their fatherland (*Intr.*). The *Collect* implores protection for those last days: "We are Your family, Lord; protect us because we rely solely upon the hope of Your heavenly grace." Mother Church wishes to impress upon our hearts two lessons: (1) the end is near, the ideal should *now* be realized; live, therefore, in such a way as if the "day of Christ" would come tomorrow. Now in the shadow of the parousia, now at the approach of the great King, "put on the garments of mercy, kindness, humility, modesty, patience."

(2) Heaven and hell *are* realities, the weeds will be burnt and the wheat will be taken to the heavenly granaries. This truth our Lord projects in a fear-inspiring scene; beneath, burning bundles of unfortunate reprobates light up the gloomy, dismal depths with their muddy-red flames, filling the abyss with wild, dissolute howlings; but high above, the saints in glory are entering the opened door of the eternal kingdom, resplendent with the brilliance of setting suns. The poignant *De Profundis* cry (*Allel., Off.*) rises as our prayer over the Gospel parable — how much cockle still remains in my soul! May today's holy

Sacrifice make reparation and steady our fickle hearts (*Secr.*). The holy Eucharist is the pledge of eternal glory (*Postc.*); given today's Gospel context, this means that the divine Reaper is now gathering the ripe sheaves into the heavenly granaries. — For further comment see Volume I, p. 347.

SIXTH SUNDAY FROM AFTER EPIPHANY

The mustard tree is the mystical Christ

The end is steadily approaching nearer and nearer, the kingdom of God is ever becoming more fully mature. Externally it resembles the mightiest of trees under whose limbs the nations of the earth dwell, while internally it is permeating the whole man even as leaven. Our part in this twofold activity consists in furthering the lay apostolate and in striving after personal perfection. Now at the end of the ecclesiastical year let us examine our conscience as to whether we have deserved the praise which Mother Church bestows upon us in the Epistle.

1. **Sunday Meditation.** It is very consoling for a Catholic to consider the growth and activity of his Church through the centuries, how as a small mustard seed it sprouted in the Upper Room on Pentecost, then steadily grew, first in Jerusalem, then in Palestine, then among the Gentiles through the labors of St. Paul. Already in the first century there was not a city in the whole Roman world where it had no branch. Three hundred years of persecution could not kill its lusty growth, because the blood of martyrs was the seed of more Christians. Then it spread its limbs out toward the Teutonic peoples and the process continued, for within a few centuries they too were Christianized. Nor was it a mere external growth but an inner transformation renewing the face of the earth. To be reassured of this, one need only consider the previous status of women, of children, of labor. Indeed, Christianity has been a leaven in the world.

Though such meditation is very edifying, still it is somewhat

extrinsic. The mustard seed is rather the mystical Christ growing unto full stature like a mighty tree. Every Christian, who through baptism has become a member of Christ, is a little twig upon this giant tree and does not become wholly dissociated even after death. The number of the chosen ones has been predetermined by God, and as soon as the last branch will have been grafted upon the mustard tree of the mystical Christ, the mission of the Church will be fulfilled. Now at the end of the Church year we look to see how great this tree has presently grown.

The leaven of the parable is the divine life within us which must permeate our entire being. What this means may best be seen in the lives of the saints, for their whole lives were energized and vitalized by it. This is the key to a personal application of today's parable, an application well adapted to the current season. Each one may ask himself: Has Christ grown in me? How has He worked within me as a leaven? In the words of the Epistle, have I always practiced "a lively faith, a self-sacrificing love, an enduring hope in the Lord Jesus Christ"?

One final thought. The holy Eucharist, too, is a mustard seed and a leaven. Each Sunday the divine Sower plants this little seed in my soul, which during the week should become a tree bearing leaves, blossoms, fruit. Each Sunday the Church (the woman of the Gospel) places the leaven of the Eucharist in my soul so that I may be wholly leavened (leaven or *fermentum* was the name given that particle of the sacred Host which the Pope in ancient times sent to all the churches of Rome). Such the purpose of the Eucharist. It is not the mustard tree, not leavened bread; rather a seed, leaven. It is strength and grace that becomes effective only with the cooperation of my human will.

2. Holy Mass (Dicit Dominus). Again we are standing beneath the shadows of the final day. In the *Introit* we hear the kind though earnest words of the Judge: "I am thinking thoughts of peace, not of punishment." In the priestly train we again see ourselves returning home to our heavenly Father's house. Conscious of that final day so quickly approaching, our petition in the *Collect* is that "in thought, word, and deed we may do what is pleasing to God." How would the Lord find the world, the Church, or my own soul, if He should come at this moment (and every holy Mass is His coming anticipated)? How strong is our faith? How perfect our love? How advanced our growth (*Gosp.*)? Are we an example to our fellow Catholics? And do we really longingly await our returning Lord and Savior? Keeping these thoughts in mind let us sing the *De Profundis* (*Allel., Off.*) full of holy desire.

The *Gospel* is suited excellently to the season's spirit. The kingdom of God upon earth must be perfected, a perfecting, however, that is twofold: external, i.e., everything capable of being saved must be incorporated into the Mystical Body of Christ, for the tree of His Church must tower in fullest grandeur; internally, too, the yeast of divine life must leaven the whole mass. When that moment shall have come, a moment hidden in the inscrutable decrees of God, the Church will return to her heavenly home for the eternal nuptials.

3. The "Fermentum." At the beginning of papal Masses in ancient times two acolytes would bring to the altar a vessel containing a particle of the holy Eucharist from the preceding Mass. This particle, called *sancta*, was placed in the chalice after the *Pater Noster* to denote the unity and intrinsic continuity of the two Sacrifices. On Sundays and principal feasts the Pope sent to the other churches of Rome portions of the Eucharistic Bread called *fermentum* as a sign of communion with the Apostolic See (*fermentum*, i.e., leaven; like the *sancta* it was to be placed in the chalice during Mass). On the Saturday before Palm Sunday the holy Father would send the *fermentum* also to the neighboring bishops for the approaching feast of Easter. This practice symbolized very beautifully the unity of the Church and the unity of the holy Sacrifice.

4. The Year's Net Gain? Now at the conclusion of the Church's year of grace, let us take an accounting of our spiritual condition. Did grace achieve its purposes within us? Did the leaven of grace produce its leavening effects in our souls? Life itself cannot be seen or measured, but its operations can. A tree's vitality can be ascertained by its fruit. A person's spiritual vitality may likewise be ascertained by its expression in virtue. St. Paul summed up the chiefest fruits of a flourishing spiritual life as the "work of faith, the labor of love and the steadfastness of hope" (*Epistle*). It is a passage that extracts the three theological virtues from the theoretical plane of dogma and injects them into the practical plane of Christian action. Faith is not mere assent to truth; it is action, sacrifice — *fides et devotio*. Abraham exemplified such activated faith. Love is not a passing physical thrill; it implies self-sacrifice, in the words of Christ: No one has love greater than he who sacrifices his life for a friend. And hope means perseverance through thick and thin. These three virtues are the principal fruits of the life of grace. These three virtues must prove their presence in a visible way: faith in the observance of the commandments; charity in unmeasured self-sacrifice; hope in patient perseverance.

TWENTY-FOURTH AND LAST SUNDAY AFTER PENTECOST

The Son of Man shall come with great power and majesty!

Is it not masterly on the part of the Church to place before our spiritual eyes on this, the last Sunday of the ecclesiastical year, the final act in the drama of salvation, the Second Advent of Christ?

1. Text Analysis. It is not wholly clear why this Mass does not have its own proper. It appears that originally it was not the final Sunday Mass of the Pentecostal cycle, but rather a complete formulary for Advent; for in centuries past people did not regard the Church year as ending on the last Sunday after Pentecost and beginning with the first Sunday of Advent. Furthermore, it seems that in certain localities there were five weeks to Advent; accordingly today's Mass text parallels that of the first Sunday of Advent. The Gospels of both Sundays treat of the end of the world, the Orations are *Excita* prayers, and the absence of a special proper likewise indicates the formulary's anomalous character.

2. Holy Mass (Dicit Dominus). It is an impressive and elevating moment when, immediately after the Consecration, holy Church professes her faith in the great mystery of redemption: "Wherefore calling to mind the sacred passion, the resurrection from the dead, and the glorious ascension of Christ. . . ." By these words the Church wishes to say: *Now* Christ is present in His *whole* work of redemption. Therefore she lists its principal phases, the passion, resurrection, ascension. In early times, and even to the present among the Greeks, Christ's Second Coming is also mentioned. The Lord who appears in the mystery of the most holy Eucharist is the Lord of the Second Advent, the Christ of "great power and majesty." The holy Sacrifice is an anticipated realization of the Lord's return. But if this be true of every Mass, it is especially true today when Mother Church commemorates the Second Advent liturgically. Today is accomplished in the sacred mysteries of the liturgy that for which we were waiting, desiring, and preparing during many weeks.

Today the curtain falls on the holy drama of the Church's year of grace.

In fear and trembling the soul approaches the house of God, which now provides the setting for the world-wide judgment. But at the very threshold our heavenly Father welcomes us and says comfortingly: "I am thinking thoughts of peace, not of punishment." Instantly our journey churchward in fear is changed into a joyous return homeward to the heavenly Jerusalem (Psalm 84, a redemption hymn, should be prayed in its entirety). The *Confiteor* is especially appropriate today, for it is a judgment scene; we are standing before the eternal Judge, the saints are both our accusers and our defendants. The *Kyrie* is our song in exile, while the *Alleluia* is the hearth-song of God's children in heaven. The *Collect*, already cast in an Advent mold (*Excita*), fittingly petitions for more zeal during the next ecclesiastical year.

Presently Mother Church steps to the fore and speaks to us in the moving words written by St. Paul when in chains (*Epist.*). She is no idle dreamer; she does not set us on the clouds of heaven, but by pleading and weeping endeavors to make us worthy to meet the returning Lord. As an anxious mother she begs and entreats. The Christian should resemble a fruitful tree; he should clothe himself with the virtues of patience and perseverance; in a spirit of joy and of gratitude he should long after the day of the Lord's return.

For all its fearsomeness the thought of the judgment should not upset us. Rather ought we be thankful that God "has made us worthy to be partakers of the lot of the saints in light and has transferred us into the kingdom of His beloved Son." Joyful over the year's triumphs, we ought sing the *Gradual*, and with hearts aglow chant the *Alleluia*, which soon will be our song with the blessed in the streets of the heavenly Sion. In the *Gospel* our Lord Himself paints for us a magnificent panorama of the final day. But He does not wish to frighten us, He wills to gather us His chosen ones together "to share the lot of the saints in light."

Now we move on to the sacrificial Banquet. With what gift to offer? Man can harbor two cravings, lust for the things of earth,

or love for the things of heaven. It is the latter that we will lay upon the paten of sacrifice today while expressing our sentiments in the *De Profundis*. At the consecration Christ the King of majesty appears under the mantle of the Eucharistic species; nevertheless, it is the same God who one day will come in great power and majesty. In the sacrificial Banquet He stoops down to every soul; from the throne of His Father He speaks consolingly: "Whatever you ask for in prayer, ask with a heart of faith, and it shall be given you." The guarantee of these words is the Eucharist itself.

3. **Divine Office.** In the breviary we read St. Basil's fear-inspiring account of the Last Judgment:

"When the lust for sin takes hold of you, turn your thoughts toward that frightful and unbearable judgment when Christ shall sit as Judge on a highly elevated throne. Before Him shall all creation stand, trembling at His majestic appearance. Individually we will be led before Him to render an account of what we have done during life. Then they who have given themselves to sin shall be surrounded by dreadful and deformed spirits having fiery eyes and fearful faces because of their hardness of heart, black as night in appearance because of their despair and hate for men.

"Picture to yourself, furthermore, the deep abyss, the impenetrable darkness, the fire without brightness which indeed can burn but which is robbed of light. Meditate upon that poison-spitting, flesh-devouring brood of worms which eats insatiably, whose appetite is never appeased, whose bite causes unspeakable pains. Finally, consider the worst of all torments, eternal shame and disgrace. Fear these things, and chastened by this fear, keep your soul as with a bridle free from all sinful lust."

4. Meditations upon the Sunday. A. The Second Advent of Christ. What should be our attitude regarding this great event which will involve us all, since all must witness it? How were people in past centuries impressed? It may help to answer the question more adequately if we give the positions of Christ, of Christian antiquity, and of the Middle Ages.

1) Quite often Christ spoke of His Second Advent. In His great eschatological discourse from which today's Gospel is taken, He spoke about it in greatest detail. The major points at least in this discourse should be familiar to every Christian who aspires to live in and with the Church. Christ did not use the occasion to satisfy men's curiosity. His purpose, rather, was to enlarge our vision of life by setting it in the perspective of eternity. He made it absolutely clear that the date of the parousia would remain unknown to men (true also of one's death, which is Christ's Second Advent for the individual soul), and He stressed the logical conclusion: *be prepared always.* To impress this conclusion upon His audience (including ourselves) Christ added four parables, all of which contain the same lesson, viz., the parables of the thief, of the steward, of the wise and foolish virgins, and of the talents.

2) What attitude did the early Christians have concerning Christ's Second Advent? We know the answer. With intense

desire and ardent love they expectantly awaited their returning Lord. With crowns of martyrdom and palms of victory they went forward joyously to meet their coming King. *Maranatha*, i.e., "Come, O Lord," was a constant refrain in all their prayers.

3) That spirit changed during the Middle Ages. A holy fear accompanied every thought of the final day. The *Dies Irae* of the Requiem Mass is an excellent example of the terror and dread that filled men's hearts: "Oh, how shall I that day endure? What patron's friendly voice secure, when scarce the just themselves are sure? . . . I groan beneath the guilt which thou canst read upon my blushing brow. . . ."

4) And we? The early Christians desired their Lord, the Christians of the Middle Ages feared Him, while we do neither. We lack both the childlike enthusiasm of the ancient Church and the naive realism of the Middle Ages. What is left for us to do? Open our New Testaments and meditate upon the last things as set forth by our Savior: Be always prepared; live your days in the light of the Second Advent. I am sure that such is the spirit of the Church according to the liturgy. By directing our gaze toward Christ's Second Coming, the Church reminds us how to become rich in the fruits of good works and in the increase of patience and perseverance (*Epist.*). We may never forget that she wants work to follow words. In the holy Sacrifice she brings the Lord in His Second Advent close to us mystically — yes, holy Mass is a Second Advent, though, of course, in its own way through grace. "I am thinking thoughts of peace, not of punishment." Holy Mass is also a judgment, the judgment of punishment He took upon Himself in death and which He is re-actualizing now. The Cross He chose for Himself, but to us He says: "Come, blessed of my Father. . . ."

B. The Year's End. The Church year is a very definite segment in the life of the mystical Christ. Our Savior lived an earthly life of some thirty-three years, but the mystical Christ will live, I know not how many millenia. He will live as the life of my soul, I know not how many decades of years. Such a year is something meaningful, something comprehensible, something real, a segment of life which our spiritual Mother, holy

Church, utilizes as such; it is a term in the school of God. Ought we not then esteem the ecclesiastical year more highly than the civil?

But the Church proposes no special liturgy for the close of an ecclesiastical year. Why? Because already here on earth she lives an eternal life. One day follows another like the links of a chain; the end of one ecclesiastical year merges into the next like an endless circle. The feasts and seasons of the Church have no finale as they fade away into eternity. Therefore the Church does not celebrate the departure of an old ecclesiastical year.

As individuals, however, we may use the occasion to make a spiritual survey of the past and to plan for the future. During this week let us set aside three peaceful days for ourselves; the first, a day of sorrow and repentance "for our innumerable sins, offenses, and negligences" during the past Church year (see the prayer at the offering of the bread at Mass); the second, a day of thanksgiving for all benefits received; the third, a day on which to look into the future, a day of petition and dedication.

First Day. Let us open the "Book of Life" to the pages of the past Church year. What do we see there? Dark spots and blotches. We have been so lazy in the service of the Lord. Indeed, the divine Sower has strewn in our hearts the seed wheat of grace, but it often fell upon hardened soil, or upon a beaten road, or upon stony ground, or among thorns. And it did not sprout. Like leaden weights passions hung upon our souls and paralyzed their buoyancy, their flight heavenward. We have not remained true to our baptismal promises. Do you renounce Satan? and all his works? and all his pomps? We have not translated our words wholly into works. We swerved toward both sides, we wished to hobble along with the devil a bit and also to gladden ourselves with Christ. We drew no sharp line between the kingdom of God and the kingdom of the world.

Did the white garment which we received at baptism remain clean and unsullied throughout the entire year? Was the Easter candle we held so exultantly never extinguished? Did we always have the oil of God's love ready to refill our spiritual lamps? Oh how small must we now feel standing before the Lord. Again during the past year 'He has given us five talents; today He comes and asks for an accounting. Am I able to answer with the faithful servant: "Here are five additional talents"? How slight indeed is the good which I have done, how great the evil I have committed.

In spirit I now stand before the eternal Judge. It is like a solemn *Confiteor.* The saints all stand before me; they are my accusers. How they pleaded for me; their merits they applied to me; their lives were a constant sermon for me. And yet I have produced so little fruit. An unfruitful tree in God's garden. *Through my fault, through my fault, through my most grievous fault!* In this way I will often pray today. "Forgive us our trespasses." I shall at least enter upon the new year without stain or fault.

Second Day. In what really did the past ecclesiastical year consist? It was a year of divine life, of the life of grace, of the life of Christ within us. Do you know what this means? Picture to yourself a tree in springtime. How the buds are swelling! The sap no longer can stay in the trunks and roots, it flows forward and very soon leaves and blossoms appear. In like manner a life of grace was pulsating in our souls. Oh could we but see with our eyes all the graces which were decreed for us during this ecclesiastical year!

Yes, let us readily admit it, we are the true children of fortune. No, not they who rustle by in mink coats and Cadillacs, or they who make the headlines — no, not they but we. Even though our phraseology is faulty, even though illness or misfortune places insurmountable hurdles in our way to success, we are the true children of fortune because we enjoy faith and grace. Royal children, God's children, heaven's children are we. Today we must again be really convinced of our high state. And if God had carpentered and had placed upon our shoulders a hard and heavy cross during the past year, it was a sign of His love; it was the badge of distinction reserved for His valiant heroes.

God is a just and upright Rewarder. Consequently no good work has fallen to earth unseen. The angels have gleaned every sigh, every prayer, every good thought, every good resolve and have brought them all before the Lord upon a golden paten. It is exactly these unpretentious actions no one prizes or esteems that are so precious in His sight. O you brave and upright Christians, your tears and your sweat, all is being gathered drop by drop into the chalice of salvation, and one day in heaven it will be more precious than gems and jewels. For all this we wish to be sincerely thankful. From the depths of our souls let us sing: "Holy God, we praise Thy Name!" "We thank Thee for Thy own great glory and majesty." "It is truly meet and just that we at all times and in all places give thanks unto Thee, O holy Lord!"

Third Day. Now let us glance ahead into the new year. What will it bring? All things lie in its lap, death and life, heaven and hell, virtue and vice, fortune and misfortune. What will it bring! Yet, we are not confronted by a blind, spiteful destiny. No, we Christians have a most optimistic outlook, for our lot is in the hands of God. A good Father is watching providentially. He is guarding us as the apple of His eye. As a hen her chicks, so does He conceal and preserve us under the shadow of His wings. He delivered His only-begotten Son, His most beloved Son over unto death for us — is this not sufficient security for His unfailing father-love?

Yes, into Thy hands, O Lord, I commend my soul and body during the coming year. Do Thou will and work still further in me that I become mature and perfect in the day of Christ. Preserve me in grace, let me never be separated from Thee. All else is secondary. If You desire that I die during this year, Your will be done. If You visit me with suffering, trials, temptations, Your will be done — only give the strength to bear them. If You favor me with earthly fortune and prosperity. Your will be done — only give me double grace to remain humble. Do with me as You will. For one thing only do I plead, that I stay in Your love. So shall I enter the new year of grace full of trust and resignation.

C. The Gospel. The time of the events narrated was during the last days of Christ's earthly life, either Tuesday or Wednesday of Holy Week. The Redeemer had been teaching in the temple the entire day; surrounding Him like wasps the pharisees had been asking intriguing questions (e.g., concerning the coin of tribute as told in the Gospel of the twenty-second Sunday after Pentecost). He had made a last endeavor to reason with the Jews and to deter them from their wickedness, but in vain. After a final appeal in which He hurled an eightfold woe against the pharisees and other Jewish leaders, He left the temple, never to enter it again. With that it ceased to be the house of His Father. As He was walking out of the temple with His apostles, one of them said to Him: Master, see these wonderful columns! Within Jesus is deeply moved. He answers: I say to you, no stone shall be left lying upon a stone.

Like a sword these words pierced the hearts of the apostles, for Jews loved their temple intensely. Silently, pensively the little band wandered down through the Cedron valley and upward on Mount Olivet. The sun was declining; its last rays were reddening the faithless city. See, the Savior is now seating Himself upon the Mount alone and gazes upon Jerusalem. Some of the apostles steal up to Him. Those words their Master had uttered in the temple courtyard had not left their minds. He had spoken of the destruction of the temple and the city. In their minds this implied the end of the world. Therefore they ask Him: Tell us, Master, when will these things happen, and what will be the sign of Your coming, and of the end of the world? The apostles were thinking that the day of judgment, the end of the world, the destruction of Jerusalem and of the temple would occur simultaneously. Then Jesus called them all together and gave a long and revealing discourse upon the subject. A portion of that discourse comprises today's Gospel.

First of all, a brief outline of its content. It is composed of four principal parts. Throughout its entirety a clear distinction must be made between the destruction of Jerusalem and the end of the world. First Christ speaks of the destruction of Jerusalem; for this there would be definite signs such as had been foretold by the prophet Daniel, e.g., the abomination of desolation erected in the temple. Then He adds a number of others in order that the Christians who lived in Judea could flee swiftly and promptly.

Finally He adds: the destruction of the city and the temple will take place during the lifetime of those then alive.

In the second part Christ described the end of the world. For that, He says, no signs are given. In the course of time astounding events will occur — world wars, earthquakes, epidemics, famines; Christians will be persecuted and put to death; during intervals of peace the Church will flourish; but there will be no way to establish the last day. Abruptly Jesus concludes: it will come unexpectedly.

In the third section our Lord paints the end scene in a few masterful strokes. The destruction of Jerusalem will be further proof of His own Second Advent.

In the fourth part He gives what may be regarded as the moral of the discourse. If the end is unknown and if it will come so unexpectedly, His followers must *always be prepared*. Christ developed the point in four parables, all of which bring home the same lesson. The Lord will come unheralded and at an hour when He is least expected. The discourse ends with a magnificent description of the general judgment; three fear-inspiring scenes are thrown before us: Christ seated upon the throne of glory in the presence of all nations; the final separation of sheep from the goats (i.e., the good from the bad); and lastly, the irrevocable sentence of judgment. Our Savior could not have concluded His speech more powerfully than with this picture of the world's last judgment.

Now we have a clearer idea of today's Gospel, which is but a portion of Christ's lengthy discourse. I shall not comment upon the entire account, but shall speak first of the destruction of Jerusalem, then of the end of the world. Our Savior told His apostles to heed the given signs. When, for instance, they would see the enemy (the Romans) pillaging the temple, without delay they should hastily flee to the hills so that Christians would not perish with Jews. False Messiahs would arise at the time, but His followers must not let themselves be deceived.

At the end of the Gospel our Lord again speaks of the destruction of the Jewish people. As one can tell the approach of summer from the fig tree (we perhaps would use the violet as an example), so from the signs He had given, Christians should know the time of the city's destruction. Yes, even in that generation Jerusalem would be destroyed! We know how our Savior's prophecy was literally fulfilled. In the year 70, hardly forty years after His death, the Romans under the Emperor Titus came, conquered, and destroyed the city and the temple, subjected the inhabitants to a horrible butchery and led those remaining away as slaves; whereupon the Jews ceased to exist as a people. Now this spectacular event and singular judgment of God should serve as a preview, or indeed even as a guarantee or dress rehearsal for the final judgment. Thereby it has unique significance for us, for everyone.

The middle portion of the Gospel, however, is the more important part for us. It is our Lord's description of the end. Employing two metaphors, He tells how the end will come suddenly, unexpectedly. As lightning brightens a dark meadow in an instant, so one day the returning Lord will suddenly stand upon earth visible to all; or as hawks and vultures swoop swiftly and unexpectedly upon an animal that has died in the hills — one does not know how they could have seen it — so shall all nations be gathered about the Judge. The Last Judgment will come suddenly, swiftly, unexpectedly.

Our Redeemer then developed these truths using familiar apocalyptic phraseology (the words are not to be taken literally, for the concrete expressions indicate abstract truth). It will be a terrifying experience — "The sun shall be darkened, the moon shall not give her light, the stars shall fall from heaven and the powers of heaven shall be moved." The Son of Man, Christ Jesus, will come on the clouds of heaven with great power and majesty. Not as in His first Advent as a small Child or as the Crucified, but as King! "And then shall appear the sign of the Son of Man in heaven." What is meant by this? Perhaps a great cross will be seen in the sky, to the consternation or joy of all men on earth. Finally Christ will send His angels with sounding trumpets to earth who will call the dead from out their graves. Here He is speaking in particular of His chosen ones, those destined to be partakers of His glory. *Amen. Maranatha.*

Scripture Readings during the Month of September

As in nature, so too in the life of the Church the autumn season begins with September. In the liturgy there now occurs the transition to the last phase of the ecclesiastical year, one definitely eschatological in character. Not entirely unrelated to this new spirit is a subtle symbolism from the world of nature. For to nature autumn has come; the nights are growing perceptibly longer, the days shorter; darkness and cold are struggling against light and warmth. This symbolizes the conflict in supernatural realms and impresses a definite character upon the current liturgy. For example, the Church enjoins the reading of books on heroes and heroines, books on battles and victories, viz., Job, Tobit, Judith, Esther — two men and two women, all champions for the right, who show how the Christian can be a hero and a fighter. Job is the hero of patience; Tobit, the hero of merciful love of neighbor; Judith and Esther are heroines in another fashion, for through a daring act that endangered their own life they saved their people. All four, unlike as they are, engender that spirit of heroism which Christianity demands. Reading these books will occasion high spiritual idealism and incentives to self-sacrifice.

SCRIPTURE READINGS DURING THE FIRST WEEK OF SEPTEMBER

THE BOOK OF JOB

Saturday Vespers. First Vespers introduce us to the Book of Job. During the next fourteen days we will have an opportunity to read and study the entire work. "When Job had heard the report of the messengers, he bore it patiently and said: If we have received good fortune at the hand of God, why should we not bear misfortune? In all these things Job sinned not by his lips nor did he speak foolishly against God."

Sunday (Job 1:1–12). The Book of Job is a lengthy treatment of the eternal problem: Why does the just man suffer? An answer is given in the introduction and more clearly in the concluding chapters (38:1—42:16). Although God utilizes suffering to punish men, to test and purify them, in particular cases this principle may not be applicable. Humble acceptance of suffering from the hands of God, without asking why or wherefore, is then the proper mode of conduct. Man should not question the ways of God who is infinitely more wise and powerful and disposes all in His good providence.

Monday (Job 1:13–22). Job loses all his possessions and his children are killed. "Naked came I out of my mother's womb and naked I will return thither. Yahweh gave, and Yahweh has taken away. Blessed be the Name of Yahweh."

Tuesday (Job 2:1–13). Job becomes leprous.

Wednesday (Job 3:1–26). Job opens his mouth and curses the day of his birth.

Thursday (Job 4–5). Job's friends blame secret sins.

Friday (Job 6). Job protests his innocence.

Saturday (Job 7). Job complains over his sufferings.

> My flesh is clothed with worms and dirt,
>   my skin hardens and festers;
> My days go swifter than a weaver's shuttle,
>   they come to their end without hope.
> Remember that my life resembles wind,
>   my eye will not see happiness again.
> A cloud dissolves and disappears —
>   so one who goes down to Sheol
>   never comes up again.

SCRIPTURE READINGS DURING THE SECOND WEEK OF SEPTEMBER

THE BOOK OF JOB

Saturday Vespers. The Magnificat antiphon summarizes the readings for the coming week: "In all these things Job sinned not by his lips, nor did he speak foolishly against God."

Sunday (Job 14). The transitoriness of human life.

Monday (Job 23). If only he (Job) could plead his case immediately before God's judgment seat!

Tuesday (Job 29). Job asserts his love for the poor:

> I was eyes to the blind,
>   feet to the lame.
> I was a father to the poor.

Wednesday (Job 31). An examination of conscience (use it sometime).

Thursday (Job 32–37). When Job had silenced his three friends by his various apologies, a new speaker not mentioned in the introduction stepped forward, Elihu. Elihu declared that he had remained silent while his seniors spoke, out of respect for their age; but since they accomplished nothing, he now wished to unravel the reason for Job's sorry lot. While the three previous speakers explained Job's suffering simply from the aspect of punishment for sin, Elihu saw it as coming from a merciful God who by tribulation would purify him from hidden sins, would test and prove him true. Without Elihu's discourse an important aspect in the divine plan of suffering would not have been treated.

Friday (Job 38—42). Job had often wished that God Himself would indict him and hear his cause. Now his wish is fulfilled as God answers him "out of a whirlwind." Few passages in Biblical literature are so magnificently cast. If man finds it so difficult to see the hand of God at work in natural phenomena, why should he complain when unable to understand the ways

of God in the affairs of men? Man's duty is simply to subject
himself humbly to the divine will. Job acknowledged his in-
significance and bowed down in silence before the Almighty.

> Then Yahweh answered Job out of a whirlwind, saying:
> Who is this that obscures divine plans
>   with ignorant words?
> Stand up now like a man, and defend yourself.
>   I will ask the questions
>   and you will answer me.
> Where were you when I fashioned the earth?
>   answer me, if you know.
> Who set its size — if you know!
>   or who stretched the measuring line over it?
> Can you send forth the lightnings on their way,
>   or will they answer you: Here we are?
> Is it you who gives the horse his strength,
>   or clothes his neck with a quivering mane?
> With fierceness and frenzy he devours the ground;
>   he stands not still at the sound of the trumpet,
>   but with each blast cries out: Aha!
> Then Job answered Yahweh and said:
>   I put my hand over my mouth.
>   I have spoken once, I will not do so again,
>   if twice, certainly I shall do so no more.

Saturday (Job 42). Job becomes healthy and wealthy again.

SCRIPTURE READINGS DURING THE THIRD WEEK
OF SEPTEMBER

THE BOOK OF TOBIT

Saturday Vespers. At Vespers today the Church prepares us
for the Scripture reading proper to the coming week; accordingly
in the spirit of Tobit we pray: "Do not remember my offences,

Lord, nor those of my parents; and do not take revenge on my sins."

Sunday (Tob. 1). This week we are to read the Book of Tobit. It is a simple story, very instructive and edifying for all classes of people. The first chapter, an introductory one, gives Tobit's family background, his deportation as a captive to Niniveh, and his good standing with Shalmaneser, the king.

Monday (Tob. 2). Tobit is stricken with blindness.

Tuesday (Tob. 4). Tobit counsels his son Tobias; a chapter noteworthy for its fine moral theology.

Wednesday (Tob. 6—9). Tobias seeks a guide, finds the angel Raphael, who accompanies him on his journey. He comes to Rages and becomes engaged to Sarah, daughter of Raguel.

Thursday (Tob. 11). After the marriage Tobias returns home with Sarah.

Friday (Tob. 12). The angel Raphael manifests himself and disappears.

Saturday (Tob. 13). The Canticle of Tobit.

> The gates of Jerusalem will be built
>   of sapphire and emerald;
>   and all her walls of precious stones.
> The streets of Jerusalem will be paved
>   with beryl and ruby and Ophir stones;
>   and ALLELUIA will be sung in the streets.

SCRIPTURE READINGS DURING THE FOURTH WEEK OF SEPTEMBER

THE BOOK OF JUDITH

Saturday Vespers. The Church has assigned the Book of Judith to the coming week. Judith, the chaste widow and courageous woman, the savior of her people from an Assyrian onslaught, beheads the leader of the enemy army, Holofernes. She is a type of the "great woman" Mary, who by her immaculate conception crushed the head of the serpent; and she also is a figure of the Church, which, chaste and pure, is victorious over all enemies. That the liturgy sees in Judith a type of Mary and of the Church should be kept in mind as we pray the Magnificat antiphon: "O Adonai, Lord and God, great and wonderful, You have placed salvation in the hands of a woman. Hear now the prayers of Your servants."

Sunday (Jud. 1–3). Account of Nabuchodonosor's plans against the West.

Monday (Jud. 4). Preparations against the enemy; prayer of the Jewish people.

Tuesday (Jud. 5–7). Holofernes besieges Bethulia; the city prepares to surrender.

Wednesday (Jud. 8). Judith before the city council.

Thursday (Jud. 9–10). Judith enters the enemy's camp and is taken before Holofernes.

Friday (Jud. 11–13). After the banquet Judith slays Holofernes and returns to her city with his head.

Saturday (Jud. 14–16). The enemy host flees; the Jews keep a thanksgiving feast.

> You are the glory of Jerusalem,
>   you are the joy of Israel,
>   you are the honor of your people.

SCRIPTURE READINGS DURING THE FIFTH WEEK OF SEPTEMBER

THE BOOK OF ESTHER

Saturday Vespers. In preparation for the Scripture lessons of the coming week we pray from the Book of Esther (like Judith,

Esther is a type of the Church and of Mary): "O Lord, almighty King, all things are in Your power, and there is no one who can resist Your will" (13:19). Our thoughts are centered on Christ, the King who will come again at the end of time.

Sunday (Esther 1–2). The Jewess Esther is made queen in the place of Vasthi by Assuerus, the Persian king.

Monday (Esther 3). Aman plots a massacre of the Jews throughout the kingdom.

Tuesday (Esther 4). In danger of her very life Esther comes into the king's presence and pleads for her people.

Wednesday (Esther 5). Aman resolves upon the death of Mardochai.

Thursday (Esther 6). The king wills that Aman honor Mardochai.

Friday (Esther 7). At a banquet Aman is unmasked by Queen Esther and upon the command of the king is hanged on the very gibbet he had prepared for Mardochai.

Saturday (Esther 8). Deliverance of the Jewish people; joy throughout the land.

SCRIPTURE READINGS DURING THE MONTH OF OCTOBER

During the month of October are read the two Books of Machabees, which describe the wars fought by the Chosen People for deliverance from the Syrian yoke. There is much for edification in these books; and in them we can learn the nature of true patriotism, its justification and necessity. These books were held in high esteem by the ancient Church, which saw her own martyrdom prefigured in their heroes. There is point, too, to the fact that the Church has selected these narratives for reading now during October. For during August when daylight and warmth dominated nature, she presented the enlightening and serene books of wisdom; during September when darkness was disputing the ground with light, she brought out four hero stories; during October, however, when night and cold gain mastery, she offers for meditation two books telling of battles and war. For the conflict between day and night in nature is for us a symbol of the battle between spiritual light and spiritual darkness. In the breviary the two Books of Machabees are so apportioned that the first is read during the first three weeks of October, and the second during the remaining two. The following excerpt is a favorite in the liturgy during the whole month:

> The sun shone upon their shields of gold
> so that the very mountains glittered;
> and the might of the Gentiles was scattered.
> For the army was exceeding great and strong —
> and Judas and his soldiers advanced for battle.

SCRIPTURE READINGS DURING THE FIRST WEEK OF OCTOBER

THE FIRST BOOK OF MACHABEES

Saturday Vespers. The Magnificat antiphon: "May the Lord open your heart unto His law and His commandments; and may the Lord God send you peace."

Sunday (1 Mach. 1:1–16). The book begins with a survey of world history from Alexander the Great to Antiochus Epiphanes.

Monday (1 Mach. 1:17–29). The Syrian king, Antiochus, conquers Egypt; he comes to Jerusalem and plunders the temple. Intense grief in Israel.

Tuesday (1 Mach. 2:1–16). With great sadness the priest Mathathias witnesses the apostasy of the Jews and their adoption of pagan practices.

Wednesday (1 Mach. 2:19–30). Mathathias kills one of the Jews who sacrifices to the gods, calls for all zealous Jews to follow him, and in the wilderness organizes the revolt.

Thursday (1 Mach. 2:49–69). Last counsels of Mathathias to his sons; his death.

Friday (1 Mach. 3:1–28). Judas, called Machabeus, becomes the leader of the opposition and prepares to fight the armies of Antiochus.

Saturday (1 Mach. 3:42–60). Trusting in God, Israel regains spirit, worships at Mispah, and arms for battle.

SCRIPTURE READINGS DURING THE SECOND WEEK OF OCTOBER

THE FIRST BOOK OF MACHABEES

Saturday Vespers. The Magnificat antiphon: "The sun shone upon their shields of gold so that the very mountains glittered; and the might of the Gentiles was scattered."

Sunday (1 Mach. 4:36–51). The temple at Jerusalem is cleansed; services are held and sacrifices again offered.

Monday (1 Mach. 4:52–61). Solemn dedication of the altar; eight days of great rejoicing; introduction of the feast of Hannukah.

Tuesday (1 Mach. 5:1–13). Skirmishes against the Syrians under the leadership of Timotheus.

Wednesday (1 Mach. 5:55–57). Disaster overtakes a contingent which fights independently; Judas continues successful.

Thursday (1 Mach. 6:1–13). Antiochus fails in his efforts to capture the Persian city of Elymais; death overtakes him on his retreat.

Friday (1 Mach. 7:1–17). Demetrius, the successor of Antiochus, sends the traitor Alcimus, who wishes to become high priest, to Judea; Bacchides leads the Syrian army.

Saturday (1 Mach. 8:1–27). Judas makes an alliance with the Romans and therewith imperial Rome enters sacred history.

SCRIPTURE READINGS DURING THE THIRD WEEK OF OCTOBER

THE FIRST BOOK OF MACHABEES

Saturday Vespers. The Magnificat antiphon: "Israel mourned for Judas with great lamentation, saying: Now even you have fallen, you so valiant in battle, you who delivered the Lord's people!"

Sunday (1 Mach. 9:1–20). Judas dies heroically; mourning over him.

Monday (1 Mach. 9:28–40). Jonathan succeeds Judas as leader (161–142 B.C.); Bacchides continues the war. Jonathan was the first Hasmonean who at the same time acted both as high priest and as civil leader.

Tuesday (1 Mach. 12:1–11). Jonathan renews the alliance with Rome.

Wednesday (1 Mach. 12:39–52). Jonathan is taken captive through a ruse of Trypho.

Thursday (1 Mach. 13:1–9). Jonathan's brother Simon assumes command; his endeavors to obtain the release of Jonathan prove fruitless.

Friday (1 Mach. 14:16–26). Simon continues the alliance with Rome and Sparta; under his rule peace is achieved.

Saturday (1 Mach. 16:14–24). Simon is deceitfully murdered by Ptolemee; the end of the Hasmoneans.

SCRIPTURE READINGS DURING THE FOURTH WEEK OF OCTOBER

THE SECOND BOOK OF MACHABEES

Saturday Vespers. With the Machabees we pray: "May the Lord hear your prayers and be reconciled with you; may the Lord our God never forsake you in an evil time."

Sunday (2 Mach. 1:1–22). The second Book of Machabees, which we begin to read this week, is not a continuation of the first; it recounts practically the same events but gives more attention to details and to spiritual aspects. The first chapter contains a letter from the Jews at Jerusalem to those in Egypt exhorting them to observe the feast of the dedication of the temple.

Monday (2 Mach. 2:1–9). Continuation of the above letter concerning the dedication of the temple.

Tuesday (2 Mach. 3:1–12). Under the high priest Onias, Simon, the overseer of the temple, informs King Seleucus (187–176) that great amounts of money were kept in the temple.

Wednesday (2 Mach. 3:23–34). Heliodorus is sent by the king to take possession of any such treasures; he is hindered by a miracle.

Thursday (2 Mach. 4:1–11). Jason dishonestly obtains the office of high priest and introduces pagan customs.

Friday (2 Mach. 5:1–10). Jason's assault upon Jerusalem; his miserable end.

Saturday (2 Mach. 6:1–12). The Jewish religion is outlawed, the temple violated.

SCRIPTURE READINGS DURING THE FIFTH WEEK OF OCTOBER

THE SECOND BOOK OF MACHABEES

Saturday Vespers. The Magnificat antiphon: "Power is Yours, and Yours is the kingdom, Lord. You are above all nations. Give peace, Lord, in our days." We will pray this prayer with the parousia in mind.

Sunday (2 Mach. 6:18–28). Today we read about the heroic death of the aged Eleazar. There are few accounts of martyrdom that move us more profoundly than that brought before our eyes today and that which serves as the Readings tomorrow and Tuesday, the story of the Seven Machabean brothers who died for the faith in their mother's presence.

Monday (2 Mach. 7:7–23). The martyrdom of the seven Machabean brothers — they died rather than sin!

Tuesday (2 Mach. 7:24–41). The heroic mother urges her sons to constancy and is martyred last of all.

Wednesday (2 Mach. 8:10–28). Judas Machabeus takes the field against Syrian tyranny; he is victorious over Nicanor.

Thursday (2 Mach. 9:1–10). The death of Antiochus Epiphanes.

Friday (2 Mach. 10:1–32). Cleansing of the temple by Judas.

Saturday (2 Mach. 15:7–19). Strengthened by a vision, Judas engages Nicanor in battle; Nicanor is slain.

SCRIPTURE READINGS DURING THE MONTH OF NOVEMBER

During the last month of the ecclesiastical year the Church centers attention upon the books of the prophets. In their words she teaches us the consummation of Christ's kingdom upon earth and its transition into the kingdom of heaven. The various prophetical books do full justice to the parousia theme.

The Old Testament contains four great and twelve lesser prophets (the terms "greater" and "lesser" do not refer to spiritual stature but to the quantity or length of their respective writings). Two of the major prophets, Isaias and Jeremias, take prominent roles during other seasons (Advent and Passiontide); the other two, Ezechiel and Daniel, are allotted the first three weeks of the present month, while the twelve minor prophets are given passing attention during the days that remain.

SCRIPTURE READINGS DURING THE FIRST WEEK OF NOVEMBER

THE BOOK OF EZECHIEL

Saturday Vespers. The Magnificat antiphon: "I saw the Lord sitting upon a throne high and elevated; all the earth was full of His glory and His train filled the temple." This text provides a good background for the reading of the prophets.

Sunday (Ezech. 1:1–12). The vision of the four living creatures that formed the framework for Yahweh's chariot. These four faces were later disjoined and used as symbols for the four evangelists.

Monday (Ezech. 2). The call of the prophet.

Tuesday (Ezech. 3:1–11). Upon God's bidding the prophet eats the scroll having on both sides words of lamentation, mourning, and woe.

Wednesday (Ezech. 7:1–13). Prophecy of the destruction of the kingdom of Judah.

Thursday (Ezech. 14:1–11). The prophet's exhortation to penance.

Friday (Ezech. 15). Like vine-cuttings Judah would be cast into the fire.

Saturday (Ezech. 19). Lamentation over the princes of Judah; the parable of the lions.

SCRIPTURE READINGS DURING THE SECOND WEEK OF NOVEMBER

THE BOOK OF EZECHIEL

Saturday Vespers. The Magnificat antiphon: "Lord, see how the city once filled with riches has become desolate; the mistress of nations sits in sadness, there is none to comfort her but You, our God."

Sunday (Ezech. 21:1–16). Prophecy of the fall of Jerusalem.

Monday (Ezech. 33:1–11). The prophet is constituted watchman over Israel.

Tuesday (Ezech. 34). Indictment of Israel's self-seeking pastors who furthered their own interests and neglected the spiritual needs of the people.

Wednesday (Ezech. 37:1–14). The well-known vision of the field of dry bones; at the Spirit's bidding they come together, take on flesh, and form an army of men — Israel restored.

Thursday (Ezech. 40:1–6). Vision of the measuring of the temple — a sign that the temple will be rebuilt.

Friday (Ezech. 43:1–12). Vision of Yahweh's entrance into the new temple.

Saturday (Ezech. 47:1–9). Vision of the waters of grace under the new temple.

SCRIPTURE READINGS DURING THE THIRD WEEK OF NOVEMBER

THE BOOK OF DANIEL

Saturday Vespers. The Magnificat antiphon: "With Yourself as an impregnable wall surround us, O Lord; and with Your powerful weapons protect us always."

Sunday (Dan. 1). The fourth major prophet was Daniel, who lived during the Babylonian exile. He was commissioned not only to maintain faith in the promises, but also to show the Gentiles the might of Israel's God over false gods. The Book of Daniel reveals how the Messianic kingdom will outlast all earthly kingdoms, itself eternal. In many sections the style is apocalyptic, an indication of composition at a relatively late date. Scholars are not too clear on what part actually stems from the prophet Daniel. There is no doubt, however, concerning the divine inspiration of all fourteen chapters.

Monday (Dan. 2). Daniel interprets Nabuchodonosor's dream.

Tuesday (Dan. 3). The three youths refuse to adore the statue and are thrown into the fiery furnace; by God's power they remain unharmed.

Wednesday (Dan. 5). King Baltassar sees hand writing on the wall during a banquet; Daniel interprets the words.

Thursday (Dan. 9). The famous Messianic prophecy of the seventy week-years.

Friday (Dan. 12). Prophecy of the end of the world and bodily resurrection.

Saturday (Dan. 14). Daniel in the lion's den.

SCRIPTURE READINGS DURING THE FOURTH WEEK OF NOVEMBER

THE MINOR PROPHETS

Saturday Vespers. Mother Church places upon our lips a glorious song to Christ the King, one which expresses well our longing for the parousia: "O Lord, King of kings, You have ascended heaven's throne and have looked upon the depths! You have weighed the mountains and You hold the earth in the palm of Your hand! Hear us, Lord, in our groaning."

Sunday (Osee 1–2). Among the so-called later prophets who left written accounts (the earlier prophets such as Elias and Eliseus left nothing in writing), Osee is one of the first. He labored in the kingdom of Israel during the eighth century before Christ. His book contains discourses on repentance preached to the unfaithful and rebellious children of Israel. Because of its picturesque language the Book of Osee takes a place among the famous works of Hebrew literature. The book is divided into two parts; in the first (ch. 1–3) the prophet recounts God's command that he perform two symbolical acts signifying the rejection and final redemption of Israel; in the second part (ch. 4–14) are gathered five sermons on penance.

The first of the two symbolical acts was meant as a sermon to bring Israel to penance (it should do the same for sinners now). The prophet was commanded to enter marriage with an adulteress; his first child was to be named "Without-Mercy," his second, "Not-My-People." Using the language of poetry Yahweh Himself instructed Osee on the meaning of these actions.

CLING TO
THE WORDS
OF LIFE!

Israel was God's unfaithful bride who had given herself to spiritual prostitution, i.e., idolatry. She therefore would find no mercy nor would she be regarded as His chosen people (1:9; 2:3). Only after Israel had returned to pure and chaste wedlock with God would she again find grace. The number of the "sons of Israel" would then be as the sands of the sea, and God would then enter into a new and eternal covenant with Judah.

Monday (Osee 14). A call to penance.

Tuesday (Joel 1–2). The prophet Joel was a contemporary of the prophet Osee. In the figure of a locust plague Joel foretells the destruction of the kingdom of Judah (1–2:11), urges the priests and people to penance (2:12–17), prophesies the re-establishment of the kingdom (2:18–32), the last judgment, and the glory of the new Jerusalem (ch. 3). The lesson today is the well-known passage with which the Church introduces the Lenten season on Ash Wednesday.

Wednesday (Joel 3). In poetical language the prophet describes the last judgment and the glorious new Jerusalem.

Thursday (Amos). Amos too belonged to the oldest circle of the literary prophets. By occupation he was a shepherd in the kingdom of Israel. In spite of the lack of formal education, he was a master of prophetic rhetoric (Augustine, a great speaker himself, praised him highly). In his book we meet excellent pictures and comparisons culled from nature and pastoral life. The first six chapters contain his prophecies against neighboring nations; the final three chapters foretell Israel's rejection.

Friday (Jonas 1–2). Scholars have difficulty in dating the Book of Jonas; a growing number no longer regard the work as historical in the usual sense, rather as an account embodying doctrinal and religious values. Christ referred to the story (Matt. 12:40–41), especially to Jonas' three days' stay in the whale's belly, as a type of His own resurrection (in the Roman catacombs, pictures of Jonas and the whale occur very frequently).

Saturday (Jonas 3–4). Jonas preaches penance to the Ninivites; in part this passage is used as the Epistle on the Monday after Passion Sunday.

SCRIPTURE READINGS DURING THE FIFTH WEEK OF NOVEMBER

THE MINOR PROPHETS

Saturday Vespers. The Magnificat antiphon: "Upon your walls, O Jerusalem, I have appointed watchmen. Throughout the day and throughout the night they shall not cease praising the Name of the Lord."

Sunday (Micheas). Micheas labored in the kingdom of Judah at the time of the prophet Isaias (last half of the eighth century). The first chapter of his book describes the appearance of the Lord to judge Israel, an appropriate passage now during the Church's harvest.

Monday (Nahum). During the second half of the seventh century the prophet Nahum prophesied the destruction of Niniveh, Assyria's capital. According to St. Jerome this prophecy in a higher sense bespeaks God's judgment upon a sinful world.

Tuesday (Habacuc). The prophet Habacuc foretold the Babylonian captivity. The book is noted for its animated style and majestic form of expression; especially noteworthy is the "Canticle of Habacuc" (see Lauds on Friday — second form).

Wednesday (Sophonias). Our prophet labored in Judea in the second half of the seventh century. He foretold the exile but added comforting words on the return to the fatherland; his Messianic oracles describe the spread of God's kingdom.

Thursday (Aggeus). Today's prophet labored about twenty years after the initial return of the Israelites from the Babylonian exile. In four sermons he urged the reconstruction of the temple. True, building operations had already begun in the second year after the return (536), but the Samaritans, who were not permitted to assist, succeeded in obtaining from the Persians an injunction against its construction. However, in 520 Darius allowed the work to be resumed. The Jews then showed little enthusiasm. In the first address Aggeus denounced their indifference and interpreted current crop failures and misfortunes as divine punishments. In the second address he comforted those who had seen Solomon's temple and wept when the new foundations were laid because they were so inglorious. The prophet pointed out how the glory of the new temple would transcend that of Solomon's because the Messiah would grace it with His presence.

Friday (Zacharias). Aggeus and Zacharias were contemporaries. The first part of Zacharias' book is devoted to the reconstruction of the temple, the second contains prophecies on the triumph of God's kingdom. Of his Messianic prophecies the most famous is: "Rejoice greatly, O daughter of Sion, shout for joy, O daughter of Jerusalem; BEHOLD THY KING will come to thee, the Just and Savior! He is poor and riding upon an ass, upon a colt the foal of an ass. . . . and He will speak peace to the Gentiles. His power will extend from sea to sea, and from the River even to the ends of the earth." The passage was fulfilled to the letter at our Lord's entrance into Jerusalem before His passion (Matt. 21:5; John 12:15). It is used twice in the Advent and Christmas liturgy (Offertory on Ember Saturday; Communion on Christmas).

Saturday (Malachias). Malachias was the last prophet of the Old Law who left us a memorial in writing. He begins lamenting the nation's ingratitude toward God. His well-known prophecy concerning the Savior's precursor is used at Mass on the feast of the Purification (3:1–5).

The Proper of the Saints

September 1

ST. GILES, Abbot
THE TWELVE BROTHER SAINTS, Martyrs
Friends in need

1. **St. Giles.** *Day of death*: September 1, about 725 (according to the Martyrology). *Grave*: the abbey church of St. Serain at Toulouse. *Life.* The acts of St. Giles are not too reliable. They say that he sprang from a royal Athenian family. From his youth he was devoted to the study of Sacred Scripture and the practice of works of mercy. After the death of his parents he distributed his inheritance among the poor, healed a sick beggar by giving him his outer garment. He lived a long time as a hermit, nourishing himself on herbs and the milk of a deer that came to him regularly at fixed times. When chased by the dogs of the king of France, this deer fled into the hermit's cave; the incident occasioned the construction of a monastery on the site in honor of Sts. Peter and Paul. Here St. Giles ruled many years as abbot. Later the city of St. Giles arose nearby. He died about 725. The Mass, from the Common of Abbots (*Os justi*), p. 421.

The twelve martyred brothers commemorated today were Africans by birth. The name of their mother is given as Thecla. About the year 760 their relics were enshrined in the church of St. Sophia at Benevento, where popular piety honors their memory.

Today marks the end of the year in the Greek calendar; a special feast is kept, called *Indiction*, to note the transition to the new year.

2. **The Fourteen Sainted Helpers.** St. Giles is one of the "Sainted Fourteen" who since the Middle Ages have been honored and invoked as helpers and intercessors in temporal needs. The fourteen include: Acacius, Giles, Barbara, Blase, Christopher, Cyriac, Denis, Erasmus, Eustace, George, Catherine, Margaret, Pantaleon, and Vitus. The cult of these helpers falls more to the province of popular piety than to that of the liturgy. Nevertheless, this question concerns all of us: may we Christians

petition God and the saints for material benefits? Could it be injurious to objective or liturgical prayer to be concerned over the small things of life?

First of all, we must remember our purpose here on earth. We are on earth not to have a pleasant time, to feel ourselves quite at home. Life is a passageway to an eternal end. Time is the way to eternity. This way may follow different routes according to God's Providence. The individual man may be either rich or poor, healthy or sick, honored or abused. Whatever it be, it is his special way to an eternal goal according to God's designs. The main thing is and will always be eternal beatitude. We know too that God adapts each man for his particular vocation, not tempting him beyond his strength or laying unbearable burdens upon him. In no way, then, is it forbidden to ask for earthly things, granting that such are in harmony with our eternal destiny. We may ask God for health, for temporal goods, for success in an enterprise, even for insignificant things such as good weather or the recovery of some trifling object, if we always add an act of resignation to God's holy will.

Christ Himself taught us to ask: *Give us this day our daily bread*! Included in this one phrase are all our earthly needs. And in the Sermon on the Mount He admonished us: Seek first the kingdom of God and His justice, and all else will be given you besides. It is as if He said: Have your eyes riveted on your final goal, the kingdom of God, and then you may also ask for material things, things which resemble the candies thrown in free by the grocer. We should remember that we are children in God's house; and God is always a Father. Children may come and ask their father for anything. Their father will judge whether the wish should be answered or not. They may ask perseveringly, with all their little hearts, even to the point of wearisomeness, but they must leave it to father as to whether or not and when he wills to answer them.

With reference to God, we must presuppose that He willingly prepares joys for His children and that He delays granting their requests only for some supernatural reason. Which answers our question. In Sacred Scripture and in the lives of the saints we could find many examples in which God answered little earthly requests, e.g., the miracle at the wedding of Cana, or the plea of St. Scholastica. And that the intercession of the saints in behalf of such needs and desires is effective, is proven by many examples. It appears too that God has given certain saints a special power of intercession for particular needs. Upon this is based the popular devotion to the Fourteen Sainted Helpers. Remaining devout children of God, intent upon our eternal goal, we may ask our heavenly Father according to our heart's desire. He will favor us not only with bread, but now and then with the candies of life also.

September 2

ST. STEPHEN, King and Confessor

He was both king and apostle to his people

1. **St. Stephen.** *Day of death*: August 15, 1038. *Canonized*: 1083. Pope Innocent IX chose September 2 as his feastday in remembrance of the Christian victory over the Turks at Budapest in 1686. *Grave*: in the church of St. Mary at Stuhlweissenburg; his incorrupt right hand in a chapel of the church of Our Lady at Budapest. *Life*. St. Stephen was the first Christian king of Hungary. He was born in 975 at Gran, the son of Prince Geisa, and was baptized in 985 by St. Adalbert. While courting Gisela, the sister of Emperor St. Henry II (see July 15), he was promised her hand in marriage provided that he remain firm in the Christian faith and lead the pagan Hungarians to Christianity. He kept his word though it cost him dearly. From the hands of Pope Sylvester II (999–1003) he received the royal crown and was solemnly enthroned at Gran on the feast of Mary's Assumption, 1001. (The alleged bull of Pope Sylvester granting to Stephen and his successors the privilege of having the cross carried before them, like metropolitans, is now regarded as a seventeenth-century forgery.)

Stephen was one of the wisest princes of his time. His royal generosity is shown in the establishment of the archbishopric of Gran and ten Hungarian bishoprics, and in his love toward the poor. Because he visited them in their houses and washed their feet, his right hand has remained incorrupt. Great was his zeal in prayer and meditation. From his marriage came a saintly son, the devout Emeric, an angel of purity, who died seven years before his father. By prayer and fasting Stephen sought the conversion of all Hungary; rightfully is he called the apostle of his nation. He chose the Mother of God as the patroness of Hungary.

Application. A saint upon the throne, who besides being king was the apostle and father of his people! Reflect his spirit in your own family and toward your associates! The Mass (*Os justi*) is from the Common of Confessors, p. 421, with the Gospel of the ten talents (for commentary, see the feast of St. Louis, August 25). The three *Orations*, too, are proper. Note in particular how the *Postcommunion* plays upon Stephen's kingship as we petition for that faith through which he "became worthy to pass from an earthly kingdom to the glory of a heavenly one." The formulary, with the needed modifications, could well be regarded as a "Common of Kings."

2. We Are Kings. Just as there is a special priesthood and a lay priesthood, so also is there a special kingship and a lay or common kingship in the Church. Christ is both Priest and King; and He permits His Mystical Body, the Church, to have a share in these two offices. Every Christian, therefore, is a king. St. Peter wrote to his followers: "You are a chosen generation, a *kingly* priesthood" (1 Pet. 2:9). In the Apocalypse the ancients sing before the Lamb: "You have made them (the redeemed) priests and kings unto our God, and they will reign upon the earth" (Apoc. 5:10). The Christian becomes a king at baptism when he is anointed with chrism.

How can we practice our royal prerogatives? We must distinguish the two great epochs of our lives, that here on earth and that hereafter in heaven. In the present life our kingship is hidden, veiled, even as Christ's kingship on earth was little manifest. In chains before Pilate, He nevertheless acknowledged: "I am a king . . . My kingdom is not of this world" (John 18:36–37). Our Christian kingship, accordingly, is not of this world and does not consist in tangible power, in riches, honors. It is a kingdom of the spirit. Nevertheless it is real.

Now every king has a kingdom; he must rule, must battle against enemies, must conquer, must exercise the office of arbiter and supreme judge. All of which holds true of the Christian. His kingdom is the realm of God which he establishes in his soul, for which he cares, which he develops and stabilizes. It is a kingdom that begins at baptism and requires a whole lifetime for expansion and development. Here human and divine energies work hand in hand. As king over this realm his duties are three: to rule, to conquer, and to judge.

To rule. In the soul's citadel the Christian must reign supreme. For this he needs a strong will. He rules through suffering, he rules through patience, he rules through obedience, he rules through love. Of this rule and its contrary, Christ said: "The truth shall make you free . . . whoever commits sin is the slave of sin" (John 8:32, 34). A Christian's ruling power consists, then, in remaining free from the slavery of sin.

To conquer. Ruling is not unrelated to fighting. The Christian must be a soldier, a conqueror. In the seven letters written to the angels of the seven Churches, there reoccurs in stereotype fashion the admonition: "He who conquers . . . to him who overcomes."

Lastly, the Christian must be a *judge.* He judges well if he always decides in favor of the good and against the bad. Thus we are kings, kings over a spiritual, an invisible kingdom. But hereafter our kingdom will become openly manifest; then we will rule with Christ, we will "judge the angels" (1 Cor. 6:3). Christ promised to those who renounced earthly ties for His sake: "You who have followed Me, in the regeneration when the Son of Man will sit on the throne of His glory, you also will sit on twelve thrones judging the twelve tribes of Israel" (Matt. 19:28). The details of our roles as kings in the heavenly kingdom we can at present only surmise.

ST. PIUS X, Pope

Renew all things in Christ

"He was one of those chosen few men whose personality is irresistible. Everyone was moved by his simplicity and his angelic kindness. Yet it was something more that carried him into all hearts: and that 'something' is best defined by saying that all who were ever admitted to his presence had a deep conviction of being face to face with a saint" (Baron von Pastor).

1. **Pope St. Pius X.** *Day of death*: August 20, 1914. *Grave*: in St. Peter's, Rome. *Canonized*: May 29, 1954. *Life*. The future Pope-Saint of the twentieth century was born at Riese in Venetia on June 2, 1835, his name, Joseph Sarto. After ordination at the age of twenty-three (by special dispensation), he labored for seventeen years as a parish priest, then as bishop of Mantua, and in 1892 was advanced to the metropolitan see of Venice with the honorary title of patriarch. On August 4, 1903, he was elected Pope, "a man of God who knew the unhappiness of the world and the hardships of life, and in the greatness of his heart wanted to comfort everybody."

The primary aim of his pontificate Pius X announced in his first encyclical letter, viz., "to renew all things in Christ." Here we need but allude to his decree on early and frequent reception of holy Communion; his *Motu Proprio* on church music; his encouragement of daily Bible reading and the establishment of various Biblical institutes; his reorganization of the Roman ecclesiastical offices; his work on the codification of Canon Law; his incisive stand against Modernism, that "synthesis of all heresies." All these were means toward the realization of his main objective of renewing all things in Christ.

The outbreak of the first World War, practically on the date of the eleventh anniversary of his election to the See of Peter, was the blow that occasioned his death. Bronchitis developed within a few days, and on August 20, Pius X succumbed to "the last affliction that the Lord will visit on me." He had said in his

will, "I was born poor, I have lived poor, I wish to die poor" —
and no one questioned the truth of his words. His sanctity and
his power to work miracles had already been recognized. Pius
X was the first Pope canonized since St. Pius V in 1672.

2. Holy Mass (Extuli electum). It is remarkable that an exception was made so quickly after the introduction of the Common of Sovereign Pontiffs, allowing our saint a proper formulary
instead of the Mass *Si diligis Me*. The tone of the composition is
in harmony with the more modern trend, expressing the office,
work and personality of Pius X.

It was Christ who chose Peter, it is Christ who speaks in the
Introit of His choice of Joseph Sarto to be Peter's successor: "I
have exalted one chosen from among My people; with My holy
oil I have anointed him and My arm will ever make him strong."
There is no saint who is not heroically humble; Pius immediately answers His Lord with a canticle of gratitude (Ps. 88):
"The favors of the Lord will I sing forever."

Pope Pius' motto, to renew all things in Christ, is woven into
our *Collect* petition; his humble, childlike, and loving spirit as
he furthered the cause of the Gospel is brought to our attention
in the *Epistle*: "We became like little ones in the midst of you,
like a mother cherishing her children . . . not only would we
gladly impart God's Gospel to you, but even our very soul, because you are become most dear to us." How well this reflects
the sainted Pontiff's dying words: "I would gladly give my life
to save my poor children from this ghastly scourge (of war)."

There is more than a veiled reference to his stand against
Modernism in the *Gradual*, "Your justice I did not hide in my
heart," or to his efforts in behalf of early and frequent holy
Communion in the *Alleluia, Offertory*, and *Communion* antiphons: "Come, children, listen to me . . . My Flesh is meat
indeed . . . You spread a table in my presence." Foremost in
our minds is his great work in behalf of liturgical reform as we
hear Jesus bid him, "Feed My lambs, feed My lambs, feed My
sheep" (*Gosp.*).

In conclusion we may observe that the very fact that a Mass
of so high a liturgical caliber could be composed in our day is

in itself in no small measure a tribute to the reforms and the inspiration of Pope St. Pius himself.

September 4

FERIAL DAY

On days when no special feast occurs, the Mass of the preceding Sunday is said.

September Spirituality. In the Church's calendar the month of September is the first of the autumn or harvest months. For now begins the change to the last phase of the ecclesiastical year, that which has as its objective holy longing for Christ's Second Advent. This change starts on the fifteenth Sunday after Pentecost. Its spirit dominates the feasts of the Exaltation of the Holy Cross and of St. Michael the Archangel; on the former there appears the Sign of the Son of Man in the heavens, on the latter Michael arms himself for the apocalyptic battle with mankind's primeval foe.

This month, however, has still other symbolism. In the world of nature, autumn is beginning; the evenings are becoming longer, the days shorter; night and cold are beginning the conflict against light and warmth. This mirrors the battle in the supernatural kingdom and leaves its impress upon September liturgy. It is the reason why "hero" books are given us by the Church, books treating of interior battle and victory: Job and Tobit, Judith and Esther, two men and two women, each a champion. In them we see how the Christian can be a hero and a soldier, Job is the champion of patience, Tobit the champion of merciful love of neighbor. Judith and Esther are heroines in a different fashion, for they, by a great deed in which they placed their lives in imminent danger, saved their people. All four, different as they are, impress us with that spirit of heroic action which Christianity demands. Serious reading of these four books will bring much edification and instruction. September spirituality, therefore, consists in cherishing a lively expectation of the parousia, and striving for the heroism characteristic of a saint.

September 5

ST. LAWRENCE JUSTINIAN, Bishop

My Savior died not on feathers but on the hard wood of the Cross!

1. **St. Lawrence.** *Day of death*: January 8, 1455 (today commemorates his consecration as bishop). *Canonized*: 1690. *Grave*: at Venice. *Life*. Lawrence, an illustrious example of humility, the "ornament and glory of bishops" (according to Pope Eugene IV), was the first patriarch of Venice. A very pious youth, he was favored in his nineteenth year with a vision of Eternal Wisdom appearing in the form of a beautiful virgin radiant with light who invited him to find peace in herself. He obeyed the invitation. Soon thereafter he became a clerk regular of St. George on the island of Alga, later bishop of Venice.

Some of St. Lawrence's special charisms were the gift of tears, power over devils, prophecy. One Christmas night the Christ-Child appeared to him. When an attempt was made during his last sickness to put him on a more comfortable bed, he refused this pleasure with the words, "My Savior died not on feathers but on the hard wood of the Cross," and requested to be laid on his usual couch. As he felt his last moments approaching, he lifted his eyes to heaven and said, "I am coming, good Jesus, to You," and slept blessedly in the Lord (January 8, 1455). At the time Venice was at the zenith of its influence and wealth. But God made that proud city understand that her greatness resulted more from the sanctity of her poor patriarch Lawrence than from the diplomacy of her doges and the power of her galleys. — The Mass, from the Common of Bishops (*Statuit*), p. 417.

2. **Wisdom's Invitation.** Eternal Wisdom appeared to our saint in the form of a beautiful virgin and spoke appealingly to him. Lawrence has woven a description of the vision into an exhortation on following his example:

"Come, any and all of you who are attracted to the good that never changes, the good that you seek in vain from this quickly passing century. I will tell you what heaven has done for me. As you have done until the present, so I too gave myself feverishly to exciting pursuits, and worldly externals would not pacify my fiery spirit. But by God's grace, which continued to feed my fears and unrest, there appeared to me at last One more beautiful than the sun, more sweet than balsam, One whose name till then had remained unknown. How lovely was her face when she came into my presence! How quieting and consoling her voice as she said to me: 'Why is your heart so restless? The peace you seek in so many ways is mine to give. Your desire can be granted. I will pledge you my troth if you take me as your bride.'

"Yes, I admit that my heart quivered at these words, for my soul was being pierced by love's arrow. How I yearned to know her name, her nobility, her origin; but she would only say that she called herself Eternal Wisdom that dwelt invisibly in the Father's bosom but now had assumed a visible form to become loved more readily. I gave my assent to her in a loud cry of joy, and having kissed me, she disappeared.

"Ever since, the flame of love toward her has been increasing, and all my thoughts are centered upon her. I am ever enraptured by her, she is my beloved bride, my inseparable companion. Now do all of you please listen to me: approach her, each of you, for she finds her happiness in never slighting anyone."

Often we too stand at the crossroads, with the world and Christ bidding for our souls. The world proffers earthly thrills, while Wisdom (Christ) offers heavenly peace for the asking. Choose wisely.

September 6

FERIAL DAY

On days when no special feast occurs, the Mass of the previous Sunday or a Votive Mass is said.

Hope. Nature enters her final phase during the month of

September, as witnessed by the shorter days and the coloring of the leaves. In the Church too the year's last phase is beginning, and we may name this period the Church's Harvest Time. It is a season having its own proper character and content, one which may be summed up in the word *hope*.

Hope ranks as one of the three theological virtues; still in a very true sense it is a stepchild. Though a stranger to many, it is the virtue that most accurately gauges the measure of one's spirituality. Perhaps this may be clarified by a consideration of its opposite. St. Paul pities the pagans who "have no hope" (1 Thess. 4:13). The worldly man who sets his hope only on money and pleasure, whose god is his belly, is the ape of the Christian ideal. The more one is sunk in earthly affairs, the less is he grounded upon Christian hope, the less a Christian is he. Therefore detachment is imperative. For then there is less danger of losing oneself in the earthly, of being enchanted with its luxury, its niceties. Doesn't this help to understand our Lord's saying: "A rich man shall hardly enter the kingdom of heaven" (Matt. 19:23)? How can those who are able to satisfy their every whim hope for something other?

The Christian filled with the virtue of supernatural hope readily sees the truth in the beatitudes Jesus proclaimed in the Sermon on the Mount (according to St. Luke): "Blessed are the poor . . . blessed are they who now hunger . . . blessed are they who now weep . . . blessed, if men now hate you." Or their contrary: "Woe to you rich . . . woe to you who are filled . . . woe to you who now laugh . . . woe to you if all the world praises you." In themselves, riches and poverty, hunger and plenty, laughter and tears, honor and persecution are neither good nor evil. In heaven kings and beggars are seated next to each other. The approaching season will provide much material and many motives for fostering the theological virtue of hope.

September 7

FERIAL DAY

What may we learn from the example of Tobit?

The Old Testament foreshadowed the New. This is true primarily when it is considered as a whole. Frequently, however, one or the other specifically Christian ideal leaps forth from the pages of a particular Old Testament book with such force and clarity as to make us believe that the good news of Christ was already being proclaimed. Included would be passages on the proper approach to material goods and earthly pleasures, and the love one must show toward fellow men in need. The aged Tobit expressed such truth when he told his son: "Do not be upset, my child, because we have become destitute. A great treasure is yours if you fear God, if you remain aloof from all sin and do what is pleasing in His sight" (Tob. 4:21).

This single passage would be sufficient to exonerate the Old Testament from the false assumption that it fosters materialism. The Book of Tobit should amply demonstrate how far superior Israel's religion was to the religions of contemporary civilized peoples. According to Plato, for example, an attempt had been made in Athens to banish all the poor from the city so as to free it from "such animals." What inhumanity that attitude reveals! How totally different the spirit of the aged Tobit in his heroic exemplification of love of neighbor! He wanted his son to reflect the highest nobility of character, an end to be achieved by observing his counsel: "Of your own store of bread give to the hungry, and from your wardrobe supply the naked. Whatever remains, regard as alms; and when you give, suppress all envy. Be most generous with your goods at the burial of a good man, but provide no support to evildoers. By so doing you will assure for yourself excellent security in the day of need. Generosity preserves one even from death, it prevents descent into the realms of darkness. In the sight of the Most High generosity is a choice offering" (Tob. 4:16f.; 4:9).

Generosity in the form of almsgiving was the characteristic

virtue of Tobit's life. How many of us Christians could truthfully say with our Old Testament hero: "I, Tobit, walked the road of truth and holiness all the days of my life; to my neighbors and to my fellow men at large I gave alms generously" (Tob. 1:3).

As he spoke, so too he lived. While still in his homeland where most Israelites not only practiced idolatry but became absorbed in the spirit of pagan cult, Tobit remained aloof from all contamination, fully devoted to the precepts of Mosaic Law: "From my total income I would give ten percent to the sons of Levi who served the Lord at Jerusalem. Another ten percent I would liquidate, journey to Jerusalem, and spend it there each year. A third tenth I would give to those who had some claim in charity" (Tob. 1:6f.).

When Samaria was destroyed, Tobit was deported to Assyria along with the other inhabitants of the Northern Kingdom. Almsgiving brings its reward, and the case of our saint was no exception. God granted him favor and honor at the royal palace, and he prospered in many ways. But the change in external circumstances occasioned no change in his spirit of generosity, "To the hungry I gave bread, to the naked, clothing. Whenever I saw the dead body of a fellow man cast alongside Nineveh's walls, I would bury it. Even after Sennacherib the King had returned from his ill-fated campaign in Judea and had ordered an execution, I buried the body secretly; for many fell victim to his wrath. If the king's servants would look for the corpse, they would find nothing. But a certain Ninevite informed the king of what I was doing. I was forced to hide. Then, upon learning that I was being sought in order to be killed, I fled in fear. All my property was seized; I had nothing left except Anna my wife and my son Tobias" (Tob. 1:17ff.).

The generous person will not be abandoned, his goodly deeds will bring ample returns. There was a palace revolution, and Sennacherib was assassinated. Essarhaddon became king and appointed Tobit's nephew keeper of the royal seal and minister of finance. Tobit returned home and his property was restored to him. There would be a feast, of course. And it was somewhat elaborate. Before touching a single morsel, Tobit said to his son:

"Go and invite here any of our neighbors who is in need and who remembers the Lord. I will wait for your return" (Tob. 2:2). Tobias returned sad, with the report that again some Israelite lay murdered in the market place. To the Oriental mind no indignity was greater than to remain unburied.

Tobit had hardly heard the news when he hastened on his wonted act of mercy, heedless of any new suffering it might bring upon him and his family. Some laughed and ridiculed him, "He is not yet afraid of being killed for such work, for already he is burying the dead again" (Tob. 2:8). Tired out by the labor of shoveling, Tobit lay down alongside a wall. Sparrows fluttered about, and into the old man's eyes fell droppings. Now he was blinded. To which came suffering and poverty. He who had dedicated himself to the service of others was forgotten. Such is a common experience; those who spend themselves in loving, selfless service will suffer like Tobit. Under such circumstances it is easy to become impatient, as shown by the retort of Tobit's pious wife: "Now where are your alms and your pious acts? Tell me, for you seem to have all the answers!" (Tob. 2:14).

Tobit, the far-famed model for love of fellow man, now has nought left but God. He knew it to be his greatest "treasure" (Tob. 4:21). While ill, he recalled a one-time loan to Gabael at Rages. Being in distress, he would send his son to that city to recover the money. And he would use the occasion to give him sound, practical advice.

Young Tobias sought a companion for the long, dangerous trip. The archangel Raphael presented himself, was "hired," and proved most helpful. Tobias returned safely, his mission well accomplished. Besides obtaining the needed money, he married a virtuous and wealthy woman at the angel's behest. And with the gall of the fish taken at Raphael's bidding, he restored vision to the blinded eyes of his aged father. Again there was joy and laughter and song in the sorrow-filled house of the generous almsgiver. The alms he had so lavishly bestowed not only brought back to him all that he had lost, but with interest. Untold blessings came in their train to him and his family. Now, when God's favor was manifesting itself so wondrously, Raphael revealed the inner theology of it all: "A little with holiness is better than much with sin. It is better to give alms than to accumulate money. Generosity will save a person from death, it will even blot out any sin. Those who practice almsgiving and seek after holiness will merit a well-rounded life. When you were burying the dead, I was standing at your side. When you rose at once and left a set table to go and lay out the deceased, your virtue did not escape me — I accompanied you. I am Raphael, one of the seven holy spirits who transport on high the prayers of the saints and go into the glorious presence of the all-holy God" (Tob. 12:8f.).

A good point to remember. Almsgiving is prayer. Like prayer it is carried before the throne of God. Almsgiving brings graces, it cleanses the soul from guilt and punishment. What good is faith without works, if we desert our fellow man in his need? (James 2:14). Autumn time, the season of abundance and divine liberality, should instill in us the spirit of magnanimity and generosity, should make it easy to be like Tobit, loving, sympathetic, generous. (— Dr. Jos. Casper).

September 8

THE NATIVITY OF MARY

Your birth, O Virgin Mother of God, heralded joy to all the world!

1. **Mary's Birthday.** To her practice of celebrating as birthday a saint's day of death instead of the day of birth, the Church makes only two exceptions, for the Blessed Virgin and for John the Baptist. The latter was freed from original sin before birth, while Mary was immaculate from the first moment of her conception, the most holy of all created beings. The feast of Mary's nativity, observed since the eighth century in the Western Church, is primarily a redemption feast, a preparation for the Messiah. It is a feast close to our heart, for as members of God's

great family we love to celebrate family events; today is our Mother's birthday. The church of St. Hadrian, once a senate chamber, was the point of gathering today for the solemn liturgy at Rome; from there clergy and people, together with the Pope, went barefoot in a brilliant procession to St. Mary Major. Upon approaching the station church, the litany was sung; on this occasion it replaced the Introit and the Kyrie.

2. Holy Mass (Salve Sancta). Since liturgy is dramatic and presents the day's saint as in our midst, we may consider today's festal Mass as a congratulatory celebration in honor of the Mother of God. Every Mass entails a sacred exchange, a giving and receiving; in the Foremass the words of men ascend to God and God's words come down to men; in the Sacrifice proper we bring our gifts at the Offertory and receive God's return Gift at the Eucharistic banquet. Note how these four sacred acts which touch the participant so directly are intimately related today to the feast being kept. In the *Introit* we greet and congratulate God's Mother: "Hail, O holy Mother. . . ." Then she replies (*Epist.* and *Gosp.*), she, our Mother standing in our midst and telling of her ancestry and of her Child's.

At the *Offertory* we show her our birthday present, a costly one and most acceptable — the paschal Lamb, her divine Son, whom we are offering to the heavenly Father in her honor! The Eucharistic Banquet is our Mother's return gift, the most precious she can give, the Body and Blood of her sacrificed Son, flesh and blood of her own flesh and blood (such exposition is not entirely in accord with best liturgical thought, I admit, since the Mass is wholly an act of cult or worship to the divine Majesty).

Portions of the Mass are taken from the Common, portions are proper to the feast. The Readings introduce Mary as wisdom speaking to us; she was in God's mind before creation: "My delight is to be with the children of men." She also has a word of admonition: "Now, children, hear me; blessed is he who keeps my way. Whoever finds me finds life, and will receive salvation from the Lord." The *Gospel* acquaints us with Joseph's illustrious lineage, which was Mary's too, at least in part. Although the Divine Office constantly alludes to Mary's birth, the Mass, apart from the various Orations, makes no reference to it.

3. Divine Office. Fervor and warmth are characteristics of today's Office. Of special note would be the beautiful responsories at Matins; all of them acclaim Mary's birthday in festal style:

> Your birth, O Virgin Mother of God,
>   heralded joy to all the world.
> For from you has risen the Sun of justice,
>   Christ our God.
> Destroying the curse, He gave blessing;
>   and damning death, He bestowed on us
>   life everlasting.
> Blessed art thou among women
>   and blessed is the fruit of thy womb.
> For from you has risen of Sun of justice,
>   Christ our God.

The Lessons of the second nocturn describe Mary's relation to Eve. "The much-desired feast of Blessed Mary ever Virgin has come; so let our land, illumined by such a birth, be glad with greatest rejoicing. For she is the flower of the field from whom bloomed the precious Lily of the valley, through whose birth that nature inherited from our first parents is changed and guilt is blotted out. Eve mourned, Mary rejoiced. Eve carried tears in her heart; Mary, joy. For Eve gave birth to men of sin, Mary to the Innocent One. The mother of our race brought punishment upon the world, the Mother of our Lord brought salvation to mankind. Eve was the authoress of sin, Mary the authoress of merit; Eve by killing was a hindrance, Mary by giving life was a help; Eve struck and Mary healed. Disobedience is displaced by obedience, and fidelity atones for infidelity.

"Now let Mary play upon musical instruments and let timbrels reverberate under the fleet fingers of this young Mother. Let joyous choirs sing together harmoniously, and let sweet songs be blended now with one melody and now with another. Hear how our timbrel-player has sung. For she said: My soul magnifies the

Lord, and my spirit rejoices in God my Savior, because He has regarded the lowliness of His handmaid; for behold, henceforth all generations shall call me blessed; because He who is mighty has done great things for me. This miraculous new birth has utterly vanquished the root of heretofore aimless wanderings; Mary's canticle has ended the lamentations of Eve" (*St. Augustine*).

4. **According to legend** St. Hadrian had been a functionary of Emperor Maximian, who enjoined upon him the persecution of Christians in Nicomedia. The steadfastness of the martyrs occasioned his conversion, and he himself then suffered a martyrdom worthy of a hero. In Hadrian's honor a former senate hall was consecrated as a church by Pope Honorius I (625–638). According to an ordinance of Pope Sergius I (687–701), the "candle procession" was to set out from this church and proceed to St. Mary Major on the four great Marian feasts (Candlemas, Annunciation, Assumption, Nativity); in these processions Pope and clergy took part barefoot. Very probably today marks the anniversary of the church's dedication.

5. **Liturgical Marian Devotion.** An examination of the liturgical texts proper to today's feast would show a double theme, one treating Mary as *theotokos*, the other stressing her illustrious human descent. Thus honor is accorded both to Mary's human lineage and to her divine prerogatives.

a) The chants of the Mass are devoted to Mary's divine Motherhood exclusively. A favorite antithesis is this: Mary, a creature, a maiden, a child of men, is the Mother of the Creator, of the King of heaven and earth, of the Sun of justice. "Hail, O holy Mother, for you gave birth to the King who rules heaven and earth forever" (*Intr.*). "O Virgin, Mother of God, the whole world could not contain Him who deigned to become man in your womb" (*Grad.*). "You are blessed, O holy Virgin Mary, and most worthy of all praise, since from you has risen the Sun of justice, Christ our God" (*Allel.*). "You are blessed, O Virgin Mary, because you are the Mother of Him who created all things. You gave birth to Him who made you, while remaining a Virgin forever" (*Off.*). "Blessed is Mary's virgin womb that bore the Son of the eternal Father" (*Comm.*). We see that the same thoughts are expressed in an unusual profusion. How beautifully the liturgy transforms the honor paid to Mary into the worship of Christ. In the liturgy Mary never appears in solitary grandeur but always in some relation to Christ.

b) The Divine Office and the Gospel text tell of Mary's family background or descent, certainly a most appropriate choice for one's birthday. The antiphons and responsories praise her royal ancestry. "It is the nativity of the glorious Virgin Mary, sprung from the seed of Abraham, of the tribe of Juda, of the renowned family of David!" "Sprung from a royal family, Mary stands in radiant splendor before us." The Gospel gives the genealogy of Jesus, which is also Mary's. Five women are listed; to these we could add Eve, Sara, Rebecca. Of those mentioned in the Gospel, two were pagans, Rahab and Ruth; and two were sinners, Thamar and the wife of Urias. Gentiles and sinners are included among those from whom Mary and Christ were descended because grace and redemption were meant to be universal, embracing Gentiles and sinners too. In the divine economy of salvation Mary has the role of "Mother of mercy," a title that would involve a special interest in pagans and sinners. What a glorious vision the liturgy reveals of our Mother! On one hand she attains the most sublime intimacy with the Godhead that any creature could possibly imagine (*theotokos*, Mother of God); on the other, she reaches down and sympathizes with human poverty and need as the Mother of sinners, Jew and Gentile. Marian devotion inspired by the liturgy would never be questioned!

September 9

ST. GORGON, Martyr

"Through the martyr Gorgon Your family, Lord, will be steeped in the sweet odor of Christ"

1. **St. Gorgon.** There are two martyrs with this name, a source of considerable confusion. The one was born in Nicomedia

and was martyred under Diocletian. Concerning him the second nocturn retains the following legendary account: "Gorgonius, a native of Nicomedia, served as a treasurer to Emperor Diocletian. Aided by one of his colleagues, Dorotheus, he converted his fellow officials to the Christian faith. On one occasion, upon witnessing the cruel torturing of a martyr in Diocletian's presence, both Gorgonius and Dorotheus were moved to become martyrs themselves. Fearlessly they addressed the Emperor: 'O Caesar, why do you restrict your punishments to this one witness? Both of us profess the same faith against which you inflict so dire a judgment. See, we are ready to undergo the same suffering.' Without delay the Emperor had them put into irons; he ordered their wounds to be washed with salt and vinegar before tying them to a heated grill. After further torture, they were hanged, about the year 303."

The other Gorgonius to whom we referred above was a Roman martyr. His first burial place was on the Via Lavicana in the cemetery between the two laurels; during the pontificate of Gregory IV (827–844) his remains were transferred to St. Peter's. Actually it was the Roman Gorgonius whose feast was kept today, and who was confused with the better known Nicomedian.

2. Holy Mass. The Mass, from the Common (*Laetabitur*), p. 407, with proper Orations. The Postcommunion is particularly beautiful: "May eternal bliss shine upon and gladden Your family, Lord; for through Your martyr Gorgon we are steeped at all times in the sweet odor of Christ." This prayer indeed indicates how highly the ancient Church respected martyrs. Let us realize that we are a great family whose most illustrious members are those who have died for the faith. From their passion we still draw benefit; and we should rejoice spiritually over them.

Enrich your repertoire of prayer by adding to it today's Benedictus antiphon: *He who hates his life in this world, keeps it unto life eternal!*

September 10

ST. NICHOLAS OF TOLENTINO, Confessor

Do not love the world,
for the world with its lusts will perish

1. **St. Nicholas.** *Day of death*: September 10, 1306. *Canonized*: 1446; feast since 1585. *Grave*: at Tolentino in middle Italy. *Life*. Nicholas was born in answer to the prayers his parents addressed to St. Nicholas of Bari; hence his name. Already during boyhood he imitated the strict fastings of his patron. He became a canon, but upon hearing a hermit of St. Augustine preach, "Do not love the world, for the world with its lusts will perish" (John 2:15), he gave the text serious thought and became a hermit of St. Augustine. Adorned with an angel-like tenderheartedness together with guileless simplicity, he would not desist from his unusual zeal in prayer although attacked by the devil to the point of blows. Each evening during the six months preceding his death he heard angels singing; the sweetness of their song allowed him to taste beforehand the joys of heaven, so that he repeatedly exclaimed in the words of St. Paul: "I long to be dissolved and be with Christ" (Phil. 1:23). — The Mass, from the Common of Confessors (*Justus*), p. 423.

2. **The Power of God's Word.** A single phrase from a sermon effected St. Nicholas' conversion and made him a saint. An excellent example of the power of God's word! Christ once said: "Not by bread alone does man live, but by every word that proceeds from the mouth of God." In other terms: Bread nourishes one's physical life, the word of God nourishes one's supernatural life. Recall the parable of the sower about the seed that fell on good ground and produced abundant returns — a parable explained by Jesus Himself. The seed is the word of God. This point is particularly important. The word of God is seed containing limitless vitality. It does not yet live, but requires the good earth to burst into life, to become a living, growing plant.

With our saint a single text was such seed; it fell upon a warm and receptive heart and produced fruit a hundredfold. God's word can make us similar to His Mother. Jesus revealed this in reply to the woman who praised Mary: "Blessed the womb that bore Thee. . . ." How did He answer? "Yes, that may be true, but even so, rather are they blessed who hear the word of God and keep it." Understand His reply correctly. He was drawing a parallel. Mary is blessed because she as a mother carried the Son of God in her womb. The Christian is blessed because he receives and carries Christ. Christ comes to us, then, in the words of God and is borne by us. With our saint this was actually the case. For he heard and heeded God's inspired words and became a chosen vessel, a Christ-bearer.

A final thought. John calls Christ the Word, the *Logos*; the second divine Person is the Father's spoken thought. Should not the word of God have in it something of the Logos, something of the divine Word? How we ought esteem the words of God! By and through them Christ comes to us, Christ the divine Logos, with the infinite vitality of the Godhead.

September 11

STS. PROTUS AND HYACINTH, Martyrs

Fidelity for its own sake

Sts. Protus and Hyacinth. The story of most martyrs of the first three centuries is so obscured by legend that it is difficult for us to cull out the historical kernel; this is true of today's saints. The breviary says that the brothers Protus and Hyacinth were chamberlains to the holy virgin Eugenia (listed as a martyr on December 25 in the Roman Martyrology) and were baptized along with their patron by Bishop Helenus. They devoted themselves zealously to the study of Sacred Scripture and lived for a time with the hermits in Egypt, illustrious for humility and holiness of life. At a later date they accompanied Eugenia to Rome and were arrested by Emperor Gallienus (260–268) for their

profession of the Christian faith. In no manner could they be
persuaded to deny the faith or worship the gods; accordingly,
after an inhuman scourging, they were beheaded on September
11.

Veneration of the two martyrs in the Church of Rome dates
to venerable antiquity. Ancient registers contain their names,
Pope Damasus praises them in verse at the end of the age of
martyrs. The cemetery of Basilla marked the site of their graves;
relics of St. Hyacinth were discovered there in 1845 and now are
honored in the chapel of the Propaganda. *Application*. Fidelity
toward our heavenly Father is indicative of fidelity toward
earthly rulers. Both brothers preserved this twofold fidelity. We
must also be loyal toward all our lawful superiors. — The Mass,
from the Common (*Salus autem*), p. 411.

September 12

THE NAME OF MARY

Star of the sea, I greet thee

1. **The Name of Mary.** "The feast of the Most Holy Name
of Mary was introduced by Pope Innocent XI after the glorious
victory over the Turks achieved through the assistance of the
Blessed Virgin at the city walls of Vienna" (*Martyrology*).
Originally it was observed on the Sunday following the feast of
Mary's nativity, but since the time of Pius X it enjoys a fixed
date, the anniversary of Vienna's liberation (September 12,
1683). The feast has a triple purpose: (a) to honor one of our
dearest names; (b) to serve as a family feast; (c) a votive celebration to commemorate a victory.

a) A person's name means much more in the liturgy and in
the Bible than to us moderns. It is an expression of one's personality, of one's whole being or nature. In many cases individuals who in sacred history were assigned special roles received
from God a name suited to their mission. We may well admit
that the name of the Mother of God did not befall her acciden-

tally but through divine design. For us Christians the name *Mary* is a sacramental which is ever spoken and honored with deepest piety. No wonder then that preachers and writers have sought to assign it meanings, to accord it highest praise. The liturgy offers various interpretations, e.g., "friend," "mistress" (Peter Chrysologus in the third nocturn), "star of the sea." This last title is widely used in the Office (although sound basis for such etymology is lacking). Upon it St. Bernard builds an edifying homily to which we listen in the second nocturn. Also in the lovely Vesper hymn of Marian Offices, *Ave, Maris Stella*, this title is used and explained in the third strophe.

b) Today's feast is also a family feast in God's great family. Mary not only is God's Mother, she is the Mother of us Christians too. Some few days ago we celebrated her birthday, today her name day. And many of us have sisters who keep this day in special union with their heavenly patroness.

c) Nor ought we be unmindful that today's feast is a thanksgiving celebration. It is the anniversary of Vienna's wonderful, almost miraculous, deliverance from the Turks on September 12, 1683. Pope Innocent XI designated this day as one of gratitude for the victory of the Cross over the crescent, due to Mary's intercession.

2. The Mass is derived from the usual Marian Masses (see p. 392f). In the *Introit* we greet God's Mother as she conducts us to Christ the King; the Bridal Song serves as chant. The three processions (*Intr., Off., Comm.*) are bridal processions, each circling a wider ambit. In the *Lesson* Mary speaks to us as Wisdom personified. The *Gospel* leads us into the home at Nazareth, where we witness the memorable dialog between Mary and Gabriel. At the *Offertory* we sing the *Ave, Maria*, the angel's immortal greeting. At the *Communion* we share the dignity of mothering the Son of God, because for us also the words are true: "Blessed the womb of the Virgin Mary that bore the Son of the eternal Father."

3. Divine Office. At Matins St. Bernard speaks: "The name of the Virgin, the evangelist tells us, was Mary. May we add a few words of comment upon this blessed name. Translated it means *Star of the Sea*, a very appropriate title for our Virgin-Mother. She may well be compared to a star, for as a star beams forth its rays without any diminution of its own lustre, so too the Virgin Mary gave birth to a Son with no loss to her virginity. The departing rays do not lessen the star's brightness, nor Mary's Son her inviolate maidenhood.

"Mary is that glorious 'star that arose from Jacob'; its rays illumine the universe, reaching into the depths, brightening the whole earth. She is, I repeat, a glorious star, a stationary light high over this vast sea of earth. There it shines, a guide to all. You, all you who are cast about upon the sea of temporalities in storms and tempests more than you walk on solid land, do not turn your eyes from this radiant star if you wish to be preserved from perishing in the depths. When the storms of temptation strike, when you run against the reefs of affliction, look to your Star, call upon Mary. When tossed to and fro by the waves of pride, of hate, of envy, of greed, look to your Star, call upon Mary. When anger, or jealousy, or the enticements of the flesh rock the boat, look upon Mary.

"If you have fallen victim to some heinous crime, if you are overwhelmed by the reproaches of an evil conscience, if you fear being engulfed in the whirlpool of doubt or an abyss of sorrows, think of Mary, call upon Mary. Let not her name leave your lips, hold it to your heart. You will win her wonderful intercession if you but follow in her footsteps. If you imitate her, you will never go astray. If you implore her help, you will never need to waver. If you keep her in your thoughts, you will never sin. If she assists you, you will never stumble. If she protects you, then never fear. If she guides you, you will never tire; if she befriends you, the attainment of the goal is assured. Make it, then, a personal experience of how rightly the evangelist wrote: *The Virgin's name was Mary.*"

Magnificat antiphon: O holy Mary, bring aid to those in misery, strength to the fainthearted, comfort to the sorrowing. Pray for your people, intercede for the clergy, plead for all women vowed to God. May all who are celebrating your wondrous Name experience your aid.

The September Ember Days

1. The September Ember Days. The Ember days of the "seventh month," September (from *septem* meaning "seven"; September was formerly the seventh month in the calendar, March being the first) have retained more of their original "ember" character (i.e., a time of thanksgiving and spiritual renewal) than the other Ember days, which reflect more or less the spirit of the current liturgical season. Three themes are prominent in the Masses, that of harvest, that of the Jewish feasts of the seventh month, that of spiritual renewal. Originally the autumn Ember days commemorated a "wine-press feast," and this accounts for the many references to the subject.

Secondly, the Jewish festivities during the seventh month were prognostic of the Christian Ember liturgy. For among the Jews three feasts were kept, the civil new year at the beginning of the month; the Day of Expiation, a day of strict penance on which the high priest entered the Holy of Holies with sacrifice blood; and, thirdly, the feast of Tabernacles, the joyful harvest festival which likewise was a memorial of the time Israel dwelt in tents while on the journey through the wilderness. Our present Ember days are not without relation to the Jewish feast of Tabernacles, the time at which the people lived in twig houses.

And lastly, the Ember days mean serious spiritual renewal, an occasion at which we ought pray and fast and do penance. The character, then, of this week is *thanksgiving* and *penance*.

In preparation for Ember week we listen to one of Pope Leo's beautiful seasonal sermons:

"The observance of fasting is assigned to the four seasons of the year in order to teach us through its regular quarterly recurrence the need of repeated purification. Throughout the entire course of our fitful lives we must ever strive by fasting and almsgiving to atone for the sins committed through the weakness of flesh and the promptings of passion. So let us go hungry a bit, my dear brethren, and let us withdraw something from our usual allowance for this brief period to be devoted to the support of the poor. The heart of a generous person rejoices in the fruits of generosity; for if you cause others to be happy you will receive what makes you happy. Love of neighbor is love of God, and God has placed the fullness of the Law and the Prophets in a single act of love with a double rhythm; therefore no one can any longer doubt but that he is dedicating to God whatever he may donate to men. Did not our Lord and Savior say in a celebrated passage on feeding and supporting the poor: 'What you do for one of these, you do for Me!' "

2. Symbols for the Four Seasons. The Ember festivities of the ancient Church were true "nature feasts" and show how deeply primitive Christian liturgy was rooted in nature. In a very real sense the liturgical year is a nature-year, and the liturgical day likewise is a nature-day. The symbols used may have been taken from the pagans, but Christianity spiritualized them with lofty content. If the various seasons were but personifications of the powers of nature to the pagan mind, or perhaps symbols of earthly life, Christian sensitivity knew them to be types of life hereafter, prognostic of bodily resurrection. The dying and reawakening in nature was a cyclic symbol of death and resurrection. In the earliest times we often find such symbols, but always near the tombs and sarcophagi in the catacombs. Only later, perhaps during the fifth century, did they spread and become used in the Church's cult-life. This is easily understood if one remembers how during the course of the fourth century Christian idealism veered from death by martyrdom toward a life of liturgical service.

At about this time the Ember observance, devised as a consecration of the various seasons of the year, began to flourish at Rome; and such products as were proper to the seasons were brought as offerings (wheat, wine, oil). These very items provide, moreover, the matter for the greatest sacraments

(Eucharist, baptism, confirmation, Orders, anointing). Thus the Christians would see in the fourfold crown of flowers, grain, grapes and olives adorning the divine Lamb, a symbol of the ecclesiastical year, of the Church's cult-life, of the sanctification of time, of labor, and of nature. Let us not overlook that spring's gifts, the rose and the lily, have a place of honor in Christian worship (the blessing of the golden rose on the fourth Sunday of Lent is a memorable instance; and according to the Egyptian Church Ordo, the rose and the lily were regarded as suitable Offertory gifts: "If flowers are brought, accept the rose and the lily" (Ch. 24, 3).

Thus the season-symbols expressed the two fundamental thought trends of Christian art to which practically all other art forms were related, viz., eschatological hope and the worship of the Church. Hope in the resurrection of the body and eternal life was oldest and most persistent; at a later date and less frequently do we find instances of the worship theme.

Now to summarize. In catacomb art of the first four centuries the seasons are represented by (1) heads or busts decorated with symbols proper to the respective season; (2) scenes in which genii are doing the work of the season, e.g., flower-dressers (spring), reapers (summer), wine-treaders, olive-pickers (autumn), huntsmen (winter); (3) ornamental bands, garlands, and crowns made from the products proper to the seasons.

In fifth-century art the four seasons are often represented in the form of a circle or crown surrounding a figure of the Lamb of God.

Whatever the manner of presentation, the general theme remains the same: flowers (roses and lilies) for spring; ears of grain (mixed with flowers) for summer; the vine and grapes (also other fruits) for autumn; olive branches for winter.

September 14

EXALTATION OF THE HOLY CROSS

You alone were worthy to bear
the price of the world's ransom

1. **Exaltation of the Holy Cross.** This feast is votive in nature, i.e., instituted to commemorate an historical event. In all such instances a distinction must be made between the event occasioning the feast and its mystery or theological content. The occasion is dependent upon the historical circumstances in which it was originally imbedded, it is only more or less interesting, could even be legendary. But the mystery is supra-temporal, affects all, is of universal benefit. Such is true of today's feast. The occasion was the finding of the true Cross (September 14, 320) by St. Helen, and the consecration of the church of the Holy Sepulcher at Jerusalem. Later the "finding" was celebrated on May 3, and the present date commemorated the recovery of the Cross from the Persians by Emperor Heraclius in the year 628. The king himself delivered the holy relics to the patriarch Zacharias on May 3, 630. Thus, the occasion for the feast underwent a change.

With the mystery it is entirely different. This the Church stresses with fullest love and enthusiasm because it glorifies Christ's Cross as the sign of redemption. With special reason she celebrates the feast now at the beginning of autumn; the Cross is "raised" against the rising darkness, a symbol of the might of hell. The Church wishes to "raise the sign of the Son of Man" which will appear at His Second Coming (awaiting the parousia is thematic to the Church's Harvest Time). The feast belongs to the most ancient legacies of the liturgy and should be accorded greater attention. Note too how the same mystery changes color when given a different light and setting — when kept during the Easter season and when kept now, late during the Pentecostal season. In May the Cross glowed in the brightness of Easter, in September it is the sign of the Son of Man at His Second Advent.

2. **Holy Mass (Nos autem).** The Mass depicts Christ's "exaltation" through the Cross. In the Cross is "salvation, life, and resurrection," and therefore we may "glory in the Cross of Jesus Christ." Both Lessons develop the theme of Christ's exaltation. As the Lord through His obedience unto death on the Cross was so "exalted" that all in heaven, on earth, and under the earth bend the knee to Him, so also it is only through humility, subjection, and suffering that we merit our exaltation (*Epist.*). The *Gradual* repeats the principal verse of the Epistle: "Therefore God exalted Him. . . ." In the *Alleluia* we praise the "sweet wood which alone was worthy to carry heaven's King!"

In the *Gospel* Christ openly speaks of His passion and of the great twofold effect of His death, triumph over the devil and the gathering of all the redeemed about His Cross: "If I be lifted up from the earth, I will draw all things to Myself." The *Offertory*, by way of exception more an oblation prayer than a chant, dates from an age at which the original signification of the Offertory was no longer paramount. The *Preface* of the Holy Cross contrasts paradise's tree of knowledge with Calvary's tree of the Cross; on the one the devil conquered, on the other he was conquered! In the holy Sacrifice and in the sacrificial Banquet we receive the blessed effects of the Cross, we too are "lifted up" and share in the Lord's exaltation.

It is exceptional for the *Communion* to be composed by the Church: "Through the sign of the Cross deliver us from our enemies, O our God!" Sacramental strength is here attributed to the sign of the Cross. The sign of the Cross has often been employed as an exorcism against the demons; the Latin Church also distributes holy Communion with this sacred sign. We would make the sign of the Cross, the most frequently used sacramental, with much more devotion if we were conscious that it had sacramental power. The ancients expressed the power of the Cross very succinctly by the Greek anagram

$$\begin{array}{c} \Phi \\ Z\Omega H \\ C \end{array}$$

for in the Cross is *light* and *life*.

3. The Cross Mystery. The liturgy wreathes a garland of poetry and deep mysticism about the Cross. One need only meditatively consider some excerpt from the various hymns or chants in the breviary to sound the sublimity and the depths of this mystery. Glancing over the texts, we may note: (a) hardly ever does the liturgy view the Cross as an instrument of torture; rather it is the sign of redemption, the sign of triumph and victory over hell. The Cross is presented under the most varied forms, e.g., as a royal banner, as the tree of life adorned with the purple of the King, as a balance upon which the ransom of mankind was weighed out, as an emblem of the victory of redemption. The Cross is also a royal throne because of David's words: "The Lord is reigning from on wood."

At times the holy sign is considered abstractly: "O Cross, more refulgent than all the stars, honored throughout the world, deeply loved by men, holiest of all things: You alone were worthy to bear the price of the world's ransom. O sweet wood, O sweet nails, that held so sweet a burden: save this flock gathered today to sing your praises." "By all kings the holy Cross is lifted on high; the royal scepter with which the Savior triumphs is erected." "O holy Cross, You have brought salvation to the languishing! How should I praise You, since You have opened the kingdom of heaven to us!"

b) The liturgy is fond of comparing the Cross to a tree,

especially the tree of knowledge in paradise. In support of this we may first of all cite the words of the Preface: "It was Your will that from the wood of the Cross man's salvation should go forth. From a tree came death, from a tree also should come forth life. He who triumphed on a tree (i.e., the devil) should also be defeated on a tree." In the Vesper hymn we praise the

> Tree of light! whose branches shine
> With purple royal and divine;
> Elect on whose triumphal breast
> Those holy limbs should find their rest!

A responsory reads: "Faithful Cross, noblest of all trees! In all the forest you have no equal in leaves, in foliage, in fruit! You alone tower over every cedar!" And the following beautiful chants: "This is that most worthy tree which stands in the midst of paradise! Upon it the Author of salvation by His own death overcame death for all." "Through a tree we were made slaves, through the tree of the Cross we were made free; the fruit of the one misled us, (the fruit of the other) the Son of God redeemed us, alleluia."

c) There are passages in which the liturgy gives evidence that the sign of the Cross has sacramental efficacy. This belief was exceptionally strong in ancient times and during the Middle Ages. The sign of the Cross puts the devil to flight, breaks the power of hell; where the Cross is planted the devil does not dare to tread. Therefore crosses on doors and gates, and the custom of frequently signing oneself. The Cross is often employed as an exorcism (e.g., the Benedictine medal). This procedure is still given prominence in the rite of baptism: "Then never dare, accursed devil, to violate this sign of the holy † Cross which we are making upon his forehead." In today's Office of the Holy Cross we find similar expressions: "Behold the Cross of the Lord! Flee, ye hostile powers! The lion of the tribe of Judah, the root of David, has conquered." "Through the sign of the Cross free us from our enemies, O our God." The sacramental power inherent in the sign of the Cross should be more highly appreciated, more often used. With its sign let us protect ourselves from the evil enemy (before work in the morning, during temptation, etc.). Against the might of hell guard your dwellings, barns, fields by replicas of Christ's saving Cross.

d) Lastly, the liturgy emphasizes the word *exaltation*. Four Lessons treat of Christ's exaltation on the Cross. The brazen serpent which Moses set up in the wilderness (Num. 21:2–9, Scripture reading at Matins) was a type of Christ's Cross and its redeeming might. In His discourse with Nicodemus, Jesus drew the parallel: "As Moses lifted up the serpent in the wilderness, so must the Son of Man be lifted up that whoever believes in Him may not perish but have life everlasting" (John 3:14). Both Lessons of the Mass likewise accent the exaltation. In the Gospel Christ voices those glorious words: "If I be lifted up from the world, I will draw all things to Myself." In all ages our crucified Lord is the great magnet attracting to Himself everyone capable of being saved. His degradation on the Cross corresponds to His exaltation: "Therefore God has exalted Him and has given Him a name that is above all names." Resemble Christ in His humiliation and you will resemble Him in His exaltation.

EMBER WEDNESDAY

Station at St. Mary Major

Do not be sad, for the joy of the Lord is our strength!

1. **Holy Mass** (Exultate). Wednesday of Ember week is always "Mary's Day"; hence at Rome the divine liturgy is celebrated in the Basilica of St. Mary Major. That the Mass is very old is evident from its three Readings, and especially from its general thought content. The liturgy is festive as befits a thanksgiving feast. The *Introit* resounds like the joyous trumpet call at Israel's solemn New Moon feast when Psalm 80 was sung (Psalm 80 was also used at the feast of Tabernacles). The *Oration*: our fallen nature must suffer, but the Church calls down God's mercy as a means of help.

In the *first Lesson* the shepherd-prophet Amos depicts the Messianic kingdom in terms of abundance in vineyard and garden; equally fruitful should the soul's garden be at the end of the ecclesiastical year. The *second Lesson* brings out an episode from Jewish history. After the return from exile Esdras read the Law to the Jews on "the first day of the seventh month," and they listened enthusiastically, breathlessly. Thus we too ought scrutinize God's Law during these days of spiritual rejuvenation and renew our covenant with Him. The second Lesson closes with the leitmotif of the Mass: "Go, eat fat meats and drink sweet wine (sacrificial Banquet), and send portions to those who are not prepared (Offertory, Communion), because it is the holy day of the Lord; and do not be sad, for the joy of the Lord is our strength." In the *Offertory* and *Communion* Banquet these words become actuality.

The first two Lessons describe the nature of spiritual renewal and note instances of it in sacred history; the *Gospel* shows the efficacy of grace. Our fallen nature is similar to a possessed body; it has indeed been cleansed through baptism, yet the holy Eucharist is necessary to keep away the devil; here the Ember days are of service, for "this kind of devil can be driven out only through prayer and fasting." Of special beauty is the *Communion* verse, which reflects the whole meaning of the Ember celebration: "Eat fat meats and drink sweet wine, and send portions to those who are not prepared, because it is the holy day of the Lord; and do not be sad, for the joy of the Lord is our strength." These words give an indication of the joyful spirit proper to ancient Christianity. Evidently this verse would not be appropriate for a modern fast day; but the ancient Ember observance was one of thanksgiving, and after Mass at None (three o'clock in the afternoon), the faithful could eat and drink. Through prayer and sacrifice we have shown our humble service, and in reward we petition a share in the spirit and life of Christ (*Postc.*).

2. Meditation. Hardly any other Ember Mass brings us as much of the spirit of the olden Ember festivals as this. The opening words put us immediately in a joyous mood. And at the climax of the celebration we proclaim with the Church: "The joy of the Lord is our true strength." It is an idea worth remembering. Christianity does not seek to lame the vital forces of life but to purify and ennoble them. Where there is life, there must be feeling, spirit, joy. One should not think that such expressions of life are questionable or proper only to the children of the world. Nor must joy confine itself to the supernatural, over the natural too we may be happy. Ember week provides a splendid occasion to show joyous gratitude for the gifts and fruits of nature.

Now a few observations on the three Lessons, for in striking gradation they bring to our attention three primary Ember blessings: bodily food — spiritual nourishment — fasting.

First Lesson. Amos, the shepherd-prophet, projects the prosperity of the Holy Land after the return from exile. He is, we know, describing in prophetical perspective the spiritual well-being of God's kingdom upon earth and the blessedness of the "new heaven and the new earth" hereafter. The early Church, however, would adapt in adopting and used the text to score the produce of nature presently being harvested. We are being urged to show a most sincere gratitude to the Father and Source of whatever comes from field, orchard, or garden. Let nature be a big picture-book illustrating the good and great God on every page. It is the warmth of His love that is ripening autumn's baskets of vegetables, grain, and fruit.

Second Lesson. Alongside these baskets of food for our bodies, the liturgy places supernatural nourishment, the word of God. For the Lord once said: "Not from bread alone does man live, but by every word that comes from the mouth of God." On few occasions in history was the word of God more highly esteemed than that recorded in the second Lesson. Esdras read from the inspired scroll; with holy reverence the people listened before worshipping God present in His words, exultingly joyous over the divine revelation. These then are the two principal blessings of the past quarter-year, bread for the body and the word of God for the soul. They have come to us in abundance. And we are grateful.

Third Lesson. How does fasting fit into the picture? Human nature is subject to the curse of original sin; like the boy in the Gospel we come under the devil's influence, and his power cannot be counteracted with the usual tools. Extraordinary tools are necessary, like "prayer and fasting." A good reason, surely, for the quarterly Ember days. With thankful hearts we may enjoy the fruits of earth, praising the good God; the inspired words of holy Scripture may bring untold spiritual blessings; nevertheless, more is needed. To tame proud and stubborn nature the mighty levers of prayer and fasting must be brought into action, not merely our own individual praying and fasting, but that of Christ too, viz., the oblation of His whole life as it comes to us through Mass and holy Communion.

EMBER FRIDAY

Station at the Twelve Apostles

**Like the repentant sinner
the Church washes the feet of her Spouse**

1. Holy Mass (Laetetur). Today is the great day of penance and expiation for the past quarter-year. We put together "the countless sins, offenses, and negligences" of the last three months and do penance for them. In spirit we are in the Church of the Twelve Apostles, where we were absolved on Holy Thursday. As sinners we enter God's house in penitential garb, and moisten the Lord's feet with our tears of sorrow. Then we hear from His lips the consoling words: "Your many sins are forgiven." This assurance that we too have actually received the grace of forgiveness occasions a strain of joy (*Intr.*) and of gratitude (*Off.*). Ember week is liturgically ideal for receiving the sacrament of penance.

We begin Mass "joyously seeking the face of God" (*Intr.*).

The whole of Psalm 104 praises the Providence of God; how good has He shown Himself to us during the past quarter! (The entire psalm is well suited as a review of the past.) The two Readings insist on penance and spiritual renewal. The prophet Osee speaks earnest words of warning: "Return, O Israel, to the Lord your God; for you have fallen down because of your iniquity. Take with you words (of sorrow) and return to the Lord and say to Him: Remove all my iniquity. . . ." Words of comfort, however, are not entirely lacking: "I will heal their wounds." Nay more, if we return to God, He Himself will be the "dew" which will make fruitful the kingdom of the soul; and Israel (the Church and the soul) will thrive like a fruitful vineyard, will bloom like the lily, like the olive.

The *Gospel* gives us the soul-stirring account of the conversion of the sinful woman; today the Church is that woman, penitent. Today the Church follows the example of her Bridegroom, who, although free from sin, covered Himself with the sins of the world and atoned for them on the Cross. So also His stainless Bride, the Bride without blemish, must suffer pain and do penance because her children are immersed in sin and imperfection. The piety and virtue of the Bride's children are the gems and bridal adornments in which the Bridegroom already now takes greatest pleasure; contrariwise, every unatoned fault dishonors the Bride, defiles her garments and robs her of her adornments. Today let us aid our Mother in removing the spots and wrinkles of the past quarter-year.

For like the woman in the Gospel, our soul comes to the house of God, repentant and full of loving devotion. "When we practice virtue, we anoint the feet of Jesus; when we stand at the Lord's feet, it is a sign that we are following in His footsteps; when we show love and sympathy to the poor, we wash His feet with tears" (*St. Gregory*, in the breviary). It is during the Eucharistic Sacrifice that He gives us the healing message: "Your sins are forgiven." Upon our souls He confers again "a new and sprightly youthfulness, resembling the eagle's" (*Off.*). Our hearts are filled with the joy of forgiveness as we approach the altar with our Offertory oblation; Psalm 102 is a thanksgiving hymn for the munificence of God, especially because He "has forgiven all your sins and has healed all your infirmities."

Our fasting too is an Offertory gift most acceptable to God and most effective in making us worthy to share in Calvary's great Sacrifice (*Secr.*). It cleanses away "the disgrace and shame" of sin and makes us love God's commands (*Comm.*). An unusual *Postcommunion* combines both gratitude and petition; we thank God for the graces of holy Mass and beg for the "greater blessings" of perfect divine sonship in heavenly beatitude.

2. Joy in Penance. When celebrating ancient Masses, we may meet types to which present attitudes are unaccustomed. A striking example occurs today. Evidently we have a penitential Mass, as witnessed by the two Readings, and therefore we would expect penitential chants. On the contrary we find joy, gratitude, praise. The Introit, which strikes the temper of the entire service, begins with the gladsome cry: "Let the heart of those who seek the Lord rejoice. . . ." The spirit of the ancient Church was so deeply rooted in faith and in consciousness of redemption that it could be happy even in penance. In the current Ember Sunday homily Pope St. Leo urges us "to accept the Ember day fasts in the spirit of faith, joyfully, mortifying body and soul. For the observance of fasting is assigned to the four seasons of the year in order to teach us through its regular quarterly recurrence the need of repeated purification. Throughout the entire course of our fitful lives we must ever strive by fasting and almsgiving to atone for the sins committed through the weaknesses of the flesh and the promptings of passion."

We may accordingly characterize Ember Friday's liturgy as "joy in penance!" In the Readings holy Church calls upon God to cleanse her children; the stains upon the hands and feet of her members must be removed. Christ's Blood washes all away, "God heals all her wounds." Abundantly He will send the dew of grace; yes, He Himself will be the dew from heaven. We see how theocentrically even sin and penance are viewed — consequently the joyful mood. In the Gospel it becomes still more evident how the liturgy stresses joy in penance. The repentant woman not only is absolved by Christ but pronounced holy. She is a type of Mother Church, who is now cleansing herself from the dust of the past quarter. The meaning of the Offertory is evident: The sacrificial gift that we carry to the altar in the form of bread is the joy of forgiveness, the happiness of being spiritually renewed.

Praise the Lord, O my soul, and forget not His many favors.
He it is who forgives all your guilt and heals all your diseases,
    who saves your life from death,
    who crowns you with kindness and compassion;
    who satisfies your desires with good things;
    your youth is renewed like the eagle's.

EMBER SATURDAY

Station at St. Peter's

A day for expiation and thanksgiving!

1. Holy Mass (Venite). Ember Saturday is the official thanksgiving day for all the blessings of the past quarter-year. Especially in autumn when we garner the fruits of nature should we be more conscious of God's Providence both in the temporal and spiritual orders. In ancient times today's Mass served as a thanksgiving sacrifice and as a renewal of the Christian covenant with God. The text presumes that the Ember days are the Christian counterpart to the Old Testament feasts of Atonement and Tabernacles, highlighting penance and gratitude respectively.

The liturgical celebration, observed during the night between Saturday and Sunday and of obligation for all the faithful, was unusually festive. The faithful gathered at St. Peter's; for an entrance song the Invitatory (Psalm 94) was sung. The first four *Lessons* belonged specifically to the night-vigil and formed a greeting worthy of the enthroned King. The Readings tap the marrow of the Ember celebration, its connection with the Jewish

Bless the Lord, all you works of the Lord,
praise and exalt Him above all forever!
Ananias, Azarias, Misael, bless the Lord;
praise and exalt Him above all forever!

feasts of the seventh month, Yom Kippur and the feast of Tabernacles. The autumn Ember days are days of penance for past failings and of gratitude for the harvest (and redemption); such too is the spiritual import of the Lessons. The first reviews the Mosaic legislation concerning the Day of Atonement, the second concerning the feast of Tabernacles, Israel's great thanksgiving feast.

The two *Graduals* echo their respective Lessons; the first, "Forgive" (Day of Atonement), the second, "How lovely are Thy tabernacles" (feast of Tabernacles). The third and fourth Lessons, from the prophets Micheas and Zacharias, are comforting messages in which God reaffirms His readiness to forgive the sins of His people and to grant them good things provided they remain faithful. God is also concerned over the manner in which we fast: "The fast of the fourth month, and the fast of the fifth, and the fast of the seventh, and the fast of the tenth shall be to the house of Judah joy and gladness and a great solemnity!" By which our Ember days, of course, are meant. The *Orations* offer God our festive fast and plead forgiveness. As on other Ember Saturdays, the *fifth Lesson* is already part of the morning service; the assembled faithful are praying Lauds; the three youths in the fiery furnace prefigure the resurrection of Christ and of Christians.

In the *Epistle* St. Paul shows how the ceremonies of the old covenant were types of the new; our day of atonement is Good Friday when Christ, the divine High Priest, entered the most holy sanctuary of heaven with His own Blood and wrought eternal redemption; every Mass is Good Friday repeated. In the *Tract* we chant the shortest Laud psalm as we express our gratefulness for God's merciful work of redemption and His fidelity in fulfilling the prophecies.

Presently the High Priest Himself appears, first "teaching on the Sabbath" (in the Foremass), then offering Himself (in the Oblation). The unfruitful "fig tree in the orchard" and the "bowed-down woman" are the faithful. God is the landlord, Christ the pleading gardener; till now we have been unfruitful. We also resemble the bowed-down woman; wholly taken up with earthly concerns, too often we are "unable to look upward"; but on this Christian Sabbath, Christ seeks "to free us from the bonds of Satan" and make us spiritually "erect." Thus the *Gospel* insinuates the workings of grace in today's holy Sacrifice.

At the sacrificial Banquet we once more recall the institution of the feast of Tabernacles as a remembrance of the deliverance from Egypt and the wanderings through the wilderness — for the Eucharist is the fulfillment of those two historical events by providing deliverance from sin and the true Manna from heaven. A classic, thought-packed *Postcommunion*: May the sacramental energy of the Eucharist realize its power in us, and may we one day enjoy face to face what now we see in a veiled manner. Three realities are noted: the first is the sign — this shows the sacrament. Underneath the sign is hidden the second reality, the sacrament's efficacy — what the sacraments contain. And lastly, the *rerum veritas*, the future unveiling.

2. A "Spiritual Renewal" Day. For a "day of recollection" no better meditation points could be found than those in the Lessons of today's Ember Mass. Of the two areas of thought proper to the formulary, viz., the Ember festivity is the Christian "Day of Atonement" and the Christian Feast of Tabernacles (or thanksgiving day at harvest time), let us pursue the former in some detail.

a) *The Old Testament type.* The Day of Atonement, *Yom Kippur*, was the great penitential observance of Mosaic Law, Israel's "confession day." With us "penance days" are not feast days, but among the Jews it was otherwise; *Yom Kippur* was a day of strict rest, absolutely no type of work was permitted, and the spirit of the occasion was festive, *celebrabitis*. The day's liturgy exemplified the nation's effort to expiate sin; on this one day of the year, the high priest would enter the Holy of Holies with sacrificial blood and sprinkle the ark of the covenant in atonement for his own and his people's sins. Meanwhile the people did penance through fasting, humbling themselves before Yahweh.

b) *The New Testament fulfillment.* Mosaic festivals were shadows which took on flesh and blood in the Church of Christ. Good Friday was the real, the unique *day of atonement* in the sight of God. How well St. Paul affirmed this truth in the Epistle of today's Mass: "Christ appeared as the high priest of coming (Messianic) blessings. He entered the greater and more perfect tabernacle not made by human hands (i.e., heavenly in nature) not with the blood of goats and steers but with His own blood — once and for all He entered the (heavenly) Holy of Holies — after He had effected an eternal redemption (i.e., one with lasting effects in contrast to the annually repeated Jewish day of atonement)." For the sacrifice on the Cross constituted the perfect reconciliation of God with mankind; and every holy Mass, as it renders present that sacrifice on Golgotha, is Yom Kippur *par excellence*.

Every Sunday then would be the Christian atonement feast. But because we Christians are so irresponsive and dull to the inner nature of spiritual realities, holy Church introduced special expiation days during the course of the Church year. Among these are the Ember days. Ember Saturdays, particularly September Ember Saturday, have preserved best this original spirit. Anyone who seeks to develop his spiritual life on a liturgical basis would have to use the Ember days during the four seasons as times of genuine spiritual renewal. The peculiar means of keeping these days is evident from the liturgy itself — acts of penance and fasting, confession of sin, humbling ourselves before God and neighbor, and nevertheless rejoicing, in the best sense of the word. Our conduct would exemplify the prophet's statement (fourth Lesson), "The fast proper to the fourth, fifth, seventh and tenth months (i.e., the four Ember weeks) should mean joy and exultation to the house of Judah (viz., Catholics) and high festival; you only need to love truth (obedience) and peace."

c) *Application.* God appeals directly to my heart in the Gospel. The two parables, one in word and one in sign, should move me deeply. *I* am that barren fig tree. The infinitely just God is the landlord, our Savior the pleading caretaker. If God should summon me to His judgment seat today (the command to destroy the tree), would there be any "fruit"? To what extent would I resemble the barren fig tree? Why does it occupy ground? But Christ intercedes, says a kindly word in my behalf: "Perhaps there will be some return — next crop! If not, it can then be cut down." The coming quarter-year must mark a change, genuine improvement.

The parable in sign is equally instructive. My soul is so badly bowed down to earth, it finds "looking upwards" toward heavenly realities extremely painful. Christ must make me stand erect again. The coming season as no other is the season of hope, of preparation for the parousia, of longing for the heavenly Jerusalem, of expectation for the returning Lord. Jesus, have mercy. Free me from stooping down to the earthly, the sensual. Straighten me out for heaven. Now! Jesus, have mercy.

September 15

THE SEVEN SORROWS OF MARY

ST. NICOMEDES, Martyr

At the Cross her station keeping,
Stood the mournful Mother weeping,
Close to Jesus to the last.

1. **Seven Sorrows.** Devotion to Mary's Seven Sorrows has its
Biblical origin in the prophetic words of the aged Simeon: "A
sword (of sorrow) will pierce your very soul" (Luke 2:35).
Already the Fathers of the Church, as Ephrem the Syrian in his
Marian "Lamentations," Ambrose, Augustine, and Bernard
composed meditations upon the sorrows of the Mother of God.
In Rome Pope Boniface IV ordered that the temple to all the
gods (the Pantheon) be transformed into a church; in 610 he
consecrated it in honor of holy Mary and all the saints, *S. Maria
ad Martyres*. Thus Mary became designated as Queen of Martyrs. Strictly speaking, however, devotion to the Seven Sorrows
was begun by the Servite Fathers. St. Philip Benitius (see
August 23) gave "the garment of Mary's widowhood" (his
name for the habit of the order) as a scapular to seculars, and
thus originated the Brotherhood of the Sorrows of Mary.

During the seventeenth century two feasts commemorating
the Seven Sorrows began to be celebrated, one on the so-called
Sorrowful Friday after Passion Sunday, the other on the third
Sunday in September. The former was approved by Pope Benedict XIII in 1724, the latter by Pope Pius VII in 1814, in memory
of his return from imprisonment under Napoleon. Everyone is
familiar with the glorious sequence *Stabat Mater* by Jacoponi da
Todi (*d*. 1306). In contrast to yesterday's feast with its emphasis
on Christ's kingship, today's concentrates on the human side of
His sufferings. Its liturgy stems from an entirely different
spiritual mentality; the feast of the Exaltation showed and
praised the Cross as the sign of objective redemption; it unfurled,
as it were, the *crux gemmata*. Today's feast sees the human, the

suffering Christ, it emphasizes Mary's role as a co-sufferer. These two feasts in honor of Christ's Cross, following so closely upon one another, clearly show two trends of Catholic spirituality, that of ancient times and that of the Middle Ages, trends which are often designated as objective and subjective spirituality. The former sees the passion as the *beata passio* (blessed suffering), the latter as the *passio amara* (bitter suffering and co-suffering).

Today's feast, occurring at the beginning of autumn, affords us a chance to reconsider the meaning and importance of suffering in union with Christ. It is a first principle in ascetics that the closer a Christian stands to His Lord, the nearer must he be to the Cross. Mary, therefore, was made to taste most deeply of Christ's sufferings. That is for all of us great consolation. Be conscious, then, that your spirituality must include not only prayer, not only charitableness, not only the ordinary acts of Christian virtue, but suffering bound up with the Cross of Christ and consecrated through the Mass. It should be noted too that our feast adds commentary to the Scripture readings of the past week. For the problem of suffering, which is solved but imperfectly in the Book of Job, is given a satisfactory answer in today's mystery.

2. Holy Mass (Stabant). The formulary is readily understood, warm and affectionate in tone, and most instructive. The *Introit* is not taken from the psalms but depicts an historical scene, Mary beneath the Cross. This setting continues throughout the entire text (Grad., Allel., Seq., Gosp., Comm.). The *Collect* recalls Simeon's prophecy on Mary's pierced heart and pleads for "the blessed fruit of Christ's sufferings." The *Epistle* presents Judith, who once saved her people, as a type of our sorrowful Mother. Israel's heroine cut off the head of the enemy Holofernes; Mary through sacrificing her divine Son crushed the head of hell's serpent. Through her sorrows she took an active share in the work of redemption. The *Alleluia* chant tells of heaven's sorrowing Queen standing beneath the Cross. The *Sequence* develops these thoughts in great detail, thus preparing us for the *Gospel*, in which the eye-witness John recounts the same memorable scene. In the *Offertory* we plead that the Queen of Sorrows intercede for us: "When you stand before the Lord, say a good word for us." In the *Communion* we praise Mary's unbloody martyrdom.

3. Nicomedes (according to the legendary Acts of Sts. Nereus and Achilleus) was a priest at the time of Emperor Domitian (81–96). He was imprisoned because he buried the body of the holy virgin Felicula, who had been martyred at the command of Comes Flaccus. Led before images of the gods, Nicomedes refused to do them sacrifice since, as he said: "I do not sacrifice except to almighty God who rules in heaven" (*Martyrology*). Thereupon he was scourged to death and his body cast into the Tiber. His remains were recovered and buried in the cemetery which received his name on the Via Nomentana, but at a later date they were transferred to St. Praxedes by Pope Paschal.

September 16

STS. CORNELIUS AND CYPRIAN, Bishops, Martyrs
ST. EUPHEMIA AND COMPANIONS, Martyrs

He who once conquered death for us triumphs in us always

1. St. Cornelius. *Day of death*: September 14, 253. *Grave*: at first in the Callistine catacomb, Rome; now in the church of St. Mary Trastevere. *Life*. Pope Cornelius (251–253) was the successor to Pope Fabian. During his reign a controversy arose concerning the manner of reinstating those who had fallen from the faith under the duress of persecution. The Novatians accused the Pope of too great indulgence and separated themselves from the Church. With the help of St. Lucina, Cornelius transferred the remains of the princes of the apostles to places of greater honor. On account of his successful preaching the pagans banished him to Centumcellae, where he died. St. Cyprian sent him a letter of condolence. At the time of Pope Cornelius there were at Rome forty-six priests, seven deacons, seven subdeacons, forty-two acolytes, fifty-two clerics and more than five hundred widows who were supported by the Church (according to Cornelius' letter to Bishop Fabian of Antioch).

2. St. Cyprian. *Day of death*: September 14, 258, at Carthage. *Grave*: at Carthage; at present his relics are honored at Lyons. *Life.* Thascius Caecilius Cyprianus, illustrious as a pagan rhetorician in Carthage, embraced the true faith in the year 246 and was soon thereafter consecrated priest and bishop of that city (248). He was an energetic shepherd of souls and a prolific writer. He defended the unity of the Church against schismatic movements in Africa and Italy, and greatly influenced the shaping of Church discipline relative to reinstating Christians who had apostatized. He fled during the Decian persecution but guided the Church by means of letters. During the Valerian persecution (258) he was beheaded. He suffered martyrdom in the presence of his flock, after giving the executioner twenty-five pieces of gold. St. Jerome says of him: "It is superfluous to speak of his greatness, for his works are more luminous than the sun." Cyprian ranks as an important Church Father, one whose writings are universally respected and often read in the Divine Office. His principal works are: *On the Unity of the Church; On Apostates;* a collection of *Letters; The Lord's Prayer; On the Value of Patience.* The Mass (*Intret*), from the Common, p. 408.

3. A Reading from St. Cyprian. It has been pointed out already how fond the Church is of having the saint whose feast is being celebrated speak to us on his feast day. It would, then, be good liturgical practice to gather some of the more important works of the saints for ready reading. A good excerpt today would be Cyprian's encouraging words to the martyrs of his day:

"How could I measure the praise that must be accorded you, most valiant martyrs! How could I duly hymn the heroism of your hearts or extol the steadfastness of your faith! Unto a glorious consummation you suffer the most dreadful torturing. Stronger than your tormentors you stand there under torment. Broken and lacerated limbs, triumph over the minions who strike

and tear with metal hooks the flesh of God's patient sufferers.
Their invincible faith would not yield to unrelenting, atrocious
treatment, even when with entrails bulging forth, they suffered
not only from the mistreatment of their bodies but from the cut-
ting pain of wounds already inflicted. In streams their blood
flowed — to extinguish the fires of presecution, to quench the
flames of hell in its glorious course.

"What a spectacle in the sight of the Lord, how incomparably
magnificent! In God's sight they are accepted as faithful and
loyal soldiers! Thus do we read in the psalms as the Holy Spirit
admonishingly tells us: Precious in the sight of the Lord is the
death of His holy ones. Precious is this death of our martyr because he bought immortality at the price of his blood; he has
received his crown at the end of a virtuous life.

"Christ was there, and how sublimely happy, how gladly did
He do battle in favor of such servants! In their struggle He stood
close, assisting; those professing and proclaiming His Name
He strengthened and encouraged and cheered on. And He who
once conquered death for us, triumphs in us always."

4. St. Euphemia and Companions. The Council of Chalce-
don was held in the church where Euphemia, a famous martyr,
was buried. As a result her cult was brought to the West, where
great veneration was accorded her, especially at Rome (the
Leonine sacramentary contains four Mass formularies in her
honor). About the martyrs Lucy and Geminianus we know
practically nothing.

September 17

IMPRESSION OF THE STIGMATA UPON
ST. FRANCIS OF ASSISI

In the flesh of Blessed Francis
You renewed the sacred marks of Your passion

1. **Stigmata of St. Francis.** Within four days three feasts
honoring the sacred Cross! On September 14 we celebrated the

Exaltation, a feast that honors the Cross as the source of "salvation, life and resurrection." On the following day we saw how Mary, the noblest of God's creatures, joined herself to the Cross and became co-redemptrix (Seven Sorrows). Today we meet a saint so wrapped in the spirit of Christ crucified that he outwardly bore His holy wounds. In the Collect the Church points out the pedagogical value of the feast; as the world began to grow cold in love toward the Crucified, God renewed the stigmata of Jesus in the flesh of St. Francis to inflame our hearts with divine love. The wondrous fact of Francis' stigmata had been widely witnessed and was irrefutably attested, especially immediately after his death. A detailed description of the occurrence is given by St. Bonaventure in the breviary:

"It was two years before his holy death in 1224 and Francis, Christ's faithful servant and disciple, was beginning a forty-day fast in honor of St. Michael (Sept. 29) in the solitude of Mount Alverno. More than otherwise he was flooded with the sweetness of heavenly contemplation; and close to the feast of the Exaltation of the Cross he saw a seraph with six shining wings fly down from heaven's heights toward him . . . when the vision vanished after words secret and intimate, there remained in the heart of the saint an ardor of love exceedingly strong; and upon his body the vision left impressed a most striking representation of Christ's sufferings, as if a seal impression had been made under the melting power of that fire. Immediately the marks of the nails appeared in his hands and feet, with the heads of the nails showing in the palms of his hands and on the upper part of his feet and the pointed end of the nails at the soles of his feet and the upper surface of his hands. His right side was also pierced as by a lance and a red scar surrounded the opening, from which blood often flowed and stained his clothing. By this most unusual marvel, unheard of since the time of Christ, Francis was transformed into a new man, one bearing the sacred wounds of the Lord. He came down from the mountain bearing the image of the Crucified, not sketched upon stone or wooden tablets by human hands, but impressed upon his very body by the finger of God."

2. Holy Mass (Mihi autem). It is a beautiful Mass, one wholly imbued with the mysticism of the Cross. Blending our voices with that of St. Francis, we begin the Mass praising the Cross and chanting the Saint's "Death Psalm" (141). When, however, do we really make our own the words: "I bear in my body the marks of the Lord"? As often as, according to the psalmist, "we pierce our flesh with the fear of the Lord" *(Ps. 118)*, i.e., when we bear suffering in the spirit of Christ; when we make progress in our love for the Crucified. Moreover, the Mass itself is a glorious means unto spiritual stigmatization. In the *Gospel* Jesus invites us to follow after Him carrying our crosses, even as Francis has given the example. At the *Offertory* procession we accompany the Lord on the way to Calvary; and at the sacrificial Banquet we may say with unsuspected truth, "I carry in my body the wounds of the Lord Jesus." This passage (Gal. 5:25—6:18) is also used as today's Scripture reading.

3. Christ's Wounds. Very, very rarely does the Church use an incident from a saint's life as the subject for a special feast. One example would be the conversion of St. Paul, January 25, because that event proved of such tremendous significance for the whole Church. Today's feast, commemorating the impression of our Savior's wounds on the body of St. Francis, is quite unique. It recalls an instance of the sublimest union between man and his Savior. Without doubt the reason why Francis was favored with the stigmata was that he completely submerged the "I" in Christ so as to become an *alter Christus*, a second Christ. He actualized most perfectly the words of St. Paul: "With Christ I am nailed to the Cross! I live, now not I, it is Christ who lives in me" (Gal. 2:19).

We do not seek to be favored with a like marvel. For such are gratuitously given to those who have attained the zenith of sanctity. Nevertheless, we do wish to stand on some lower rung of union with our blessed Lord. We too will seek to enter deeper and deeper into Christ's spirit, for we too must be submerged in Christ. Nor is it a mere psychological union through meditation alone that is the objective. The way to true union with Christ is twofold: action on our part, action on God's part. The first is the way of imitation, a way which Christ often stressed. We must be Christians wholeheartedly; we must keep "His" commandment, love. We must take upon us the cross, must exemplify the Sermon on the Mount. We must untangle ourselves from the world and its snares. This Francis accomplished to perfection. To the highest degree possible he extracted the "I" from the vessel of his soul and invited Christ to enter.

But this was only part, the human part; of itself it would never have led him to the heights. The more important element was God's work. The Church proffers us ontological union through her mysteries and through grace; and this becoming one, this spiritual stigmatization is the more fundamental, the more worth striving after. Through grace we become incorporated into Christ, become one Body with Him. Here we discover the great mission of the Church, viz., to effect union with Christ and to perfect that union. Constantly we are drawn deeper into this divine union. The first step was baptism, at which time the impression of Christ's wounds began. Confirmation and Holy Orders add distinguishing steps. The celebration of the Eucharist each Sunday has for its special end to perfect mystical incorporation. It is a slow but a sure spiritual assimilation. We may call it the liturgical way toward stigmatization. Through it we actually bear Christ's wounds in our body, although not visibly or externally, nor merely through a mental or psychological mode of being.

September 18

ST. JOSEPH OF CUPERTINO, Confessor

**Though I should speak
with the tongues of men and of angels. . . .**

1. **St. Joseph.** *Day of death*: September 18, 1663. *Canonized*: 1767; feast 1769. *Grave*: at Osimo (near Ancona, Italy) in the chapel of the Immaculate Conception. *Life*. Joseph of Cuper-

tino is known for his extraordinary mystical gifts and for his
evangelical simplicity. Born in 1603 of poor parents (his father
was a carpenter), he entered the Order of St. Francis after over-
coming many difficulties. First a lay brother, later a priest. His
ardent love of God overflowed into wonderful ecstasies. He was
especially given to obedience and humility. "He extended loving sympathy to everyone, even to those who had assailed him
with rebukes, insults, and all types of injury" (*Second Nocturn*).
Suffering and persecution were not wanting. On account of his
mystical favors he was brought before the Inquisition and transferred to a remote monastery to remove him from the eyes of
the people.

Application. Our saint suffered severely at the hands of his
own ecclesiastical superiors. It is a bitter thing to find no aid or
comfort among one's own brethren, and, moreover, to be mis-
understood and condemned by them. Even this, however, is
permitted by God; and it may serve for the cleansing and perfecting of the soul, as shown in the life of our saint.

2. Holy Mass (Dilectio Dei). A proper Mass, rich in well-
selected Scripture passages that portray Joseph's life. Joseph's
most extraordinary gifts were love of God and humility; the
former is emphasized in the Foremass, the latter in the variable
parts of the Sacrifice proper. The *Introit* would remind us that
the wisdom of our saint was his love of God; it was this that
brought him very special gifts of grace. Psalm 83, with its intense longing for union with God, makes us feel the warmth of
Joseph's soul:

> My heart and flesh shout for joy to the living God.
> The sparrow finds a house, the swallow a nest
>   where she may put her young —
> Your altars, Yahweh Sabaoth,
>   my King and my God!

The divine charity with which he was all afire is further described in the *Epistle* (taken from St. Paul's Canticle of Love):
"Though I should speak with the tongues of men and of angels,

and have not charity, I am become as sounding brass or a tinkling cymbal . . . charity is kind, is patient; charity does not envy, does not deal perversely, is not puffed up. Charity is not ambitious, does not seek her own; is not provoked to anger; thinks no evil . . . bears all things, believes all things, hopes all things, endures all things. Charity never falls away." Such was the spirit of our seraphic saint.

The *Gospel*, too, is meant to tell of God's love, since the parable on the wedding garment is so interpreted by the Fathers; note, for instance, St. Gregory's homily at today's Matins.

"What, beloved brethren, is signified by the wedding garment? Let us say it refers to baptism and faith. For could anyone take part in that wedding feast without faith and baptism? Yet one who does not believe remains voluntarily outside. In the parable, however, the man did not remain outside. By the wedding garment, therefore, we cannot think of anything else than love.

"A member of the Church who has faith but not love resembles the man who entered the nuptial banquet without the proper nuptial attire. It is quite fitting to call love a wedding garment; for our very Creator clothed Himself with it when He came to espouse Himself to the Church in the divine nuptials. It is due to God's love alone that His only-begotten Son joins Himself to the hearts of the predestined. What did St. John say? God so loved the world that He delivered His only-begotten Son for us (John 3:16). He who came to men because of love has indicated clearly enough that love is the wedding garment. Everyone of you who believes in God and belongs to the Church has indeed entered God's wedding halls; but anyone who is present without the charism of divine love resembles the man whom the king upbraided for not being properly clothed.

"Here is a point we ought always remember. Just as cloth is woven on a loom with a double beam accounting for its warp and woof, so too love is inextricably interwoven in two commandments, love of God and love of neighbor. This twofold rhythm is clearly indicated in the Scripture text: The Lord your

God you must love with your whole heart, with your whole
soul, with your whole mind and with your whole strength; and
you must love your neighbor as yourself (Mark 12:30). With
regard to the love of neighbor you will note that a standard of
measurement is given, namely, you must love your neighbor
as yourself. But no such measure is attached to the love of God.
It simply says: the Lord your God you must love with your
whole heart, with your whole soul, and with your whole mind
and with your whole strength. There is no comparison when it
is a matter of loving God; the sacred words simply state the
manner in which He should be loved, viz., with your whole being. Genuine love of God withholds nothing for self. These two
commandments on love must be observed by everyone who
wishes to be clothed in a wedding garment at God's great nuptial
feast."

Just as the Foremass revealed one fount of our saint's sanctity,
so the Mass proper indicates another, viz., humility, poverty, patience. By these virtues men are made like unto their crucified
Savior, a living sacrifice. At the *Offertory* St. Joseph Cupertino
places his humiliations upon the altar and thus helps to fill up
what is lacking to the Body of Christ: "I put on haircloth; I
humbled my soul with fasting. . . ." Joseph was poor, humble,
obedient, bowed down through the great mortifications which
impressed the stigmata of Christ on his body. Again at the
sacrificial Banquet we put on the saint's humble garb: "I am so
poor, so weighted down with suffering; may Your salvation
help me, God. . . ."

September 19

ST. JANUARIUS AND COMPANIONS, Bishop, Martyrs

The shining host of martyrs

1. St. Januarius and Companions. *Grave*: at first in the
catacombs at Naples; since 1497 the relics have remained with-

out interruption in the cathedral church of Naples. *Life*. Together with his deacons Socius and Festus, and his lector
Desiderius, Januarius, bishop of Beneventum, was subjected to
most atrocious torturing during the Diocletian persecution
(about 304). Nevertheless, with God's aid they were preserved
unmaimed. The wild animals let loose upon them would not
attack. Beheaded at Puteoli, their bodies were reverently interred in the neighboring cities. Eventually the remains of St.
Januarius became the prized possession of the city of Naples.

"Even to the present time the blood of the saint that is preserved in a glass phial will become fluid shortly after it is brought
close to the head of the saint; then it bubbles up in a remarkable
manner, as if it had just been shed" (*Breviary*). Cardinal Schuster makes this statement in his *Liber Sacramentorum* (vol. 8, p.
233): "The author has seen the marvel of the blood liquefaction
at closest range and can give witness to the fact. Taking into
consideration all the scientific investigations that have been
made, he would say that a natural explanation of the phenomena
does not seem possible." — The Mass is from the Common
(*Salus autem*), p. 411.

2. Liturgy Lived. Bishop, deacon, and reader, three saints
holding liturgical offices, joyfully give their lives for Christ!
What an example for their flock! They preached not only with
words but also with deeds! They brought not only a spiritual
sacrifice during Mass but imitated the Lord through a bloody
death. Bishop, deacon, and reader — such were the original,
official, ecclesiastical offices. In any attempt to restore life to the
liturgy, it would be necessary for the holders of liturgical offices
to distinguish and sublet duties not directly inherent in their
offices.

The resulting good would be twofold: (a) we would again
become conscious of our proper tasks; the bishop and priests are
liturgists primarily, heralds of God's word; the Eucharistic
sacrifice and the homily are their first and all-important duties;
(b) perhaps those liturgical offices of secondary importance
which at present are only formalities could be restored to the
laity. The living parish needs a deacon or deaconess to whom

the poor may go, needs men who will perform important functions at the divine services. Readers and chanters are called for;
without them it is impossible to have liturgical efficiency. We
must institute schools for these purposes; we must educate young
men of the parish to master the missal, men who are able to read
in public and direct public praying. Especially great is the need
for experienced organists and choral directors of good liturgical
calibre. When we have restored to the parish its three proper
offices, that of the priest and preacher of God's word, that of
caretaker of God's poor, and that of reader-chanter at the divine
services, then our parishes will be liturgically mature.

September 20

ST. EUSTACE AND COMPANIONS, Bishop, Martyrs

Nostra culpa!

St. Eustace, a bishop of Antioch, died in exile at Trajanopolis
in Thrace (fourth century) for professing the Nicene faith.
Legend, however, has transformed him into a famous general
and father of a family. Once while pursuing a deer of extraordinary size, the story continues, he suddenly saw between
its horns a shining replica of the crucified Savior and heard a
voice from heaven inviting him to embrace the life that never
ends. Following this counsel he received baptism together with
his wife Theopista and two sons Agapitus and Theopistus. Immediately he returned to the place where the vision had occurred, as the Lord had commanded him, and there was told the
unspeakable sufferings he would have to bear for the glory of
Christ. All these trials the saintly confessor endured with wonderful patience. Finally the whole family suffered martyrdom,
shut up in a red-hot brazen bull. Eustace is one of the Fourteen
Holy Helpers, and he is venerated as the patron of hunters.

Aren't you thinking: how can the Divine Office contain such

fiction? The breviary does contain some hagiography, we must admit, that runs wide of fact or historical truth. Should we blame the Church? *We* are the Church. We must blame ourselves, strike our own breast. Every age has the liturgy it deserves. During times of interest and study, dross and weaknesses are eliminated. We may as well admit that for hundreds of years no one has bothered much about liturgical propriety or truthfulness. Liturgy became fossilized and Catholics treated it accordingly. The breviary especially remained a thorn to clerical comfort, and about it and within it there grew up a hedge of oddities. Years ago Pope Pius X appointed a commission for revising the historical accounts given in the second nocturn. Results? So far none, because the clergy have evinced so little interest. If priests and bishops were genuinely concerned, the necessary changes would have been made long ago. *Nostra culpa*! — The Mass (*Sapientiam*) from the Common of Martyrs, see p. 410.

September 21

ST. MATTHEW, Apostle and Evangelist

Follow Me — and Matthew rose up and followed Him

1. St. Matthew. *Grave*: in Persia, according to the *Hieronymianum*; his relics are said to have been transferred to Salerno (Italy) by Pope Gregory VII (May 6, 1084). *Life.* Matthew is a lovable personality both as a man and as an apostle and evangelist. We know the story of his conversion and call. Saints upon whom sanctity was not bestowed in the cradle and who were obliged to sever themselves from the service of the world and follow Christ attract us more because they seem nearer to us. Matthew belonged to the contemned and, in part, sinful group of publicans; assuredly there were many among them who were better than their occupation would indicate. We know nothing about him before his conversion. Most probably he had already made the acquaintance of Jesus and had listened to His words. Perhaps he had previously been one of John the Baptist's disciples. Our Savior's glance and call perfected his conversion. A beautiful passage in the first Gospel tells of the farewell meal Matthew gave to other members of his profession and at which Jesus and the disciples were present.

Following these initial incidents we find nothing more of him in Sacred Scripture; legend says he went into pagan lands like the rest of the apostles, and points to Persia as the region where he gained the martyr's palm. His body was brought to Salerno (1084) and later placed in a church consecrated by Pope Gregory VII (see *Martyrology* on May 6). From St. Matthew we possess a most precious legacy, the first of the four Gospels.

2. **Holy Mass (Os justi).** The Mass differs considerably from other apostle-Mass formularies; the call and conversion of Matthew is its primary burden (*Gosp.*). Listen as he himself recounts his conversion and call. Note how the Gospel itself serves as a fine illustration of the Mass; for at the holy Sacrifice we too sit at table with publicans and receive from the Lord the assurance that He is calling sinners. The *Lesson* describes the cherubim who formed the base for Yahweh's throne in Ezechiel's inaugural vision. The faces of the four living creatures are related to the four evangelists by the Fathers of the Church and ecclesiastical tradition; hence the selection of the passage and its use today. As the Mass service begins we honor the holy evangelist who meditated so profoundly upon the wisdom of His Master (*Intr.*); at the *Offertory* and at the sacrificial Banquet we behold him in his glory.

3. **The Gospel According to St. Matthew.** Lovers of liturgy will be noted for their zeal in studying the four Gospels and in knowing their distinguishing characteristics. Originally written in Aramaic, St. Matthew's Gospel only later was translated into Greek. A misfortune that we no longer possess the original text. For it contains the most detailed description of Christ's life. Matthew is said to have composed his Gospel as a farewell letter to the Jews before leaving Palestine; he wished to reassure

who is like god?

them that Jesus of Nazareth was the promised Messiah, even though rejected by His own people. His book follows a topical order rather than a chronological one, i.e., it orders the events of Christ's life not according to the time at which they occurred but according to subject matter. This is evident particularly in the so-called miracle chapters (8 and 9) where miracles occurring at various times are grouped together.

Of note, too, is the artful structure of narratives in which the symbolism of numbers (so highly respected among the Jews) has a role. St. Matthew's Gospel may be divided into seven major parts; of these each has two subdivisions, a discourse by Jesus and an historical narrative. A good example is had in the second major division (ch. 5–9); first we hear the Sermon on the Mount (ch. 5–7), then we see the Miracle-worker in action (ch. 8–9). It is as if Matthew wanted to say: Jesus indeed preaches, but His miracles prove that what He says is true.

The book contains five major discourses evenly distributed. The two most important are at the beginning and at the end, the Sermon on the Mount and the discourse on the Last Things. The parables at the seashore fall in the middle (ch. 13) between two discourses to the disciples. These five discourses Matthew has recorded in a most detailed manner. In general he depicts the humanity of the Messiah; therefore too his emphasis on Christ's physical sufferings. And finally it is to be noted that our evangelist makes frequent reference to the fulfillment of prophecies, because he wrote to Jews and to Jewish Christians.

Application. Take time today to read St. Matthew's Gospel, keeping the above introduction in mind. You do have a well edited New Testament? and respectable in appearance? Give it the place of honor in your home or room. And recollect yourself spiritually before beginning to read.

4. **Follow Me.** The feast of the holy apostle Matthew brings to mind his memorable call and his glorious work. It was a great hour indeed in Matthew's life when Jesus approached the tax-gatherer's desk, gazed into his eyes and said: "Follow Me." We need not hold that these words came to him wholly unprepared. Matthew had already known Jesus. Perhaps he had been at the

Jordan with John the Baptist and was baptized. Then he became a zealous listener to Jesus' preaching in Galilee. And now the Master says to him: "Follow Me." And he followed.

It was not a resolution easily made to give up a goodly position, to leave a pleasant family, and to plunge into an unknown future. Yet Matthew followed. It was a hard but happy exchange he was making. For he received in return the friendship of Jesus, the glory of apostleship, the honor of an evangelist. For a tax-gatherer's table he would receive a judgment seat over Israel, for its load of wares, immortal souls; in place of money, heavenly treasures became his portion!

Follow Me! The words bring to mind my vocation. I too was called. Also to me Jesus said: Follow Me. At baptism He first invited me, and often has He repeated that invitation. Many an event in life is a call from God. As I entered this Order, as I became a priest, God's call was the important thing: Follow Me! Is there, however, a common calling, one given to all, whether priests, laymen, married, or nuns? St. Ignatius says: "Yes — to praise God, to serve Him and save one's soul." A familiar phrase. We are *called* to belong to the family of God. As the apostle Paul proclaims on apostle feasts: "You are now no longer guests and strangers, you are citizens of God's people, members of His family."

We are called to be children of God, already a high end; yet not the highest. The highest is that we are called to be numbered among Christ's members, incorporated most intimately into Him. We are cells in Christ's Mystical Body, His divine life should diffuse itself in us. Such is the highest purpose of our calling. In itself it makes little difference what particular role in Christ's Body I play or what portion of the Body's work falls to me. The important thing is that Christ's strength is operative in me, that Christ spreads Himself through me. This calling is a grace, a gift, but also a duty. It is bound up inextricably with my cooperation. Linked to the great central power station, I must allow that power to operate. I must identify myself with Christ in every action. Such is the tremendous task assigned me. Paul repeats it again and again, and in various ways, e.g., to become a new creature; to put on the new man; to rise with Christ. Matthew obeyed the call faithfully. And I?

September 22

ST. THOMAS OF VILLANOVA, Bishop and Confessor
ST. MAURICE AND COMPANIONS, Martyrs

Liberally he gave to the poor

1. **St. Thomas.** *Day of death*: September 8, 1555. *Grave*: in the church of St. Augustine at Valencia. *Life.* Our saint, born in Spain in 1488, inherited a special love toward the poor from his parents; he often gave away his very clothes. After the death of his father and mother, he used his inheritance to sustain poor virgins. He became a lecturer in the higher schools at Alcala, entered the order of the Hermits of St. Augustine in 1516 at Villanova, acted as court preacher to Charles V. Against his will he was made archbishop of Valencia (1544), then exercised the office as a zealous shepherd of souls and a great friend of the poor. The bed in which he died was borrowed back from the one to whom he had given it as alms shortly before. During the sixteenth century he was called the "apostle of the Spaniards." The Mass, from the Common of Bishops (*Statuit*), is explained on p. 417.

2. **St. Maurice and Companions**. Returning from Gaul, Emperor Maximian (286–305) led his soldiers to Sitten, Switzerland, and there arranged a victory sacrifice to the gods. The Christian legion from the Egyptian Thebaid refused to participate in the idolatrous service. Their leader Maurice exhorted them to perseverance. As a consequence the Theban legion was decimated, then massacred (about 300). The Roman Martyrology mentions Exuperius, Candidus, Victor, Innocent and Vitalis by name. These martyrs were later referred to as Agaunum's glorious legion. Their relics are venerated at St. Maurice

in the canton of Wallis, Switzerland, in a famous Augustinian abbey.

3. Love of the Poor. Thomas' most cherished virtue, love of the poor, is brought to our attention in the Collect of the Mass and in the Hours of the Divine Office. "God adorned the bishop Thomas with the virtue of heroic mercy toward the poor (*insignis misericordia*)"; with confidence, then, we petition Him to "pour forth upon all the riches of His mercy." The Biblical basis for the prayer is Christ's words: "Be merciful as your heavenly Father is merciful." *Benedictus antiphon*: "Of his almsgiving all the members of the Church are speaking." *Magnificat antiphon*: "Lavishly did he give to the poor; his holiness will last forever." At about this time the Church, while keeping the Ember days, urges us to supplement almsgiving with fasting. What we deny our appetites should be given to the poor.

Did Christ teach anything special about loving the poor? He who Himself was so poor as not to have whereon to lay His head, for whom there was no cradle at birth and no bed at death, He who had come to bring the glad tidings of the riches of God's kingdom, He speaks startlingly on the subject. He says: "To give is more blessed than to receive" (Acts 20:35). Recall His awesome words on the final judgment: "When the Son of Man will come in majesty . . . and all nations are gathered together before Him, then will He separate them as a shepherd separates the sheep from the goats . . . then the King will say to those at His right: Come, blessed of My Father . . . I was hungry and you gave Me to eat; I was thirsty and you gave Me to drink. I was a stranger and you asked Me in. Naked, and you clothed Me. I was sick and you visited Me. In prison, and you came to to see Me. Then the just will ask: Lord, when did we see You hungry and give You food, or thirsty and give You to drink? . . . And the King will answer: Truly, I say to you: As long as you did it to one of these My least brethren, you did it to Me" (Matt. 25:31–40).

This passage merits soul-searching thought. Moralists of today and yesterday would picture the judgment in a wholly different fashion. Wholly different virtues and vices would be featured.

But Christ puts love of neighbor first. Further, He shows that love of neighbor is loving Christ and serving Christ. Christ is hidden away in one's neighbor, and in the poor Christ is concealed even to a greater extent. Acts of merciful love will decide the issue between heavenly happiness and eternal punishment. As comment on Christ's teaching we can only quote the psalmist: "The words of the Lord are pure words, as silver tried by the fire, purified in the crucible refined seven times" (Ps. 11:7).

September 23

ST. LINUS, Pope and Martyr

ST. THECLA, Virgin and Martyr

St. Peter's first successor

1. St. Linus. *Day of death:* September 23, about the year 79. *Grave:* in the Vatican next to that of St. Peter. *Life.* Linus, Pope and martyr, was the immediate successor of St. Peter. The historical accounts of his life leave much to be desired. The fact that since most ancient times his name is listed among the popes in the Canon of the Mass is of greatest weight, but otherwise he does not seem to be mentioned in the oldest lists of Roman bishops. The Divine Office relates the following, though we need not regard the details as genuine history:

"Pope Linus hailed from Volterra in Etruria and governed the Church immediately after blessed Peter. So great were his sanctity and faith that he not only drove out evil spirits but brought the dead back to life. He decreed that women present at the divine services must have their heads covered. Because of his steadfast fidelity to the faith, he was beheaded at the command of the wicked and ungrateful consul Saturnius, whose daughter he had freed from an evil spirit."

Application. Linus is credited with the ordinance that women should wear head-covering at divine services. This ancient cus-

tom has been insisted upon again and again by the Church down
to the present day. The more we imbibe the spirit of the liturgy,
the more easily will we realize that during divine services
Christians should be clothed differently than modern fashion
would frequently favor. What a spirit of reverence is manifested
by this ordinance of Pope St. Linus!—The Mass, from the
Common of Sovereign Pontiffs (*Si diligis Me*), p. 398.

2. **St. Thecla.** *Day of death*: September 23, about the year
100 (according to the *Martyrology*). *Grave*: at Iconium, her
birthplace. *Life*. This child of St. Paul is honored by the Fathers
of the Eastern Church as proto-martyr and "near apostle." Already during the second century legends concerning her were
current and her grave was much visited by pilgrims. It is historically certain that she lived, but the *Acts* of her life are largely
legendary. According to these she was born at Iconium, where
she was converted to Christianity by the preaching of St. Paul.
It is related that she was "accused of being a Christian by her
own parents after she had refused to marry Thamiris, in order
to give herself wholly to Christ. But the pyre enkindled for her
burning was extinguished by a sudden downpour of rain as she
threw herself into it, making the sign of the Cross. Then she
fled to Antioch, where the ferocious beasts and bulls to which
she was tied would do her no harm. Nor did she suffer injury
during confinement in a snake pit. Because of these marvels
many pagans accepted the faith. Thereafter Thecla returned to
her native land, where she lived in solitude upon a hill. At the
age of ninety she died a peaceful death."

Application. Since most ancient times St. Thecla has been
highly venerated, especially as patron of the dying. Her intercession is still invoked in the litany during the rites for the dying
and in the Church's official prayer for a departing soul: "As
Thou didst deliver the holy virgin and martyr Thecla from three
most gruesome torments, so deliver the soul of this Thy servant;
and let him (her) enjoy with Thee the blessings of heaven.
Amen."

3. **Prepare for Death**. Now during the Church's Harvest
Time it is very appropriate "to prepare Christ's throne" by mak-

ing provisions for a happy death. The Church has a series of very special helps to aid one's passage through death's dark door, viz., the Last Anointing, holy Viaticum, the Apostolic Blessing, the *Commendatio Animae* (Commending the Dying Soul to God). This last rite is too little known among the laity and too seldom made accessible to them. Mother Church wishes to be present at the death of her children in the person of the priest and by prayer to brighten their last moments.

There is depth and beauty to the prayers forming the *Commendatio*, and there is purpose to their length; moreover, they may be extended if death is slow in coming. Why not read meditatively through one or the other of these prayers today, e.g., the *Proficiscere*, "Depart from this world, O Christian soul, in the Name of the almighty Father who created thee, in the Name of Jesus Christ, the Son of the living God, who suffered for thee, in the Name of the Holy Spirit who is poured forth in thee. . . ." To comfort and encourage the dying Christian a whole galaxy of Old and New Testament personages are invoked, saints whom God once helped in need. While still in good health we ought become familiar with these prayers so as to grasp them easily when the occasion actually arises. In this way *prepare the throne for the Lord!*

September 24

OUR LADY OF RANSOM (DE MERCEDE)

Free us, Mary, from the bonds of Satan

1. Our Lady of Ransom. This feast commemorates the founding of the Order of Our Lady of Ransom (Mercedarians) which had as its primary purpose the ransoming of captive Christian slaves from the Saracens. For the Church wants us to remember the very special protection Mary bestowed upon a work that was all-important at the time. The two founders of the Order, Peter Nolasco (Jan. 28) and Raymond of Pennafort (Jan. 23), are also venerated by the universal Church. The Order sprang into existence on August 10, 1218. The Office tells how Mary herself requested St. Peter Nolasco to make the foundation; during the same night St. Raymond and King James I received like visions, whereupon the Order was called into existence.

2. The Mass and Office, with the exception of the three lessons of the second nocturn and the Collect, are taken from the Common of the Blessed Virgin. "Common" here is not used in the usual sense of a group of saints receiving a like Office or Mass formulary. Mary's place is unique, she can be merged into no group. Far above all she stands as Queen of apostles, Queen of martyrs, Queen of confessors, Queen of virgins, even as we pray and sing in the Laurentian litany. The word *common* is used in the sense that fundamental Marian theology forms an integral whole, while on the various feasts we meditate upon and celebrate one or the other Marian privilege. From which it becomes clear how important the Common is for the full understanding of Marian Offices. When we have grasped the basic truths presented in the Common, we will be able to understand better the facts illustrated by particular feasts.

The Mass (*Salve Sancta*) p. 392f. An Oration proper to today's mystery pleads that God may free us from the captivity of Satan through Mary's intercession.

3. The Mystery of Evil. "May we be delivered from all sin and from Satan's bondage." Thus we plead in the Collect. Even as there is a *mysterium Christi* in the sense that the absolute efficacy of grace or the Church as the Mystical Body cannot be fully comprehended, so too there is a *mysterium iniquitatis*, a mystery of evil. It will never be wholly clear why the devil is allowed to wield such tremendous power. Before Christ and apart from Christ the world falls under Satan's influence. Christ made this abundantly clear in the parable of the strong man overcome by the stronger, and in another passage He gives the devil the title "prince of this world." Paganism and all its ramifications had been the devil's playground. It is interesting to note the various diabolical machinations alluded to in the rite for baptism: "Break all the nets of Satan in which he (she) has been entangled . . . come forth, depart from this servant of God, spirit accursed and damned . . . never dare, accursed devil, to violate this sign of the holy Cross which we are making upon his (her) forehead."

But the devil still possesses very definite power against the Church, though, of course, his power is not unlimited. The devil is now like a chained dog and can only injure those who come too near. The Apocalypse affords good insight into the devil's activity against the Church. He seeks to harm the Church and Christians in a twofold way, through persecution and through temptation. Persecution really does the Church no harm, rather it greatly increases her glory. Through persecution the devil "sifts Christians as wheat," but from the treasury of the Church he can take nothing.

Much more dangerous are his attacks through sin. He seeks to cool the zeal of Christians, to weaken their wills, to confuse their thinking. His allies are the world and self, through which he seeks to rob Christians of the kingdom of God and to win for himself spiritual dominion. This is what the Collect calls the "bondage of the evil one." Against "the wiles and wickedness of the devil" we must be on guard continually and utilize the many means of grace at our disposal. Such are the intercession of the saints, whom we ought to invoke daily, the sacraments and sacramentals, especially the holy Eucharist. The last mentioned is the finest antidote against the machinations of hell. Yes, the whole liturgy, with the ecclesiastical year, the Divine Office, etc., are means with which to nullify the mystery of evil.

4. **The Scripture Readings** during September, the first of the autumn months, are cast in a captivating style and bring home their moral with impact. Two men and two women appear — Job and Tobit, Judith and Esther. They are types of heroes in the best sense, and make good escorts through the Church's Harvest Season. The virtue common to all four is perseverance in the midst of trials, hardships, and suffering. Job is the proverbial type of patience, a virtue we need daily, hourly. Christ

said: "In patience you will possess your souls." Tobit was a
good, kindly man, an ideal father of a family, full of divine
faith and fear. His special virtues were mildness and merciful
love of neighbor. Both Job and Tobit were obliged to undergo
bitter suffering to be proven true and rewarded.

A second round features Judith and Esther, two illustrious
women. Judith in particular impresses us, Judith the abstemious
widow, the wise woman. She staked her life and her honor for
her kinsfolk, her God and her religion. Now she ranks as a type
or figure of the Church (and the soul) — of anyone who must
"cut off Holofernes' head," i.e., overcome Satan and temptation.
Esther too sacrificed herself for her people. It is woman's vocation to forget self, to immolate self for children and family. Not
in egoism but by heroic self-sacrifice does she realize her vocation. Thus four model Biblical personages lead us through the
Church's Harvest Season, showing us how to prepare the throne
for our returning Lord.

September 25

FERIAL DAY

The Heroine Judith.[1] The heroism of this Old Testament Joan
of Arc should not be gauged according to present-day Christian
standards of morality. Judith was a heroine, a model heroine,
though some facets of her activity reflect the thinking of another
age. For her kinsfolk, her country, and her God she was ready
to do the impossible. So she ventured out on a most unusual
errand, she, a lonely widow; for she alone sought to undo the
foe of her people and her religion with God's assistance.

An Assyrian army under the leadership of Holofernes was
advancing toward the Mediterranean Sea, subjecting new lands

[1] From the writings of Dr. Joseph Casper, Vienna.

and nations to the king of Nineveh. Presently they encamped in the plains of Damascus; Aram's cities were sacked, her fields devastated, her youths slain with the sword. Fear and horror of Holofernes fell on all who dwelt on the seacoast (2:27f.). The march continued southwards, toward Jerusalem. To the mountain citadel of Bethulia Holofernes set siege. The inhabitants of the town "were seized by an indescribable fear and confusion because of Jerusalem and because of the temple of the Lord." From a military viewpoint Bethulia was of high strategic importance for the capture of Jerusalem. With the fall of Bethulia the fate of Jerusalem would probably have been sealed, God's temple becoming fuel for fire and the city open to ravage and plunder. Therefore the conflict may rightly be called a religious war, and in this war Judith, the deliverer of Bethulia, acted as the protectress of the temple and of true worship.

As the plight of Bethulia's residents became more and more desperate, the elders decided, "We will delay the surrender of the city for five additional days; by that time Yahweh, our God, will show us His mercy, for He will not abandon us utterly. But if no aid comes and the five days have passed, then we will surrender" (7:30f.).

Judith, who after the death of her husband had lived in strict seclusion, was informed of this latest development. Immediately she summoned the elders and reproached them, saying: "Your action is not good . . . for who are you to try your God this very day, and place yourselves before men in God's stead? . . . You may not force the decisions of Yahweh, our God, because God cannot be threatened like a man, or cajoled. Therefore we ought await deliverance from Him and call to Him for aid. He will indeed respond when it pleases Him." Her admonition was well taken; and acknowledging their mistake, the elders entrusted the city to the prayers of courageous Judith.

Judith prayed, and during her prayer determined that she herself would deliver the people. She put on festive attire and accompanied by a maidservant, proceeded toward the Assyrian camp. Brought before Holofernes, she won his good pleasure,

was invited to remain as a guest, and granted permission to proceed to a nearby vale each night and pray. Some days passed; in
Holofernes' presence she would eat the food brought along, and
at night she would leave the camp to plead with her God. The
fourth day came and Holofernes ordered a camp banquet. Wine
flowed freely, and all drank to satiety. In a drunken stupor the
general was left alone with Judith in his tent.

There he lay as Judith approached. With the sword at hand,
she cut off his head, put it in a sack, handed it to her servant.
Then, as on previous evenings, she walked past the guards out
toward her accustomed place of prayer. Her act had made her
"the glory of Jerusalem, the joy of Israel" (15:9). Before morning she had returned to Bethulia and her deed transformed the
oppressed and despairing inhabitants into men of spirit and
courage. Soon the counterattack was shaping, while the Assyri-
ans, suddenly aware of having a headless leader, panicked and
fled in wild disorder. Thus did Judith accomplish the deliverance of her people. And all Israel hailed her blessed.

Judith had conquered the foe, and her valiant act prefigured
the victory of Christ. She is a type, moreover, of all who fight
and triumph in union with Christ, of all Christian heroes and
saints, and *par excellence* of Mary, Christ's Mother, who co-
operated so perfectly in God's great work of redemption. Mary
indeed contributed more and entered more deeply into that saving work than we can ever surmise. There is profound reason
for the praise liturgy accords her in using the acclamation of
the women of Bethulia: "You are the glory of Jerusalem, you
are the joy of Israel" (15:9). Judith likewise rises before us as
our model, for we too must resemble her, we too must vanquish
the primeval foe, granting him no resting place, no vantage of
any sort. Ours must be a full and absolute triumph over Satan,
like that of the heroine Judith.

September 26

STS. ISAAC JOGUES, JOHN DE BRÉBEUF AND COMPANIONS, Martyrs

It would be unjust that a martyr for Christ should not drink the Blood of Christ

1. **The Church in the United States and Canada** keeps a proper feast today, that of the eight North American Martyrs. And its rank in the calendar as a Double of the Second Class gives it due stature. Honored are the Jesuit missionary priests, Fathers Isaac Jogues, John de Brébeuf, Anthony Daniel, Gabriel Lalemant, Charles Garnier and Noel Chabanel; and two associates, Brother René Goupil and the oblate John de Lalande. All eight were French; all worked amidst great privations for the conversion of the Huron Indians in the area that is now New York state and northwards into Canada; all were beset upon or taken prisoners by the fierce Iroquois between the years 1642 to 1649 and died under savage torture.

The story of Isaac Jogues is perhaps the most heroic. In 1642, after bringing desperately needed supplies to the Huron mission from Quebec, his band was attacked and captured by the Iroquois. Jogues' companion, René Goupil, was tomahawked — the first of the canonized group to die, after both he and Jogues had been savagely maltreated and beaten, hair, beard, and nails torn off, and forefingers bitten through. With Dutch aid, Jogues succeeded in escaping and returning to Europe. His mutilated fingers prevented him from offering holy Mass; but Pope Urban VIII waived the canonical restriction with the words: "It would be unjust that a martyr for Christ should not drink the Blood of Christ."

Early in 1644 Father Jogues was back in his beloved mission country. He participated in a peace parley between the Iroquois and the French, but old enmities flared up again after a crop failure in Mohawk territory and the outbreak of an epidemic. A box the missioner had left behind was considered the cause

of these misfortunes. Accordingly, when the priest fearlessly returned a third time into the hostile district, it was to certain
death. Captured, tortured mercilessly, tomahawked; his head
was cut off, and according to Indian superstition, placed on a
pole facing the route by which he had come. Isaac's martyrdom
took place on the evening of October 18, 1646, in an area covered
by the diocese of Albany, New York.

2. Holy Mass (Hi sunt qui). The texts seem to strike a happy
medium between the objective theological types of ancient
formularies cast in mysterium mold, and the modern biograph-
ically descriptive types featuring a mosaic of passages illustrating
the virtues and accomplishments of the day's saint. The apocalyptic vision of heaven opens the Mass liturgy as above the altar
we see those "who have come out of the great tribulation and
have washed their robes and made them white in the Blood of
the Lamb" (*Intr.*). Their preaching and their blood hallowed the
first-fruits of the faith in "the northern regions of America";
may their intercession continue and produce an abundant harvest (*Coll.*). According to good liturgical precedent, the *Epistle*
was chosen because of a phrase that bears easy accommodation:
"Behold, this is the *third* time that I am ready to come to you."
St. Isaac's third visit spelled his martyrdom. Yet "most gladly
did he spend himself and be spent for souls, even though loving
them, he was loved less." There is true mysticism in the soul
that can truly pray the *Gradual*, that can see the glory of heavenly liberty in the liberation of the soul from the body, as a bird
freed from its cage. Especially when that liberation equals suffering (*Allel., Off., Comm.*). The Eucharist is the "Bread of the
strong." It gave all necessary strength to the eight we honor
today to do the work of martyrs even before becoming martyrs.
The Bread of the strong will also enable us to "bear one another's
burdens and to love our neighbors sincerely and through deeds"
(*Postc.*).

3. Divine Office. The Lessons of the second and third nocturns are proper, also a few antiphons; otherwise the Office is
taken from the Common of Several Martyrs. Details on the

lives, work, and heroic deaths of all eight North American martyrs are given in three lengthy Readings at Matins. Here is a summary: "These martyrs, members of the Society of Jesus, were sent by their superiors to the Canadian Missions. In 1642, on a journey from Quebec into Huron country, Frs. Isaac Jogues and René Goupil were captured by enemy Iroquois and subjected to horrible torments. On September 29 René was killed for his faith near what is now Auriesville, New York. The next year Isaac escaped, only to return with Fr. John Lalande to make a second and third trip to the savages. On October 18, 1646, he was struck with a tomahawk, and obtained the palm of martyrdom, as did John on the following day.

"On July 4, 1648, Fr. Anthony Daniel was killed by a rain of bullets and arrows while defending his Huron flock from the Iroquois at the village of St. Joseph. On March 16, 1649, Fr. John de Brébeuf and Fr. Gabriel Lalemant were captured by the Iroquois at St. Ignace, in what is now Ontario. Brébeuf, the apostle of the Hurons, died a glorious death under the most atrocious torments, and Lalemant suffered the same cruel martyrdom on the next day. That same year Fr. Charles Garnier was killed by a hatchet blow on the eve of the Immaculate Conception and Fr. Noel Chabanel was slain by an apostate Huron and thrown into a river on the feast itself. These eight martyrs, the first in North America, were beatified in 1925 by Pope Pius XI and canonized by him five years later."

"Theirs indeed is the kingdom of heaven! Rejecting a worldly life, they attained the rewards of this kingdom. In the Blood of the Lamb they washed their robes" (*Magn. Ant.*). It would be interesting to count the number of times this last sentence, "In the Blood of the Lamb they washed their robes," occurs in today's liturgy.

"The very hairs of your head are all numbered. Therefore do not be afraid; you are of more value than many sparrows" (*Ben. Ant.*). Men who rejoiced to run the way of martyrdom would surely sense the humor in the breviary's allusion to their scalps falling under the tomahawk's blow.

4. Sts. Cyprian and Justina. The legend concerning these
two saints was already widespread in the fourth century; it is
extremely difficult to extract the historical kernel. The Divine
Office gives the following:

Cyprian, once a magician, later a martyr, had resorted to every
possible means to make the Christian virgin Justina interested
in a pagan youth who was aflame with passion toward her. When
all his efforts had proven fruitless, he asked counsel from the
evil one. Satan replied that he possessed no power over such who
worshipped Christ in truth. Shaken by the answer, Cyprian
began to rue and detest his former wicked way of life. He abandoned black magic completely and turned sincerely and wholly
to the Christian faith. He was, therefore, arrested with the virgin Justina, and both won the crown of martyrdom (about 304).
For six days their bodies remained uninterred, when at night
certain Christians transported them to Italy by ship and buried
them on the estate of the noble matron Rufina. Later their relics
were transferred to the Holy City and posited near the baptismal
font in the Lateran Basilica. — Some future breviary reform
will certainly eliminate this feast also. — The Mass, from the
Common of Martyrs (*Salus autem*), p. 411.

September 27

STS. COSMAS AND DAMIAN, Martyrs

I was sick and you visited Me

1. Sts. Cosmas and Damian. *Grave*: at Cyrrhus in Syria,
where Emperor Justinian built a large basilica over their grave.
Later their relics came into the possession of various European
churches, e.g., to Bremen in the year 965. *Life.* These two saints,
celebrated "physicians" of the ancient Church who used their
art in the service of converting souls to Christ, are venerated as
patrons by doctors and pharmacists. Their names occur in the
Canon of the Mass and in the Litany of the Saints. The *Martyr-*

ology reads: "In Aegea (Asia Minor) the holy martyr-brothers Cosmas and Damian. In the Diocletian persecution they were subjected to various tortures; they were cast into chains, locked in prison, thrown into the sea, tormented with fire, nailed to crosses, and shot at with arrows. Since with divine help they suffered all this unmaimed, they were beheaded" (about 300).

Application. In imitation of their Savior our two physician-saints sought to heal sick bodies in order to win and heal sick souls. The same procedure is still followed in mission lands. Care of sick bodies and care of sick souls lie very close to the Church's heart, because no one is more ready for God's kingdom than the sick. Every true Christian should have one or the other ill or disabled person to take care of.

2. Holy Mass (Sapientiam). This Mass, which in the course of time attained a place in the Common of Martyrs, originally served as the festal Mass for today's saints. In the *Introit* the "people" (i.e., we the faithful) hasten to the burial church of Cosmas and Damian, voicing wonder at their wisdom. Then with second breath we bid them "rejoice in the Lord." In the *Lesson* the Church praises our saints: "The just will live forever and their reward is with the Lord. . . . Therefore they will receive a glorious kingdom and a precious crown from the hand of the Lord." The *Alleluia* chant stresses the "true brotherhood" which overcomes the world's wickedness.

To understand the *Gospel* we must remember that in ancient times it was customary to bring the sick to the graves of the martyrs; linens also that had touched the tomb were placed upon them. People were convinced that "strength went out from the bodies of the saints." The Gospel, moreover, presents a splendid mystery-action, i.e., the account assumes mystical reality in the Sacrifice proper: "a very great multitude" (viz., all of us) are assembled to be healed from spiritual sickness. Jesus "comes down from the (heavenly) mountain into a plain" (our church). "And all the people sought to touch Him (in ancient times each one received the sacred Host in his hand), for strength went out from Him (from the holy Eucharist)." Continuing His work, our Lord declares the martyrs Cosmas and Damian blessed, for during life they practiced the beatitudes, especially the fourth: Blessed are you if men hate you, repudiate you, disgrace you or rob you of your good name, for the Son of Man's sake; be glad and rejoice, for your reward is great in heaven."

The *Communion* — what a contrast! While eating the Body of the Lord the Church reminds us that the bodies of the saints were thrown to the birds of the air and wild beasts. The phrase *carnes sanctorum* (flesh of the saints) may have occasioned its selection.

> This is true brotherhood,
>   one that could be destroyed not even by war.
> They shed their blood and followed the Lord.
> They despised the courts of kings
>   and attained the kingdom of heaven.
> Behold, how beautiful, how lovely it is
>   when brothers live harmoniously together (*Resp.*)

3. The Station Church of Sts. Cosmas and Damian. Pope Felix IV (526–530) consecrated "the temple of the holy city" in the Roman forum to the honor of Sts. Cosmas and Damian. In the course of time this church became the most famous sanctuary dedicated to our saints, and likewise a stational church. That the Roman people had great trust in our sainted doctors is evident from the Mass formulary. In their church we still may see the glorious mosaic placed in the apse by Pope Felix IV, one that belongs to the best of the preserved Roman mosaics. It is a piece of art that could well serve for a treatise on ancient symbolism.

In the middle the figure of the glorified Savior stands upon the clouds, His right hand upraised, in the left the scroll of Sacred Scripture. His garments are of gold embellished with red stripes. Through a flowery field (symbolic of paradise) Peter and Paul are leading toward the Lord two martyrs, Cosmas and Damian (again deeply symbolic: two saints from distant Asia are led by the princes of the Roman Church!). Dressed in royal fashion, the two saints carry their crowns of victory with cov-

ered hands (a favorite way of picturing saints in ancient art).
Medicine cases, indicative of their profession, may be detected.
Through the meadow flows a river which, as the inscription
says, is the Jordan — again a symbol, indicating the graces of
baptism and divine life. On the banks of the river are fruit-
laden palm trees, signs of a life pleasing to God. Upon one of
them rests the mythical phoenix, a figure of resurrection and
transfiguration. Even the star above St. Paul has meaning, it
represents heaven. Above Christ can be seen the hand of God
reaching down the crown of victory.

In a lower rung the Lamb of God is seen standing upon a rock
from which the four rivers of paradise flow. Compare the two
areas; above the glorified Christ in heaven, below the Lamb of
God, Christ in the holy Sacrifice. Towards Christ, from the
right and from the left, twelve lambs come out of the cities of
Jerusalem and Bethlehem; they symbolize the Church militant
assimilating members from Judaism and paganism. Thus the
mosaic beautifully portrays the Church triumphant and militant,
the former surrounding Christ glorified in heaven, the latter
assembled about the divine Lamb in the Eucharist. This venerable mosaic is most instructive in that it shows us what values
were precious to the ancient Christians, viz., Christ as Teacher
and as glorified King; the sacramental life of the Church, baptism and the Eucharist; the Christ-life typified by the palm
tree; and lastly hope in the hereafter (the phoenix). These four
treasures would provide ample food for many a fruitful meditation.

September 28

ST. WENCEL, Martyr

**With his own hands Wencel sowed the wheat and pressed the
grapes for the bread and wine used at holy Mass**

1. **St. Wencel.** *Day of death*: according to the *Martyrology*,
September 28, 929, at Stara Boleslav; feast since 1729. *Grave*: at

Prague, in the cathedral of St. Vitus. *Life*. Wencel, duke of
Bohemia, received from his grandmother, St. Ludmilla, a devout
rearing. Throughout his life he preserved his virginity un-
blemished. As duke he was a father to his subjects, generous
toward orphans, widows, and the poor. On his own shoulders
he frequently carried wood to the houses of the needy. He often
attended the funerals of the poor, ransomed captives, visited
those suffering in prison. He was filled with a deep reverence
toward the clergy; with his own hands he sowed the wheat for
making altar breads and pressed the grapes for the wine used
in the holy Sacrifice. During winter he would visit the churches
barefoot through snow and ice, not seldom leaving behind
bloody footprints. Angels were the protectors of his person. A
powerful pagan element, at the head of which was his younger
brother Boleslaus, opposed his Christianizing efforts. Wencel
attended a banquet to which his brother had invited him, but
when warned of the danger about him, he took no counter-
measures. On his way to Mass he was set upon by Boleslaus and
slain as he reached the church door. "May God forgive you,
brother," was his last prayer.

2. Holy Mass (In virtute). The Mass is from the Common
of One Martyr, p. 406. Wencel experienced what today's Gospel
demands of a Christian, for he was hated for Christ's sake by
his relatives, his brother, his mother, a hatred that brought him
the crown of martyrdom. He indeed kept holy Christ's words:
"Who receives you, receives Me," for he took more than a cup
of cool water to Christ's servants. You too ought resemble Wencel in doing what you can in and for the Church — cleaning
the building, supplying candles, etc. Place yourself at the service
of the pastor. Nor will the practice of charity toward one's neighbor be neglected by any true liturgist. For in no other way can
the prejudices against the Christian religion be better overcome
than by acts of mercy. Make this a resolution: as often as I assist at the holy Sacrifice, I will bring as an Offertory gift some
corporal or spiritual work of mercy.

DEDICATION OF ST. MICHAEL THE ARCHANGEL

Who is like God!

1. The Archangel Michael. Today's feast commemorates the consecration of the basilica of St. Michael on the Via Saleria, Rome. But present-day Christian attitude regards it as a feast in honor of the holy angels. Michael is, indeed, the best known of all the angels and the one most often spoken of. He was the leader when the heavenly hosts battled Lucifer and his followers. The name of our Archangel means "Who is like God!" He was considered the protecting angel of the synagogue (Dan. 10; 12) and is honored as the protector and patron of the universal Church, as also the guide of departed souls to paradise (see Offertory of the Requiem Mass). His feast is the oldest, originally the only angel feast. The liturgy presents our Archangel in dramatic fashion according to the threefold service he renders to the Church as (a) soldier, (b) intercessor, and (c) companion and guide at death.

a) Most often we see him battling Satan. "While Michael the Archangel was fighting against the dragon, there was heard the voice of those who said: Salvation to our God, alleluia!" (2. Ant., Lauds). "There was silence in heaven while the dragon fought with the Archangel Michael. Then the voice of thousands upon thousands was heard, saying: Salvation and honor and power to almighty God." "Whenever some work of heroic proportions is to be performed, Michael is commissioned. Thus from the work and from the name of the Angel we are given to understand that nobody is able to do such things as only God can accomplish" (St. Gregory, at the second nocturn). "Many wondrous deeds are recounted about the Archangel Michael, who because of his bravery in battle obtained the victory" (9. Ant. at Matins). "Holy Archangel Michael, defend us in battle that we may not perish in that dreadful judgment."

b) Michael also functions as one of the great intercessors in behalf of the Church. The liturgy often pictures him standing

with censer in hand at the altar, bearing the prayers of the faithful and mediating before God. "An angel stood before the altar
of the temple, having a golden censer in his hand; there was
given to him much incense, and the smoke of the perfumes
ascended before God, alleluia" (*Off.*; Apoc. 8:3-4). "O most
glorious prince, Michael the Archangel, be ever mindful of us,
both here and everywhere entreating the Son of God for us, alleluia, alleluia" (Magn. Ant.) "Fragrant incense rose up to God
from the hand of the angel" (Versicle). "This is the Archangel
Michael, the leader of the angelic hosts; his veneration brings
rich blessings to the nations, and his intercession leads to the
kingdom of heaven" (Resp.). "The Archangel Michael came to
help the people of God; he rendered assistance to the souls of the
just."

c) The third task of our Archangel, a particularly beautiful
one, is described in the Requiem Offertory: "O Lord Jesus
Christ, King of glory, deliver the souls of all the faithful departed
from the lion's jaws that hell may not swallow them up . . .
rather may the standard-bearer St. Michael lead them into the
holy light." "Archangel Michael, I have appointed you prince
and guardian over all souls on their journey home" (3. Ant.,
Lauds).

2. Holy Mass (Benedicite). The liturgy does not restrict today's celebration to St. Michael; all angels are included, especially those assigned to the protection of men (see *Collect*). In
the *Introit* we call upon all the angels to praise God, they who
are mighty and hearken to His orders. The *Lesson*, giving the
first five verses of the Apocalypse, mentions angels twice, but the
Church would have us recall the entire book (the beginning for
the whole — a favorite procedure in the liturgy). The Apocalypse is, *par excellence*, the "angel book" of the Bible; in no other
is so much space devoted to them. The theme of our passage is:
the angels are zealous in perfecting the work of redemption and
in battling against the devils; Michael stands at their head.

The *Gospel* pericope owes its selection to the final verse: Their
angels (guarding little children, i.e., all Christians) are standing before God's heavenly throne as advocates and defenders.

How well these few words express the role of angels in our regard — especially when contrasted with the doctrine of diabolical temptation. During the *Offertory* chant, how our hearts thrill at the scene of angels offering clouds of incense at the altar of God — an act mystically visible at solemn Masses.

3. War in the Spirit World. With the name of the Archangel Michael there is associated the idea of battle or war, a conflict that may truly be called cosmic, for all other battles or wars are but its extension or a phase in its evolution. It is the war in the spirit world, a conflict raging since the beginning of creation and to have no resolution until the end of time. In this cosmic conflict we may distinguish four phases. The first phase has its setting in heaven. The Book of Revelation affords these details: "There was a battle in heaven — Michael and his angels fought against the dragon; and the dragon and his angels fought back. But they were unable to win, and their places were no longer found in heaven. So the great dragon, the ancient serpent who is also called the devil or Satan, but one who seduces the whole world, was hurled down to earth, and his colleagues were hurled down with him" (Apoc. 12:7f.). We do not know the reasons provoking this first spirit clash. Some rebellion against God on the part of one or more members of the angel hosts is probable. Disregarding its original or literal message (i.e., a taunt against Babylon's king) spiritual writers and speakers have applied Is. 14:12–15 to the fall of Lucifer:

How you have fallen from heaven, you Morning-star!
How you have been smitten to earth,
   you conqueror of nations!
You thought to yourself: I will scale the heavens,
   I will set my throne above the stars of God;
   I will reign on the Mount of Assembly
     in the farthest north;
   I will ascend the heights of the clouds,
   I will become like (God) the Most High.
But now you have been brought down to Sheol,
   to the depths of the pit.

The second phase of that cosmic conflict has its setting upon earth. The devil obtained very definite power over the world. He brought strife upon the face of the earth on the day when he led Eve into sin, and Adam through her agency. Evil then made a triumphal entry and Satan became "the Prince of this World." His power was described by Christ in the parable of the strong man overcome by one stronger. Over all mankind Satan extended his sway. Paganism with its idolatry, its cruelty and lust was his domain. Until One stronger came, Christ. On Golgotha they clashed, and Satan lost. Christ had foretold it before His passion: "Now has judgment come upon the world; now the prince of this world is cast out" (John 12:31). The second phase likewise ended with the defeat of the devil.

The third phase consists in the war the devil is waging against the Church until the end of time. Here the Apocalypse is very enlightening. For this entire book is actually a war annal. "A great sign appeared in the heavens — a woman clothed with the sun, the moon at her feet, about her head a crown of twelve stars. And soon she was to have a child." This woman represents the People of God. "Another sign appeared in the heavens: a great fire-red dragon. It had seven heads and ten horns and upon its heads seven diadems. His tail swept away a third of heaven's stars and flung them on the earth. The dragon placed himself before the woman heavy with child so that when she had given birth, he could devour her child. . . . The dragon became enraged against the woman and went off to make war against her other children, against those who obey God's commandments" (Apoc. 12:1f.). This war continues in all fury down through the ages. The devil resorts to every means, including the services of men; as his instruments he uses civil and religious organizations, as represented by the two beasts, and the notorious harlot Babylon comes under his hire. As the end approaches, the devil will become still more furious, fighting with greater ferocity.

This third phase leaves a backwash in the soul of every human being. Deep in your heart, too, the war comes to a crisis. The line of conflict is easily recognized, though it cuts through one's very marrow. It is a conflict of spirits; on one side the devil, on the other Michael and his angels, the angel guardians sent by him. My child, fight the good fight, so that you may win the victory-crown of life. You have not been abandoned to yourself, God is close to you. On the battlefield of your soul, as Psalm 90 describes it, "A thousand fall to your right, ten thousand to your left." Your path lies through the midst. "But God has ordered His angels to bear you up in their hands, that you do not strike your foot against a stone." Upon the outcome of this war depends your eternity. Satan resembles a chained dog; he can attack only those who come too close, against others he is powerless.

The fourth phase will bring the final clash. There can be no other eventuality than the full and absolute defeat of Satan and his colleagues. "The devil who seduced them was cast into the sea of fire and brimstone, where the beast and the false prophet were, there to be tormented day and night forever and ever" (Apoc. 20:10). "Depart from Me, you cursed, into the eternal fire prepared for the devil and his angels." In that final conflict too Michael will take the leading role. Thereafter all war will cease, and God will reign alone in peace.

September 30

ST. JEROME, Priest and Doctor of the Church

Ignorance of Scripture is ignorance of Christ

1. **St. Jerome.** *Day of death*: September 30, 419 or 420. *Grave*: in Bethlehem, near the crib of the Savior. *Life*. Sophronius Eusebius Hieronymus, born in Stridon, Dalmatia, was baptized at Rome as an adult by Pope Liberius; he then devoted himself to scriptural and theological studies. In the Holy Land he learned the Hebrew language; after being ordained priest at Antioch, he returned to Rome, was commissioned by Pope

Damasus to translate the Holy Bible. Returning to Palestine in 386, he chose Bethlehem as his residence. Here, near the Savior's cradle, a community of monks soon arose under his surveillance, and a nunnery under the direction of the widow Paula. Jerome died at the ripe old age of nearly ninety years. To him we are grateful for introducing the Alleluia chant into the Sunday Mass, for sponsoring monastic life among the Roman patricians, and for the daily celebration of the Divine Office.[1]

Jerome is one of the four great Fathers of the western Church. His principal contribution to Christendom is his translation of Sacred Scripture, the mature fruit of painstaking studies. Known as the *Vulgate*, his work remains to this very day the official version of the Latin Church. As a scripturist he far excelled all his contemporaries. His many letters were highly prized far into the Middle Ages. Already during his lifetime Jerome was considered the greatest philologist of his day; he had mastered the Greek tongue and Greek literature even as his native Latin, and as an accomplished scholar of the Hebrew language he stands alone in ancient times. By temperament he was sanguine, controversial. To Pope Damasus he wrote the memorable words: "I seek my soul's food from that city in which I first put on the garment of Christ. . . . I, following no other leader but Christ, wish to remain ever in communion with Your Holiness, that is, obedient to the Chair of Peter. For I know the Church was built upon that rock. . . . Outside the Church there is no salvation. Anyone outside the house of the Lamb is unclean; anyone outside the Church cannot be holy" (Ep. 15, c. 2).

2. Mass and Divine Office. The Mass (*In medio*) is from the Common of Doctors, p. 419. Note how the *Collect* centers our thoughts on the "great expounder of holy Scripture"; yes, may his feast stimulate us to devote more time and attention to God's inspired words. *Nulla dies sine linea* — no day without Bible reading! It is an excellent custom of Mother Church, a custom dating from the earliest times, to read something from a saint's writings on his anniversary. Accordingly we find in the Divine Office a homily by St. Jerome on today's Gospel:

[1] Schuster, Bk. 8, p. 255.

"Apostles and teachers are called salt because by them the entire human race is seasoned. *But if salt loses its strength, how can it be restored?* If the teacher errs, by what means can he be corrected? *It (the salt) is no longer good for anything except to be thrown away and trodden upon by men.* The reference is to common practice. For salt has no other use than to serve as a condiment for food or its preservation. Yes, you may point to the scrolls which tell about certain cities having been sown over with salt by angry conquerors so as to prevent any seed to germinate. But that is beside the point. So let teachers and bishops beware and let them realize that those who are extraordinarily blessed will be extraordinarily punished; that if the leaders themselves go astray, no salvation at all is possible; that their ruin leads directly to hell.

"*You are the light of the world. A city situated upon a mountain cannot remain hid; nor does a man light a lamp to put it under a bushel, rather upon a stand so as to cast its beams upon all present in the house.* Jesus is inculcating trust and confidence in the work of preaching; for from motives of fear the apostles were not to go in hiding and thereby resemble a lighted lamp under the cover of a bushel. Rather, they were to show themselves courageously and proclaim on the housetops the truths they had heard in private."

October 1

ST. REMIGIUS, Bishop and Confessor

Enter into the joy of the Lord

1. **St. Remigius.** *Day of death*: January 13, 535. *Grave*: in the year 1049 Pope Leo IX placed his remains in the Benedictine abbey church at Rheims. *Life.* Born about the year 440 at Laon, Remigius was bishop at Rheims during the reign of Clovis, king of the Franks (c. 460–535). Through preaching and miracle-

working he converted the Franks to the Christian faith. Well known are the words Remigius is reported to have spoken when he baptized the king: "Humble yourself, Sicambrian. Adore that which you formerly burned, and burn that which you formerly adored" (496). On one occasion his prayer brought back to life a young girl. Of his literary work four authentic letters are still extant.

Accounts of his life contain much that is legendary. The *Martyrology* reads: "He wielded the bishop's crosier for an unusually great number of years before he departed from this life, highly esteemed for his holiness and for amazing miracles. The day of his death is January 13; today is the anniversary of the transfer of his remains to a specially constructed crypt in the church of St. Christopher." *Reflection.* A great missionary and shepherd of souls! St. Remigius is honored as the apostle of the Franks, the forefathers of the present French people. In every century the Church of France contributed significantly to the progress of religion and produced numerous illustrious saints. The Mass is from the Common of Confessors (*Statuit*), see p. 417.

Do not overlook the fact that the parable of the five talents has a distinct coloring now during the parousia weeks of the ecclesiastical year. We are to prepare ourselves for judgment, "Enter into the joy of the Lord, *Intra in gaudium Domini tui.*"

2. Symbolism of the Month of October. The month of October is popularly known as the "month of the holy Rosary" because the feast of the Most Holy Rosary occurs on October 7 and because Pope Leo XIII enjoined that the Rosary be prayed daily in all churches during this month. Since 1925, when Pius XI placed the feast of Christ the King on the last Sunday of October, it has become easy to associate the month with the kingship of Christ. We, however, prefer to consider these weeks as an organic unit of the ecclesiastical year. October forms the middle portion of the Church's Harvest Time. In nature, cold and darkness are triumphing over warmth and light; there may be days of fine autumn sunshine, but cold rains, storms and chilling winds have become common.

These changes in nature should be interpreted as symbolical of a new phase in the Church's life. The words of Christ are finding fulfillment: "I am not come to bring peace but the sword" (Matt. 10:34). The road of the Church in this world leads through thorns, spotted with blood. The nearer the Church approaches her final destiny, the greater will her sufferings and persecutions be. The Book of Revelation permits a passing glimpse at the tribulations of the last days. To encourage us Mother Church places in our hands the two Books of Machabees; here the liberation of the Jews from the domination of pagans is described. The Church has honored these books since most ancient times; in them she sees prefigured the martyrdom of her children. The Books of Machabees can teach us many lessons, as for instance, love of our holy faith; devotion to the Church, for which we must be willing to suffer and sacrifice; the place patriotism has in civil life, and how necessary it at times becomes. Give the book serious study during the coming days.

October 2

THE HOLY GUARDIAN ANGELS

He has given His angels charge over you
to keep you in all your ways

• **1. The Feast of Guardian Angels.** The Church lives in the realm of the supernatural and therefore has full confidence in those who dwell there, the angels. We need only recall the Ordinary of the Mass where we meet the angels again and again, proclaiming their presence (*Confiteor*), singing their hymns (*Gloria, Sanctus*), or admiring them as they perform their services to God and man (*Supplices te rogamus*). Today, however, the Church wishes to celebrate a particularly lovable revelation of divine Providence, viz., that God has ordained for each one of us a special angel guardian, who accompanies us through life from the cradle to the grave. True, the feast is not of ancient origin, but since its introduction it has become very popular. It appeared first in Spain during the sixteenth century; Paul V in 1608 permitted it *ad libitum* on the first ferial day after the feast of St. Michael; in 1670 it was extended to the universal Church and made obligatory. Evidently it has relations with the older angel feast, that in honor of the Archangel Michael, guardian of the universal Church (see September 29).

2. Holy Mass (Benedicite). In part the text of today's feast is borrowed from that in honor of St. Michael (Gospel and chants). The *Lesson* admonishes us to give ear to the voice of our guardian angel: "Behold, I will send My angel, who will go before you to guard you on your journey and bring you into the place I have prepared (the liturgy, of course, means heaven). Be mindful of him, obey his voice; do not regard him as one to be contemned." For comment on the remaining prayers, see September 29.

3. Divine Office. The psalms of Matins would seem to form a "Common of Angels." For such psalms are chosen as mention the angels (8, 10, 33, 102), or in which some reference is made to heaven (14, 18, 23). These reasons, however, are quite extrinsic; as prayer forms they are psalms of praise and trust; we should pray as members of the choir of angels and confident of their protection. The Lessons touch the heart. In the second nocturn it is St. Bernard, the "Mellifluous Doctor," who speaks:

"Be alert in your every action as one should be who is accompanied by angels *in all your ways,* for that mission has been enjoined upon them. In whatever lodging, in whatever nook or corner you may find yourself, cherish a reverence for your guardian angel. In his presence do not dare to do anything you would not do in mine. Or do you doubt his presence because you do not see him? Would it really help if you did hear him, or touch him, or smell him? Remember, there are realities whose existence has not been proven by mere sight.

"Brethren, we will love God's angels with a most affectionate love; for they will be our heavenly co-heirs some day, these spirits who now are sent by the Father to be our protectors and our guides. With such bodyguards, what are we to fear? They can neither be subdued nor deceived; nor is there any possibility at all that they should go astray who are to guard us in all our ways. They are trustworthy, they are intelligent, they are strong — why, then, do we tremble? We need only to follow them, remain close to them, and we will *dwell in the protection of the Most High God.* So as often as you sense the approach of any grave temptation or some crushing sorrow hangs over you, invoke your protector, your leader, your helper in every situation. Call out to him and say: Lord, save us, we are perishing."

4. **The Spirit World.** Upon a stone arch in the chapel of St. Gertrude at Klosterneuburg there was found a fresco from the Middle Ages showing the ladder of Jacob with angels ascending and descending. The theology implied in the scene deserves attention. In a very real sense there is a Jacob's ladder over every altar, and upon it angels ascend and descend, carrying heavenward our gifts and earthward God's graces. Christ Himself had this beautiful picture in mind when He said: "You will see the heavens opened and the angels of God ascending and descending upon the Son of man" (John 1:51). He was telling His disciples: Through My saving work the thru-way between heaven and earth has been opened, and angels are commuting upon it.

This brings us to a fundamental of which we liturgists should be more aware, i.e, there *is* a spirit world. It is a world teeming with beings both good and evil; and these beings are all about us. Holy Scripture gives abundant proof. It is time now to stir up our faith and with the eye of the spirit recognize the angels and devils present in our very midst. We are far too prone to consider them distant as heaven, unreal upon earth. They are *very* real. Angels and demons encircle us from the cradle to the grave; and about every person rages a spirit battle, like that between Lucifer and Michael.

In a special way the parish church is peopled with good angels. At Mass they surround the sanctuary with a spirit rampart (*Off.*, 14. Sunday after Pentecost) and form another Jacob's ladder to God on high. This is shown in the five passages of the

Ordinary which mention angels. When at the steps of the altar we prepare ourselves for the holy Sacrifice through repentance, Michael stands before us as plaintiff and intercessor (*Confiteor*). He is our captain in the battle against hell. How often have we been cowards! The *Gloria* is an "angels' song," and our minds and hearts, if not our voices, blend with the angels' on the plains of Bethlehem.

At the Offertory the "Archangel Michael stands at the right of the altar of incense" and in union with all the elect intercedes for us during the incensation. Here again is reflected the Biblical picture of angels carrying the prayers and good works of men before the throne of God. As the preface ends and the Canon begins, it is a scene of thousands of angels "adoring, praising, filled with reverent awe, aglow with a common joy." Humbly we enter their midst at the *Sanctus*. Every fiber of our being should thrill over the fact that at the consecration the King of heaven comes to the altar accompanied by a countless host. From the angels we may learn a great art, prayer.

When the Canon has reached its climax we are reminded how our sacrifice is carried "by the hand of God's holy angel upon the heavenly altar before the eyes of the divine majesty." And finally when Mass is over, the Church wishes that once more we turn to the Archangel Michael and implore him "to defend us in battle . . . against the wiles and wickedness of the devil." Cherish a lively faith in the spirit world so truly close about us.

October 3

ST. THERESE OF THE CHILD JESUS, Virgin

Become as little children

1. **St. Therese.** *Day of death*: September 30, 1897, at the age of twenty-four. *Grave*: at Lisieux, France. *Life*. Therese Martin, the Little Flower of the Child Jesus, has become one of Christen-

He who is mighty
has done great things for me
and holy is His Name ✚

dom's best loved saints. The Catholic world has been deeply impressed that she, a contemporary, has received the honors of the altar, crowned one of heaven's saints. Therese was born of saintly parents at Alencon, France, on January 2, 1873. At the age of nine her education began under the direction of the Benedictine nuns at Lisieux. At ten she recovered miraculously from a severe illness. When fifteen, she personally received from Pope Leo XIII the permission to enter the Carmelite convent at Lisieux.

"Therese had found in Sacred Scripture a catchy text: 'Whoever is truly a little one, he will come to Me' (Prov. 9:4). She therefore determined to become a little child in spirit and dedicated herself with childlike confidence to God as her most loving Father. Her *Way of Spiritual Childhood* she taught to others, especially to the novices; their education to a zealous practice of the Order's ideals, Therese had accepted in holy obedience. Filled with true apostolic zeal, she showed a world puffed up with pride and vanity the way of evangelical simplicity. Moreover, it caused her extreme pain that the love of God was so widely regarded as of little worth; accordingly, two years before her death she offered herself as a victim to the love of our merciful God.

"Shortly thereafter, according to her own narrative, she was wounded by a heavenly fire and died, consumed by divine charity. Enraptured with holy passion, her last sigh was: 'My God, I love You!' Thus at the age of twenty-four, on September 30, 1897, she hastened to her heavenly Bridegroom. At the point of death Therese, the Little Flower, promised that she would cause a continual shower of roses (heavenly blessings) to fall upon the earth. That promise she fulfilled after she had been taken into heaven, and by countless wonders she continues to fulfill it even to our very day" (see Second Nocturn).

2. Holy Mass (Veni). The Mass is composed of texts portraying the spirit of our little saint. At the very beginning we hear the Lord's invitation to His bride: "O come from Lebanon, you My bride! You have wounded My heart." The psalm invites all children to praise God: "Praise the Lord, ye children." The

Collect voices our petition for the childlike spirit of little Therese, "her humility and simplicity of heart." Truly beautiful is the *Lesson* from Isaias:

> Indeed, I will extend peace to her like a river,
>> like a flowing stream the glory of the nations.
> You shall drink thereof,
>> you shall be carried on the hip and dandled in her lap.
> As an infant fondled by its mother,
>> so will I fondle you;
>> yes, you shall be comforted in Jerusalem.
> When you see this, your heart will rejoice,
>> and your bones will flourish like an herb.
> And the hands of the Lord will be known towards
>> his servants.

The *Gospel* emphasizes the need of a childlike spirit: "Jesus called a little child, set it in the midst of them, and said: Amen, I say to you, if you do not change your way of living and become as little children, you will not enter the kingdom of heaven." We hear our saint sing the Magnificat at the *Offertory*: "He has regarded the humility of His handmaid." Notice how affectionately the *Communion* antiphon applies a verse from Deuteronomy: "He led her about and taught her, and He kept her as the apple of His eye. As the eagle enticing her young to fly and hovering over them, He spread His wings, took her and carried her on His shoulders." The singular warmth and tenderness of all these texts bring us close to the heart of the Little Flower.

3. A Child of God. The Collect, the Gospel, the saint's whole life story, all point to the one dominant trait of our beloved Therese — her effort to be childlike in God's sight. What this implies can more easily be described than defined. First, let us recall the spirit of Jesus. What infinite love and tenderness He manifested toward children. Whenever He met them, it was an occasion for joy. At times the disciples became annoyed and did not wish mothers with children to approach too closely. But Jesus rebuked them: "Allow the little children to come near

Me, do not forbid them. For of such consists the kingdom of God. Amen, I say to you, whoever does not approach the kingdom of God as a little child will not enter into it. Then He embraced them and laid His hands upon them, and He blessed them" (Mark 10:13–16). The two other Synoptics recount the same episode.

Our Gospel contains a double lesson: (a) Jesus' great love for children. This was a new virtue; neither in paganism nor in Judaism do we find proper esteem for the dignity of children; the whole Old Testament presents no parallel passage. (b) In the child, Jesus sees a creature of heaven; in the child He finds the required disposition for admission into the kingdom of God. This is clearly shown in the passage providing today's Gospel. The disciples were arguing about precedence in the kingdom; Jesus placed a little child in their midst and said: "Amen, I say to you, if you do not change your way of living and become as little children, you will not enter the kingdom of heaven. Therefore, anyone who humbles himself as this little child, he is the greater in the kingdom of heaven" (Matt. 18:1–5).

To become more definite, we may inquire what constitutes the point of comparison in the figure, the *tertium comparationis*. Bodily or mental immaturity and helplessness certainly are not meant, and therefore must be immediately excluded. It is a matter of virtue or of a *spiritual disposition*. Proper to children is a catalog of virtues that we need if we wish to be true Christians. Two of these virtues Christ singled out in the above passages, childlike, unreserved *faith* ("He who does not receive the kingdom of God as a little child") and *humility* ("Whoever will humble himself as this little child, he is the greater . . ."). A third virtue is indicated in today's Collect, simplicity of heart. The child makes no mental reservations, is not skeptical; his heart is wide open to receive the words of others. Further virtues may easily be detected by a little observation. Only yesterday at Matins St. Hilary spoke on the subject:

"Through childlike simplicity we must atone for that wherein we have failed in body and soul. A child obeys its father, loves its mother; it is not aware of how one might wish his neighbor evil, is not concerned about striving after material wealth. Children are not presumptuous; they do not hate, they do not lie. They give their trust at once and regard everything they hear as true. All of us should cherish and emulate such childlike simplicity. If we possess this virtue, we will have that humility which the Lord described."

Lastly, let us recall what St. John Chrysostom said on being a child of God (Matins: St. Joseph Calasanctius, August 27):

"The soul of a child is still untouched by passion; the child does not mull over injustices or injuries done it, but runs to those who treated it harshly as if they were friends, as if nothing at all had happened. Even after being severely punished by mother, the child will anxiously seek after her and prefer her to anyone else. You may show it a queen adorned in regal splendor and wearing every diadem, but the child will choose its mother wrapped in cheapest broadcloth — yes, it will rather look upon its mother in rags than upon a queen in embroidered purple. For it chooses between things close or distant, not by the appearance of poverty or wealth but by the reality of love. Nor does the child demand more than is needed, for as soon as it has enough milk, it no longer clings to mother's breasts. The child does not become a slave to human lusts, as for instance, the love of money. Unlike ourselves, it finds no happiness in transitory earthly pursuits nor does it marvel at the sight of physical beauty."

October 4

ST. FRANCIS OF ASSISI, Confessor

Poor and humble Francis enters heaven with full honors, greeted by celestial songs

1. **St. Francis.** *Day of death*: October 3, 1226. *Grave*: in his honor Pope Gregory IX built a magnificent church at Assisi; to it his body was transferred in 1230. Since for some centuries

there had been an effort to conceal the place of his burial, it became difficult to identify the exact spot until after arduous excavation the holy remains were found under the high altar in 1818. *Picture*: as a Friar Minor with a cross, often with the stigmata. *Life*. Today we honor a prince in the kingdom of heaven, Francis of Assisi, the seraphic saint. He was the inspiration and founder of the Friars Minor, the Poor Clares, and the Third Order Secular. He is known as the troubador of divine love, as the beggar who espoused Lady Poverty as his bride, as nature's great friend who spoke of the sun, moon, and stars as his brothers and sisters, and to whom birds flew unfrightened, and as the first ecstatic who bore the wounds of Christ in his body.

Among the countless saints of the Catholic Church, Francis is unique. He is one of the very few really great reformers, exerting a far-reaching influence upon the Middle Ages and the centuries following to our very day. Down through the years since he walked the fields of Umbria, our saint has been the inspiration of artists, poets, writers. He was the originator of a new type of piety. Due to his inspiration our Savior was again brought down from remote pedestals and loved in a human way as the Child of Bethlehem and as the Man of Sorrows who suffered unspeakable agony upon the Cross. He who was neither rich nor learned has drawn all to himself.

Francis was born at Assisi in 1182 and given the baptismal name Giovanni; out of affection for the French tongue, however, he preferred being called Francesco. As a young man he decided to be a merchant like his father and accorded customary attention to the frivolities of a worldly life until taken captive in Perugia in 1201, when he became more serious minded, more zealous in the practice of generosity and charity. As months passed his father became increasingly annoyed and finally disinherited him before the bishop. Thereupon Francis returned his wardrobe to his father, happy in the thought of now being able to call God alone his Father.

With twelve others of like mind he founded the Order of Friars Minor, after interpreting a recourse to Matthew 10:9 as a definitive divine call. A first refusal was followed by approbation for his institute from Innocent III in 1209. In a dream the Pope saw how a poor, barefooted man with a girdle about his loins propped up the tumbling Lateran palace with his shoulders. This dream symbolized the saint's work of spiritual renovation in the Church. Francis directed his brethren to go into the towns and crossroads of the world to preach the Gospel. Two years before his death he received the sacred stigmata of our Savior (see September 17). Seriously ill, he was carried to the church of St. Mary of the Angels at Assisi, the chapel where he originally received his vocation. While Psalm 141 was being prayed, he died on October 3, 1226. Pope Gregory IX canonized his holy friend in the year 1228, two years after his death.

2. **Holy Mass (Mihi autem absit).** The Mass prayers reflect the spirit of our illustrious saint. The inspiration and seal of his whole life was love of the Cross; therefore he walks before us at the *Introit* with the words: "God forbid that I should glory, except in the Cross of our Lord Jesus." We respond with the song sung at his death, Psalm 141 (it should be prayed in its entirety). The Mass is the *mysterium* of his death; during the holy Sacrifice we relive with him the words: "The just are waiting for me till You bring me home." In the *Epistle* Francis comes to the fore and preaches on the Cross; he bears the "marks of the Lord Jesus" in his body; neither are these marks absent from us if we carry the cross of life in a manner pleasing to God.

In a few beautiful words the *Alleluia* antiphon characterizes the "poor man" of Assisi. One of the loveliest passages in the New Testament serves as *Gospel*, a self-portrait by Jesus; it is also the portrait of Francis, who brought the human nature of Jesus so close to us (crib, Cross). Christ is thanking His heavenly Father for having revealed the kingdom to "little" Francis; and Francis has learned from Him how to be "meek and humble of heart." The fruit of today's holy Mass is love of the Cross, love of poverty, love of humility.

3. **Francis Celebrates Christmas.** "Following his pilgrimage to the Holy Land and his visit at Bethlehem, Francis had been engrossed by a special love of the Christmas mystery. He often

expressed it this way: 'If I knew the emperor, I would ask him to proclaim that on Christmas day everyone should throw out corn to the birds, especially to our sisters the larks, and that those who had beasts in the stable should give them specially good fodder, for love of the Child Jesus born in a manger. And on this day the rich should feast all the poor.'

"In the year 1223 Francis proposed to himself to celebrate Christmas in a way the world had never yet seen. In Greccio he had a friend and supporter, John Vellita, who had given him and his brethren a vale of trees and rocks near Greccio as a place to live. Francis now summoned this man to Fonte Colombo and said to him: 'I want to celebrate the holy night of Christmas together with you. Now listen how I would like to do it. In the woods by the monastery you will find a cave, and there I would like you to arrange a manger filled with hay. We should also have an ox and an ass, just as at Bethlehem. For once do I want to keep the coming of the Son of God upon earth real seriously and see with my own eyes how poor and weak He wished to be for our sake.'

"John Vellita carried out all of Francis' wishes; and toward midnight on Christmas eve the brethren at Fonte Colombo and all the people dwelling about came together to celebrate the feast. They carried lighted torches, and around the manger the brethren stood holding candles; it was light as day under the dark vaulting of the trees. Mass was said over the manger, which served as an altar, so that the divine Child under the forms of bread and wine should be present there as once He was bodily present in the stable of Bethlehem. Indeed, for a moment it actually seemed to John Vellita as though he saw a real child lying in the manger, like to one dead or sleeping. Then Brother Francis stepped forward and took It lovingly in his arms, and the Child awoke and smiled at Francis, and with His little hands stroked his bearded chin and his coarse gray habit . . . nor did this vision astonish Giovanni Vellita. For Jesus had been dead or at least asleep in many hearts, but Brother Francis by his words and his example had restored the divine Child to life or had awakened It from slumber.

"After the Gospel had been sung, Francis stepped forward, clothed in deacon's vestments. 'Breathing heavily, bent over by the weight of devotion, his soul flooded with ecstatic joy, God's holy one stood by the manger,' says Thomas of Celano. 'And his voice, strong and sweet, clear and resonant, challenged all to seek the highest good.'

"Brother Francis spoke about the Child Jesus. With words that dripped sweetness he told of the poor King who was born that night, He who truly was the Lord Jesus, in the city of David. And every time he would try to utter the Name Jesus, the ardor of his love overpowered him, and he called Him instead the Child of Bethlehem. The word *Bethlehem*, as he pronounced it, had the ring of a lamb bleating; and when he did say the Name of Jesus, he let his tongue glide over his lips as if to taste the sweetness the sacred word had left as it passed over them. It was very late when that holy vigil was over, but everyone returned home filled with joy.

"At a later date the place where the manger stood was dedicated to God as a church, and over the manger an altar was erected to the honor of our blessed Father Francis. Accordingly where once dumb animals ate hay out of a manger, men now receive the spotless Lamb, our Lord Jesus Christ, for the well-being of soul and body — the same One who in unspeakable love shed His Blood for the life of the world and who with the Father and the Holy Spirit in glory eternal and divine lives and reigns for ever and ever. Amen." (From *Der hl. Franz von Assisi* by Johannes Jörgensen).

October 5

ST. PLACID AND COMPANIONS, Martyrs

The blessing of obedience

1. **St. Placid and Companions.** *Life.* There had been a group of fourth-century Sicilian martyrs of whom one had the

name Placid. This Placid was erroneously identified with the disciple of St. Benedict; thus arose the legend that the monk Placid, his sister, and thirty monks suffered martyrdom in the port of Messina at the hands of pirates.

Today's saint, brought to St. Benedict by his father while yet a child, to be trained in monastic life, became the most illustrious member in the circle of Benedict's first followers. Alongside the awe-inspiring figure of the holy patriarch stands little Placid, and with the innocent simplicity of a child he does much to soften the austerity emanating from the patriarch of monks. Pope St. Gregory devotes several chapters to Placid in his second book of Dialogues. — The Mass is from the Common of Martyrs (*Sapientiam*), see p. 410.

2. **From the Life of the Saint.** "Once while blessed Benedict was in his room, one of his monks, the boy Placid, went down to get some water. In letting the bucket fill too rapidly, he lost his balance and was pulled into the lake, where the current quickly seized him and carried him about a stone's throw from the shore. Though inside the monastery at the time, the man of God was instantly aware of what had happened and called out to Maurus: 'Hurry, Brother Maurus! The boy who just went down for water has fallen into the lake, and the current is carrying him away.'

"What followed was remarkable indeed, and unheard of since the time of Peter the apostle! Maurus asked for the blessing and on receiving it hurried out to fulfill his abbot's command. He kept on running even over the water till he reached the place where Placid was drifting along helplessly. Pulling him up by the hair, Maurus rushed back to shore, still under the impression that he was on dry land. It was only when he set foot on the ground that he came to himself and looking back realized that he had been running on the surface of the water. Overcome with fear and amazement at a deed he would never have thought possible, he returned to his abbot and told him what had taken place.

"The holy man would not take any personal credit for the deed but attributed it to the obedience of his disciple. Maurus on the contrary claimed that it was due entirely to his abbot's command. He could not have been responsible for the miracle himself, he said, since he had not even known he was performing it. While they were carrying on this friendly contest of humility, the question was settled by the boy who had been rescued. 'When I was being drawn out of the water,' he told them, 'I saw the abbot's cloak over my head; he is the one I thought was bringing me to shore.'" (From *The Life and Miracles of St. Benedict* by Pope Gregory the Great, translated by Odo Zimmermann, O.S.B. and Benedict Avery, O.S.B.)

October 6

ST. BRUNO, Confessor

Solitude and silence

1. St. Bruno. *Day of death*: October 6, 1101. *Grave*: in the monastery of St. Stephen, La Torre, Calabria. *Life*. Bruno, born in Cologne about 1030, was the founder of a religious Order, the Carthusians; excepting St. Norbert, he is the only German having that honor. His contemporaries called him the light of the Church, the flower of the clergy, the glory of Germany and France. Early in life he was a canon at Cologne and Rheims. Persecution by the simoniacal archbishop of Rheims, Manasses, hastened his resolve to enter a life of solitude (1084). Legend puts it this way. A famous professor had died. While the Office of the Dead was being chanted at his funeral, he suddenly raised himself up from the coffin and said: "By the just judgment of God have I been accused, judged, damned." Thereupon Bruno renounced the world. He received from Hugo, bishop of Grenoble, a site called Chartreuse (from the color of the surrounding hills) as a place of residence.

The Order founded by Bruno is one of the strictest in the Church. Carthusians follow the Rule of St. Benedict, but accord it a most austere interpretation; there is perpetual silence and complete abstinence from flesh meat (only bread, legumes, and water are taken for nourishment). Bruno sought to revive the ancient eremitical way of life. His Order enjoys the distinction of never becoming unfaithful to the spirit of its founder, never needing a reform. Six years after initiating the foundation, Bruno was called to Rome by Pope Urban II as personal counselor. He complied with a heavy heart. However, when the Pope was forced to flee to Campania because of Emperor Henry IV, Bruno found a wilderness similar to that of Chartreuse at La Torre; there he made a second foundation, which blossomed into a flourishing community. Here in September, 1101, he became severely ill. Having called together his followers, Bruno made a public confession and died on October 6, 1101, at the age of seventy-one. The Mass is taken from the Common of Confessors (*Os justi*), see p. 421.

2. **Solitude and Silence.** St. Bruno founded an Order which practices unbroken silence, unbroken fasting, unbroken solitude. For us Christians living in the world such practices are not for imitation but for admiration and edification. Nevertheless, the daily observances of the Carthusians should now and then form part of a Christian's routine. No one is able to enjoy the goods of this world reasonably who has not learned the virtue of detachment. Temperance actually is a school for proper pleasure. No one is able to command wisely or prudently who has not learned to obey; no one is able to speak becomingly who has not learned how to remain silent; no one is able to take food and drink in proper measure who has not learned to fast; no one is able to be a perfect community man who refuses to practice solitude occasionally.

Solitude and silence mother noble thoughts, salutary resolves, and meaningful deeds. The great saints have become great not in the turmoil of the world but apart from it. Major discoveries of profane science, major works of art and poetry are born in solitude — how much more that which is of importance and worth in the kingdom of God.

For proof consider the example of our Lord Jesus. In the quiet stillness of night He was born; till the age of thirty, His was a hidden life. Forty days of silence, solitude, and self-denial mark the beginning of His public ministry. Frequently He would leave the noisy crowds and withdraw with His disciples to be alone with His Father, to pray. Christ did not will to follow the example of His forerunner, practicing severe penances, living as a hermit; in fact, He described the contrast in their lives in a memorable sentence: "John came neither eating nor drinking — the Son of Man came eating and drinking" (Matt. 11:18f.). Jesus taught an ordered use of the goods of this world. He also taught that an orderly use can be attained only through occasional self-denial and mortification.

Read what the *Imitation of Christ* has to say concerning love of solitude and silence (Bk. I, ch. 20). "Seek a convenient time to attend to thyself and reflect often upon the benefits of God to thee. Let curiosities alone. Read such matters as may produce compunction rather than give occupation. If thou wilt withdraw from superfluous talking, and idle visitings, and from hearing new things and rumors, thou wilt find time sufficient and proper to spend in good meditations. The greatest saints shunned the company of men when they could, and chose rather to live unto God in secret. As often as I have been amongst men, said one, I have returned less a man.

"This we too often experience when we talk long. It is easier to keep silence altogether than not to fall into excess in speaking. It is easier to keep retired at home than to be enough upon one's guard abroad. He, therefore, who aims at inward and spiritual things must, with Jesus, turn aside from the crowd. No man can safely appear in public but he who loves seclusion. No man can safely speak but he who loves silence. No man can safely be a superior but he who hath learned how to obey well. No man can rejoice securely but he who hath the testimony of a good conscience within. Yet even the security of the saints was always full of the fear of God. Neither were they the less careful and humble in themselves, because they shone with great virtues and grace. But the security of the wicked ariseth from their pride and presumption, and in the end turns to their own deception.

"Never promise thyself security in this life, however good a religious or devout a solitary thou mayest seem to be. Oftentimes the highest in men's estimation have been in the greater danger, by reason of their too much confidence. And hence it is more useful for many not to be wholly without temptations, but to be very often assaulted, lest they be too secure, lest perhaps they be lifted up unto pride, and even turn aside, with too little restraint, after exterior consolations. Oh, how good a conscience would he keep who should never seek transitory joys, and never busy himself about the world! Oh, how great peace and tranquility would he have who should cut off all vain solicitude, and think only of the things of God and his salvation, and place his whole hope in God!

"No one is worthy of heavenly consolation who hath not diligently exercised himself in holy compunction. If thou wouldst feel compunction to thy very heart, enter into thy chamber and shut out the tumult of the world; as it is written: "Be sorry in your beds." Thou wilt find in thy cell what thou wilt too often lose abroad. The cell continually dwelt in, groweth sweet; but ill guarded, it begetteth weariness. If, in the beginning of thy religious life, thou dwell in it and keep it well, it will be to thee afterwards as a dear friend and most delightful solace. In silence and quiet the devout soul maketh progress and learneth the hidden things of Scripture. There she findeth floods of tears, wherein each night she may wash and be cleansed, and so become the more familiar with her Creator, the further she dwelleth from all the tumult of the world. For whoso withdraweth himself from acquaintances and friends, to him will God, with His holy angels, draw near.

"Better is it to lie hid and take diligent care of thyself, than, neglecting thyself, to work miracles. It is praiseworthy for a religious but seldom to go abroad, to shun being seen, and to have no wish to see men. Why dost thou wish to see what it is not lawful for thee to have? The world passeth away and its concupiscence. The longings of sense draw thee to roam abroad; but when the hour hath passed away, what dost thou bring back with thee but a weight upon thy conscience, and a dissipated heart? Oftentimes a joyous going abroad begetteth a sorrowful return home; and a merry evening maketh a sorrowful morning. So all carnal joys enter pleasantly; but at the end bring remorse and death.

"What canst thou see elsewhere that thou dost not see here? Behold the heavens, and the earth, and all the elements; for out of these are all things made. What canst thou see anywhere that can last long under the sun? Thou trusted that perchance thou wilt be satisfied; but thou wilt never be able to reach it. If thou couldst see all things at once before thee, what would it be but an empty vision? Lift up thine eyes to God on high, and pray for thy sins and negligences. Leave vain things to vain people; look thou to those things which God hath commanded thee. Shut thy door upon thee, and call unto thee Jesus thy beloved. Stay with Him in thy cell; for nowhere else shalt thou find so great peace. If thou hadst never left it, nor hearkened to any rumors, thou wouldst have remained longer in happy peace. But the moment thou delightest to give ear to novelty, thou must suffer from thence disquietude of heart."

October 7

FEAST OF THE MOST HOLY ROSARY

Let us imitate what they contain so as to obtain what they promise

1. **The Feast of the Most Holy Rosary.** This feast was instituted to honor the Blessed Virgin in gratitude for the protection she tenders the Church in answer to the recitation of the Rosary. It was introduced to commemorate the miraculous victory of the Christian forces at Lepanto on October 7, 1571, and other triumphs over the Turks. Pope Leo XIII gave the feast its present rank (1887) and Office (1888). A distinction must be made between today's feast of the Rosary and the Rosary as a prayer.

As prayer it follows a method which evolved out of medieval devotion to Mary. Legend tells how this prayer was introduced by St. Dominic, to whom the Mother of God entrusted it as aid and protection in the conflicts with the Albigensians. The Dominican Pope Pius V did much to further the spread of Rosary devotion, and thereafter it became one of the most popular devotions in Christendom. Although enriched with countless indulgences, it never attained liturgical status; at times the holy Rosary is called the "layman's breviary."

2. Holy Mass (Gaudeamus). The changeable parts of the Mass honor Mary's high dignity (*Intr.*) and inculcate the use of the Rosary as meditative prayer. A beautifully phrased *Collect* brings home to us the purpose of praying the Rosary as we ask that "meditating upon these mysteries of the most holy Rosary we may imitate what they contain and obtain what they promise." In the *Lesson* Mary appears as "wisdom" which stood before God from all eternity; whoever listens to her will become perfect. The immortal annunciation story has been chosen as the *Gospel* because the *Ave* forms the principal part of the Rosary. The mystic soul will quickly detect subtle allusions to "*rose*-ary" in the *Communion* antiphon: "Bloom, ye flowers, as the lily, produce perfumes in stately verdure. Join us in singing canticles, blessing the Lord in all His works."

3. The Rosary and the Liturgy. It is sometimes said that those who promote the liturgical apostolate look askance at the Rosary. Is this really the case? First we will note some fundamental distinctions. (a) The Divine Office and the Mass form part of the liturgy, i.e., the Church worshiping God. The Rosary is private, popular prayer which has been approved and prescribed by the Church. By nature liturgical prayer ranks higher and must be esteemed more highly than private prayer. The one is basically distinct from the other. But it does not follow that the Rosary is therefore frowned upon or considered of little worth by intelligent and sensible liturgists.

b) The practice of saying the Rosary during holy Mass can hardly be harmonized with the ideal of active participation by the faithful in Christ's Sacrifice; in fact, praying the Rosary

during Mass tends to offset such participation. Mass is sacrifice
and action, praying the Rosary is meditative prayer. We do not
deny that the Rosary can be a good preparation and a fitting
conclusion to the Mass, for its purpose is to make present "the
life, death, and resurrection" of the Lord even as the Mass does.
So much for fundamentals.

But we may go further and see other, positive relationships
between the liturgy and the Rosary. Actually, the Rosary had its
origin in the liturgical mentality of former ages. Even at the
present time it is called "Mary's Psalter." There still are Catholics
who consider the 150 Hail Marys a substitute for the 150 psalms
for those persons who neither have the time, the education, nor
the opportunity to pray the Hours of the Divine Office. Thus
"Mary's Psalter" is a shortened, simplified "breviary" — alongside the common Hour-prayer of the Church.

In details, too, there is a rapport between liturgical worship
and the Rosary. The Creed comes at the beginning of the Rosary
and at the end of the Mass of the Catechumens; the Our Father
occurs at important points in the Office, even as at the beginning
of the various decades; and the Hail Mary is not absent from
liturgical services. Every psalm ends with a doxology glorifying
the triune God; every decade of the Rosary comes to a solemn
close with "Glory be. . . ." The fifteen mysteries which form
the soul of the Rosary cast in noble relief the whole life of Jesus
and Mary; they rest directly upon the Gospel, the Bible, and
orthodox tradition; only in the Biblical account itself can a more
detailed picture be found. Sometimes, toc, a Scriptural passage
is read before each decade to aid and nourish meditation — all
in the spirit of the liturgy.

At this point we could consider the Rosary as a method of
prayer, and here too there would be relations with the liturgy.
For while praying the Rosary a person does not think separately
upon each Hail Mary or upon isolated words; rather one's
thoughts and affections are directed to some major theme while
his lips repeat the form. Attention is not centered upon the
form, any more than one who recites the psalms centers attention upon each verse. While praying the psalms we are fre-

quently concerned with the principal ideas, and sometimes greater thought is given to the antiphon than to the psalm itself. Thus he who prays the Rosary is no stranger to the method of liturgical prayer; rather, he often has the same spiritual approach. But the liturgical offices are much richer, more varied, more beautiful, more profound.

Accordingly the Rosary may easily lead to liturgical prayer, and then continue on hand in hand with it. A layman well educated in the liturgical spirit will join the Church in one or the other Hour of Office, especially on Sundays or feasts. He will add a reading from the Bible, from the Fathers, or the lives of the saints. On days when this is not possible, particularly in times of sickness, the Rosary will remain his faithful companion. "Mary's Psalter" and the day Hours are friendly companion: "Mary's Psalter" and the Day Hours are friendly com- There is but one grand prayer-choir; for while thousands pray the Rosary, other thousands are chanting the Divine Office. The voices of those who pray and those who chant must resound together harmoniously before heaven's throne.

Benedictus antiphon: This day let us devoutly celebrate the solmenity of the most holy Rosary of Mary the Mother of God, so that she may intercede for us with the Lord Jesus Christ.

4. Saints of the Day. St. Mark, pope and confessor, ruled from the See of Peter only eight months, February to October 7, 336, at the time of Emperor Constantine. The Church was then just beginning to flourish after the persecutions. Pope St. Mark built two churches, one at the cemetery of Balbina, the other where his remains were later interred. In spite of his short reign he procured for himself a lasting remembrance through holiness of life. His feast is numbered among the oldest in honor of non-martyr saints.

Sts. Sergius and Bacchus. The story of these holy martyrs has been highly colored by legend. It is said that they belonged to the Roman nobility and were put to death for their faith under Emperor Maximian. Bacchus was scourged with rough cords until his whole body was pitiably torn; invoking the Name of Christ, he surrendered his soul to God. Sergius suffered by being forced to wear shoes into which nails had been driven; as he would not renounce his faith, he was condemned to be beheaded. The place of his burial was named Sergiopolis. Because of the many miracles that occurred there, it became a popular place of pilgrimage.

October 8

ST. BRIDGET, Widow

Heavenly mysteries were revealed to Saint Bridget

1. St. Bridget. *Day of death*: July 23, 1373 (October 8 commemorates the day of her canonization in 1391). *Grave*: she died in Rome; her body was transferred to Wadstena, Sweden. *Life*. St. Bridget, patroness of Sweden and one of the great mystics of the Middle Ages, was born about the year 1303 at Upsala, Sweden. While still in the womb, she saved her royal mother from shipwreck at sea. A sermon on the sufferings of Christ made a lasting impression on her as a ten-year-old child; the following night she was privileged with a vision of the crucified Savior, who invited her to meditate constantly on His bitter passion.

Later she married a nobleman and did eminently well in the difficult art of rearing children; for her daughter Katherine also received the honors of the altar. In 1344 her husband entered the Cistercian Order, where he soon died. Thereafter she was favored with extraordinary revelations. Following the wishes of our Savior, she founded a religious Order. She used her influence with Pope Urban V to encourage him to leave Avignon and return to Rome; but after a three-year residence at Rome, he left again for Avignon. In other respects, too, Bridget strove zealously for the reform of bishops and members of diocesan curias, of priests and monks.

2. Holy Women and the Church's Harvest Time. Today's Mass, *Cognovi*, is from the Common of Holy Women, see p. 428. Let us try to isolate the ideas peculiar to the Church's Harvest Time in this formulary. We notice at once that it is the spirit of widowhood that the Church is now advocating. The widow no longer is attached to things earthly, she expects nothing more from the world, her care and longing is for the Lord: "The true widow, one who is all alone in this world, places her trust in God and passes her nights and days in prayer and supplication. But one who surrenders to the lusts of the world is a living corpse" (*Epist.*). Paul's words aptly describe the Church as such, for toward the world she shows a widow's attitude by longing constantly after her heavenly Spouse.

The Introit gives another expression to the same theology in words that voice the spirit proper to the current season: "I know, Lord, that Your decisions are just; You have good reasons for humbling me. Pierce my flesh with holy fear; indeed do I dread Your judgments." The Christian who is deeply rooted in things eternal receives the visitations of God with resignation; he knows that suffering and poverty are excellent means to tear one loose from the world. Salutary fear of God is the greatest protection from sin. A similar Introit will be found on the twentieth Sunday after Pentecost. A special Collect ends with a positive formulation of the parousia theme: "At the revelation of Your eternal glory may we rejoice and be glad."

In today's Gospel we accord attention to a parable that is often overlooked, the Parable of the Net. The explanation is given by Christ Himself: "So will it be at the end of the world. The angels will go and separate the wicked from the just, and will cast them into the furnace of fire, where there will be weeping and gnashing of teeth." This is the dark side of the Lord's Second Advent. We ought apply the parable to ourselves. The net with the fish is our workaday world with all our deeds; these deeds will be put to the test at death; some will be worthless for heaven and some will occasion reward. Frequently activities that appear laudable to the world are "bad fish" not worth the weighing; often the unnoticed and unpretentious deeds are the "good fish" gathered in vessels for heaven. With the parousia in mind, let us imitate St. Bridget in her zeal for "every good work."

October 9

ST. JOHN LEONARDI, Priest

A true reformer

1. **St. John Leonardi.** *Day of death*: October 9, 1609, at Rome. *Grave*: in the church of S. Maria in Campitelli, Rome; beatified in 1861, canonized in 1938. *Life.* Today we honor one of the more recent names added to the calendar of feasts in the Roman liturgy (1941). John Leonardi was born in 1543 at Decimi (near Lucca, Italy). As a boy he was unusually devout and charitable; at the age of twenty-six he felt the call to the clerical state and did not hesitate to study Latin in a class with youths years younger. He progressed swiftly, was ordained within four years (1571). With extraordinary zeal he then gave himself to the care of souls in hospitals and prisons, and by catechizing, preaching, and hearing confessions.

In 1583 he founded a community of priests known as the Clerks Regular of the Mother of God, who devoted themselves zealously to pastoral work. St. Philip Neri did much to further the institute. From Rome as its center St. John directed the activity of his community. From the Sovereign Pontiff of Christendom he received various important missions touching reform in the Church and in religious Orders. Of course, opposition was not lacking, attempts to nullify his work and his ideals. St. Philip Neri lauded John as "a true reformer." Another area of efforts centered in the establishment of an institute for educating and aiding foreign missionaries; because of this he is called the originator of the *College de Propaganda Fide*. Our saint died on October 9, 1609, from sickness contracted while caring for the plague-stricken. A proper Collect takes notes of his zeal for mission work and his establishment of the Clerks Regular.

2. **Holy Mass (In sermonibus Domini).** There are many texts proper to this Mass and their purpose is to bring to mind the life and work of our saint. The *Introit*, however, surprises us because it seemingly makes no allusion to the day's saint; it is simply a statement of nature's praise of God: "By God's word

were all His works created. The sun's brilliance makes all things resplendent, while all His works are filled with the glory of the Lord."

Today's *Epistle*, an excerpt from Second Corinthians, occurs no place else in the missal; our saint is describing his own conduct as he speaks of the self-sacrifice and zeal that should characterize a priest; in particular he will preach the word of God to those who open the eyes of their hearts to divine grace "to see the light of the Gospel of the glory of Christ . . . for God who in the beginning of creation said: Let there light, has also enkindled in our hearts a light to enable us to behold His majesty." However, because God is invisible, Christ appeared upon earth as a man, and accordingly we see "the glory of God in the face of Christ Jesus." Now to proclaim the glorious dignity of man's supernatural status the heralds of the Gospel — St. John Leonardi, for instance — will spare no pains. His life and troubles prove the truth of the words: "Therefore we do not lose heart even though our outer man is decaying." It does not worry him, for "the things that are seen are temporal, while the things that are not seen are eternal . . . and our inner man is being renewed day by day." As Jesus commissions His disciples to go forth in the *Gospel*, our saint is among them; his soul too was filled with a burning zeal for souls, his heart knew the meaning of Jesus' words: "The harvest is great, the laborers few. Petition the Lord of the harvest to send laborers into the ripened fields."

The various chants provide an insight into the spirit of St. John Leonardi. *Zeal for souls*: "My heart is aflame, all within me is atremble, because zeal for Your house (the Church) is consuming me." For this reason "God makes my tongue a sharp sword." But he also tells about his sufferings: "To many I seemed a dreadful monster, but, Lord, You were my strong support."

As we proceed to associate ourselves more intimately with the sacrifice of Christ in the *Offertory*, St. John Leonardi leads the way, convinced that his vocation was from God: "I am become Christ's servant through the divine mission entrusted to me, to proclaim the word of God in all its plenitude" (Col. 1:25). It is a reminder that the Offertory provides a splendid occasion for us to bring to the altar our mission in life. The *Secret* voices the mission plea "that there be offered the clean oblation everywhere on earth." Upon finding the pearl of great price, the holy Eucharist, we say with St. Paul, "Whatever had seemed advantageous to me, I now count as trash, in the light of Christ" (*Comm.*). The fruit of the sacred Meal should be "to profess the faith that he held and to practice the virtues he taught" (*Postc.*).

3. St. Dionysius and Companions. Since the introduction of the feast of St. John Leonardi, the older feast of St. Dionysius and companions has been reduced to a simple commemoration. It is a happy change, particularly because of the historical uncertainties touching the latter. Three distinct persons come into consideration under the one name Dionysius. First there is Dionysius the Areopagite who was converted by St. Paul in Athens. Hence the Epistle was taken from Paul's speech in Athens: "Certain men followed Paul and believed; among these there was Dionysius the Areopagite." According to the *Martyrology* this same Dionysius became the first bishop of Athens. Quite another individual was the martyr-bishop of Paris during the third century; legend tells how he walked two miles carrying his head after his decapitation. In the course of time these two saints were identified, and to the first were ascribed four celebrated treatises on mystical theology written by a third party, a neo-Platonist of the fifth century in Syria. These treatises rank among the most significant from Christian antiquity. Since the seventh century, Rusticus and Eleutherius have been associated with "Dionysius." Dionysius the Areopagite is a very popular saint in the Orient.

4. The Writings of Pseudo-Dionysius. As already mentioned, important treatises have come down to us attributed to Dionysius the Areopagite, but actually written by an unknown author about the year 500. Among these, that entitled *Concerning the Ecclesiastical Hierarchy* is a particularly important one for the history of the liturgy. We find there a detailed description of the ceremonies of baptism, the sacrifice of Mass, the consecration of the holy oils; we read about the three degrees of the priest-hood (deacon, priest, bishop), and their power and efficacy. The work ends with a description of funeral ceremonies — the body of one in holy Orders is carried before the altar, the body of a monk or lay person before priests.

Then begin the prayers and thanksgivings. "The spiritual hierarch approaches, pronounces a prayer over the one sleeping, and after the prayer kisses him; all present do likewise in order. The prayer begs divine Goodness to forgive the sleeping one all that he sinned out of human weakness and to allot him a place in light, in the land of the living, in the bosom of Abraham, Isaac, and Jacob, in the place from which pain, suffering, and sorrow have fled. After the kiss of peace the hierarch pours oil on the body . . . the oil signifies that the deceased was victorious in the holy battle." After the anointing the body is interred in an appropriate place.

October 10

ST. FRANCIS BORGIA, Confessor

Lord Jesus Christ, You are the model and the reward of true humility

1. St. Francis Borgia. *Day of death*: September 30, 1572; canonized 1671; feast celebrated since 1688. *Grave*: at first in Rome; since 1617 in the house of the Jesuits in Madrid (it was almost entirely destroyed when the church burned in 1931). *Life.* Francis Borgia, viscount of Catalonia and third general of the Jesuits, was born in 1510. On his father's side he was a great-grandchild of Pope Alexander VI; on his mother's side he was the great-grandchild of a son of Ferdinand the Catholic. His holy life atoned for the sins of his ancestors.

As viscount and duke at the palace of Emperor Charles V, Francis stood in high honor. The sudden death of the beautiful

Empress Isabella (May 1, 1539) and the sight of her disfigured face as her body was taken to Granada made him resolve to leave the world and serve the King of kings alone. After the death of his wife (1546), he entered the Society of Jesus with the holy resolve of leading a hidden life and of closing the door forever to all earthly honors. His example of humility exercized an influence upon Charles V when he considered renouncing the throne. Devoted to labor and severe mortification, Francis held himself in such little esteem that he called himself the "poor sinner." In 1565 he became General of the Order. He died at Rome. — The Mass is from the Common of Abbots (*Os Justi*), see p. 421.

   2. Humility. Profound humility, the principal virtue of our saint, should be the object of our prayer and practice today. The Collect points to "Jesus Christ, the model and reward of true humility." Humility consists in acknowledging one's own helplessness, yet can readily be found in one conscious of a great vocation. *Nothing due to me — all from God!* Therefore our blessed Mother in one and the same breath could say: "He has regarded the humility of His handmaid: from henceforth all generations will call me blessed." Therefore Paul could say: "I am as one born out of due time, not worthy to be called an apostle"; but he also added, "I have labored more abundantly than all the other apostles. "

   Humility is not just another Christian virtue, it is fundamental. The citizens of God's kingdom *must* be humble; pride and arrogance belong to Satan and his colleagues. The primeval sin among men as well as among the angels was that of pride. I will not serve, cried Lucifer. You will be like gods, knowing good and evil, the serpent told Eve. The way to redemption, therefore, must be along the lowly path of humility. St. Paul could find no words more beautiful to describe Christ's saving work than these: "Cherish the same spirit that Christ Jesus did; although He possessed a divine nature, He would not cling to equality with God, but emptied Himself and took on the nature of a servant, becoming like other men. Further, after assuming human form, He humbled Himself still more and became obedient unto death, even unto death on a cross" (Phil. 2:5ff.). The life of Christ, from Bethlehem to Golgotha, was one extended act of humility. Of old the prophets had heralded Him as the "Servant of Yahweh"; repeatedly He affirmed that He was doing the will of His Father, that the will of God was "His meat."

Indeed, Christ is the great model of true humility, and He confided His spirit as an heirloom to His Bride, the Church. The pearl of humility may well be regarded as a "mark" of the true Church, a sign of genuine holiness. The saints, all of them, wend their way through this world clad in the garment of humility. The Collect reminds us of another noteworthy point; Christ is Himself the "*reward* of true humility." If we follow our Savior humbly bearing our cross, we will receive as reward the Lord Himself — now in grace, hereafter in glory. Christ enters only the humble soul; only a humble person can be a member of His Body. But in the next life the lowly member will be exalted with Christ, will rule with Christ, will receive Christ Himself as the crown of victory.

October 11

THE MOTHERHOOD OF MARY

A memorial to the Council of Ephesus

This feast, one of the more recent in Mary's honor, was introduced into the calendar of the universal Church by order of Pope Pius XI.

1. **Occasion.** The sixth Lesson at Matins gives the following as background for today's feast:

In the year 1931 a jubilee marking the fifteenth centenary of the Council of Ephesus was celebrated to the great joy of the whole Catholic world. The fathers at that Council, under the guidance of Pope Celestine, formally condemned the errors of Nestorius and declared as Catholic faith the doctrine that the Blessed Virgin Mary, who gave birth to Jesus, was truly the

Mother of God. Prompted by holy zeal, Pope Pius XI determined that the memory of so important an event continue alive in the Church. Accordingly he ordered the renovation of Rome's famous memorial to the Council of Ephesus, namely, the triumphal arch and transept in the Basilica of St. Mary Major on the Esquiline. His predecessor Pope St. Sixtus III (432–440) had embellished that arch with a beautiful mosaic, but time had done it damage.

In an encyclical Pius XI, moreover, underscored the principal teachings of the General Council at Ephesus, developing in detail and with loving affection the singular privilege of divine Motherhood granted to the Blessed Virgin Mary. For so sublime a mystery should ever become more firmly anchored in the hearts of the faithful. At the same time the Pope singled out Mary, the Mother of God and the one blessed among women together with the holy Family of Nazareth as the foremost model for the dignity and sanctity of chaste married life and for the religious education of youth. Lastly, in order that this event should likewise have its liturgical memorial, the Pope decreed that a feast in honor of the divine Motherhood of the Blessed Virgin Mary with a proper Mass and Office rated as a double of the second class be celebrated annually throughout the Church on October 11.

2. **Holy Mass (Ecce Virgo).** The changeable parts of the formulary refer to Mary's Motherhood. The first two chants (*Intr.* and *Grad.*) are from the Old Testament, while the chants of the Mass of the Faithful are from the New. It is the voice of Isaias we hear at the *Introit*: "Behold, a virgin will conceive and bear a son." The Christmas-psalm (97) is then chanted: "Sing to the Lord a new canticle because He has performed wonders." The wonder today is Christ's virginal birth. The *Collect*, from the Rorate Mass, expresses our faith in Mary as *Theotokos*: "We believe that she is truly the Mother of God."

The *Lesson* contains some of the most beautiful Old Testament texts which the liturgy applies to Mary. The Messianic prophecy in the *Gradual* tells who this "fruit" is: "A blossom will come forth from Jesse's root," the Son of God. Mary, the "mother of fair love," is inviting us: "Come to me, all who desire me, and fill yourselves on my fruits." The *Alleluia* antiphon praises the "Mother of God." Perhaps we had expected the annunciation account as Gospel; instead we hear the story of the loss of the Boy Jesus, an incident that gives a touching insight into Mary's motherly heart; moreover, we hear Jesus acknowledge God as His Father for the first time: "Did you not know that I must be about My Father's business?" The *Offertory* antiphon recalls one of Mary's greatest sorrows, Joseph's doubt. We share the happiness of Mary while singing the lovely *Communion* antiphon: "Blessed is the womb of the virgin Mary that bore the Son of the eternal Father." The Mass is not a new composition; it had been given in the appendix of the missal.

3. A Monument to the Council of Ephesus. How deeply the decision of the Council of Ephesus affected the people of the time may be seen in the basilica of St. Mary Major in Rome. The edifice dates to the fourth century but was renovated by Pope Sixtus III (432–440) and dedicated to Mary. It may well be regarded as a memorial to the Council of Ephesus, especially the arch before the apse adorned with a glorious mosaic by order of Pope Sixtus III. At the time of the centenary of the Council in 1931, Pius XI ordered the restoration of this mosaic and explicitly called it a "monument to the Council." A few observations on this masterpiece of mosaic art will be in place.

It is the only extant mosaic from the time of Pope Sixtus III. Its eleven scenes present excellent historical corroboration of the decrees of the Council. In the main, the scenes are from the childhood of the Savior, selected to proclaim two truths of our holy faith, the divinity of Christ and the divine Motherhood of Mary. The themes are taken from the Gospels (and one from the apocryphal gospel of Matthew). In the center of the arch is a throne (*hetoimasia*) with all the insignia of Christ's kingship (a truth solemnly proclaimed at Ephesus). About the throne are the four symbols of the evangelists and symbols proper to the two princes of the apostles. Below is the inscription: "Xystus, Bishop of God's People." The pictures on either side are arranged panel-wise in four rows. The lowest shows the traditional representation of the Church, sheep leaving Jerusalem (Jews) and Bethlehem (Gentiles). On the eight scenes from the childhood of Jesus which form the remaining portion of the mosaic, Wilpert gives the following comment:

"The series begins by picturing the moment when the Logos assumed flesh in the womb of Mary. Joseph, to whom Mary was allotted after the miraculous flowering of his rod, was the first to take offense at the supernatural conception of his bride till an angel clarified the matter. At the presentation the divinity of the Child was acknowledged not only by Simeon and the prophetess Anna but by the head of the temple, too, according to the artist; therefore there could be no more excuse for the Jews who because of their blindness would not accept Christ. The Gentiles likewise have every reason to abandon their idols and attach themselves to Christ. For the Wise Men, pagans from the east, read the birth of the Son of God in the stars and came to do homage to the Child. Even an Egyptian ruler with his advisers and friends accepted Christ after they had seen how 365 idols fell upon their faces before the Child and His Virgin Mother."

Three scenes show Mary clothed in regal garments, indicative of her divine Motherhood, *Theotokos*. Perhaps the reader will want further information regarding the apocryphal picture. In Pseudo-Matthew we read:

"The holy family arrived in the city 'Sotin,' and having no acquaintances with whom they could lodge, they entered a temple in which 365 idols were placed for adoration. Hardly had Mary and the Child passed through its portals when all the idols fell to earth on their faces and broke into pieces. When this news reached Aphrodosius, the prince of Sotin, he and his whole court hastened to the temple. Seeing the fallen idols with his own eyes, he approached Mary and adored the Child she was carrying at her breast. He then briefly addressed his friends and followers, pointing out to them the divinity of the Child and advising conversion. As a result the inhabitants of the city professed faith in Christ." Thus the mosaic is a hymn to the divinity of Christ and the divine Motherhood of Mary.

October 12

FERIAL DAY

Martyrs in the Books of Machabees. *The Aged Eleazar.* In times when faith and morals are put to the test, there have been and always will be those who waver and fall; but there are others, too, who remain firm and constant, courageous heroes of the faith. These are the men of strength, and they obtained that charism by prayer to God, the fountain of strength. It will help us immeasurably if we meditate on the heroic example they bequeathed to us. The faith of Mathathias will strengthen our faith as we read his last testament to his five sons:

"Give your lives for the covenant of your fathers! Call to remembrance the works of the fathers, the deeds they accomplished in their generations. Then you will receive great glory and an everlasting name . . . Joseph in the time of his distress kept the commandment, and he was made lord of Egypt . . . Ananias and Azarias and Misael by believing were saved from the flames. Daniel in his innocency was delivered out of the mouth of the lions . . . therefore, my sons, take courage!" (1 Mach. 2:49f.). Many others besides the sons of Mathathias remained courageous, and their strength spelled victory for the people.

Eleazar is to be numbered among the most valiant. His exemplary life and death encouraged many to faithful observance and perseverance. Eleazar was ninety years old, a revered doctor of the Law, when his persecutors endeavored to make him deny the religion of his fathers. But he remained steadfast. Cleverly and calculatingly the enemies of Yahweh proceeded. As a sign of apostasy they did not demand an abjuration of faith nor words of blasphemy. They did not require a sacrifice to Jupiter or to some other god in the pagan pantheon; they only insisted upon a violation of the Mosaic abstinence law (2 Mach. 6:18f.). Now according to God's plan of salvation, the Israelites, as bearers of revealed religion, were to live in the midst of Gentile nations and be separate. To be clean or unclean, i.e., to be qualified or not for participation in liturgical worship, was an absolute requirement to prevent the people from being absorbed by surrounding, externally more aggressive and powerful nations. To these safeguards belonged the law forbidding the consumption of unclean flesh (among which swine-flesh was listed).

Had Eleazar yielded to the opposition, even apparently, the scandal would have been truly grave, because he was a recognized doctor of the Law. The door would have been opened for general apostasy. Every imaginable means was used to make him falter. His mouth was torn open and a piece of the forbidden flesh forced in; the old man spat it out. The persecutors became furious; a rack was brought to tear his limbs apart. And a glorious future was promised him if he would only concede to their wishes. Eleazar, however, remained steadfast. Then his own friends suggested a compromise. "Taking him aside they desired that flesh be brought which was lawful for him to eat; then he might act as if he had eaten as the king had commanded of the flesh of the sacrifice, and by so doing be delivered from death."

Surely there have been occasions in our life when the aged man's reply ought to have been ours: "It doth not become our age to dissemble, whereby many young persons might think that Eleazar at the age of four score and ten years was gone over to the life of the heathens; and so they through my dissimulation, and for a little time of a corruptible life, should be deceived, and hereby should bring a stain and a curse upon my old age. For though, for the present time, I should be delivered from the punishment of men, yet should I not escape the hand of the Almighty, neither alive nor dead. Wherefore by departing manfully out of this life, I shall show myself worthy of my old age; and I shall leave an example of fortitude to young men, if with a ready mind and constancy I suffer an honorable death for the most venerable and most holy laws" (6:24–28).

Particularly those in authority must keep these words in mind. Dignities bring duties in their train. There is need for other Eleazars today, heroic characters who will profess their faith in the face of opposition. In case of necessity we too must be ready to surrender ourselves into the hangman's hands. "When he was now ready to die because of the flogging, he groaned and said: Lord, in Your holy knowledge You know that I might have escaped death instead of suffering these dreadful pains in my body; but in my soul I am well content to suffer these things because I fear You" (2 Mach. 6:30). Sacred Scripture accords him the finest epitaph: "Thus did this man die, leaving not only to young men but to the whole nation the memory of his death as an example of virtue and fortitude."

May the spirit of Eleazar inspire us! For woe to him who gives scandal. Blessed is he who confesses Christ before men and suffers persecution because of Him!

October 13

ST. EDWARD, King and Confessor

Blessed are the pure of heart, for they shall see God

1. **St. Edward.** *Day of death*: January 5, 1066; canonized 1161 (the present day commemorates the transfer of his remains in 1163). *Grave*: in Westminster Abbey, London. *Life*. Edward, the last king of the Anglo-Saxons, a grandson of the martyr-king Edward, passed his youth in exile with his uncle, the Norman leader. In an environment of sin he preserved innocence of life. Called to the throne of England in 1042, he sought to put into practice the Christian ideals for a ruler, with the help of God's grace. His first efforts were directed toward a renewal of religion in the hearts of his people. Priests were invited into his kingdom, churches were built. Yielding to pressure, he married, but is said to have retained virginity during his whole married life.

His favorite saint was St. John the Evangelist; he would not deny any request asked in his name. One day the Beloved Disciple appeared to him in the form of a beggar and asked alms in the name of the fourth evangelist; as Edward had no ready money, he gave up the ring on his finger. Shortly thereafter St. John returned the ring with the message that his death was near. The king ordered public prayers to be said for himself and died in the Lord on the day foretold, January 5, 1066. The Mass is from the Common of Confessors (*Os justi*), see p. 421.

2. Reflections upon the Feast. (a) How highly this holy king esteemed purity and innocence! His favorite saint was the virgin-disciple of the Lord. He maintained his virginity although married. His body remained wholly incorrupt. Persons who are pure live a heavenly life upon earth.

b) Note the special concern the liturgy has for kingship. In ancient times kings were regarded as sharers in God's sovereignty. Ancient Christian art represents kings with the nimbus of saints. For example, Justinian and Theodora are pictured with nimbi in the church of St. Vitale in Ravenna; even Herod is accorded this honor in the mosaic of Sixtus III in St. Mary Major, Rome.

October 14

ST. CALLISTUS, Pope and Martyr

Show concern for the dead

1. St. Callistus. *Day of death*: September 28, 222 (today commemorates his burial). *Grave*: in the basilica of *S. Maria in Trastevere*, whither his body was taken from the cemetery on the Via Aurelia; he rests under the high altar. *Life.* Callistus I succeeded Pope Zephyrin (see August 26) and ruled from 217 to 222. Born as a slave, he spent his youth amid great hardship; due to Jewish intrigue he was forced to do compulsory labor in the mines of Sicily.

After obtaining his freedom he became archdeacon to Pope Zephyrin and superintendent of the great cemetery which later bore his name. Finally he was made bishop of Rome, in which office he was obliged to contend with many errors and much opposition. (His opponent was Hippolytus, anti-pope, philosopher, martyr!) The mild treatment Callistus accorded those who had fallen into grievous sins occasioned severe attacks by his enemies. It is said that he introduced the Ember days and the decoration of churches. On the Via Appia he enlarged an ancient cemetery in which many holy priests and martyrs had been buried; therefore it was named after him. He died as a martyr, probably during a tumult; his body was cast into a well which is still pointed out to pilgrims.

Application. Today we honor a martyr-pope whose name is linked with the ancient Christian burial grounds, the catacombs. Respect for the bodies of the deceased is a Christian virtue. What is our conduct at a funeral? Do we visit cemeteries, care for the graves, remember the dead? — Mass from the Common of Sovereign Pontiffs (*Si diligis Me*) see p. 398.

2. **The Catacombs.** When we hear the word *catacombs* (the word *cemetery* would be better), a feeling of holy awe comes upon us and our thoughts go back to the age of heroes in the youthful Church. In particular we think of the martyrs whose bones rest or rested in those honorable burial places. We also think of the subterranean divine services that took place there in the time of persecution, even though this did not happen frequently because room for a goodly number of worshippers was lacking. Nevertheless, it is certain that the liturgy was at times celebrated in the catacombs during the first centuries.

Very significant is the ancient Christian art found there, art that loudly proclaims the liturgical spirit of the ancient Church. Practically all the pictures fall into one of two categories; either they represent the cult life of Christians, e.g., baptism and Eucharist, or they express early Christian belief in a future life and in the final resurrection. The piety of the ancient Church is well summarized by these two concepts, the life of grace and the life of glory; in brief, "life" was the sum and substance of their faith.

Baptism was the primary source of this life; to preserve the grace of baptism and to augment it was their constant care. Into a Christian's life there flows another stream of grace, the Eucharist. Baptism and Eucharist still form the substance of the Church's cult life. All Lent is a time of baptismal renewal, all Eastertide centers about baptismal consciousness, every Sunday points to baptism and its implications. The Eucharist promotes and nourishes that which baptism bestowed in germ. How powerfully the art in the catacombs preaches hope and yearning for heaven! We see there how longing for the parousia was a driving force in early Christianity, that it spurred Christians on to forsake the world, to suffer martyrdom, to lead a holy life. Between earth and heaven ancient Christian piety had built a bridge with three arches: baptism, Eucharist, parousia.

Years ago Abbot Ildephonse Herwegen made the following observation on catacomb art: "The matter for early Christian pictorial representations is for the most part limited to a small canon of Old and New Testament topics. Their principal purpose was not to illustrate holy Scripture or simply to give a picture of Biblical accounts. Rather, they sought to visualize present actuality, i.e., to unleash the full meaning inherent in Biblical types.

"An example. Pictures of Moses striking the rock from which water begins to flow occur frequently. We recall the event during the Exodus journey when Moses struck the rock in the wilderness and gave the people who were dying from thirst refreshing water. But in the catacombs this episode proclaims our liberation from death, our resurrection to a new life. Moreover, the same picture will also remind us of baptism, for the waters flow from the rock, Christ. As miraculous nourishment the picture points to the Eucharist. The rod of Moses symbolizes the Cross of Christ. Although the whole ensemble bespeaks the Christian interpretation of the Old Testament event, nevertheless it often happens that the name Peter is inscribed close to the figure of Moses, making the application absolutely certain.

"This one example of early Christian art teaches us that the artists of the time saw close relationships between the Bible, the mysteries of Christianity, and the cult life of the Christian com-

munity. They derived their inspiration from the community at
prayer, i.e., from the common service of God, the liturgy"
(Herwegen: *Vom christlichen Sein und Leben*, p. 188).

October 15

ST. TERESA, Virgin

Lord, either to suffer or to die!

1. **St. Teresa.** *Day of death*: October 4, 1582 (because the
calendar reform became effective the following day, her feast
was placed on October 15); canonized 1622. *Grave*: in the
Carmelite church at Alba, Spain. *Life*. St. Teresa of Jesus, honored by the Church as the "seraphic virgin," *virgo seraphica*, and
reformer of the Carmelite Order, ranks first among women for
wisdom and learning. She is called *doctrix mystica*, doctor of
mystical theology; in a report to Pope Paul V the Roman Rota
declared: "Teresa has been given to the Church by God as a
teacher of the spiritual life. The mysteries of the inner mystical
life which the holy Fathers propounded unsystematically and
without orderly sequence, she has presented with unparalleled
clarity." Her writings are still the classic works on mysticism,
and from her all later teachers have drawn, e.g., Francis of Sales,
Alphonsus Liguori. Characteristic of her mysticism is the sub-
jective-individualistic approach; there is little integration with
the liturgy and social piety, and thus she reflects the spirit of the
sixteenth and following centuries.

Teresa was born at Avila, Spain, in the year 1515. At the age of
seven she set out for Africa to die for Christ, but was brought
back by her uncle. When she lost her mother at twelve, she
implored Mary for her maternal protection. In 1533 she entered
the Carmelite Order; for eighteen years she suffered physical
pain and spiritual dryness. Under divine inspiration and with
the approval of Pope Pius IV, she began the work of reforming

the Carmelite Order. In spite of heavy opposition and constant difficulties, she founded thirty-two reformed convents.

Truly wonderful were the exterior and interior manifestations of her mystical union with God, especially during the last decade of her life. These graces reached a climax when her heart was transfixed (*transverberatio cordis*), an event that is commemorated in the Carmelite Order by a special feast on August 27. She practiced great devotion to the foster-father of Jesus, whose cult was greatly furthered throughout the Church through her efforts. When dying she often repeated the words: "Lord, I am a daughter of the Church!" Her holy body rests upon the high altar of the Carmelite church in Alba, Spain; her heart with its mysterious wound is reserved in a precious reliquary on the Epistle side of the altar.

St. Teresa composed the following well-known lines:

> Let nothing affright thee,
> Nothing dismay thee.
> All is passing,
> God ever remains.
> Patience obtains all.
> Whoever possesses God
> Cannot lack anything —
> God alone suffices.

The Mass (*Dilexisti*) is from the Common, see p. 425. A proper *Collect* implores that we might "be nourished on the food of her heavenly doctrine," the only instance in which the liturgy proposes a woman as a teacher. Among women mystics Teresa is the greatest. Bossuet says: "In matters mystical Teresa holds an unique position, even as Thomas Aquinas does in matters theological."

2. The Parable of the Wise Virgins in Autumn Time. Let us meditate more deeply upon this parable. To understand a parable one must have a clear notion of (a) the story, and (b) its spiritual message. *The story*. According to ancient Oriental custom, wedding celebrations were rather elaborate affairs. During the day games were played by the groom and his friends. Toward evening or sometime during the night he would go and conduct his bride from the house of her parents. At the bride's home there would be a group of maidens, friends of the bride, who were waiting and who would accompany the pair in festive procession to the house of the groom. If the bridegroom delayed his coming to the early hours of morning, it could happen that the maidens-in-waiting would become drowsy. Only at his appearance would they ready themselves and form the wedding train.

In the Gospel story some of the maidens had a supply of extra oil in little jugs in order to refill the lamps, if such became necessary; the others had no reserve, thinking that the oil in the lamps would suffice. Because the bridegroom came later than expected and all the oil had burned away, these thoughtless girls would have to go and procure further stock (some details in any parable could easily be fictitious — no shops, for instance, were open for business at midnight). Meanwhile, however, the wedding procession had formed and had come to the house of the bridegroom. The doors were shut and no one further was welcome at that hour. Such is the story of the parable, an account that blends custom and imagination in a manner that may seem strange to us Westerners.

The *spiritual message* of any parable hinges upon the point of comparison, the *tertium comparationis*; here it is the *sudden* and *unexpected arrival* of the bridegroom. With this in mind we are able to make further personal associations and applications. We are the bride's maidens; the bridegroom is Christ; the bride, the Church. Our task is to await the Bridegroom with lighted lamps. And since the Bridegroom will arrive at an undetermined moment, we must always have oil on hand. One of the Fathers associates this oil with grace, the love of God, the service of God. We must persevere in being living Christians at all times. The Bridegroom will come suddenly, unexpectedly, i.e., Christ's coming at one's death. If at His advent He does not find the oil of grace, such a one will be excluded from the heavenly nuptials. Our Lord Himself pointed out the true lesson of the parable:

Watch, for you do not know the day or the hour. The lesson is identical with the theme proper to the Church's Harvest Time, viz., preparation for the Lord's Second Advent. Cherish a bridal relationship to Christ. As chaste virgins full of love and longing, we should pass the night of life, having our lamps constantly aglow with divine love and grace, wearing our wedding garments unstained (see 19th Sunday after Pentecost). Our one concern should be to keep our lamps filled with oil, i.e., to persevere unto the very end. Then when the Bridegroom comes He will conduct us straightway into the heavenly nuptials.

October 16

ST. HEDWIG, Widow

Leave the attractions of this world to embrace the Cross

1. **St. Hedwig.** *Day of death:* October 15, 1243; canonized 1267; feast celebrated since 1706. *Grave:* in the monastery at Trebnitz, Silesia. *Life.* Hedwig, an aunt of St. Elizabeth of Thuringia, was born about the year 1174. The three states of life possible to a woman — virginity, wifehood, widowhood — have her as model. After bearing six children and educating them in piety, she persuaded her husband to make a vow of continency (1208); after his death she took the veil and lived a life of strictest mortification. It was her joy to put herself at the service of all and to perform the most menial tasks, serving the poor on her knees, washing the bodies of lepers, cleansing and kissing their wounds.

A fine instance of her spiritual courage occurred at the death of her son Henry II in the war against the Tartars; her gratitude to the Lord rose superior to her sorrow as she prayed: "It is the will of God and acceptable to us that He has taken him. I thank you, Lord, that you gave me such a son; in life he always loved me, showed me great honor and respect, and never provoked my least displeasure. Although I would love to see him living, this thought gives me great joy, that through shedding his blood for You, O Creator, he is already united with You in heaven." The Mass (*Cognovi*) is from the Common of Holy Women, see p. 428.

2. "Surmount all obstacles by embracing the Cross." Because of its many fine thoughts today's Collect merits our special attention. First of all, it points out that St. Hedwig was taught by Christ to renounce the attractions of the world and humbly to embrace the Cross. Her life story shows how in a heroic way she detached herself from human comforts, property, social status, family joys, even that which is most difficult, her own will. She appears greatest in her act of offering her own son. Many pious Christians accept misfortune simply as something inevitable. True Christian piety, however, regards misfortune as the will of God, even though it is humanly unintelligible why God should want it so.

The Collect implores grace to "trample upon all passing pleasures and to surmount all obstacles by embracing the Cross" (a common picture of the saint shows her clasping a crucifix). The first petition is easy to make but difficult to practice. *Trample upon all passing pleasures*: perhaps we could meet the ideal with a lesser objective — by humbly enduring the restrictions and disappointments which circumstances bring upon us. The second plea presents a still higher challenge: *surmount all obstacles by embracing the Cross*. Here we have genuine Pauline theology. "With Christ I am nailed to the Cross . . . I bear the marks of Christ in my body." Pain and suffering become understandable and meaningful in the perspective of the Cross, or better, in the *embrace* of the Cross. Then does it become a part of Christ's great oblation and we contribute in supplying what is lacking to the Body of Christ (Col. 1:24). We may look upon the Collect as a rewording of Christ's words: "Whoever wishes to be My disciple must mortify himself, must take up his cross and follow Me" (Mark 8:34).

October 17

ST. MARGARET MARY ALACOQUE, Virgin

May we find in Your heart an eternal dwelling-place

1. St. Margaret. *Day of death*: October 17, 1690. *Grave*: at
Paray-le-Monial, in the convent of the Visitation. *Life*. Margaret,
the fifth of seven children, was born on July 22, 1647, at Janots
in Burgundy. After some years of trials and uncertainty, she
entered the Visitation convent at Paray-le-Monial in 1671, a community noted for its zeal and strict observance. God had gifted
her not so much with a strong body for the regular labor as with
exceptional gifts of grace, which for a long time stirred up mis-
givings in her superiors. She is of importance to the universal
Church in that through her, devotion to the Sacred Heart was
greatly furthered, a devotion that finally issued in the institution
of a major feast honoring the Sacred Heart. Three great revelations were granted to our quiet and humble virgin; by these
divine communications the import of Sacred Heart devotion
was revealed together with its rewards as listed in the "Great
Promises." Of special significance was the vision on June 16,
1675, the occasion on which our Lord requested the institution
of the feast of the Sacred Heart. Pope Benedict XV added her
name to the canon of the saints in 1920; Pius XI made the Office
and Mass universal in 1929.

Devotion to the Sacred Heart of Jesus has its source in the
boundless love which the God-Man bears in His heart toward
mankind and which He manifested so wondrously in His passion and in the holy Eucharist. The humanity of Christ, His
love and His sufferings, are the subjects given prominence in
the Hours of the Divine Office.

2. Holy Mass (Sub umbra). Appropriate texts well suited to
express St. Margaret's bridal love toward her Lord make up the
formulary for today's Mass. The chants in particular have the
ring of loving intimacy with Christ. *Introit*: united mystically
with Margaret, the Christian soul feels itself in the house of
God as under the shade of a divine tree (i.e., Christ) and asks

for its sweet fruit (Eucharist); for the psalm a finer choice could
not have been made: "How lovely are Thy tabernacles."

In the *Collect* we ask for the grace of loving Christ "in all
things and above all things, and to find in Your Heart an eternal
dwelling-place." A boundless supernatural charity is the fruit of
devotion to the Sacred Heart. Our humble little saint, using the
words of St. Paul, is still trying "to announce to the nations the
unfathomable riches of Christ" (*Epist.*), i.e., to spread devotion
to the Sacred Heart. Now in heaven she "bends the knee" as
she intercedes for us "that Christ may live in our hearts, and
that we might be rooted and grounded in love, and that we
might understand the love of Christ, which surpasses all understanding." Between the Epistle and Gospel our hearts dwell
upon three of the most beautiful Old Testament passages on the
love of Christ; two are from the Canticle of Canticles and voice
bridal love, a third is from the psalter (Ps. 72:26).

The *Gospel* brings to our attention one of the most touching
prayers uttered by Christ, a passage that surely deserves our
loving consideration today. Jesus is thanking His Father for
revealing the mysteries of God to little ones, to Margaret, to us.
He then sketches a self-portrait, a true "Sacred Heart picture."
He states the source of His divine mission, "All things have
been entrusted to Me by My Father," then His oneness of nature
with the Godhead, "No one knows (i.e., has unity of nature
with) the Son but the Father." Now He turns to us poor men:
"Come to Me all you who labor and are heavily burdened, and
I will refresh you. Take up My yoke (i.e., the cross, the commandments) upon you and learn of Me, because I am meek
and humble of heart; and you will find rest for your souls. For
My yoke is sweet and My burden light."

As the sacrificial Banquet begins, the Church chants a passage
from the prophets which had not been used previously in the
liturgy; our most precious good is "the Bread of the elect and
the Wine that produces virgins." The *Secret*: "May the divine
fire bursting forth from the heart of Jesus inflame us" through
our sharing in this holy Sacrifice. An apt choice, too, is the
Communion antiphon because it voices the holy sentiments be-

tween Christ and the Christian soul in the heavenly Banquet; moreover, the condition for such intimacy is added in poetic terms: "the soul must *feed among the lilies*." The fruit of the Sacrifice is that we truly "put on the meekness and humility of the divine Heart," as counseled in the Gospel. It is, indeed, an excellently arranged formulary, each part deftly placed to constitute one organic whole.

3. The homily at Matins today is taken from the writings of St. Francis of Sales; it seldom happens that so recent a saint (seventeenth century) is granted this privilege. St. Francis founded the Order of the Visitation to which St. Margaret belonged.

"No other wisdom exists except that which has its source in the Holy Spirit. His wisdom, however, is granted exclusively to the humble. Have you not known some great theologians who could speak brilliantly on the virtues but practiced none themselves? On the other hand, there are women who cannot construct a correct sentence on the subject, but they understand full well how to perform them. Such persons the Holy Spirit fills with wisdom, for they possess the fear of God; they are pious as well as humble. Our Lord, the great and highly esteemed Physician of all human ills, made public through His prophets before He came into this world His program of action: *that which is broken I will bind up, that which is weak I will make strong.* Then, on one occasion, He added: *Come to Me all you who are sorrowing and are heavily burdened; I will refresh you.*

"Are we then amazed to see Him surrounded by the sick, by sinners, and by tax-gatherers? Does not a physician's glory consist exactly in that the ill look for him? Jesus carries our burdens, yes, He ennobles them; upon His own heart He places our troubles, for, see, His side is wide open. We must return again and love such a person, for He shows us His wounds now in love — but someday it may be in wrath and retribution. Good Jesus, grant that we may receive the peace that You are extending to us; that we may look upon Your wounds; and as long as there is faith, hope and charity, may we await Your Advent filled with joyous hope and love. At Your Coming may we behold You as the Lamb on the right and not as the Lion on the left. Then instead of believing we will see with our own eyes; instead of hoping we will be in possession; and in the place of our imperfect love we will be able to love in a never-ending embrace of bliss. Amen."

October 18

ST. LUKE, Evangelist

The Gospel of mercy and love

1. St. Luke. St. Luke is dear to us because of his two books, the Third Gospel and the Acts of the Apostles. The Acts of the Apostles in particular is dear to liturgists because it portrays so well the spirit of the ancient Church which gave birth to the liturgy. Luke was a companion and co-laborer of Paul, and Paul's spirit too is reflected in his writings. By birth a Gentile, by vocation a physician from Antioch (Col. 4:14), Luke embraced the faith at some unrecorded occasion. We first meet him as disciple and fellow-traveler of St. Paul during the Apostle's second missionary journey. The so-called we-sections of the Acts (16:10–17; 20:5–15; 21:1–18; 27:1–28:16) prove that he accompanied the great Apostle until his first imprisonment in Rome. The Acts of the Apostles may well have been written during that two-year period.

Luke remained unmarried and is said to have reached the ripe old age of eighty-four; he died as a martyr at Patara in Achaia and was buried at Thebes in Boetia. In the year 357 his remains, together with those of the apostle Andrew, were transferred to Constantinople at the bidding of Emperor Constantine. Various cities, such as Venice and Padua, claim to possess his relics.

2. Holy Mass (Mihi autem). The chants are identical with those in the Common of Apostles, since evangelists enjoy the status of apostles. We honor Luke as a friend of God and prince of God's kingdom (*Intr., Off.*). The *Epistle* is taken from Second Corinthians because of a seeming allusion to Luke: "We have sent also with Titus the brother who is famous in all the churches because of his work in behalf of the gospel" (that Luke is actually meant by "the brother" cannot be proven; nor can the word "gospel" be in any way understood as a reference to the third written Gospel). According to the admonition given in the Epistle, "think on that which may be good not only before God but also before men."

While praying the *Gradual* we see Luke going forth "into all the world," proclaiming the word of God. Christ chose our evangelist "from out the world" (*Allel.*) and made him a sower of the faith in order "to bear fruit, fruit that should remain." The *Gospel*, describing the mission of the seventy-two disciples, places Luke in the ranks of the messengers of the faith; by his Gospel he indeed will remain a preacher unto all ages. The *Communion* antiphon exalts our evangelist to a heavenly throne; in this exaltation we share through the Mass-mystery, for such is its peculiar fruit today.

3. Scripture Reading (Ez. 1:1-12). This passage, chosen with purpose, describes the vision granted to Ezechiel at his call to the prophetical office. Ezechiel saw four cherubim, each having four faces, "there was the face of a man and the face of a lion and the face of an ox and the face of an eagle." To the Oriental mind these faces symbolized the most important features or faculties with which creatures are endowed. Man possesses intelligence; the lion stands for fearsome majesty; the ox, might and strength; the eagle, speed and superiority over matter. Above these cherubim Yahweh sat enthroned. Yahweh accordingly possesses all these attributes and *in an eminent degree.*

Since most ancient times spiritual writers have linked the four faces to the four evangelists. Luke is represented by the ox. An explanation for the various symbols, once given by a bishop to catechumens on Wednesday after the fourth Sunday of Lent, goes in part as follows: "The evangelist Luke is symbolized by an ox. The sacrifice of oxen prefigured the sacrifice of our Redeemer on the Cross. Luke begins his Gospel with the account concerning Zacharias and Elizabeth, who when well advanced in years became the parents of St. John the Baptist. Luke is associated with an ox because he combines so perfectly the two horns (the two Testaments) and the four hoofs (the four Gospels)."

4. St. Luke's Gospel. The Gospel of St. Luke may have originated in the following manner. Because the apostle Paul did not know the Savior personally and because he conversed very little with the Chosen Twelve or with the disciples who had followed Christ, he charged Luke, certainly the best educated among his followers, to write the life and deeds of Jesus. Luke gathered all the extant records; he did not confine himself to the two Gospels already written, Matthew and Mark, but drew from other sources, both written and oral; for eye-witnesses of the acts of Jesus were still living. Undoubtedly he consulted the apostles, especially John; assuredly also Mary. Thus he became qualified to author a precious volume, one which someone has praised as the "most lovable book ever written."

In St. Luke's Gospel our Savior is pictured as the merciful Physician of bodily and spiritual ills. It has, therefore, been called "the Gospel of mercy and love." The beautiful passages of God's loving-kindness touch us deeply, for example, the parables of the prodigal son and the good Samaritan, the account of the penitent woman, and the good thief on the cross. Of inestimable value are the first two chapters on the incarnation and childhood of Jesus. Here Luke preserved for us the three precious canticles that we pray daily in the Divine Office, the *Benedictus*, the *Magnificat*, and the *Nunc Dimittis*. In these two chapters Luke describes our Blessed Mother so vividly that a legend arose, making him an artist who painted a picture of the Virgin (the painting itself could then easily appear). Certainly this detail lacks historical justification; but the Gospel does provide excellent insights into Mary's soul.

Every promoter of the liturgical movement should read the Sacred Scriptures willingly, diligently; especially should he cherish a reverent love toward the Gospels, since these bring to us not only the word and deeds of Christ, but in the liturgy the Gospel makes Christ present, at the Gospel Christ Himself appears and speaks.

October 19

ST. PETER OF ALCANTARA, Confessor

O happy penances which won for me such blessedness

1. **St. Peter.** *Day of death*: October 18, 1562; canonized 1669. *Grave*: in the monastery of Viciosa at Pedrosa, Portugal. *Life*. Peter, surnamed Alcantara after the town of his birth, was eminent among the saints of the sixteenth century for an extraordinary spirit of penance and for attaining the heights of contemplation (*Coll.*). Born in 1499, at the age of sixteen he entered the Order of Friars Minor. He was an apostle of spiritual reform in his own community and aided St. Teresa in her reform of the Carmelites. God revealed to her that no one would remain unheard who begged in the name of Peter; thereafter she was most eager to have his prayers and honored him as a saint while he was still alive. With great humility Peter shunned all favors from eminent personages, even though they esteemed him as the mouthpiece of God or asked his counsel; for instance, he declined the request to act as confessor to Charles V. The fervor of love toward God and neighbor which smoldered in his breast at times forced him to leave his tiny cell and seek cooler air outside. Although she was at quite a distance at the time of his death, St. Teresa saw his soul entering heaven. Later he appeared to her and said: "O happy penances which won for me such blessedness!" Peter was a great mystic.

Application. Penances, i.e., mortification of one's lower nature, together with intimate union with God are two virtues which must stand out prominently in the life of one who really is a liturgist. For such was the example given by the greatest liturgist, Christ, and by all the saints who followed Him.

2. **Holy Mass (Justus).** Apart from the Collect and the Epistle, which are proper, the Mass is from the Common of Confessors (see p. 423). The *Collect* places before us an an ideal the "admirable penances and lofty contemplation" of St. Peter Alcantara, while his spirit is singularly well described in the *Epistle*, taken from Paul's letter to the Philippians (one of the finest pas-

sages in the Apostle's writings): "Whatever was to my advantage, that I regarded as a disadvantage for the sake of Christ . . . for Him I suffered the loss of all things and I reckoned them but as dung to be certain of gaining Christ . . . so that I might know Him and the power of His resurrection."

Only one who had died perfectly to the world could speak such words, one wholly poor in spirit. Only one for whom Christ has become all things, in whom self has been crucified and Christ alone is sovereign will think in such a manner. For in this consists highest mysticism, when with Christ the earthly man has been put to death. Peter Alcantara attained the heights. For him honors, the favors of the mighty, earthly amusements were "dung." Therefore he received countless mystical graces and attained a perfect union with Christ while still on earth.

October 20

ST. JOHN CANTIUS, Confessor

I was an eye to the blind, a foot to the lame, a father to the poor

1. **St. John.** *Day of death*: December 24, 1473; canonized 1767; feast introduced 1770. *Grave*: at Cracow, in the church of St. Anne. *Life*. John Cantius was born in the year 1397 in the Polish town of Kenty (whence his surname). He became a professor of theology, then parish priest; soon, however, he returned to the professor's chair at the University of Cracow. On foot he visited the holy places of Rome and Palestine. One day, after robbers had deprived him of all his effects, they asked him whether he had anything more. The saint said no, but hardly had they gone when he remembered having sewn some gold pieces inside his clothing; immediately he followed and overtook them. The robbers, astonished at the man's sense of truthfulness, refused to accept the money and returned to him the stolen luggage.

To guard himself and his household from evil gossip he wrote upon the wall of his room (after the example of St. Augustine): *Conturbare cave, non est placare suave, diffamare cave, nam revocare grave*, i.e. "Guard against causing trouble and slandering others, for it is difficult to right the evil done." His love of neighbor was most edifying. Often he gave away his own clothing and shoes; then, not to appear barefoot, he lowered his cassock so as to have it drag along the ground. Sensing that his death was near at hand, he distributed whatever he still had to the poor and died peacefully in the Lord at an advanced age. He is honored as one of the principal patrons of Poland.

2. Holy Mass (Miseratio hominis). The Mass, which is proper, belongs to that peculiar modern type which, departing from classical forms, emphasizes the saint's life and virtues. Today's formulary concentrates on St. John's loving-kindness — *misericordia* is the key word. From the Introit to the Communion there is repeated reference to merciful love on the part of God and man. The *Epistle*, from the letter of St. James, teaches that faith is worthwhile only when linked to love of neighbor. A most appropriate text is chanted as we proceed with our gifts for the poor to the *Offertory* table: "I was an eye to the blind, a foot to the lame, a father to the poor" (Job). And at *Communion*, while we receive the most excellent Gift imaginable, we are reminded to give ourselves first to our fellow man; then will it be given to us richly in return. The *Gospel* is the lovely parable of the watchful servant. The special fruit of today's Sacrifice is grace to act kindly toward our neighbor, according to the heroic example of St. John Cantius.

3. Meditation. The feast occasions a number of lesser reflections. (a) Saintly professors are not abundant, for mere knowledge of sacred things by no means implies holiness. On the contrary, only the "wisdom of the saints" is sanctity. Every teacher, however, should be a *doctor vitae*, a "teacher of divine life." Virtue and holiness of life make the words of a teacher really effective. (b) The episode of the robbers shows that our saint was an "extremist" for truth. We are tempted to smile upon hearing the story. Surely in similar circumstances we would not be duty bound to act as he did. But we are bound to act and live the truth at all times in accord with Christian prudence. Much, accordingly, needs reform. What is my attitude toward half-truths, exaggerations, pretences, "diplomacy"? (c) The verses cited above from St. Augustine could well hang on many walls. A little reflection will show that most of our conversation centers around absent brethren. We are so apt to be harsh in criticizing others and so indignant when someone criticizes us. (d) The principal virtue of today's saint is loving-kindness. Let us list some of the beautiful passages from the Mass describing this virtue. They are precious gems:

"Lovingly does He teach and correct, for He is the shepherd of His flock" (*Intr.*).

"Mercy boasts in the face of judgment" (*Epist.*).

"He opens his hands to the needy and stretches out his arms to the poor" (*Allel.*).

"I was an eye to the blind, a foot to the lame, a father to the poor" (*Off.*).

"Give, and it will be given to you; in goodly measure, pressed down, shaken together and running over will they pour it into your lap" (*Comm.*).

October 21

ST. HILARY, Abbot
ST. URSULA AND COMPANIONS, Martyrs

Go thither, my soul, why do you fear?

1. **St. Hilary.** Abbot St. Hilary was born at Tabatha near Gaza, Palestine, in the year 291. His pagan parents sent him, while still a youth, to study at Alexandria. He was remarkable for his diligence and good manners, became a convert to Christianity, made great progress in faith and charity. He was zealous in visiting churches, in fasting and prayer, in scorning all earthly joys and pleasures. Lured by the fame of St. Antony, Egypt's

illustrious hermit (see January 17), he entered the desert and
for two months remained his disciple. While absent, his parents
died. Now Hilary gave all he had to the poor, and although
hardly fifteen years old (306), he returned to the desert, built a
little hut scarcely large enough to accommodate himself, and
slept on the bare ground. Never did he wash the coarse peni-
tenial garb which he wore, nor did he ever exchange it for another because, as he was accustomed to say, "It were vanity to
be concerned about cleanliness when doing penance."

Most of his time was spent in reading and in meditating upon
holy Scripture. A few figs and a little soup from herbs sufficed
for his nourishment, but this he never took before the setting of
the sun. Because of his mortifications and humility, he triumphed
over fierce assaults by the evil one and healed many who were
possessed. After founding numerous hermitages (he had two
thousand followers) and working countless miracles, he became
ill at the age of eighty. In his last agony he encouraged himself
by saying: "Go thither, my soul, why do you fear? Why do you
tremble? Seventy years you have served Christ, and now you
fear death?" The day of Hilary's death is given as October 21,
371. His grave is on the island of Cyprus. St. Jerome wrote the
life of the holy hermit twenty years after his death. The Mass is
from the Common of Abbots (*Os justi*), see p. 421.

2. St. Ursula and Companions. There is a kernel of truth in
the legend concerning the martyrdom of these Christian virgins,
viz., they were put to death at Cologne during the Diocletian
persecution. Data as to names, numbers (given as eleven thousand), or other details are fictitious, some points being derived
from a Breton saga according to which eleven thousand maidens
of the nobility once left Brittany with a large escort; some
perished when a tempest demolished their ships, some were put
to death by the Huns. *Application.* In St. Ursula and her companions we honor all those virgins who for Christ's sake have
renounced the pleasures of marriage and the amusements of
life. They are the silent preachers of purity and modesty without which a people can be neither happy nor healthy. They are
true benefactors of their people.

October 22

FERIAL DAY

Martyrs in the Books of Machabees. *A Mother and Her Seven Sons.*[1] On August 1 we honor the memory of this heroic mother who exhorted her seven sons to die rather than offend God. St. Gregory of Nazianzen says of them:

"They deserve to be honored by all because for justice' sake and the laws of their fathers they fought resolutely and showed themselves heroes. True, they died a bloody death years before the passion of Christ, but what would they not have suffered if they had had the death of Christ as a model! It has significance for us — this deep mystery; they suffered before Christ, but certainly not without faith in Christ" (Oration XV *In Machabaeo-rum laudem*, PG 35, 913f.).

The martyrdom of the mother did not consist in her physical death. Only a mother's heart can understand what it means to see seven sons cruelly murdered. Meditate on the suffering of the seven sons, read the account as it is described so powerfully, so realistically in 2 Mach. 7; even the most unemotional must sense the courage and faith which was in that mother's soul.

Lashing with whips and scourges began the ordeal. Then one of them called: "We are ready to die rather than to transgress the laws of God received from our fathers." The king was enraged. To intimidate the others, the executioner was ordered to tear out his tongue, cut off his hands and feet, and roast him slowly over the fire. His mother was forced to witness the death agony of her child.

Scarcely had the first child died when the second was seized. The Bible tells us: "When they had pulled off both the skin and hair from his head, they asked him if he would eat before he was punished throughout the whole body in every limb. But he answered in his own language, and said: "I will not do it. And when he was at the last gasp he said: O most wicked man, you indeed are destroying our present life, but the King of the world

[1] By Dr. Joseph Casper (Vienna).

will raise us up, we who die for His laws, in the resurrection of eternal life."

The third son laughed at his suffering like a Mucius Scaevula (Faulhaber). If he had known Christ, he would have said he was taking seriously the command: "If your right eye scandalizes you, pluck it out and cast it away . . . and if your right hand scandalizes you, cut it off and cast it away; for it is better for you that one of your members should perish rather than that your whole body go into hell" (Matt. 5:29f). The fourth followed in turn, and when dying proclaimed the Old Testament belief in the resurrection: "Willingly does one die at the hands of men if he looks hopefully to God to be raised up again. But for you there will be no resurrection unto life." In the face of death the fifth son said: "The mills of God grind slowly, but they grind exceedingly fine." The sixth suffered patiently, offering himself as expiation.

The youngest still remained with his mother. Next to God, each of the six had received strength from her. "She bravely exhorted every one of them in her own language, being filled with wisdom and joining a woman's heart to a man's courage." For the seventh, peculiar trials were kept in store. The torturers did not immediately attack him physically but appealed to common passions, to avarice and ambition. The king tried to weaken him by many sorts of promises and enticements. But sons of such a mother were stronger than any king. The youngest chose as did his brothers. Could a king promise him anything like his courageous mother: "My son, have pity upon me. For I carried you nine months in my womb, and nursed you three years, and reared you to your present age. Now I beseech you, my son, look upon heaven and earth, and all that is in them; remember that God made them out of nothing and mankind too. So do not fear those tormentors, but be a worthy partner with your brothers. Accept death that I may receive you again with your brothers in the day of mercy."

In clear, decisive tones the mother's words re-echo from the mouth of her child: "I, even as my brothers, offer up my life and my body for the laws of our fathers; and I call upon God soon to be merciful to our nation." Incensed by such spirit, the king "raged against him more cruelly than all the rest." And lastly, the mother too died, "wholly trusting in the Lord."

What is the lesson taught us by this mother, or what lessons are to be learned from those bloody deaths? From the statements of the seven sons we may easily deduce the type of education she had given them. Her house must have been a house of prayer. That mother "prayed the psalms with her sons" (Faulhaber). For the psalms proclaim: "Blessed the man . . . whose will is in the law of the Lord" (Ps. 1:5). "I declared Your testimonies before kings" (Ps. 11:46). "You will not bring me down to sheol, nor permit Your holy one to suffer corruption" (Ps. 15:10). "As smoke vanishes . . . so do the wicked perish at the presence of God" (Ps. 67:3).

The Machabean mother had introduced her sons to the whole of Sacred Scripture. In her home she was a priestess to them, their leader unto God. She showed them holy models. The death of her sons is "a triumph of the priestly art of education" (Faulhaber). In the Catholic Church the Machabean mother has many imitators. I am now thinking, for example, of St. Symphorosa, whose feast we celebrated on July 18. Such heroic mothers and such heroic sons the Church can produce in every age, during every persecution. Holy mothers, holy sons, holy people! Perhaps we have so many apostates because we have so few priestly mothers. *Sanguis martyrum, semen Christianorum!*

October 24

ST. RAPHAEL, Archangel

Descend from heaven,
O Raphael, Angel-Physician,
to heal our ills,
to guide our erring steps.
— Vesper Hymn

1. The Archangel Raphael is one of the three archangels to whom Sacred Scripture accords a proper name (the other two: Michael and Gabriel). He appears only in the Book of Tobit, where in the form of Azarias, the son of the great Ananias, he is sent by God to cure Tobit of his blindness, to help Sara, Raguel's daughter, out of a sorry situation, and to accompany young Tobias on his journey. In the twelfth chapter of the book Raphael says the following about himself and his work: "When you prayed with tears and buried the dead and left your dinner unfinished in order to hide the dead by day in your house and bury them by night, I offered your prayer to the Lord . . . I am the angel Raphael, one of the seven who stand before the Lord . . . when I was with you, I was there by the will of God . . . I seemed indeed to eat and to drink with you, but I use an invisible meat and drink which cannot be seen by men. It is time, therefore, that I return to Him who sent me. Bless God, and publish all His wonderful works" (Tob. 12:12ff.). The Church honors Raphael as a patron of travelers, as may be seen in the liturgical prayer for travelers. Today's feast appears in the liturgical books of the tenth and eleventh centuries; in 1921 Benedict XV extended it to the entire Church.

2. Holy Mass (Benedicite). The formulary is in part from a "Common of Angels," in part it is proper. The *Introit* summons all the angels to the praise of God; it points out that the angels are "mighty in strength, execute His word, and hearken to the voice of His orders." What a beautiful prayer-picture! The angels are praising God as we approach and join them.

The *Collect* recalls how Raphael "was given as a guide to Tobias on his journey" and implores the same angel's assistance and protection on our own life's way. The *Lesson*, a very enlightening passage from the Book of Tobit, reveals how the angels bring to God our prayers and our good works; the final verses recall Raphael's work of "healing" physical and spiritual ills. In the *Gradual* we see our Archangel contending against the evil enemy (he took "the devil and bound him"). The *Gospel* tells about the healing waters in the pool of Bethsaida in Jerusalem: "An angel of the Lord descended at certain times upon the pond;

and the water was moved. And whoever went down first into the pond after the motion of the water was made whole of any infirmity he lay under." The liturgy would identify that angel with Raphael (the word *Raphael* means "God heals"), and, moreover, would widen his field of activity by making him the guardian spirit over every healing art, whether miraculous or natural. The *Postcommunion*: it is the task of the angels to bring our weak prayers before the throne of God, and we beg Raphael to do this for us. Thus today's Mass covers the various activities of our Archangel, viz., traveler's guide and guardian; physician; banisher of demons; mediator before God.

3. The Itinerarium. The liturgy endeavors to sanctify every activity of life. Hence a special prayer upon beginning a journey. In former times travel entailed greater hardships, inconveniences and dangers than at present. A special blessing for travelers, therefore, was more necessary. The liturgical *Itinerarium* elevates travel into the sphere of the supernatural. Travel becomes a type and figure of the great journey of life to our eternal home.

The opening prayer is the *Benedictus,* Zachary's song of praise, which describes the divine plan of salvation in terms of the Orient from on high who illumines life's journey and directs "our feet in the way of peace." The antiphon makes reference to the trip about to begin and begs "the angel Raphael to accompany us on the way that we may return home in peace, safety, and joy." In the prayers that follow, life's journey unto God repeatedly serves as the setting for the trip presently undertaken: "Show us Your ways, O Lord . . . teach us to walk in Your paths . . . that which is crooked, may it become straight . . . that which is rough, may it become an even road."

Three Biblical journeys are alluded to, namely, the crossing of the Red Sea, the journey of the Magi under the guidance of a star, and Abraham's journey to the Promised Land. In spite of many difficulties these journeys had a blessed ending. They give us confidence to implore the divine protection upon our own traveling. May God aid us at our departure, be our comfort on the way, our shade in heat, a protecting roof in the cold, in fatigue a cooling spring, defense when enemies attack, a staff

on slippery ground, in shipwreck a port of safety. In the last
prayer the journey is again considered as a type and as a part of
life's great journey. Make the resolution to pray the *Itinerarium*
before longer trips, and see in such earthbound actions the sign
of a supernatural reality.

October 25

STS. CHRYSANTHUS AND DARIA, Martyrs

**Let us show ourselves as God's servants, in much patience,
in tribulation, in necessities, in distress**

1. **Sts. Chrysanthus and Daria.** According to legend these two
saints belonged to the nobility. Daria received baptism through
the efforts of her husband Chrysanthus. In Rome they were instrumental in bringing many to the faith, for which cause they
were cruelly martyred. Chrysanthus was sewn inside an ox's hide
and placed where the sun shone hottest. Taken to a house of
ill-fame, Daria was protected by a lion while she passed the
time in prayer. Finally both were buried alive in a sand-pit and
thereby together gained the crown of martyrdom (283). They
were buried in the Jordan cemetery on the Via Saleria, Rome;
at the same site were buried sixty-two soldiers who died as
martyrs and also a group of faithful who had gathered together
for the holy Sacrifice on the anniversary of saints' deaths but
were cut down by the enemies of Christ. All these saints are
commemorated today.

2. **Holy Mass (Intret).** The formulary is, in part, from the
Common, see p. 408; in part it is proper. At the *Introit* we hear
the cry of the persecuted Church. What Paul says of himself in
the Epistle, our martyr-couple could well repeat: "Dying? See,
we live! Tortured? We are not dead! Sorrowful? Yes, and still
always rejoicing; needy, and nevertheless enriching many; having nothing while possessing all things!" In the *Gospel* Christ
pronounces woe upon the murderers of the prophets. All the

The splendor of divine light
beams forth in a multitude of rays,
for personal merit is nought else
but the glory of Christ ✚

martyrs take part in that glorious procession of saints who shed their blood for the kingdom of God from Abel down through the ages.

October 26

ST. EVARISTUS, Pope and Martyr

Blessed is the man who endures temptation, for when he has been proven he will receive the crown of life

St. Evaristus, one of the first popes (c. 99–107), was the son of a Hellenistic Jew. According to the none-too-reliable *Liber Pontificalis,* he divided the city of Rome into four distinct parishes and assigned priests to the various churches. He also appointed seven deacons, who were to accompany the bishop when he performed his duty of preaching. He insisted that apostolic tradition be observed regarding the form of marriage; it was to take place publicly and be blessed by a priest. "Under Emperor Trajan he watered the soil of God's Church with his blood" (*Martyrology*) and was buried at the Vatican near the grave of St. Peter on October 26. The division of Rome ascribed to Pope Evaristus became basic in liturgical observance for centuries. The priests of the titular churches performed the ordinary liturgy and were responsible for the care of souls, while the Pope reserved to himself solemn functions, e.g., stational church observance, baptism, reinstatement of penitents.

Observation. Already in the first century we find expressed the mind of the ancient Church on an important problem; liturgy favors communal activity and centralization, while the care of souls calls for personal contacts and decentralization. In the above arrangement Rome found the proper solution for these two basic needs; there should be small parishes to facilitate the care of souls, while unity in liturgical matters is imperative for the diocese at large. — The Mass (*Si diligis Me*) is from the Common of Sovereign Pontiffs, see p. 398.

October 28

STS. SIMON AND JUDE, Apostles

He will present you without blame
at the coming of Jesus Christ

It is a fundamental principle of liturgy that factors which
once were instrumental in founding the Church should now
serve to perfect the kingdom of God. The apostles were made the
foundation of the Church; in the liturgy they still continue
that function. They are and will remain foundation-stones upon
which the living stones of countless generations will be laid to
form one mighty and glorious edifice. Such is the significance of
feasts honoring the apostles. These days must be viewed sacramentally, i.e., as celebrations spread throughout the year which
in themselves give grace and are effective in building up the
Mystical Body of Christ.

1. **Sts. Simon and Jude.** Since earliest times these two apostles have been commemorated together on the same day. Simon
bears the surname, the Zealot; it may be that previous to his
call he belonged to the fanatical party of the Zealots, who proposed to introduce the Messianic era through violence. Better
known, especially in Austria where he is very popular, is Jude,
called Thaddeus (i.e., "the courageous"). He was a brother to
the apostle James the Less, a relative of Jesus. His mother was
Mary, a sister or cousin of the Blessed Virgin; his father Alphaeus
was related to St. Joseph. One of the seven "Catholic Letters" in
the New Testament was written by St. Jude. Popular devotion
honors him as the helper in "hopeless cases." Simon and Jude
first preached the gospel in countries widely distant from one
another, Simon in Egypt and Jude in Mesopotamia. It is said
that later both went to Persia and after extensive missionary
work were put to death for the faith.

2. **Holy Mass (Mihi autem).** The formulary is the usual one
for apostles; apart from the Gospel, it also serves as a votive
Mass. The vocation, dignity, and hardships of that high office
are noted. As the clergy enter, we greet the apostles reverently

as friends of Christ and co-rulers with Him. The *Collect* expresses three truths well worth pondering: (a) our faith rests upon the work of the apostles; (b) we celebrate feasts not merely as occasions for prayer but for the purpose of becoming more virtuous; (c) every feast is a rung in the ladder of perfection.

The *Epistle* explains the work of an apostle from the Mystical Body viewpoint. Every member of Christ has a definite duty "according to the measure of the giving of Christ." The special task of an apostle is "to prepare the saints (i.e., Christians) for the (sublime) work of worship." It consists in "building up the (mystical) Body of Christ, until we all attain unity in faith and in the knowledge of the Son of God, and having become fully mature, reach the perfect measure of development destined for (the mystical) Christ." The apostles, we learn, were not only the founders or the foundation-stones of the Church — in a sacramental way their mission continues until the Body of Christ arrives at its final, consummate perfection.

The *Gospel*, taken from Christ's "farewell address," foretells a martyr-death as the lot of the apostles. Union-in-love with Christ calls for union-in-suffering with Him. The apostles, and we too, will be hated by the world because Christianity and the world stand at odds. The apostles have attested their union-in-love with Christ by union-in-suffering unto martyrdom. The *Offertory* antiphon shows the apostles traveling through all the world, proclaiming Christ and His truth (Psalm 18 was formerly called "the Apostle"). The *Communion* antiphon reminds us of how we share in the glory and sovereign power of the apostles.

3. The Letter of St. Jude. It is one of the lovable practices of the liturgy to have the saint speak to us on his feast day if at all possible; therefore the Church departs from the regular Scripture reading today in favor of the Letter of St. Jude. Let us listen as though he were addressing us directly. His words ring like a prophet's call, stern and grave. The inscription is particularly solemn: "Jude, a servant of Jesus Christ (he was a cousin of our Lord!) and brother of James, to the elect — those beloved by

God the Father and preserved in Jesus Christ. (May God have) mercy on you; and may peace and charity be yours in fullest measure."

Then he beseeches his readers "to contend manfully for the faith that was definitely given to the saints (i.e., Christians)." There follows a warning against the snares of false teachers who misuse Christian freedom from Mosaic Law by allowing licentious conduct. As warning, he recalls several examples of divine punishment from the Old Testament. "The angels who did not maintain their high estate but left their proper dwellings, God put in everlasting chains, keeping them in darkness for judgment on the great Day" (a very important text on the fall of the angels; the passage recalls the major theme during the Church's Harvest Time). St. Jude's letter contains another passage proper to the present period of the ecclesiastical year: "Enoch, also, the seventh from Adam, prophesied, saying: Behold, the Lord is coming with thousands of His saints to execute judgment upon all and to reprove all the ungodly for all the works of their ungodliness. . . ."

The Apostle brings his letter to a beautiful conclusion: "But you, my dear friends, must build yourselves up by means of your most holy *faith*; you must pray in the Holy Spirit and keep yourselves in the *love* of God while you *await* the mercy of our Lord Jesus Christ which effects life everlasting. . . . To Him who is able to preserve you without sin and to present you spotless before His glorious presence with exceeding joy — to the only God our Savior through Jesus Christ our Lord, be glory and magnificence, empire and power, before all ages, now and forever. Amen."

October 30

FERIAL DAY

The Spirit of the Liturgy during the Month of November. The last month of the ecclesiastical year is regarded as "Poor Souls' month" in popular piety. In the liturgy this is not the case. Recall what has been said already on the Church's Harvest Time. November brings parousia expectation and preparation to their climax. The liturgy directs our gaze forward to the end of time. Already the first day of the month, the feast of All Saints, draws aside heaven's curtain and makes us participate in the heavenly liturgy. Two Dedication feasts follow, not without genuine allusions to the Second Advent theme; you need only read the Scripture Lessons proper to them (Apoc. 21:9–18, 18–27). To which add the last Sunday of the ecclesiastical year with its awesome description of the General Judgment.

The month of November is also dedicated to the *prophets* of the Old Testament. The Church conducts us into the assembly of Israel's inspired seers and bids them speak to us. Their message serves excellently in educating us in parousia theology. For the prophets described the consummation of the kingdom of God and its transition from its earthly phase to its heavenly one. Twelve lesser and four greater prophets are found in the canon of the Old Testament. The terms *greater* and *lesser* do not refer to mental or spiritual endowments, but simply to the quantity of writing still extant. Two of the greater prophets, Isaias and Jeremias, speak to us at other seasons, Advent and Passiontide respectively; the other two, Ezechiel and Daniel, are accorded the first three weeks of November, while the remaining twelve lesser prophets are given some passing attention during the month's final two weeks.

The pericopes from the prophets would become more attractive if we knew what task they accomplished for their own times and what purpose they now fulfill in the Church. (1) *For their own times*. After the reign of King Solomon, conditions among the Israelites worsened constantly, one of the results of the division into two kingdoms. The people fell into idolatry and all its concomitant vices. God did not fail to send warnings or to threaten punishment. He raised up prophets in Israel, more numerous than ever before. Supernaturally illumined, they not only foretold the future but labored to reform current evils, to abolish idolatry, to urge penance. These divinely sent teachers and admonishers of kings, priests, and people would point to the future, proclaiming a day of wrath upon the un-repentant; and the devout they would comfort by inspiring hope in a Messiah whose coming they delineated with ever-increasing clearness and certainty. For their times, therefore, the prophets were the voice of God warning, reforming, consoling.

2) *For our times.* But why does the Church have the prophets address *us*? Isaias has the pulpit from Advent to Christmas and again on Epiphany; Jeremias during Passiontide; and the others during the month of November. First, the prophets strengthen and confirm our faith, as we see how all has come to pass as they foretold. Then they have left us prophecies concerning the end of the world; and lastly, they exhort us to do penance, e.g., in Lent.

The primary purpose of the liturgical Lessons from the prophets, however, is something quite different. The prophets are and will ever remain the great *preachers of God's holy Will.* The voice of God rings through their words into our ears to this very day. "Thus saith the Lord," a phrase so frequently found in the prophets, now brings God's message in its fullest sense. The word of God proclaimed by the prophets and working sacramentally is "more piercing than any two-edged sword . . . it reaches unto the division of the soul and the spirit" (Heb. 4:12). Like the apostles, the prophets have a permanent office in the kingdom of God. As certainly as the apostles are the foundation-stones upon which we are erected into a living struc-ture, the prophets are the great heralds of the divine Will.

Finally, the prophets can only be fully understood from the viewpoint of the Redeemer, Christ Jesus. He is the center, the focal point of God's kingdom. Upon the prophets fell the duty of preparing the people of their generation for the Messiah. But since the Messiah's work is not yet completed, their voices are not yet silenced. The prophets are calling out to us as truly as they called out to their contemporaries: *Do penance, for the kingdom of God is at hand!* And a further point that receives too little attention, viz., by their very lives some of them pre-figured the Redeemer. Thus Jeremias in his meekness, in his sufferings, in his lamentations and utter desolation abandoned by all was a prophetic type of our suffering Savior.

October 31

FIRST VESPERS OF ALL SAINTS

**The Lord has wonderfully magnified His saints,
and He hears them when they call upon Him**

Readying Ourselves for the Feast. We should try to sense the joy and holy blessedness that thrills through the heart of Mother Church as she glances over her children who have attained their eternal destiny, who have entered the heavenly fatherland to enjoy the eternal vision of God. Mother Church must always be filled with fear concerning the salvation of her children who are still upon earth, children who must fight the ancient enemy. Our Mother, who suffers intensely because of the weakness and infidelity of many, tonight chants a grateful *Magnificat* and a joyful *Te Deum* over those who have fought the good fight and have received the crown of life. She fixes her gaze upon the elect; with a mother's joyful pride she inspects the celestial ranks again and again. As we preview tomorrow's liturgy, three scenes which seem representative take attention.

1) The first scene is a wholly joyful one, a view of heaven. What do we see there? The Church takes us by the hand and shows us the heavenly liturgy as painted in brilliant colors by St. John the Evangelist, the seer of Patmos. We enter the celestial basilica; a lofty throne rises before us surrounded by cherubim, there in state the eternal Father is seated. Before the throne stands an altar upon which lies the immolated Lamb, our Redeemer Christ Jesus. Around the altar are gathered twenty-four elders, representative of the old and new kingdoms of God upon earth; on all sides stand the elect, a countless multitude of Jews and Gentiles, saints from every tribe and people and nation. They are clad in white garments and hold palms in their hands and sing a new canticle: "You have redeemed us for God in Your Blood, out of every tribe, and tongue, and people, and nation. You have made us unto our God into a kingdom of priests; and we will reign on the earth." The four cherubim add the *Amen*, while the twenty-four elders fall down adoring God

and the Lamb. *Alleluia* continues without an end. To this multitude we should and must someday belong. Throw off the chains that bind to earth! In spirit ascend to heaven!

2) For the second picture of her holy children, Mother Church leads us back to earth and shows us her saints in the process of becoming such. We see them exercising the eight beatitudes promulgated in the Sermon on the Mount. We see the step-children of this world who often labor under extreme difficulties to obtain daily nourishment. Here a father, there a mother earning some scanty food for their children; slaves, passing their lives without rights; silent heroes who make no complaints over the intense physical pain they are enduring; the bed-ridden; those whose cheeks are furrowed with hot tears. Surely pain alone does not produce holiness, but these have accepted it from the hand of God and have made it a scaffold to perfection. They are the "peace-loving," the "merciful," the "upright and clean of heart." The "Way of the Cross" is passing before our eyes, a procession of plain and common people to whom the world means nothing. Do you see yourself among them?

3) The Church has still another way to gain a general view of her holy ones. She loves to group together those who have been heroic after the same pattern. During the course of the year she focuses attention on various groupings, but today she glances over them all. Particularly at Matins do the saints pass in classified review. In the center of the scene is God the Father "sitting on a high and elevated throne; the border of His garments fills the temple; seraphim hover about Him" (*1. Resp.*). As first among the saints, Mary, the Mother of God, approaches the throne; choirs of angels hail her with the *Ave* — "Hail, Mary, full of grace, the Lord is with thee" (*2. Resp.*). The angels, too, belong to the multitudes of God's holy ones: "In the presence of the angels we will sing to You; we will adore in Your holy temple" (*3. Resp.*).

Now comes one who belongs to no particular class, the precursor who was acclaimed by Christ in the words: "Among those born of women, there is not a greater than John the Baptist" (*4. Resp.*). Now we see a band deserving of every honor, they who planted the Gospel with their own life's blood: "They have drunk the chalice of the Lord, they have become God's friends. Their voice has rung out into all the world, their words to its farthest boundaries" (5. *Resp.*). These are the apostles, who have a very special position in the Church of God.

After them follow an army of martyrs. They are clad in white garments and have palms in their hands. The battle was fierce, but the reward princely; Christ now invites them: "Come, blessed of My Father! Take possession of the kingdom" (6. *Resp.*). Another army advances with "girt loins and burning lamps in their hands." These confessors of the faith watched and waited till the Lord returned for the nuptials (7. *Resp.*). And lastly, the choirs of virgins. They too carry lamps in their hands and go to meet the Bridegroom with bridal love and longing (8. *Resp.*).

What group do I wish to belong to? Do I wish to be decorated with the red rose of martyrdom, the lily of a stainless life, the violet of penance? It requires effort, mere wishfulness is not enough. We are still on the way, still in the fray. Patiently we must persevere. *Omnes Sancti Dei, intercedite pro nobis*!

November 1

ALL SAINTS

Oh how glorious is the kingdom where all the saints rejoice with Christ! Clothed in white robes, they follow the Lamb wherever He goes!

1. **History of the Feast.** The practice of honoring all the saints by a common feast extends back to the fourth century in the Orient. At first, however, only martyrs were so honored; the feast occurred on the first Sunday after Pentecost, the date which still holds among the Greeks. In Syria the commemoration took place on the Friday after Easter (the Roman Missal gives the

station church on the Friday after Easter as that of *Sancta Maria ad Martyres*).

Early in the seventh century Pope Boniface IV ordered the Pantheon at Rome, which had been given him by Emperor Phocas, transformed into a church (this temple had been built by Marcus Agrippa to commemorate Augustus' victory at Actium in 27 B.C.). After a great stock of relics had been transferred to the purified temple (allegedly twenty-eight wagons full), Pope Boniface dedicated it on May 13, 610, in honor of the Mother of God and all the holy martyrs (see Roman Martyrology for May 13). Accordingly the feast of All Martyrs was celebrated on May 13, very appropriately soon after the resurrection of our Blessed Savior. Due perhaps to the difficulty of procuring food in Rome for great numbers of pilgrims in the springtime, Gregory IV (827–844) transferred the feast to November 1 and extended it to include all the saints. Thus it received its place toward the end of the Church year and serves well as an occasion to anticipate the consummation of Christ's kingdom and His Second Coming.

2. Hours of the Office. In varying ways those who love the liturgy will take part in today's Divine Office. The texts are easy to understand and spiritually inspiring. The celebration begins on the previous evening with First Vespers. In spirit the seer from Patmos leads us into heaven and shows us the services before the throne of God and the Lamb, "I saw a great multitude which no man could number, out of all nations, standing before the throne. . . . And all the angels were standing round about the throne, and they fell on their faces before the throne and worshipped God." We hear the hymn of the redeemed, "You have redeemed us, O Lord, with Your Blood, out of every tribe and tongue and people and nation, and have made us into a kingdom for our God." Thus the antiphons, interspersed between the usual Vesper psalms.

The hymn praises the various classes of saints about our heavenly Queen: the angels, the apostles, martyrs, confessors, virgins. In the Magnificat antiphon we assure ourselves of the intercession of all these saints. Matins, chanted during the night, in many points resembles the Common of Martyrs; this follows from the fact that our feast began as a celebration honoring martyrs only. How Christocentric the Church feels as she honors the saints is very beautifully shown by the Invitatory, "Come, let us adore the Lord, King of kings, for He Himself is the crown of all the saints." The first nocturn Lessons take us before these saints; the Lessons of the second nocturn contain a lovely sermon by St. Bede the Venerable:

"Today, dearly beloved, on one solemn day of rejoicing, we celebrate the feast of all the saints in heaven. In their communion heaven exults; in their patronage earth rejoices; in their triumph holy Church is crowned with glory. Their testimony becomes more glorious with honor in proportion to the intensity of their agony. As the battle waged fiercer, the greater was the glory which came to those who fought; the more terrible their tortures, the more illustrious the triumph of their martyrdom; the greater their torments, the greater their rewards.

"As our holy Mother the Catholic Church — now spread far and wide throughout the whole world — has been taught by Christ Jesus her Head, not to fear shame, or the cross or death, but to become stronger and stronger, not by resisting but by enduring, so has she breathed into her children, welded by the cruel prison into a glorious band, a triumphant spirit equal to her own in its fire and in courage to carry on the conflict.

"O Mother Church truly holy, whose glory God deigns to illumine, whom the glorious blood of conquering martyrs adorns, whom the white robes of virgins clothe with an inviolate confession of faith, roses and lilies are not wanting to your garlands. Dearly beloved, let each one of us fight that he may gain the high dignity of one or the other of these honors, either the white crown of virginity, or the red crown of martyrdom. In the heavenly camps both peace and war have their own garlands with which the soldiers of Christ are crowned.

"For the ineffable and limitless goodness of God has provided that the time of both toil and struggle shall not be prolonged unduly, nor drawn out and without end, but brief, and as I might say, of a moment. Therefore, although in this short and difficult life there may be labors and struggles, in that life which is eternal there are crowns and rewards for merit. The struggles are soon over, the rewards for merit last forever. God in His goodness has provided, too, that after the darkness of this life they shall see an exceedingly great radiance, they shall receive blessedness far beyond the bitterness of all their torment. The Apostle bears witness of this when he says: The sufferings of this time are not worthy to be compared with the glory to come, that shall be revealed in us" (translation from: *Roman Breviary in English*, publ. by Benziger Brothers, Inc.).

During the third nocturn St. Augustine explains the eight beatitudes. At our morning prayer, Lauds, we ascend to heaven under the guidance of the seer John and chant the *Benedictus* with the saints assembled there. "The glorious choir of the apostles, the admirable company of the prophets, the white-robed army of martyrs, the saints with all the elect join their voices to praise You, O blessed Trinity, one God" (*Ben. Ant.*).

3. Holy Mass (Gaudeamus). A joyous invitation goes out to all to join us in celebrating this wonderful family feast. There is joy upon earth and joy in heaven. This thrilling *Introit* text, *Gaudeamus*, was borrowed from the Greek liturgy and first used for the feast of St. Agatha (Feb. 5). With genuine mother's pride the Church glances over all her glorified children and feels assured of their intercession (*Coll.*). The *Epistle* opens heaven before us and we see a great host gathered about the throne of God, singing sacred songs. One division of the elect stems from the Chosen People of old, but innumerable are the hosts stemming from non-Jewish quarters. All have been cleansed from sin by the blood of the Lamb and carry victory-palms in their hands.

With the *Gradual* and the *Alleluia* verse we are back again upon earth to learn the way to heaven, i.e., serve God and carry your cross. The eight beatitudes, "the royal highway of Christ, the golden ladder to eternal blessedness" (Meschler), outline the sure way by which to become saints. A saint's life is nothing more than the beatitudes in action. At the sacrificial Banquet the beatitudes are engendered, nourished, and preserved; the blessed

Eucharist is the source of all their effectiveness, "Blessed are the pure of heart, for they shall see God. Blessed are the peacemakers, for they shall be called children of God. Blessed are they who suffer persecution for justice' sake, for theirs is the kingdom of heaven." Today's Mass, accordingly, is bifocal; now we see the saints in heaven (*Epist.*), now the saints upon earth (*Gosp.*). As the feast draws to a close (2. Vespers) we cry out in amazement, "Oh how glorious is the kingdom where all the saints rejoice with Christ! Clothed in white robes, they follow the Lamb wherever He goes!"

4. Vespers on All Saints — an Hour in Heaven. "No Vespers during the whole year makes so deep an impression upon me as Vespers of All Saints. Artistic reliquaries decorate the altar; in the relics the saints themselves are present, and Christ their leader is the altar. The latter is adorned in feast-day robes, golden antependium, glistening snow-white linens. Upon six golden candlesticks burn six huge candles. Behind them resplendent is the Lamb of the Apocalypse. Upon the throne as representative of the eternal Father sits the abbot in a golden-threaded cope. About him are the "seniors" of the monastery in white robes, while below four chanters, clothed in flowing pluvials, lead the monastic choir in the heavenly melodies. Out in the nave stand or sit 'the multitude of faithful which no man can number, from all peoples.' And throughout the edifice resound the jubilantly sonorous harmonies from the organ. It is an hour in heaven" (from a description by Fr. Kutzer of Mindelzell).

November 2

ALL SOULS

Eternal rest grant unto them, O Lord

The Martyrology today begins with these beautiful words, "Today we keep the commemoration of all the deceased faithful.

After the Church as the loving Mother of all strove to honor with worthy solemnity all her children who already enjoy themselves in heaven, she seeks to aid those souls who yet suffer in the place of purgation by her powerful intercession with the Lord and Bride Christ, so that as speedily as possible they may join the community of heaven's citizens."

1. Historical Background. The introduction of a day commemorating all the faithful who departed from this life in the state of grace is due to the meek and holy Abbot Odilo of Cluny (d. 1048). In 998 he ordained that the Office of the Dead be said after Vespers on November 1 in all the monasteries of Cluny. This custom was widely imitated and finally officially adopted by the whole Latin Church. All Souls' day or the "Commemoration of All the Faithful Departed" was raised to its present high rank by Pope St. Pius X. On this day every priest has the right to celebrate Mass three times. The 1955 breviary reform abolished First Vespers of the Office of the Dead after Vespers of All Saints.

2. The Office of the Dead is a prayer service filled with deep compassion, a spirit of willingness to aid the needy, true sympathy, genuine sorrow, but restrained by deep Christ-like love. As we pray the Hours we assume a position between the all-just, all-merciful God and the souls near and dear to us in purgatory. Our position, however, does not remain stationary; as comforting angels we approach now closer to God, now closer to our suffering brothers and sisters. God appears in mighty power to punish, in His holiness, in His boundless goodness. As you pray the Office, keep facing God, keep approaching Him. He wants to take His servants and friends who have died in the state of grace into everlasting beatitude as quickly as possible. He wants them to behold His presence and to be united with Him as soon as they are cleansed from all stain of sin. The Office of the Dead unites us with the suffering souls so that we may feel their pain and torment; indeed, in spirit we may transport ourselves to their places in purgatory to cry in their stead, to beseech some alleviation.

There is considerable similarity between the Office of the Dead and the Office on the last three days of Holy Week. Most of the ordinary introductory and concluding formulas are omitted, e.g., the opening versicle, hymn, doxologies, blessings before Lessons. It is permeated by serious, measured sorrow; all that is of a festive nature is absent. The final Oration of each Hour is said kneeling, for we are weeping intercessors in behalf of our beloved dead.

Before the reform of Pope Pius X, the Office of the Dead only contained Vespers, Matins, and Lauds, the three oldest prayer Hours. All the other Hours were then added, so that All Souls' now has a complete Office. The old Office of the Dead comprising Vespers, Matins, and Lauds is a memorial of the Church's most ancient liturgy.

The Office begins with Matins' hope-inspiring Invitatory, "The King for whom all things live, come, let us adore!" In every instance the doxology is replaced by the invocation, "Eternal rest grant unto them, O Lord. . . ." In the Lessons of the first nocturn, Job, a remarkable earthly replica of the souls suffering in purgatory, pleads for deliverance. In the second nocturn we read from the works of St. Augustine a passage on the care that is to be bestowed on the deceased. This ancient and venerable document shows how important the human body is, how the body should be piously buried, and how the deceased should be aided through prayer, because holy Church seeks to help all who can be helped by prayer and sacrifice. The Apostle of the Gentiles speaks in the third nocturn and foretells our resurrection in Christ. Particularly stirring are the responsories as they echo from the lips of the suffering souls. The psalms reflect now a spirit of repentance (first and third nocturns), now hope for forgiveness (second nocturn).

Lauds bring to a zenith our spirit of joyous hope. After the usual penitential psalm (50), the themes are those of joy in harvest time (Ps. 64), glowing yearning for union with God (Ps. 62), jubilation in the assurance of resurrection (Cant. and Ps. 150). The Canticle of Ezechias, in particular, very forcefully describes the transition from suffering in purgatory to beatitude in heaven.

Vespers according to the Office of the Dead are very impressive. The psalms, recited with and for the poor souls, make our thoughts dwell on human misery and human weakness, on the terrors of the hour of death and the Last Judgment, on the last agony, but also on the boundless goodness of God who comforts and beckons heavenward. When Vespers come to a climax at the *Magnificat,* our hope mounts, for our divine Redeemer Himself appears and promises to take all whom the Father has given Him into His heavenly kingdom. "All that the Father gives to Me shall come to Me, and him who comes to Me I will not cast out."

3. Holy Mass (Requiem aeternam). Like the other Masses for the Dead, today's formulary reflects two distinct strata as to spirit and content. The more ancient stratum dates back to Christian antiquity, is joyful in spirit, and tells the happy message of bodily resurrection. To this thought area belongs the *Introit* with its joyous harvest hymn, Psalm 64; for the Church is meditating upon her spiritual harvest (the whole psalm must, of course, be prayed to get the implications). The Introit antiphon, taken from the apocryphal Fourth Book of Esdras (2:34–35), has been used in the liturgy at least since the sixth century.

To the older stratum also belong the two Lessons, both joyful revelations of resurrection with glorified bodies. In the *Epistle* the Apostle explains the manner of this resurrection. The body will rise, but not in a corruptible state; a glorified body will be joined to the soul. In the *Gospel* Christ stands before us as the one who awakens from a twofold death; upon earth He awakens men to a life of grace, on the day of judgment to a life of glory. This level also includes the *Preface of the Dead,* a recent composition modeled upon ancient Mozarabic liturgy. Inimitably beautiful is its terse phraseology:

> In Christ
>   the hope-star of a blessed resurrection has shone upon us.
> Though the certainty of dying may sadden us,
>   the assurance of future immortality gladdens us.

For to those who have faith in You, Lord,
    life does not cease —
    it merely changes!
And when our earthly dwelling falls to ruins,
    we find an eternal home in heaven.

The other stratum of the Requiem Mass has its source in the sin-conscious spirit of the Middle Ages. It is neither joyful nor triumphant in tone, but is filled with concern over the suffering souls; this part paints death and judgment in dark and fearsome colors. Characteristic here is the sequence, *Dies Irae*, a highly poetical description of the Last Judgment (Michelangelo's painting of the Last Judgment in the Sistine chapel was influenced by the *Dies Irae*).

The *Offertory* chant shows us St. Michael in the role of escort of souls past the gates of hell into their heavenly home. This is the only example in the missal of an Offertory containing a separate versicle. The explanation may be: in Masses for the Dead the Offertory procession was longest retained, necessitating a lengthier chant. The theme stems from the ancient pagan notion that souls after death must be accompanied by someone. Also the petition that they "fall not into oblivion" is a pagan concept borrowed from myths concerning the river Lethe. To summarize: belief in bodily resurrection and prayer for the liberation of our beloved dead are the two themes of today's Mass.

A *Collect* cast in classic form first states the reason why God love us, i.e., He created and redeemed us; secondly, the plea for forgiveness and liberation is based upon "our devout supplication" and the spirit of loving trust in God manifested by the deceased. The Communion of Saints receives due recognition. The *Secret* again points out the gift of Christian faith as that which makes us worthy of reward. It should be noted that the lighted candles held during a Requiem Mass do not symbolize the grace of baptism as at other times during the year; today they represent the suffering souls whose places we are taking and for whom we are begging "eternal light."

November 3

FERIAL DAY

O Lord, hope and strong citadel of the saints, You give the earth to those who fear Your Name. They shall dwell in Your tabernacle forever.

1. Reflections on the Season. At the present phase of the liturgical year, a very appropriate topic for spiritual meditation would be the glory of heaven. Before 1955 the Divine Office for November 3 contained a homily by St. Bede the Venerable on the subject:

"Then shall there never be any discord anywhere; all shall be in harmony. Then shall there be but one concord of all the saints, holding only peace and joy. Then shall all things be calm and at rest. Splendor shall be everlasting, not such as we see now, but brighter, because it shall be more blessed. For we read that the city does not need the light of the sun; the Lord almighty shall lighten it, and the Lamb is the lamp thereof. Then shall the saints shine like stars for all eternity. Those who have taught many shall be as the brightness of the sky.

"And there shall be no night, nor darkness, nor lowering clouds, no extremes of heat and cold. But there shall be such a harmony of things as no eye has ever seen, nor ear heard, nor the heart of man conceived, except those only whose names are written in the book of life, they who have washed their robes in the Blood of the Lamb, and are before the throne of God, serving Him day and night. There shall be no old age, nor the misery of it, for all shall have come to perfect manhood, to the measure of the age of the fullness of Christ.

"There is more! Greater than all these things is it to be in communion with the hosts of angels and archangels, to enjoy the companionship also of the Thrones, Dominations, Principalities and Powers, and of all the heavenly Virtues. Greater, too, is it to behold the army of the saints, shining more gloriously than stars; the patriarchs radiant with faith, the prophets rejoicing in hope, the apostles judging the world in the twelve tribes of

Israel, the martyrs resplendent in their ruddy crowns of victory, and to see the virgins in choir upon choir wearing garlands of purest white" (translation of homily from: *Roman Breviary in English*, publ. by Benziger Brothers, Inc.).

2. The "Seven Last Liturgical Things." Although the theme of the present season, the Church's Harvest Time, is a constant reminder of death and afterlife, the commemoration of All Saints and more so that of All Souls is Mother Church's most eloquent single sermon on death and thereafter. These days, then, are ideal for meditation on what the future holds in store for us. At the end of our earthly pilgrimage comes a sacramental anointing, Extreme Unction, and a series of liturgical acts designed to help us pass from this world to the next. At that most crucial moment, upon which hangs the fate of an eternity, Mother Church stands with holy rites and efficacious signs, and with the power of her liturgical prayer — at your deathbed. I would put the stress on liturgical prayer. It is indeed a magnificent scene! The Church, the great and universal Church, the globe-encircling Church, comes into my small house with her mighty blessings. We must understand LITURGY in its full and deep significance and see its real greatness at the time of death. So let us examine the liturgy as it touches the last things in life, or better, the liturgy of the last liturgical things. How many are there? Perhaps one or the other could be taken together; whatever their number, the logical sequence is: Penance, Viaticum, Extreme Unction, Apostolic Blessing, Commending the Dying to God, Requiem Mass, Burial.

An Ideal Death. It is morning. In the parish church holy Mass is being celebrated. About the altar are gathered the members of the parish. They are praying, they are sacrificing in common. At the *Memento vivorum* the lector says: Remember, O Lord, our sick brother (our sick sister) N., to whom we will bring holy Viaticum today. All are listening, all is quiet; in spirit all are at the sickbed. A parish Mass with the parishioners present! A community spirit is engendered which rises up and flows out beyond the walls of the church. And the sick man upon his bed, with missal in hand, believes himself in the house of God; for him it is the last Eucharistic Sacrifice with his fellow parishioners.

The Banquet is over. The priest, after all have communicated, lays the Body of the Lord in the pix. The Mass comes to an end. A white cope is brought, Mass servers come with candle and bell, the people form a procession. The "praying and sacrificing" Church proceeds to the home of a dying member. The Banquet did not come to an end in the church, no, it is concluded in the sick man's room. The room with its bed becomes a sanctuary, the table an altar, the porch and its approaches a nave from which the faithful participate in the service.

The *Asperges* reminds the dying man of baptism; let him be clean, let him purify himself at the end of life as at the beginning. You are baptized, redeemed — that is the message from the holy water sprinkler as it purifies with its blessed water. The *Confiteor*, the principal unit in the Prayers at the Foot of the Altar, represents the Foremass here. "Behold the Lamb of God, who takes away the sins of the world," the priest begins while holding up the sacred Host. "O Lord, I am not worthy," reply the sick man and the faithful. "Receive, brother (sister), the Body of our Lord Jesus Christ as Viaticum. May it preserve you from the evil enemy and lead you to eternal life." With these words the sick man receives the Body of the Lord. The prayer following has the character of a Postcommunion.

A table in the room had served as altar. Persons with a love for things liturgical will prepare that table while still in good health. The women will provide a linen covering cloth like those used at church. A crucifix with two candleholders are essential appurtenances of this home altar. In the candleholders there should burn blessed candles, preferably blessed on Candlemas. Upon a special stand, resembling the Easter Candle, the sick man's baptismal candle could be burning. It and the other lights now symbolize the burning lamps with which to approach the Lord at the parousia. If there is to be an anointing with holy oils, a plate with six cotton balls, and a second plate with bread crumbs or salt for cleansing the oil from the priest's hands should be ready. The cotton, bread and salt will be burned after use.

For a sick person who swallows with difficulty, place a glass

of water on the table, to be given immediately after receiving
holy Viaticum. Choice bouquets of flowers may certainly be displayed as a greeting to the Eucharistic Guest. A small container
with water for the ablution of the priest's fingers and a small
cloth ought not be lacking. Nor holy water. A large linen sheet
spread over the bed would not be inappropriate. Before the sick
table a carpet may be placed, and at a convenient position a
kneeler, if one is handy.

November 4

ST. CHARLES BORROMEO, Bishop and Confessor
STS. VITALIS AND AGRICOLA, Martyrs

Truly a great shepherd of souls

1. St. Charles. *Day of death*: November 3, 1584; canonized
1610. *Grave*: in the cathedral at Milan. *Life.* Our saint, one of
the glories of the Catholic Church in the sixteenth century, was
noted for (a) *Church reform*, a very urgent need at that time;
(b) *care of souls* in Milan. At first he labored at the side of his
uncle, Pope Pius IV, to bring to a successful conclusion the
Council of Trent; his pastoral instructions have remained classic
to the present day. Born in 1538 of a noble Milanese family and
dedicated to spiritual things at an early age, he became a cardinal
at twenty-three (1560); soon after, archbishop of Milan. His
greatest concern was to put into effect throughout his province
the decrees of the Council of Trent. Due to his reforming efforts
there soon arose enemies and opponents of high civil and ecclesiastical rank.

Great was Charles' love of neighbor and liberality toward the
poor. When the plague raged in Milan, he sold his household
furniture, even his bed, to aid the sick and needy, and thereafter slept upon bare boards. He visited those stricken by the
disease, consoled them as a tender father, conferred upon them
the sacraments with his own hands. A true mediator, he im-

plored forgiveness day and night from the throne of grace. He once ordered an atonement procession and appeared in it with a rope about his neck, with bare and bloody feet, a cross upon his shoulder — thus presenting himself as an expiatory sacrifice for his people to ward off divine punishment. He died, dressed in sackcloth and ashes, holding a picture of the Crucified in his hands. His last words were, "See, Lord, I am coming, I am coming soon." His tomb in the cathedral of Milan is of white marble. The Mass is from the Common of Bishops (*Statuit*), p. 417. A proper *Collect* stresses his zeal for souls, *pastoralis solicitudo*.

2. **Sts. Vitalis and Agricola.** *Grave*: at Bologna. Their bodies had been interred in a Jewish cemetery but later were exhumed by St. Ambrose and the bishop of Bologna and accorded due veneration. *Life*. The Office gives a legendary account:

Vitalis, a slave, and Agricola, his master, were cruelly tortured under Diocletian. In vain was Vitalis tempted by promises to renounce his faith; he merely showed himself more constant as a confessor of Christ. He was tortured most dreadfully, but bore all with incomparable patience till in prayer he gave up the spirit. Agricola's sentence was delayed in the hope that the torments of his slave would frighten him into a denial of Christ, but the constancy of Vitalis confirmed him in the faith. He was nailed to a cross and thereby became a comrade and sharer with his servant in the crown of martyrdom (*c.* 304). Later times distinguished two persons by the name Vitalis, one the martyr of Ravenna, the other Agricola's companion at Bologna; actually there is question of but one and the same individual.

Application. Today's is surely a glorious drama: a slave and his master dying together for Christ! Christianity must bridge social divisions and raise all men to the same high status. Servant and servant are brothers in Christ, and their master is Christ's slave. The slave obeys his lord as Christ's representative, the master honors his slave as Christ's member. Both are to share eternal joys together if both perform the duties proper to their state in life.

3. The Pastor and the People. Some thought upon the nature of our pastor's work is appropriate today as we commemorate that eminent shepherd of souls, Charles Borromeo. For we ought to know what it means to have the charge of souls and how we may help along in the noble work. (a) What is meant by the "care of souls"? No one is entirely ignorant of a pastor's duties. Preaching, hearing confessions, celebrating Mass, visiting the sick, teaching catechism. But what, we may ask, is the ultimate point or purpose? To plant the life of grace and to help it grow. It is the same work as Christ performed, "For this have I come, that they may have LIFE and have it more abundantly."

Pastoral work continues Christ's redemptive work; men must be incorporated into the Body of Christ, and this incorporation must be fostered and furthered. That is the essence of pastoral work. And the means? For life to develop, light and nourishment are necessary, "Your word is a light unto my feet" (*Ps. 118*). Nourishment is provided by the bread of the Eucharist. God's word and God's food, Bible and liturgy, are the two most important means for achieving true success in pastoral work.

b) Can we help along in this work of caring for souls? Certainly. Observe a kind of "spiritual circle": a good parish produces many worthy priests, and good priests produce virtuous parishioners. Christ is urging us forward, "The harvest indeed is great, but the laborers are few. Ask the Lord of the harvest to send laborers." Pray for priestly vocations.

Finally, the laity too are priests, pastors of souls through participation in the common priesthood bestowed at baptism and confirmation. Parents have the priestly duty to give their children life overflowing with God. Every person by example and prayer has a priest's vocation in his environment. This is the meaning of Catholic Action to which our Holy Father summons every Catholic; in his own state and situation he should be a "shepherd of souls" — to his neighbor and to those under his care. Every Catholic is responsible for the salvation of those with whom he lives!

c) It is also our grave duty to use well the graces coming to us from our pastor's work, particularly those which flow from the primary sources, i.e., the liturgy and the Bible. Good shepherds are close about us; we must be docile lambs, willing to be led into rich meadows.

November 5

FERIAL DAY

Blessed are the pure of heart, they shall see God!
Blessed are the peacemakers, they shall be called chil-
dren of God! Blessed are they who suffer persecution
for justice' sake, theirs is the kingdom of heaven!

1. Reflections on the Season. During these days it is our privilege to keep our thoughts upon the saints in heaven. We will make use of the opportunity in order better to comprehend the season's theme, the Church's Harvest Time. Note how the feast of All Saints, since its transference to November 1, has received an eschatological coloring. The saints form the train of the returning King who at the end of time will appear "in the brightness of His holy ones." This is quite evident in the Invitatory, "Come, let us adore the Lord, King of kings, for He Himself is the crown of all the saints."

Pius XI embellished the idea by introducing the feast of Christ the King on the Sunday before All Saints. These two feasts are related and keep before us a theme beloved by the early Christians, viz., Christ the King returning in the company of His saints. Moreover, these feasts afford us a goodly view into heaven, acquaint us with our native country and our true fellow citizens. Genuine homesickness fills our hearts, "O how glorious is the kingdom where all the saints rejoice with Christ! Clothed in white robes, they follow the Lamb wherever He goes!"

St. Bede continues his homily, urging us to follow the example given by the saints:

"Let it be our happy aim to win the prize. Let us strive cheerfully and willingly. Let us run in the race of justice, in the sight of God and Christ. Let us who have already begun to rise above the things of time and the world not impede our progress by worldly desires. If the final day of our lives finds us ready and still running swiftly in the race of good works, our Lord will never fail to reward us as we deserve.

"He who will give a purple crown for suffering in persecution will give a white one to those who conquer in peace, as a reward of their righteousness. For Abraham, Isaac, and Jacob are honored — they deserve to be — as first among patriarchs, although they did not suffer martyrdom. Everyone who is found faithful, just, and praiseworthy sits down at their banquet. We must be mindful to do God's will and not our own, for he who does God's will, will abide with God forever, even as God lives forever.

"Therefore, dearly beloved, let us be ready for whatever God wills, whole-souled, firm in faith, staunch in virtue, perfect in charity. Let us keep the commandments of the Lord bravely, practising innocence with simplicity, concord in charity, modesty in humility, diligence in ministering, eager to help those who labor, compassionate in our aid to the poor, courageous in defending the truth, austere in our rule of life. Then shall we not fail to set an example of good deeds. Behold these are the footprints the saints have left as they journeyed along their way to the heavenly fatherland. Let us tread in those steps that we may follow them to their joy" (translation from: *Roman Breviary in English*, publ. by Benziger Brothers, Inc.).

2. Extreme Unction and the Apostolic Blessing. History records how the gladiators in ancient Greece and Rome rubbed their limbs with oil. This anointing aided them in two ways when fighting, by strengthening the members of the body, keeping them fresh and supple, and by rendering it more difficult for the enemy to get hold of a smooth and slippery skin. The decisive battle in a Christian's life comes at death. Then Mother Church approaches with holy Oils to anoint her child well for the last round. The oils of Extreme Unction, consecrated by the bishop on Holy Thursday before the little elevation of the sacred

Host, have the power to strengthen a dying Christian for the crisis, and to render impossible any serious hold or vicious attack by Satan.

The oil for the sick is consecrated during Mass on Holy Thursday — and we wish to emphasize the point. For from the Sacrifice of Mass comes the power inherent in the sacred anointing. At the Last Supper in the Coenaculum, our Lord celebrated the mystery of His departure; it was followed by His dedication to death in the garden of Olives. What a meaningful parallel for the last liturgical things in the life of a Christian! After receiving holy Viaticum, the last sharing in the earthly sacrificial Banquet, follows the liturgical dedication unto death. The anointing with chrism at confirmation consecrated the dying man a soldier of Christ; there now takes place the last holy anointing, to a hero's death. A solemn *mysterium* at the end of each Christian's life! The Ritual officially calls it *Extrema Unctio*, last anointing.

For liturgically-minded persons, for those who await and desire the Lord's parousia, the last anointing is full of consolation. They see in it a consecration unto death with Christ. They do not fear death, for they see in this sacrament the Church's great motherly care and interest as she plucks from death its bitterness, its tears and fears, as she transforms death itself into a door leading to a new existence. For those who have the spirit of the Church the last anointing is an anointing unto incorruptibility and resurrection, an adorning and beautifying for the impending parousia, an occasion to join the great chorus crying, *Maranatha*, Come, Lord Jesus! The liturgically-minded Christian accordingly informs himself while still in good health about the rite of Extreme Unction.[1] Now and then he reads it through — translations abound — and with text in hand follows the sacred actions when his turn comes or when it is administered to another.

Usually a very consoling rite takes place immediately after the administration of Extreme Unction. Our Holy Father himself

[1] Copies in pamphlet form are available from: The Liturgical Press, Collegeville, Minnesota.

comes to the sick bed. Only the great number of his lambs prevents him from doing so personally. So he delegates the liturgist at the sickbed to take his place and equips him with the greatest and most embracive powers. He bids him empty the Church's spiritual treasury to the very bottom. As the sick man piously invokes the Name of Jesus and accepts death with patient resignation, the priest with the sign of redemption in his hand and the Church's official prayer on his lips grants a plenary indulgence effective at the moment of death. Truly, Mother Church makes dying easy, makes it beautiful, makes it redemptive.

November 6

FERIAL DAY

In fear serve the Lord, all you His saints! To those who fear Him nothing is lacking. See, God's eye rests kindly upon the just; willingly He bends His ear to their petitions.

1. Reflections on the Season. Let us keep our thoughts in heaven; a word from St. Bernard, the "Mellifluous Doctor," will help.

"Does our thinking about the saints help them any? or our praising them? or our glorifying them and keeping a solemnity to their honor? How would they profit by earthly honors whom the heavenly Father honors in exact fulfillment of His Son's promise? Our eulogies, what good are they to the saints? They do not need them. Exactly. The saints, dearly beloved, in no way need anything from us, nor does our veneration of them add to their beatitude. Rather, if we celebrate their memory, it is to our benefit, not theirs. Do you wish to know how much it is to our benefit? In my own case I must confess that thinking about them gives rise to a burning desire, one best described as threefold. Remember the saying: Seeing is believing? Now my memory is like seeing to me; and to think about the saints is hardly different from seeing them. So by keeping them in mind we already have a portion in the land of the living; nor is it something tiny if we but give our full affection to it. Thus, may I say, our state of life is heavenly — though not, of course, identical with the saints in all respects. For the reality is theirs and it is present to them, ours is still desire; they are actually present, while we are there in thought."

2. **Commending a Dying Soul to God.** Often death does not follow immediately after the administration of Extreme Unction and the Apostolic Blessing. In many cases the dying person will live at least for some time. He is fully equipped. Church and Church members have done what was to be done according to the liturgy. The moment of the Lord's parousia is drawing near. It is heralded by increasing agony; there are recognizable signs that the Lord of life is approaching to take His faithful follower even in cases where death resembles a peaceful falling asleep. Mother Church did not leave her child after the anointing with holy oils like one who says: I have done my duty. She is only retreating somewhat so that at the moment of final crisis she may fortify once more the dying child of Adam with her prayer and sacred rites. The Ritual has a special section devoted to the last agony of a dying person and his departure from this life. According to the official title it is called *Commendatio Animae*, Commending the Dying Soul to God.

In too many dioceses this service has fallen into disuse. The Roman Ritual (Tit. VI, ch. 7) gives this directive: "Let the priest about to perform the *Commendatio Animae* be accompanied by a cleric carrying a vessel with holy water; he is to be clothed with surplice and purple stole." Evidently this rubric directs that the priest be present when a sick man is at the point of death in order to act as the official liturgist, commending the soul to God in the name of the Church. In large cities where the demands upon those in charge of souls are so manifold, this directive of the Ritual becomes very difficult to comply with, but there are places (institutions) and smaller parishes where calls to the sick and dying are relatively rare; it would not be too much for the

Church's official liturgist to be present for the *Commendatio Animae*.

What is the essence of this dedication of the soul to God? Perhaps it can be illustrated by a comparison. An American emigrates to Australia. He builds a homestead, makes friends and acquaintances who love and help him. Yet in spite of his good fortune an attachment to America still burns within him. After some years he resolves to return. At the port he shakes hands, embraces and kisses his friends farewell. Tearing himself away, he ascends the gangplank, and from the deck waves a final adieu to those below. A push from the tug, the ship begins the journey to his native land. At the deck in San Francisco his father and mother are waiting, friends and brothers greet him on his return, take him into their arms and accompany him to the family home.

Now we Christians are foreigners upon earth, homeless men, or at least we should be such. We have here no lasting city. By ritual and rite Mother Church keeps alive in our breasts a longing for our true fatherland. She keeps burning a desire for the parousia. Death culminates that yearning. Into the wide unknown, into the unbounded sea with misty shores we steer as we leave the port of this world. Close friends stand about to wish us a happy voyage, to give parting advice, to say adieu (*etym: ad Deum*, to God); over beyond are other friends, those in full possession of their homeland, to welcome and receive us. "Escorts at Departure, Escorts at Arrival" would be an appropriate explanatory subtitle for the *Commendatio Animae*. For it presents the drama of the Christian soul's return to its Creator and Redeemer.

Keep in mind the comparison. Two choirs pray in this final rite. The first choir is composed of acquaintances and friends praying about the sickbed, wishing the departing soul beatitude. It is the choir from this world. To the second choir belong the blessed in heaven, the redeemed who, led by Christ the King, escort the soul into the realms of joy and peace. The *Commendatio Animae* has a positive and a negative aspect. When the text treats of forgiveness of sin or of merciful judgment, we citizens of this earth are praying. When the text treats of the reception into the next world, when the saints of the Old and the New Testaments are called upon, we, so to speak, let them pray with our mouths. The Church militant and the Church triumphant clasp hands across two distant shores when a Christian soul returns to his Father's home.

November 7

FERIAL DAY

Lord, they put justice into practice; now they dwell in Your tabernacle and rest upon Your holy mountain!

1. Reflections on the Season. Today we ask the "golden-mouthed" John Chrysostom to lead the meditation. He will develop this theme: If you do not imitate the deeds of the saints, you are not allowed to praise them.

"The man who, with reverential love, admires the merits of the saints, who continually sings the praises of these just ones, should imitate their saintly ways and their righteous lives. Should he find delight in the virtue of some particular saint, let him find an equal delight in obedience in God's service. Does he praise a saint? Then let him imitate that saint. If he is not ready to imitate him he should not praise him. Who praises another, let him make himself worthy of like praise. Let him who admires the meritorious life of a holy man, himself become worthy of admiration by a like holiness of life. If we love the good and faithful because we admire their goodness and fidelity, we may, by doing what they did, become like them.

"Nor is it difficult for us to imitate what they did. Observe that these saints of ancient days did their heroic deeds without the benefit of any example. They did not imitate others. They left themselves to us as examples of virtues to emulate. So, while we derive profit from them, others may derive benefit from us, that through His servants Christ may ever be glorified in His holy Church. In the beginning of the world, blameless Abel was slain, Enoch with whom God was pleased was taken away, Noah was found righteous, Abraham faithful, Moses meek, Josue chaste, David mild, Elias acceptable, Daniel holy, and the three children rendered victorious.

"The apostles, disciples of Christ, are held to be teachers of the faithful; the valiant confessors give battle, the heroic martyrs triumph, and Christian hosts, armed by God, always prevail over the devil. All these have been men, alike in valor, unlike in their strife, glorious in their victory. Hence, O Christian, you are but a fainthearted soldier if you think you can conquer without a battle, triumph without a struggle. Use your strength, fight manfully, wage a fierce battle. Remember your covenant, consider your situation, study your battlefield. You have pledged yourself to a contract, you have taken up a responsibility, you have enlisted in an army" (translation from: *Roman Breviary in English*, publ. by Benziger Brothers, Inc.).

2. Christian Burial. Let this be the guiding principle for all who wish to bury their near and dear ones in the spirit of holy Church: Everything related to the funeral must reflect simplicity, sincerity, and liturgical propriety. This principle will be operative as the obituaries are written and the funeral arrangements made. There should be no grandiose preparations foreshadowing a pompous funeral or one resounding with woes and lamentations. It will be enough to extend a simple "invitation to a Christian burial."

Immediate relatives or acquaintances should assume care over the body, themselves doing some of the preliminaries. These last acts of love and piety should not be completely handed over to professional morticians. The deceased should be clothed in his best, that worn on Sundays as he attended holy Mass. An infant clothed with baptismal robe as it lies in the coffin would indeed be most impressive. A wreath or veil, signs of virginity, could well be given an unmarried girl. The custom of putting a crucifix into the cold hands stems from deep faith.

Let the coffin and its ornamentation be of genuine material. The liturgy hates all pretense. A plain, brown wooden box is more appropriate than a coffin covered with silvery confetti, and

linen cloth is better than lace. Some Christian symbol should
adorn man's last earthly home. Do not make the room where
the body lies resemble a dark, foreboding corner, as if there
were no hope or solace. Black carpets and hangings are out of
place. The coffin should be placed before the home-altar where
there is one; where not, let the room have more the character
of a chapel than of a funeral chamber. Flowers and lights — dis-
creetly arranged — manifest the primitive Christian sense of
death as the hour of victory and triumph.

After these first arrangements for a becoming burial have
been made and the house becomes somewhat quiet, the family
will turn to the spiritual needs of the deceased. How appropriate it
would be if on the day of death the family with near relatives and
friends gathered about the bier for the common recitation of
Vespers of the Dead! Vespers, the Church's evening thanksgiving prayer, always have a festive ring as they bid goodbye to a
day of salvation. And today was a day of salvation in the house
of the deceased. Blessed they who are so deeply anchored in
eternity that at a coffin they can sing Mary's hymn of salvation.
They do not lack the spirit of the primitive Church.

On the evening before the funeral, Matins of the Dead could
be recited near the body of the deceased; and in the morning,
Lauds. Mother Church comes personally with all her sympathy
and all her love in this Office of the Dead. It is the vigil service
which prepares for and inaugurates the Eucharistic Sacrifice for
the burial.

November 8

THE FOUR CROWNED BROTHERS, Martyrs

*Oh, how glorious is the kingdom where all the saints
rejoice with Christ! Clothed in white robes, they follow
the Lamb wherever He goes!*

1. Reflections on the Season. It is already a week since the
great vision of heaven on All Saints. It was a week with "our

conversation in heaven." Let us listen as St. Cyprian continues that conversation.

"My dearest brethren! We must take this to heart and ponder over it repeatedly, that we have renounced the world and have become sojourners on earth, living here as guests and aliens. We look forward anxiously to the day that will bring each one to his true home, the day on which we will be removed from hence, the day that will free us from earth-shackling bonds, the day that will restore paradise to us and all of heaven's realms. Who, when in a strange country, does not hasten to return to his fatherland? Who, when sailing homeward, does not ardently desire favorable winds so as to embrace beloved ones more quickly? Now we know that our homeland is paradise, and our parents are the patriarchs. Why then do we not hasten, why are we not running swiftly forward to see our homeland, to greet our parents? A tremendous number of our beloved ones are there expecting us, parents, brothers, sisters; sons and daughters are yearning to meet us. All these are already sure of their own immortality, while they are anxiously concerned over ours.

"What joy it would be both for them and for us if we could but see them, embrace them! What pleasure it would be to live in those celestial realms eternally, with never a fear of death! In perfect beatitude forever! That glorious choir of apostles is there. Those joyous bands of prophets are there. Martyrs in countless throngs are there, adorned with crowns because of their victory over persecution and death. Virgins are there in triumph, they who subdued the lusts of flesh and body by the might of continence. The merciful are there, rewarded for having provided the poor with food and supplies, thereby practicing the works of justice; for they observed the Lord's precepts and stored up their earthly possessions in the heavenly granaries. To these, beloved brethren, we must hasten with yearning desire and holy impatience; with them we want to be as soon as possible so that, we hope, it will be our good fortune to be more quickly with Christ."

St. Cyprian discourses well on the parousia. We will try to

remember his words during the remaining days of the Church's Harvest Time.

2. The Four Crowned Brothers. The history of these holy martyrs is very confusing. The *Martyrology* has this: "At Rome on the Via Lavicana the day of the death of four holy martyrs, .he brothers Severus, Severianus, Carpophorus, and Victorinus. Under Emperor Diocletian they were scourged to death with lead rods. Their names were first made known many years later through a divine revelation. As no one knew their names previously, the annual feastday to their honor was celebrated under the title: The Four Crowned Brothers. The designation was retained even after the revelation."

The basilica of the Four Crowned Martyrs also contains the relics of five sculptors who under Diocletian refused to make idols or to venerate sun-god pictures. Reports say they were scourged, placed in lead coffins and submerged in a stream (*c.* 300). Hagiographers are trying to disentangle the conflicting statements on the relation of these two groups to one another, whether two groups actually existed, whether they were Pannomians or Romans, soldiers or stone-masons, etc.

3. Burial Service. Our Catholic burial service is actually a triple service, first at the home of the deceased, then around the altar, lastly in the cemetery. The most important part is unquestionably the Requiem Mass in church. The very act of bringing the body to the parish church does not remain untouched by liturgy. Relatives and parishioners gather at the home. The deceased must be brought to the house of God in a solemn manner. The last trip to holy Mass retains something of the ancient stational service, when kept according to the manner prescribed. The deceased's house resembles the *ecclesia collecta*, the place where the faithful gather and at which the liturgical procession forms and leaves for Mass at the station (parish) church. These preparatory acts form the solemn Introit to the holy Sacrifice. There is sprinkling with holy water and prayer, and the funeral procession is formed. The psalm *De Profundis* unites us with the deceased suffering in purgatory, who are awaiting the merits of the holy Sacrifice.

With the singing of the words, *"Subvenite. . . . Come, you saints of God, hasten to meet this soul . . .,"* the body enters the church for the last time. It will rest near the altar while the great Sacrifice of atonement is offered. The rubrics of the Roman Ritual here prescribe the Office of the Dead as preparation for the Mass of Requiem. Seldom, however, is this possible because of its length or the lack of chanters. The Requiem Mass, set in the midst of the burial service and constituting its climax, brings out clearly that through the power of the holy Sacrifice the deceased obtains salvation and admittance into the peace and joy of the Lord. Let us never forget that the very core and substance of the burial rite is torn away if the holy Sacrifice is first cele-brated after interment. The parishioners are holding a final community celebration with their departed member at which they obtain for his soul and for the souls of all departed Chris-tians the fruits of Calvary. A Sacrifice offered in this spirit is very moving. To such a Sacrifice there naturally belongs a meaning-ful Offertory and a Eucharistic Banquet. The funeral sermon would have its place after the Gospel. It should not consist in a eulogy of the departed but in a homily explaining the liturgy or in an exposition of the *mysterium* of redemption now being consummated.

After the Mass of the Dead there follows the *Libera*. This heavy chant does not at first glance square too well with the redemption-*mysterium* fulfilled in the deceased. Its setting is the final judgment, the day on which the corpse here present will rise again and share in the soul's lot of eternal joy or damnation. If the holy Sacrifice benefits the soul directly, we may perhaps re-gard the *Libera* as an absolution over the body, its companion in sin. The sprinkling and incense tend to confirm this interpre-tation. The Church washes it clean with holy water, honors it with incense. Like the incense smoke which disappears, the body will vanish; like the incense which is transformed into the sur-rounding atmosphere, so the body after death and corruption will be transformed into glory. The soul is redeemed, the body purified, the *mysterium* of the last journey enters its final phase.

With the chanting of *In paradisum*. . . . "May the angels conduct you into paradise," all proceed to the cemetery.

The funeral procession from the house to the church was symbolic, likewise that from the church to the cemetery. The former represented the soul coming before Christ, the latter its entrance into the joys of paradise. The thought-content of the prayers preceding the Mass differs fundamentally from those following. The former come from hearts that are heavy, serious, sorrowful. The latter are joyous, triumphant, light, almost festive in spirit. Lauds in the Office of the Dead reflect best the attitude among early Christians toward death and dying, and much of that attitude is retained in the last phase of the burial ritual. It cannot, may not be different. If the soul was well prepared at the moment of death, it cannot lose its precious treasure. The mystery of holy Mass made that clear. Accordingly, the change now in our spirit of prayer.

The *In paradisum* which accompanies the body out of church has a lightsome and happy melody. We quoted part above. One senses a resemblance to the last prayers of the *Commendatio*; the act of carrying the body to its resting place could well symbolize the soul's entrance into eternal happiness, "the place of coolness, light, and peace," as the Canon phrases it. "May the angels conduct you into paradise, at your coming may the martyrs receive you and accompany you into the holy city Jerusalem (heaven). May choirs of angels receive you and with once poor Lazarus may you have rest everlasting." There is moral certainty that our deceased member will be numbered in the choir of the blessed.

While the heavenly citizens hurry to meet and accompany it to eternal beatitude, we, their counterparts here below, surround the body to carry it to its temporary resting place. On the way to church the Ritual called for penitential prayer. On the way to the cemetery nothing of the kind. Comforted, erect, we follow the coffin, in hope. At God's acre the body is consigned to the earth. How beautiful, I might say, how liturgical is this phrase, "God's acre." Spontaneously it brings to mind that the body is *seed* for a more beautiful life. It is sown in the furrows of holy ground, seed budding into divine life. The body is not abandoned to death, it is not left to destruction. *Vita mutatur, non tollitur* we prayed in the Preface, "Life does not cease, it merely changes." This is true of the body now being lowered into the grave. The grave into which the body of a Christian is placed is first blessed. Holy things are hid in holy places. The body sanctified through the mysteries of holy Church rests in sacred ground. "I am the Resurrection and the Life. . . ."

November 9

DEDICATION OF THE LATERAN BASILICA IN ROME ST. THEODORE, Martyr

This place is an ineffable mystery

1. The Feast of Dedication. We are celebrating the dedication of the mother church of Latin Catholicism, the Lateran Basilica in Rome. According to an inscription at the entrance of the building, it ranks as the "Mother and Head of All Churches in the (Holy) City and throughout the World" — OMNIUM URBIS ET ORBIS ECCLESIARUM MATER ET CAPUT. This, not St. Peter's, is the Pope's cathedral. Also called the Church of Holy Savior or the Church of St. John Baptist, it was the baptism church of ancient Rome.

As one of the more important station churches, it was the scene of common meeting for the great festivals closely related to the Easter (baptism) mystery. Here on the first Sunday of Lent we begin our spiritual warfare; here on Palm Sunday we prepare the triumph for the King of martyrs. Here on Holy Thursday we celebrate the memorial of the Last Supper on an ancient wooden altar. And here we solemnize the greatest of all mysteries on Easter eve as we are reborn in the saving waters of baptism. Truly we have reason today to be sincerely grateful for manifold graces. The Basilica of Holy Savior was constructed by Emperor Constantine on the spot where he had received the sacrament of holy baptism from the hands of Pope Sylvester. The wooden altar in this edifice recalls the days of persecution during which the Roman bishops had no permanent place to offer the holy Sacrifice. For comment on the dedication of a church and on its Mass formulary, see p. 429.

2. **Holy Scripture** (Apoc. 21:9-18). Before our eyes today the Church unfurls a view of the heavenly Jerusalem; it is her way of indicating that the material edifice dedicated to divine worship symbolizes heaven. "Then one of the seven angels who had the seven bowls full of the seven last plagues approached and said to me: Come, I will show you the bride, the spouse of the Lamb. In spirit he carried me away to a mountain, great and high, and showed me the holy city Jerusalem, coming down out of heaven from God, having the glory of God. Its light was like to a precious stone, as it were, a jasper-stone, clear as crystal. It had a great and high wall with twelve gates, and at the gates twelve angels; there were carved on them the names of the twelve tribes of the children of Israel. On the east were three gates, on the north three gates, on the south three gates, and on the west three gates. The wall of the city had twelve foundation-stones, and on them the twelve names of the Lamb's twelve apostles" (Apoc. 21:9–14).

It is not without reason that the liturgy disregards the usual Lessons for dedication feasts today (and November 18) and places before us the material edifice as a type of heaven. For by so doing she wishes to link these two feasts with the Church's Harvest Time. Standing before the cornerstone of the Lateran, the inference comes easily to mind: this basilica represents the place of baptism and the place of glory!

3. **St. Theodore.** St. Theodore was a Christian soldier who set on fire the temple of the mother-goddess Cybele at Amasea (303 A.D.). The prefect of the legion promised mercy if he repented his act and renounced the Christian faith. Theodore persevered bravely; accordingly he was cast into prison and his flesh ripped by iron hooks so that his ribs were exposed. In the midst of indescribable torture he sang joyfully, "I will bless the Lord at all times; His praise will ever be in my mouth" (Ps. 33).

Praying and singing the glories of Christ, he was burned alive on November 9. A panegyric by St. Gregory of Nyssa on his virtues is extant. Theodore's head has been venerated at Cajeta since the Middle Ages. In ancient times, particularly among the Greeks, this soldier-martyr was honored as patron of armies. During the seventh century a church was dedicated to him in Rome, and his picture appears upon the apse mosaic in the church of Sts. Cosmas and Damian. *Application*. We marvel at the heroic courage St. Theodore showed in the midst of pain. While suffering horribly he sang songs of praise! While we are so frightened by the smallest ache, become uncomfortable at the very mention of suffering! God does not ask such suffering from us as He did from Theodore, yet He asks that we accept some troubles patiently. The example of today's martyr is another source of strength.

November 10

ST. ANDREW AVELLINO, Confessor

A lying mouth kills the soul

1. **St. Andrew.** *Day of death*: November 10, 1608 (at the age of eighty-seven). *Grave*: at Naples, in the Theatine Church of St. Paul. *Life.* As a young priest Andrew served at an ecclesiastical court. While making a defense, a small lie slipped by his lips; soon afterward he accidentally read the words, "A lying mouth kills the soul" (Wis. 1:11). Deeply moved, he resigned his position and dedicated himself solely to the service of God and the welfare of souls. In 1566 he entered the Order of Theatines and chose the name Andrew out of love for the Cross of Christ. He labored most zealously as a shepherd of souls. With fatherly love and prudence he spent countless hours hearing confessions. He frequently visited the towns and villages in the neighborhood of Naples to preach the saving message of the Gospel.

By means of miracles God Himself often glorified the love of neighbor burning in the heart of His holy priest. Once as he was returning home from a round of duties, the rain and wind extinguished the lantern he was carrying; he and his companion, however, were not soaked by the downpour; in fact, rays of light proceeded from his body and guided them through the dense darkness. Many came to him to settle cases of conscience, his letters number thousands. Worn out by work and enfeebled by age, he suffered a stroke at the foot of the altar just as he was beginning holy Mass and died as he repeated for the third time, "I will go unto the altar of God." He is venerated as patron against sudden death.

Application. The life of a saint is like a course at school. From each day's saint we ought to assimilate some practical lesson. What, for instance, is our attitude on speaking the truth? The words, "A lying mouth kills the soul," might well resound in our ears all through the day. And in what condition is my love toward Christ and His Cross? Would I choose the name Andrew out of love for the Cross? What a beautiful death — to die at the altar! I will pray for an equally happy death, well prepared, and with the mercy of the last sacraments. The Mass is from the Common of Confessors, *Os justi*, see p. 421. A proper *Collect* praises Andrew's zeal for advancing daily in virtue and asks a similar grace for us.

2. Sts. Tryphon, Respicius, and Nympha. Tryphon, said to have been a Phrygian goose-herd as a boy, was martyred under Emperor Decius (*c.* 250); of the martyr Respicius nothing is known. The virgin Nympha, according to one account, was put to death at Palermo during the fourth century. All three were buried in the station church of St. Tryphon at Rome. When the building had become delapidated, their relics were transferred to the neighboring church of St. Augustine (see Saturday after Ash Wednesday).

3. Speech. Our lesson today is the text from Sacred Scripture, "A lying mouth kills the soul." What *is* our attitude on speaking the truth? Or, more positively, what is our attitude toward the sanctity of speech? Every human word echoes a divine word.

Human speech has been sanctified by the Word of God. For when human nature found its highest nobility through the incarnation of the Word of God, human words too were consecrated and ennobled. Poor human nature becomes the home and weak human words become the echo of divine omnipotence and omniscience!

How the human body, how human speech have been sanctified! With what reverence ought we use lips and tongue! In God's plan they are designed to spread wisdom, truth, and love: "The mouth of the just man speaks wisdom, and his tongue righteousness." The words begin today's Mass. Recall how St. James spoke of the tongue, "Let every man be swift to hear, slow to speak . . . if anyone thinks himself to be religious but does not restrain his tongue, that man's religion is vain . . . if anyone does not offend in word, he is a perfect man, able also to lead round by a bridle the whole body . . . with it we bless God the Father; and with it we curse men, who have been made after the likeness of God. Out of the same mouth proceed blessing and cursing. These things, my brethren, ought not to be so. Does the fountain send forth sweet and bitter water from the same opening?" How holy the tongue sanctified by God's Word and God's Presence! What care should be exercized over a member of the body that so often serves a sacred purpose!

November 11

ST. MARTIN, Bishop and Confessor

O blessed man, whose soul possesses paradise! Therefore angels exult, archangels rejoice, choirs of saints sing, and hosts of virgins say: Stay with us forever (Ben. Ant.).

O blessed bishop, who loved Christ the King wholeheartedly and did not fear the might of princes! O

holy soul, you were not stricken by the persecutor's
sword, yet did not lose the palm of martyrdom! (Magn.
Ant., 2. Vesp.)

1. **St. Martin.** Next to St. Sylvester and St. Antony the hermit, St. Martin was one of the first to receive the honors of a saint
without suffering martyrdom. The great veneration tendered
him in ancient times is reflected in today's beautiful Office; from
it we come to know many details of his life. *Life.* Martin was
born (*c.* 316) at Sabaria, a town in Pannonia near the famous
Benedictine monastery dedicated to his name. Against the wishes
of his parents he associated with Christians and became a
catechumen at the age of ten. At fifteen he entered the army and
served under the Emperors Constantius and Julian. While in
the service he met a poor, naked beggar at the gates of Amiens
who asked alms in Christ's Name. Martin had nothing with
him except his weapons and soldier's mantle; but he took his
sword, cut the latter in two, and gave half to the poor man. During the following night Christ appeared to him clothed with
half a mantle and said, "Martin, the catechumen, has clothed
Me with this mantle!"

Martin was eighteen years old when he received the sacrament of holy baptism. At the pleading of his superior officer, he
remained two years longer in the army. Then, upon requesting
dismissal, Julian accused him of cowardice. "With the sign of
the Cross," Martin answered, "I shall more certainly break
through the ranks of the enemy than if armed with shield and
sword." When released he sought out St. Hilary, bishop of
Poitiers (see January 14), was ordained exorcist. Later he was
made bishop of Tours. Close to the city he built a monastery
(Marmoutier), where with eighty monks he led a most holy life.
On one of his numerous visits to the imperial court at Trier, a
certain man besought him to help his daughter, "I firmly believe in the Lord that my daughter will be healed through your
prayer!" Martin healed the girl with consecrated oil. Tetradius,
who witnessed this extraordinary manifestation of divine power,
asked for baptism.

Martin also possessed the gift of discerning spirits. Once the devil appeared to him radiant and clothed in royal apparel, and spoke as if he were Christ. Martin, recognizing the deceit, replied, "The Lord Jesus Christ never prophesied that He would come in purple robes and royal crown." The apparition immediately vanished. Three dead persons he raised to life. While celebrating holy Mass a luminous sphere appeared over his head. He was far advanced in age when he fell into a grievous fever during a visitation at Candes, an outlying parish of his diocese. Unceasingly he begged God to release him from this mortal prison. His disciples, however, implored him with tears, "Father, why are you leaving us? To whom will you entrust the care of your disconsolate children?" Deeply moved, Martin turned to God: "Lord, if I am still necessary for Your people, I will not refuse the labor. Your will be done!"

When the bystanders saw that despite his great fever he remained lying on his back, they besought him to change position to alleviate somewhat the pain. But Martin answered, "Brothers, rather let me look toward heaven than to earth so that my soul in its journey home may take a direct flight to the Lord." Shortly before death he saw the evil spirit. "What do you want, horrible beast? You will find nothing in me that's yours!" With those words the aged saint breathed forth his soul on November 11, 397, at the age of eighty-one.

We will keep in mind St. Martin's longing for the parousia. His faithful biographer and trusted friend was Sulpicius Severus, an eyewitness to some of the saint's words and miracles. Devotion to St. Martin soon spread over all western Europe and his feast was kept with unusual solemnity. For centuries Christians ate roasted goose on his feastday (for which reason he is pictured with a goose). Perhaps this custom served as a kind of Mardi Gras before the beginning of the Advent fast, which during the Middle Ages began earlier than at present.

2. Holy Mass (Statuit). The Mass is from the Common of Confessor-Bishops, see p. 417. Before us stands a high priest, one of the most venerable in Church history; accordingly the *Introit* and *Epistle* have a distinctive character. A proper *Gospel* shows us Martin as a "light of the Church" that illumines far and wide;

it reminds us of the baptismal "light" in our soul. To keep this burning for the advent of the Bridegroom is our one great duty. The *Alleluia* verse describes Martin's assumption into heaven, "The holy man, St. Martin, bishop of the city of Tours, has fallen asleep. Angels and archangels, thrones, dominations and virtues have received him." The hymn *Iste Confessor* was originally composed in honor of today's saint.

3. St. Mennas, according to legend a Christian soldier from Egypt, left the Roman army during the persecution of Diocletian and Maximian to go into the desert and do penance. On the Emperor's birthday, which the people celebrated with outdoor spectacles, he entered the theatre at Cotyaeum and openly mocked belief in pagan gods. He was seized and cruelly scourged by Pyrrhus, the official in charge. Tied to the rack, his whole body was burned with torches, brushed with thorns, torn with leaden whips. He was finally beheaded and his body thrown into the fire. Christians took what remained and gave it honorable burial. His grave, close to Alexandria, became such a famous place of pilgrimage that, as at Lourdes today, a whole town arose to accommodate the pilgrims. Many small phials or *eulogia* have been found there which show St. Mennas between two kneeling camels. *Application.* God does not ask of us the heroic acts performed by today's spiritual champion. The saints came directly under the influence of the Holy Spirit; we cannot imitate them in everything, but we can admire them and be confirmed in love and obedience toward God.

November 12

ST. MARTIN I, Pope and Martyr

Rejoice when you share in the sufferings of Christ

1. **St. Martin I.** *Day of death*: September 16, 655. *Grave*: at Rome, in the church of Sts. Sylvester and Martin. *Life.* Pope Martin I (649–655) was outstanding for virtue and knowledge.

He was selected by divine Providence to be the supreme defender of the doctrine that in Christ there are two wills, a divine and a human, against the monothelite teaching of one will favored at Constantinople. Immediately after ascending the papal throne, he convoked a synod at the Lateran which put the true teaching in its proper light and condemned the opposing error. Emperor Constans II supported the monothelite patriarch of Constantinople and commissioned the Exarch Olympios to assassinate the Pope. The Exarch entrusted the task to a lictor who planned to murder Martin during Mass in the church of St. Mary of the Crib. The lictor could not accomplish the mission because he was suddenly struck blind. From that moment many misfortunes befell the Emperor, but no change in attitude resulted. Instead he sent the Exarch Theodor Kalliopes to Rome with orders to arrest the Pope.

Martin was carried to Constantinople to begin a tedious martrydom. He was given over to the scoffing of the rabble as he lay ill on the ship. For three months he languished in prison. Called before a tribunal, he was condemned, robbed of his episcopal garments, put into chains. Finally he was banished to Kherson in the Crimea and died there due to inhuman privations. Two letters written before his death give evidence of how he suffered under the dreadful treatment. *Application.* As head of the Church, St. Martin condemned false doctrine and thereby brought upon himself the wrath of the Emperor. He would not yield a hairbreadth from the way of truth, even when such a stand entailed suffering, imprisonment, exile, death. Here is a model for fidelity to one's vocation. In every state of life there are opportunities for martyrdom.

2. **Holy Mass** is from the Common of Sovereign Pontiffs, *Si diligis Me*, see p. 398. It is easy to think of Pope Martin as we listen to the *Epistle*, "I, a witness to the sufferings of Christ . . . after we have suffered a little while the God of all grace will perfect, strengthen, and establish us." Martin relied upon God for his vindication and his trust did not prove vain. He is the last of the Popes to be venerated as a martyr; the Byzantine liturgy acclaims him as a "glorious defender of the true faith" and an "ornament of the divine See of Peter."

November 13

ST. DIDACUS, Confessor

O sweet wood, O sweet nails

1. St. Didacus. *Day of death*: November 12, 1463; canonized 1588; feast introduced into the missal in 1671. *Grave*: at Alcala in Castile. *Life*. Didacus (or Diego, Jacob) was born in the town of San Nicolas, Andalusia. From early youth he showed a love for solitude. At Arrizafa, near Cordova, he became a Franciscan brother and was outstanding in humility and obedience. He had little formal education, yet through divine enlightenment in no way lacked wisdom. As a missionary he visited the Canary Islands and was appointed first superior of the new foundation there. In 1450 Pope Nicholas V confided to his care the sick in the celebrated convent of Ara Caeli. With his tongue he often cleansed the wounds of the sick; many he miraculously healed with oil from the lamp which burned before a picture of the Blessed Virgin or with the sign of the Cross.

During a stay at the friary at Alcala in 1463, Didacus felt the approach of his last hour. Wrapped in discarded rags, with eyes fixed immovably upon a crucifix, he died while fervently praying the words of the hymn *Dulce lignum, dulces clavos*, O sweet wood, O sweet nails that held so sweet a burden! You alone were worthy to bear the King and Lord of heaven! For a long time his body remained incorrupt. The Mass is from the Common of Confessors, *Justus ut palma*, see p. 423. The formulary mirrors the mortified life of today's saint; the *Collect* accents his humility and makes it pivotal to our petition for heavenly glory.

2. The Little Flock. "Do not be afraid, little flock, for it has pleased your Father to give you the kingdom." Meditation upon these words from the Gospel will show two marks of true Christianity: (a) the Christian will always walk alone, for the world follows the broad, level and easy roads, while he must take the steep and narrow path. Do not marvel, then, if your environment does not understand you or regards you as "queer"; for so it treated the apostles (see today's Epistle), and so it treated the saints. As a Christian you belong to God's household. (b) Christ's flock is little in another sense, i.e., it is humble, keeps its virtues concealed. Be utterly convinced that only such things are truly pleasing to God which men do not see or praise. But from such little ones God raises up witnesses to His grace and power, "In Your wonderful Providence You choose the weak things of the world to put to shame all that is strong" (*Coll.*). Let us humbly be Christ's "little flock."

November 14

ST. JOSAPHAT, Bishop and Confessor

A martyr to the cause of Church unity

1. **St. Josaphat.** *Day of death*: November 12, 1623; canonized 1867. *Grave*: originally in Polotzk; his relics were hidden in 1875 when Russia suppressed the last Uniate diocese; during World War I they were brought to Vienna (1915), where they are venerated in the Greek Uniate Church of St. Barbara. There the body lies in a glass reliquary, clothed in episcopal robes, partially incorrupt. *Life*. In our age when greater efforts are being made for the cause of reuniting separated Eastern Churches, this outstanding patron of reunion should receive greater veneration.

Josaphat Kuncewitcz was born about the year 1580 at Vladimir, Volhynia, and given the name John at baptism. While being instructed as a child on the sufferings of our Savior, his heart is said to have been wounded by an arrow from the sacred side of the Crucified. In 1604 he became a Basilian monk, lived a very mortified life, went barefoot even in winter, refrained from the use of wine and flesh-meat, always wore a penitential garb. In 1614 he was appointed archimandrite of Vilna, and four years later archbishop of Polotzk; in this position he worked untiringly for Church reunion. He was a great friend of the poor, once even pledged his archepiscopal omophorion (pallium) to support a poor widow. The foes of union decided to assassinate him. In a sermon he himself spoke of his death as imminent. When he visited Vitebsk, his enemies attacked his lodging and murdered a number of his companions. Meekly the man of God hastened toward the mob and, full of love, cried, "My children, what are you doing? If you have something against me, see, here I am." With furious cries of "Kill the papist," they rushed upon him with gun and sword. Josaphat's body was thrown into the river but emerged, surrounded by rays of light, and was recovered. His murderers, when sentenced to death, repented their crime and became Catholics.

2. Holy Mass (Gaudeamus). There is intentional dependence of today's Mass formulary upon Greek liturgy, e.g., the *Introit* is derived from the East, and the Readings are used for martyr-bishops in Greek feast-day Masses. The liturgy begins on a festive note, "Let all rejoice in the Lord as we celebrate a feast-day in honor of the blessed martyr Josaphat." The thematic words, "I am the Good Shepherd; I know Mine . . .," are repeated three times, viz., in the *Collect, Gospel,* and *Communion* verse. The parable of the Good Shepherd is doubly true today, for Christ lays down His life anew through the Mass and through Josaphat, His member. We who mystically unite ourselves with Christ in the Sacrifice (and with Josaphat too) seek to share in His shepherdly spirit of love, fidelity, and self-immolation. Meditate, too, on the beautiful *Epistle* from Paul's letter to the Hebrews, for it tells of Christ's new High Priesthood. He, the eternal High Priest, offers Himself as a bloody Sacrifice; that immolation continues in the Mass as it is offered by the special priesthood of ordained ministers and the common priesthood of the laity.

3. The Greek Liturgy. A liturgist's interests should include a love for the Greek liturgy with its deep Oriental piety and early Christian enthusiasm. When you have the opportunity to be present at Mass celebrated in a Greek Catholic rite, prepare for it by obtaining a translation of the liturgy to be used. Every Catholic is allowed to receive holy Communion under both species at such a service. A good way to acquire an understanding of the Greek liturgy is to compare its structure with the Latin, noting similarities and divergencies. Like the Latin, the Greek Mass has two main parts, a Foremass and a Mass of the Faithful. The first part is mostly a prayer service (longer than the Latin Mass) and a reading service with two lessons, Epistle and Gospel. A point of difference is that the Greek Foremass is preceded by a long preparation called *proskomidie*; during it the priest vests at the altar and prepares the bread and wine.

In the Greek Mass of the Faithful we may distinguish three parts as in the Latin, a kind of Offertory, a Canon (called *Anaphora*), and Communion. The Offertory is considerably different from the Latin because the bread and wine are already prepared at the beginning of the service and there is no Offertory procession of the faithful. Instead we find a most impressive ceremony, the Great Entrance with its so-called cherubic chant. The priest brings the bread and wine from the Offertory table and goes to the altar through the Royal Door, while choir and people chant, "Let us, who mystically represent the cherubim and offer a thrice holy hymn to the life-giving Trinity, now put aside all earthly cares. That we may receive the King of all, who comes invisibly attended by hosts of angels. Alleluia, alleluia, alleluia." In this part the Creed is said and the kiss of peace given.

The part during which the consecration occurs has many similarities with ancient Mass ordos, e.g., consecration, anamnesis, epiclesis, and then only the mementos which in our Latin Canon come before and after the consecration. The Communion service is essentially the same as ours. I might point out three salient points in the Greek Mass: (a) it contains practically no changeable texts (apart from the Lessons, which are a type of

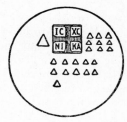

The arrangement of the particles upon the *diskos* at a Mass in the Greek Rite

lectio continua); (b) its prayers have a much wider range; (c) the people participate far more actively, the language being immediately intelligible to them.

November 15

ST. ALBERT THE GREAT, Bishop and Doctor

Blessed are the peacemakers

St. Albert. *Day of death*: November 15, 1280. *Grave*: church of St. Andrew in Cologne. *Life*. Albert, the "light of Germany," called the Great because of his encyclopedic knowledge, was born in 1193 at Lauingen, Donau. He studied at Padua, where under the influence of the second Dominican general, he joined the newly-founded Order of Preachers (1223). Soon he was sent to Germany, taught in various cities, particularly Cologne; Thomas of Aquin was his student. In 1248 he received the honor of Master in Sacred Theology at Paris. Throngs attended his lectures.

In 1254 Albert was chosen provincial of his Order in Germany. For a time he lived at the court of Pope Alexander II, who in 1260 made him bishop of Regensburg; two years later, however, he returned to his community at Cologne. There he acted as counselor, peacemaker, and shepherd of souls with great success. He died at the age of eighty-seven. Pope Pius XI numbered him among the ranks of the saints on December 16, 1931, and declared him a doctor of the Church. Much of his life was given to writing. His twenty-one folio volumes are devoted to commentaries on Aristotle (whose works were just then becoming known in the West) and the Bible. Legend credits him with drawing the ground plans for the cathedral at Cologne. Albert, the greatest German scholar of the Middle Ages, was outstanding in the fields of natural science, theology, and philosophy. (Holy Mass, from the Common of Doctors, see p. 419.)

November 16

ST. GERTRUDE, Virgin

In His saints God prepares a lovely dwelling-place

1. **St. Gertrude.** *Day of death*: November 17 (?), 1302; feast celebrated since 1739. *Grave*: at Helfta. *Life*. St. Gertrude the Great, a Cistercian nun, is one of the most lovable German saints from medieval times, and through her writings she will remain for all ages a guide to the interior life. She was born in 1256 at Eisleben and at the age of five taken to the convent at Rossdorf, where Gertrude of Hackeborn was abbess. Similarity in name has often occasioned confusion between the two Gertrudes. Our St. Gertrude never functioned as superior.

In spite of much ill-health, Gertrude used her exceptional natural talents well, knew Latin fluently. When she was twenty-five years old (1281), Christ began to appear to her and to disclose to her the secrets of mystical union. Obeying a divine wish, she put into writing the favors of grace bestowed upon her. Her most important work, *Legatus Divinae Pietatis*, "The Herald of Divine Love," is distinguished for theological profundity, sublime poetry, and unusual clarity. How it stimulates love of God can be felt only by reading it; Abbot Blosius is said to have read it twelve times each year. St. Gertrude died in 1302, more consumed by the fire of God's love than by fever.

Application. The Collect says that "God prepared for Himself a lovely dwelling-place in His saint." This is a profound observation; God dwells in His children. Virtues and graces make this dwelling lovely, while sin makes it a den of robbers. What an incentive for us to live piously, virtuously. The Mass is from the Common of Virgins, *Dilexisti*, see p. 425.

2. **Mysticism and Liturgy.** Mysticism means union with God, a union less by means of reason and will as through affection, feeling and love. Mysticism has always been a mark of Catholicism. John the Evangelist and Paul were the first great mystics. The Fathers of the Church, Ignatius of Antioch, Ireneus, Jerome, Augustine, Gregory the Great were mystics. The medieval Doc-

tors Bernard, Bonaventure, Thomas Aquinas were mystics, as
also Ignatius Loyola, Teresa and John of the Cross, down to such
modern-day representatives as Möhler, Scheeben, and Newman.
The mystics of ancient times thrived on piety based on the Mystical Body of Christ and the liturgy; this preserved them from
exaggerated individualism.

But when interest in liturgical piety declined in the later
Middle Ages, mysticism became more personal and stressed
direct union with Jesus. The liturgical revival of our day has the
task to give mysticism the proper balance between the excesses
of subjectivism and collectivism. There already have been noteworthy results. The doctrine of the Mystical Body and of the
lay priesthood are again becoming the common heritage of
Christians. The liturgy affords the specific type of mysticism
advocated by the Church; the sacramental system, understood
in its widest sense, is the most perfect and most effective means
unto mystical union with God.

The cult of the Sacred Heart in recent times has in some regards followed the road of subjective mysticism. On this point
it is instructive to hear that St. Gertrude, who belonged to the
older type of piety, spread devotion to the Sacred Heart long
before St. Margaret Mary Alacoque. A lengthy quotation from
Cardinal Schuster is here in place:

"The mission of this celebrated Benedictine nun in the thir-
teenth century was very similar to that of Margaret Mary
Alacoque. There is this difference, however, between the two
mystics: the great revelations of the Heart of Jesus to the Benedictine saint were intended for a band of privileged souls; those
of Paray-le-Monial were to enrich the whole Catholic world.
The object of the apparitions granted to both mystics was the
same: the ineffable love of Jesus, of which His Heart is the organ
and the physical sign. But the manner of conceiving this devotion is as different in the two saints as was their spiritual education.

"A member of an Order which for more than seven centuries
had been the heir of patristic tradition and in which the liturgy
was almost exclusively the source of spiritual life, Gertrude con-

ceived devotion to the Sacred Heart not as a separate devotion, but as a deeper intelligence of the great, all-embracing mystery of Christ living again in the Church by means of the Catholic liturgy. It is essentially the love of Jesus which through the universal prayer of the Church explains and illustrates the whole drama of His incarnation and the treasures of His Heart.

"The mysticism of St. Gertrude is entirely founded on the liturgical life of the Church. She knew few religious practices except the Divine Office and the solemn Masses at which she and St. Mechtilde, the *cantrix Mechtildis*, sang daily in the choir, together with the community of the Abbey of Helfta. The revelations granted to her by God were generally in relation to these Offices, and Jesus explained to her their more hidden meaning, or taught her more sublime ways of following them and of nourishing her spiritual life upon them.

"The atmosphere in Gertrude's mystical writings is almost always serene and radiant. Jesus revealed to her His Heart as a mystery of grace and love rather than as an abyss of sorrow. She did not see the divine Heart encircled with a crown of thorns, neither was she called to the special vocation of victim for the sins of the world as was St. Margaret Mary Alacoque. She sometimes beheld the Sacred Heart pierced for us, but that wound was a golden door through which she entered joyfully into the secret sanctuary of the Godhead, the chamber of the Spouse.

"Like John, who at the Last Supper rested calmly on the breast of the Savior, whilst the other apostles were alarmed and distressed by the announcement made by Christ of the treachery of Judas and of His own death, the mystic of Helfta found in the Sacred Heart a secret tabernacle, where nothing disturbed her profound contemplation.

"At times she would see that Heart like a golden cup at which all the saints slaked their thirst. At other times a chain of gold came from the Heart of Christ to bind the world in bonds of love. Again, the divine Heart resembled a thurible sending up incense before the throne of the heavenly Father, whilst at another moment it would appear like a precious casket containing all the merits of the incarnation freely granted to souls.

"Therefore the devotion of the Benedictine virgin to the Sacred Heart as a symbol of sorrow and of love reflects the attitude of fervent worship of the humanity of the Redeemer adopted by Catholic piety at the end of the Middle Ages.

"In writing the history of the devotion to the Sacred Heart, it is right to consider the ancient spiritual tradition of the Benedictine Order, as well as the zeal displayed in spreading the apostolate of the Heart of Jesus by more modern religious congregations, without setting one devotion against another, since all contribute to illustrate one Catholic Faith. In the same manner as the incarnation or the holy Eucharist, so too the most Sacred Heart of Jesus is a gift common to the whole Church and cannot be regarded as the exclusive possession of any particular Order. St. Gertrude therefore joins hands with Margaret Mary Alacoque, and her revelations find their complete fulfillment in those granted four centuries later to the heroic daughter of the Visitation" (from: *The Sacramentary* by Ildefonso Schuster, vol. 5, pp. 276–277, 278).

November 17

ST. GREGORY THAUMATURGUS, Bishop and Confessor

Whoever says to this mountain, 'Arise, and hurl yourself into the sea,' and does not waver in his heart, but believes that whatever he says will be done, it shall be done for him!

1. **St. Gregory Thaumaturgus,** i.e., the Miracle-worker, bishop of Neo-Caesarea in Pontus (Asia Minor), was graced to an extraordinary degree with the charism of performing miracles. Basil the Great compared him to Moses, the prophets, and the apostles. For instance, by his prayer he moved a hill which obstructed the construction of a church (see the Gospel of the Mass), dried

up a swamp which had occasioned dissension between two brothers, drove devils from men and idols. His miracles and prophetic
gifts converted many to Christ. As he neared death (*c.* 270), he
asked how many unbelievers remained in Neo-Caesarea and was
told seventeen. He thanked God and said, "That many believers
I found here when I became bishop." Holy Mass, *Statuit*, from
the Common of Bishops, see p. 417.

2. **The Faith that Moves Mountains.** The Gospel on "faith
that moves mountains" was selected because such a miracle
occurred in St. Gregory's life. "Have faith in God. Amen, I say
to you, whoever says to this mountain, 'Arise, and hurl yourself
into the sea,' and does not waver in his heart, but believes that
whatever he says will be done, it shall be done for him!" In the
homily St. Bede relates the story:

"We read that at the request of St. Gregory, bishop of Neo-
Caesarea, who was a man remarkable for his labor and virtue, a
hill did recede as much as the inhabitants of the city considered
necessary. For he wished to build a church at a particular site;
but when he realized that the plot was too small, the seashore
being on one side and the hill on the other, he returned at night,
knelt down and reminded the Lord of His promise that hills
would flee at the request of one who asked with faith. When he
arrived there next morning, he found a large level area, with the
hill moved as far away as the builders needed."

November 18

DEDICATION OF THE CHURCHES OF ST. PETER AND OF ST. PAUL

The heavenly Jerusalem

1. **The Feast.** Today's feast is a spiritual journey to two holy
tombs, that of St. Peter and that of St. Paul in Rome. These two
basilicas, marking the place of each apostle's martyrdom, are the

common heritage and glory of Christendom; it is, therefore, easily seen why we observe their dedication. At St. Peter's we celebrate the greatest feasts of the ecclesiastical year. Fourteen times annually we assemble there as at the stational church for the day's liturgy. To it we come for the joyful *Gaudete* Sunday in Advent, for the third Mass on Christmas, for Epiphany, Quinquagesima, Passion Sunday, Easter Monday, Ascension, Pentecost; also for Ember Saturday each quarter-year. In St. Peter's we receive the greatest feast-day graces of the Church year. For this we are thankful today.

In St. Paul's Outside the Walls we meet four times annually. St. Paul is our baptism patron; with him we renew our baptismal blessings on Sexagesima Sunday, on the Wednesday after the fourth Sunday in Lent, on Easter Tuesday; he is also our guest lecturer on Sundays, because most of the Epistles come from his lips.

Abbot Herwegen makes the following observations on St. Peter's in Rome. The Eternal City has two principal churches, St. John Lateran and St. Peter's. Since ancient times the Lateran basilica, the mother of all churches on earth, has been the church proper to the bishop of Rome in his position as head of the local community. Here the Lenten season was opened and the Easter liturgy solemnized. The basilica of St. Peter, on the other hand, was the church of non-Romans, of pilgrims who journeyed to the city where the two great apostles were martyred. Here those celebrations were held which expressed the universal character of the Roman Church, e.g., Epiphany and the noon Mass on Christmas. The Introits, Lessons, and chants of both these feasts are best explained as proclaiming Christ's universal dominion and His royal majesty.

To cite a few texts. "A Child is born to us and a Son is given us! Sovereignty rests upon His shoulders" (*Intr.*, Christmas). "The Son, He who is the radiance of His Father's glory and the image of His essence, He who upholds the universe by the power of His word, it is He who has cleansed us from sin and who is enthroned on high at the right hand of God's majesty. . . . To the Son He says: Your throne, O God, is forever and ever, a righteous sceptre is the sceptre of Your kingship" (*Epist.*). "All the ends of the earth see the salvation of our God . . . the Lord has made known His salvation before the eyes of all the Gentile nations" (*Grad.*). "Behold," reads the Introit of Epiphany, "the Lord, the Ruler, is come! Kingship rests in His hand, and might and universal rule. O God, give Your judgment to the King, Your justice to the King's Son." "Arise," the Epistle continues, "shine, O Jerusalem, for your light is come, and the glory of the Lord is risen upon you." The Gospel tells of the newborn King of the Jews who in the Offertory is adored by the kings of Tarsis and Arabia and by gift-bringing caravans from Saba. "All the kings of the earth adore Him, all nations serve Him." Both Masses, as is easily seen, are replete with Biblical texts on the kingship of Christ.

2. **The Lessons** of the second nocturn give the history regarding the construction of the two basilicas. Among the holy places which the first Christians held in honor, those sites were especially dear where the bodies of holy martyrs lay. Great veneration was accorded that area of the Vatican Hill where the grave of St. Peter was located. From all lands Christians made pilgrimages to it as to the rock of faith and the foundation of the Church. In due time the legend arose that Emperor Constantine the Great, eight days after his baptism, took off his diadem, threw himself humbly upon the earth, and shed many tears. Then with pick and shovel he started digging and, in memory of the twelve apostles, carried away twelve baskets of ground; thereby he set the boundaries of the basilica to be built in honor of St. Peter. When finished, the edifice was solemnly consecrated by Pope Sylvester I.

Pope Sylvester had ordered the altar to be of stone; he anointed it with chrism and decreed that in the future only stone altars were to be used. A new church, the present St. Peter's, was consecrated by Pope Urban VIII on November 18, 1626. The ancient basilica of St. Paul was destroyed by fire in 1823; a new structure was consecrated by Pius IX on December 10, 1854, the occasion of the proclamation of the dogma of the Immaculate Conception. — On the significance of the Dedication of a Church and the

Mass, see p. 429. In earlier times the dedication of a church was not a feast in honor of the Lord as it is today, but one in honor of the building's patron saint.

3. Scripture Reading (Apoc. 21:18-27). The Church interrupts the regular sequence of Scripture Readings today and unfurls before us an apocalyptic picture of the heavenly Jerusalem. The passage harmonizes well with the theme proper to the present phase of the Church year. Notice how the passages have been selected; for the November 9 Dedication feast we had Apoc. 21:9–18, today Apoc. 21:18–27. The Lessons of the third nocturn are taken from the octave day of the Common, another indication of the close relationship between these two feasts. These Lessons describe the heavenly Jerusalem in its final phase.

"And the material of its wall was jasper; but the city itself was pure gold, like pure glass. The foundations of the wall of the city were adorned with every precious stone. The first foundation, jasper; the second, sapphire; the third, agate; the fourth, emerald; the fifth, sardonyx; the sixth, sardius; the seventh, chrysolite; the eighth, beryl; the ninth, topaz; the tenth, chrysoprase; the eleventh, jacinth; the twelfth, amethyst. And the twelve gates were twelve pearls; that is, each gate was of a single pearl. And the street of the city was pure gold, as it were transparent glass.

"I saw no temple in it, because the Lord God Almighty and the Lamb are its temple. Neither has the city any need of the sun or the moon to shine upon it; for the glory of God illumines it, and the Lamb is its lamp. The nations too walk by its light, and the kings of the earth bring their glory and honor into it. Its gates will not be shut by day, because there will be no night there. And they will bring the glory and the honor of nations into it. Nor will anything defiled enter into it, nor he who practices abomination and falsehood, but those only who are written in the life-book of the Lamb" (Apoc. 21:18–27).

This passage alone would be sufficient evidence for seeing an intrinsic relation between the two Dedication feasts and the symbolism inherent in the Church's Harvest Time; for the visible church is put before us as the figure of the heavenly Jerusalem.

November 19

ST. ELIZABETH, Widow

God's nightingale

1. **St. Elizabeth.** *Day of death*: November 17, 1231; canonized 1235; feast introduced 1670. *Grave*: until 1539 her relics remained in the church of St. Elizabeth at Marburg; at the present time her head is in the church of St. Elizabeth in Vienna while her body rests in Brussels. *Picture*: as a queen distributing alms. *Life.* Elizabeth was the daughter of the Hungarian king Andrew II. At the age of four (b. 1207), she was brought to the court of her future husband, Ludwig, landgrave of Thuringia. After her marriage in 1221, she very conscientiously fulfilled her duties both toward her husband and as a servant of God. During the night she would rise from bed and spend long periods at prayer. Zealously she performed all types of charitable acts; she put herself at the service of widows, orphans, the sick, the needy. During a famine she generously distributed all the grain from her stocks, cared for lepers in one of the hospitals she established, kissed their hands and feet. For the benefit of the indigent she provided suitable lodging.

After the early death of her husband (in 1227 while on a crusade led by Emperor Frederick II), Elizabeth laid aside all royal dignities in order to serve God more freely. She put on simple clothing, became a tertiary of St. Francis, and showed great patience and humility. Nor was she spared intense suffering. The goods belonging to her as a widow were withheld, she was forced to leave Wartburg. In Eisenach no one dared receive her out of fear of her enemies. Upon much pleading a shepherd of the landgrave permitted her to use an abandoned pig sty. No one was allowed to visit or aid her; with her three children, of whom the youngest was not more than a few months old, she was forced to wander about in the winter's cold.

In 1228 she took the veil of the Sisters of the Third Order of St. Francis at Marburg and there built a hospital with some property still belonging to her. She retained for herself only a small mud house. All her strength and care were now devoted to the poor and the sick, while she obtained the few things she needed by spinning. Young in years but rich in good works, she slept in the Lord in 1231, only twenty-four years old. The Mass is from the Common of Holy Women (*Cognovi*), see p. 428.

2.   St. Pontianus, pope and martyr, ruled from 230 to 235 and then resigned. He was banished to Sardinia by Emperor Alexander Severus with the priest Hippolytus, the famous writer (see August 22). The hardships Pontianus was obliged to endure soon caused his death; his body was brought back to Rome and interred in the catacomb of Callistus. An inscription marking the place of his burial was found in the chapel of St. Cecilia.

November 20

ST. FELIX OF VALOIS, Confessor

From the slavery of Satan

1.   St. Felix. *Day of death*: November 4, 1212. *Grave*: in the monastery of Cerfroi (Meaux). *Picture*: as a Trinitarian (white habit with red and blue cross), and a white deer beside him. *Life.* Felix, born in 1127, and John of Matha (see February 8) founded the Order of Trinitarians for liberating captured Christians from Saracen slavery. He belonged to the royal family of Valois. The breviary recounts several marvelous events from his life. As a boy he frequently gave away his clothes to clothe the naked. He pleaded for the life of a murderer condemned to death and foretold that he would reform and lead a highly edifying life — which prophecy proved true. With St. John of Matha he journeyed to Rome at the bidding of an angel and requested permission from Pope Innocent III to found a religious Order (1198). During holy Mass the Pope was granted a revelation regarding the proposed foundation; an angel appeared to him clothed in white with a red and blue cross. At Innocent's bidding the Order took the name of the Blessed Trinity.

In the newly-founded monastery at Cerfroi, Felix was favored with a visit by the Blessed Virgin. During the night preceding the feast of Mary's Nativity all the brethren slept through Matins by a special divine dispensation. Felix alone appeared at choir, where he found the Blessed Virgin clothed in the habit of the Trinitarians, accompanied by a great throng of angels similarly dressed. United with them, with Mary as hebdomadary, Felix recited the Office as usual. When he was about to leave the earthly choirs to join those of heaven, an angel foretold to him the day of his departure; he admonished his brethren to persevere in love toward captives and the poor, and died on November 4, 1212, mature in age and merit.

2. Holy Mass (Justus ut palma). The Mass is the second formulary in the Common of Confessors (such is frequently the case with saints distinguished for mortification and love of solitude), see p. 423. A proper *Oration* emphasizes two outstanding virtues, viz., Felix' life of solitude and his efforts at liberating captives. The practical application follows easily: Freed from the captivity of sin may we be taken into our heavenly fatherland. The Church is again pointing out the theme proper to this time of the year.

November 21

PRESENTATION OF THE BLESSED VIRGIN

May we too be brought into the temple of God's glory

1. The Feast. Sacred Scripture contains no text concerning the event commemorated in today's liturgy. For something of a historical background one may consult the apocryphal works, particularly the Protoevangel of St. James (ch. 4:1ff). After an angel had revealed her pregnancy, Anna is said to have vowed her future child Mary to the Lord. Soon after birth the infant was brought to the sacred precincts at which only the best of Israel's daughters were admitted. At the age of three she was transferred to the temple proper (7:2). Here she was reared like a dove and received her nourishment from the hand of an angel (8:1). Thus legend.

In the East, where the feast, celebrated since the eighth century, is kept as a public holiday, it bears the name, "The Entrance of the Mother of God into the Temple." It was introduced at Rome by a Cypriotic legate to the papal court of Avignon in 1371. In 1472, Sixtus IV extended its observance to the whole Church. Abolished by Pius V, it was reintroduced some years later (1585). The Mass is from the Common (*Salve Sancta*), see p. 392f. A proper *Oration* asks that "we too may merit to be brought into the temple of God's glory." Note how the liturgy slants everything toward our glorification and final state in heaven (i.e., the season's theme). With special fervor we will make today's Offertory oblation in union with Mary. How many sacrifices and holy acts flowed from Mary's presentation to God!

2. Divine Office. The Office is almost wholly from the Common. Only the Lessons of the second nocturn and the antiphon for the Magnificat are proper. St. John Damascene gives us the points for meditation today:

"Joachim married Anna, a most excellent and praiseworthy woman. Once there had lived another Anna who overcame physical sterility through prayer and a promise to God, and then gave birth to Samuel. In a similar way our Anna received from God the Mother of God through a vow and heartfelt petition; for she would not yield in any way to the illustrious women of previous ages. Accordingly grace (for the word Anna means grace) gave birth to the Lady (this is signified by the name Mary). Truly Mary became the Lady above all creation in her role as the Mother of the Creator.

"She was born in Joachim's house near the Probatica, and was presented in the temple. Thereupon 'planted in the house of God' and nurtured by His Spirit, like a fruitful olive tree she flowered forth in every virtue. From her mind she drove every

worldly or sensual desire; she preserved virginity of soul as well
as of body, as was becoming to one destined to carry God in her
very bosom."

November 22

ST. CECILIA, Virgin and Martyr

Bride of God

Cecilia, virgin and martyr, was so highly venerated by the
ancient Roman Church that her name was placed in the Canon
of the Mass. Already in the fourth century there was a church
of St. Cecilia in Trastevere, erected on the site where her home
had stood. Her martyrdom probably occurred during the reign
of Emperor Alexander Severus, about the year 230. In 1599 her
grave was opened and her body found in a coffin of cypress wood.
It lay incorrupt, as if she had just breathed forth her soul. Stephen
Maderna, who often saw the body, chiseled a statue that resembled the body as closely as possible. Since the Middle Ages,
Cecilia has been honored as patroness of Church music, a practice having its source in a false application of a passage from
the Office (*cantantibus organis*). This very poetic Office also
contains excerpts from the legendary *Passio Sanctorum*.

Apart from the fact of her martyrdom, we know practically
nothing about her that is historically genuine. Among other
details the breviary offers the following. Cecilia led a life of
prayer and meditation, "This glorious virgin always carried the
Gospel of Christ on her breast and neither day nor night ceased
from divine colloquy and prayer. With extended arms she prayed
to the Lord and her heart burned with heavenly fire" (*3. Resp.*).
Under her clothes she wore penitential garb, "With haircloth
Cecilia tamed her members; she prayed to God with tears" (*4.
Resp.*).

Cecilia had vowed lifelong virginity, but a youth by the name
of Valerian, relying upon the approval of her parents, hoped to
marry her. All was ready for the marriage, "While the musical

instruments were playing, the virgin Cecilia sang in her heart to her only Lord: May my heart, O Lord, and my body be immaculate, that I may not be put to shame (*Ps. 118:80*). For two days, for three days together she would pray with fasting, and she commended to the Lord the trouble in her heart" (*1. Resp.*). When the wedding night arrived, she confided to Valerian, "There is a secret, Valerian, I wish to tell you. I have as a lover an angel of God who jealously guards my body" (*Magn. Ant., 1. Vespers*). Valerian promised to believe in Christ if he would be enabled to see that angel. Cecilia explained how such was impossible without baptism, and Valerian consented to be baptized.

With a companion she joyously sent him to Pope Urban, who was hiding in the catacombs. Upon seeing the youth, Urban fell on his knees and thanked God for Cecilia, the seed that now was bearing fruit: "Lord Jesus Christ, good Shepherd, sower of chaste counsel, receive the fruit of the seed which You have sown in Cecilia. Cecilia, Your servant, serves You as a busy bee; for the spouse whom she received as a ferocious lion she has dedicated to You as a gentle lamb" (*6. Resp.*). Then Pope Urban baptized him. When Valerian returned, "He found Cecilia in her little room lost in prayer, and next to her the angel of the Lord was standing. When Valerian saw the angel, he was seized with great terror" (*5. Resp.*). The angel handed to them a bouquet of fiery red roses and snow-white lilies as a reward for Cecilia's love of chastity, a bouquet that would not wither, yet would be visible only to those who love chastity. As a further favor Valerian besought the conversion of his brother Tiburtius.

Upon arriving to congratulate the newlyweds, Tiburtius was astounded by the unspeakably beautiful roses and lilies. As soon as he was informed regarding their origin, he too asked for the waters of baptism. "St. Cecilia said to Tiburtius: Today I acknowledge you as a brother-in-law, because the love of God has made you despise the idols. Just as the love of God gave me your brother as a spouse, so it has given you to me as a brother-in-law" (*7. Resp.*). When Almachius, the prefect, heard of the conversions, he ordered Maximus, his officer, to arrest and im-

Lord,
may those
whom You have called
home
rest in the radiance
of heaven's light✝

prison all of them. Before being put to death, they instructed Maximus and his family, and baptized them during the night preceding execution.

At dawn Cecilia roused the two brothers to struggle heroically for Christ, "As the glow of morning disappeared, Cecilia called: Arise, soldiers of Christ, throw away the works of darkness and put on the armor of light" (this *Benedictus antiphon*, a most apt selection, brings to mind the Epistle of the coming first Sunday of Advent). Cecilia pursued her victory as the soldiers willingly listened, "We believe that Christ is true Son of God, who has chosen such a servant" (*Ant.*). Led before the prefect, she professed her faith in Christ, "We profess His holy Name and we will not deny Him" (*Ant.*).

In order to avoid further show, the prefect commanded her to be suffocated in the baths. She remained unharmed and prayed, "I thank You, Father of my Lord Jesus Christ, that through Your Son the fire was extinguished at my side" (*Ant.*). Beheading was next in order. The executioner made three attempts (the law prohibited more) and let her lie in her blood. She lived for three days, encouraging the poor and dedicating her home into a church, "I have received a three-day respite from the Lord so that I might consecrate my house into a church" (*Ant.*). The Mass is from the Common of Virgin-Martyrs (*Loquebar*), see p. 424.

November 23

ST. CLEMENT, Pope and Martyr

A bubbling fountain appeared at the feet of the Lamb of God

1. **St. Clement I of Rome** (92–101) was one of the first popes; according to St. Ireneus, he was the third after Peter. Clement most probably died as a martyr. Otherwise little is known of his life. It is not certain whether he is the one Paul mentions as his

companion in Phil. 4:3. St. Clement's letter to the Corinthians is
authentic; in it he authoritatively intervenes in that strife-torn
community, a memorable act in the early history of the papacy.

The breviary gives these legendary details. Because of his zeal
for souls, Pope Clement was banished to distant Chersonese;
there he found two-thousand Christians who had received a
similar sentence. When he came to these exiles he comforted
them. "They all cried with one voice: Pray for us, blessed
Clement, that we may become worthy of the promises of Christ.
He replied: Without any merit of my own, the Lord sent me to
you to share in your crowns" (*5. Resp.*). When they complained
because they had to carry the water six miles, he encouraged
them, "Let us all pray to the Lord Jesus Christ that He may open
to His witnesses a fountain of water" (*1. Magn. Ant.*). "While
blessed Clement was praying, the Lamb of God appeared to him;
and at His feet a bubbling fountain of fresh water was flowing"
(*4. Resp.*). Seeing the miracle, "All the pagans of the neighborhood began to believe" (*Ant.*).

When Trajan heard of these marvels, he ordered Clement to
be drowned with an iron anchor about his neck. "While he was
making his way to the sea, the people cried with a loud voice:
Lord Jesus Christ, save him! But Clement prayed in tears:
Father, receive my spirit" (*Ben. Ant.*). At the shore the Christians asked God to give them the body. The sea receded for three
miles and there they found the body of the saint in a stone coffin
within a small marble chapel; alongside lay the anchor. "You
have given a dwelling to Your martyr Clement in the sea, O Lord,
a temple of marble built by the hands of angels" (*6. Resp.*). The
body was taken to Rome under Nicholas I (858–867) by Sts. Cyril
and Methodius and placed in a church dedicated to his honor
(S. Clemente). This is one of the most venerable of the churches
in Rome because it retains all the liturgical arrangements of
ancient times.

2. **Holy Mass (Dicit Dominus).** Most of the Mass is culled from
Common texts, but some parts are proper (*Intr., Epist.*). We see
the high priest Clement modeled after the divine High Priest.
In the *Introit* we hear our saint called to his office after the man-

ner of the ancient prophets. God is speaking to him: Clement's word is God's word and Clement's offering will be accepted. For the psalm we sing the "Praises of the Good Man," (i.e., Pope Clement) who was faithful to God and kind toward fellow men. In the *Collect* we implore our saint to help the Church. The *Epistle* (the same as on the twenty-third Sunday after Pentecost) was chosen because the name Clement occurs in it, "His name is in the book of life." We could also regard the Epistle as a sermon addressed to us by the saint; we pay special attention because he treats the parousia theme.

As the *Alleluia* is sung, Clement is the "rock" before us. The *Gospel* and the *Communion*, taken from the Common of Sovereign Pontiffs (see p. 398), bring before us the familiar scene at Caesarea Philippi. Today it is to Clement that Christ is giving the power of the keys in heaven and upon earth — and the privilege to open the treasury of the Church's saving graces. The whole Office of St. Clement radiates parousia spirit. The Lamb, at whose feet bubbles a fountain of water, is an excellent picture of the sacrifice of Mass which brings refreshment to us exiles and thirsting children of men.

3. St. Felicitas. On July 10 we had the feast of the Seven Martyred Brothers; today their saintly mother receives special honor. Her body, together with that of her youngest son Silvanus, rests in the cemetery of Maximus; later her remains were transferred to the church of St. Susanna, where they still are honored.

4. Excerpts from the Letters of St. Clement. It is good liturgical practice to read something from the writings of a saint on his feastday. Let us listen to St. Clement as he says, "Let us, therefore, be humble-minded, brothers, putting away all boasting and conceit and silliness and anger, and let us do what is written, for the Holy Spirit says: 'Let not the wise man glory in his wisdom, nor let the strong man glory in his strength, nor the rich man in his riches, but let him that glories glory in the Lord, to seek Him and to do judgment and justice' (ch. 13).

"Christ belongs to the humble-minded, not to those who exalt themselves above His flock. The sceptre of the majesty of God, the Lord Jesus Christ, came not in the pomp of boasting or of arrogance, though He was mighty; but He was humble-minded, as the Holy Spirit spoke concerning Him (ch. 16).

"With this hope (in Christ's resurrection) let our souls be bound to Him who is faithful in His promises and just in His judgments. He who commanded us not to lie will be far from lying Himself. For nothing is impossible to God, except to lie. Let faith in Him, then, be enkindled in us, and let us recollect that all things are near to Him. By the word of His majesty He has set up all things, and by a word He can overturn them. 'Who shall say to Him, "What hast Thou done?" or who shall stand against the force of His power?' When He wishes, and as He wishes, He will do all things, and none of the things decreed by Him shall fail. All things are before Him, and nothing is hid from His planning (ch. 57).

"Seeing, then, that all things are seen and heard, let us fear Him and abandon the unclean lust of evil deeds, that we may be shielded by His mercy from the future judgments to come. For where can any of us flee from His mighty hand? (ch. 28).

"This is the way, beloved, by which we found our Savior, Jesus Christ, the High Priest of our offerings, the protector and helper of our weakness. Through Him let us strain our eyes toward the heights of heaven; through Him we see mirrored His spotless and glorious countenance. Through Him the eyes of our heart have been opened; through Him our foolish and dark understanding shoots up into the light; through Him the Lord willed that we should taste knowledge, 'Who, being the brightness of His majesty is so much greater than the angels as He hath inherited a more excellent Name' (ch. 36).

"Therefore, let our whole body be saved in Christ Jesus, and let each be subject to his neighbor, according to the position which grace bestowed on each. Let not the strong neglect the weak, and let the weak respect the strong. Let the rich man supply the wants of the poor, and let the poor man give thanks to God, because He has given him someone to supply his needs. Let the wise show his wisdom not in words but in good works. Let the humble-minded not testify to his own humility, but allow others to bear him witness. Let him who is pure in the flesh be so without boasting, knowing that it is Another who grants him this continence (ch. 38).

"The apostles received the Gospel for us from the Lord Jesus Christ; Jesus Christ was sent from God; Christ, therefore, is from God and the apostles are from Christ. Both, accordingly, came in proper order by the will of God (ch. 42).

"Let him who has charity in Christ keep Christ's commandments. Who can explain the bond of the charity of God? Who can express the splendor of its beauty? The height to which charity lifts us is inexpressible. Charity unites us to God, 'Charity covers a multitude of sins'; charity bears all things, is long-suffering in all things. There is nothing mean in charity, nothing arrogant. Charity knows no schism, does not rebel, does all things in concord. In charity all the elect of God have been made perfect. Without charity nothing is pleasing to God. In charity the Lord received us; out of charity which He had for us Jesus Christ our Lord gave His blood for us by the will of God, and His flesh for our flesh, and His life for our lives (ch. 49).

"Let us not merely call Him Lord, then, for this will not save us. For He says: 'Not everyone who says to Me Lord, Lord, shall be saved, but he who works justice.' So, then, brothers, let us confess Him in our works by loving one another (Second Letter, ch. 4).

"Therefore, brothers, leaving behind life as strangers in this world, let us do the will of Him who called us, and let us not be afraid to go forth from this world. For the Lord said: 'You shall be as lambs in the midst of wolves.' And Peter answered and said to Him: 'What if the wolves should tear the lambs?' Jesus said to Peter: 'The lambs should not fear the wolves after they are dead. And so with you — fear not those who kill you and can do nothing more to you; but fear Him who after your death has power over soul and body, to cast them into hell fire.' And understand, brothers, that the lingering of our flesh in this world is short and passing, but the promise of Christ is great and wonderful and is a repose in the kingdom to come and in eternal life (Second Letter, ch. 5).

"This world and the future world are two enemies. This world talks of adultery and corruption and love of money and deceit, but that world says farewell to these things. We cannot, then, be friends of both, but we must say farewell to this to possess the other. We think that it is better to despise the things which are here, for they are small and passing and perishable, and to love the things which are there, things good and imperishable (Second Letter, ch. 6).

"Let us, then, wait for the kingdom of God, from hour to hour, in love and justice, since we know not the day of God's manifestation" (Second Letter, ch. 12). (The above excerpts from St. Clement's letters are taken from: *The Apostolic Fathers*, trans. by Francis X. Glimm, Joseph M. F. Marique, S.J., Gerald G. Walsh, S.J.; publ. by the Cima Publishing Co., Inc., New York.)

November 24

ST. JOHN OF THE CROSS, Confessor and Doctor of the Church
ST. CHRYSOGONUS, Martyr

Lord, to suffer and be despised for Your sake

1. **St. John of the Cross.** *Day of death*: December 14, 1591; canonized 1726; feast 1738. *Grave*: Segovia, Spain. *Life*. Born in 1542 at Fontiveros near Avila, John as a youth was a nurse, later (1563) entered the Carmelite Order. In obedience he received the sacrament of Holy Orders. He aided St. Teresa in the reform of the Carmelite Order, an activity that occasioned much suffering. Rightfully he merits to be called, next to St. Teresa, founder and father of the Discalced Carmelites. He ranks with the great teachers of mysticism; his principal works on the subject are: *The Ascent of Mt. Carmel, The Dark Night of the Soul, The Spiritual Dialogues between the Soul and Christ, The Living Flame of Love*, and *Thorns of the Soul*. Because of these classic works Pius XI raised him to the dignity of a Doctor of the Church.

Toward the end of his life much physical suffering was his lot. Once when Christ asked him what reward he wanted for so many labors, he replied, "Lord, to suffer and be despised for Your sake!" At Ubeda in Andalusia he fell grievously ill; five painful, festering sores on his leg he bore with great patience in order to quiet his desire for suffering. Fortified with the last sacraments, he slept in the embrace of the Crucified, whom he had constantly carried in his heart. With the words, "Into Your hands, Lord, I commend my spirit," he died at the hour foretold to him; it was December 14, 1591, and he was in his forty-ninth year. The Mass is from the Common of Doctors (*In medio*), see p. 419.

2. **St. Chrysogonus** probably was a native of Aquileia, although he was venerated in Rome already in the fourth century. According to legend he was brought to Rome under Emperor Diocletian and thrown into prison; there he stayed two years, sustained by St. Anastasia (see December 25). That pious woman was obliged to endure many hardships from her husband Publius because of the Christian faith, but she derived much comfort from these short visits and acts of mercy. When all imprisoned Christians were ordered to be executed, Chrysogonus was brought to Aquileia. There Diocletian addressed him, "I have called you before me, Chrysogonus, to load you with honors provided you are willing to adore the gods." The saint replied, "Only the true God will I adore. Idols which neither have existence nor life and only represent devils, I hate and curse." Embittered by such an answer, the Emperor commanded him to be beheaded on November 24. His body was submerged in the sea; when found shortly after on the shore, it was interred by the priest Zoilus in his house (*c.* 304). Great honor was paid Chrysogonus by the Church of Rome; his name was inserted in the Canon, and a station church in his honor was erected.

3. **The Night of the Senses.** "This night produces in spiritual men two sorts of darkness or purgations conformable to the two divisions of man's nature into sensual and spiritual. Thus the first night, or sensual purgation, wherein the soul is purified or detached, will be of the senses, subjecting them to the spirit. The

other is that night or spiritual purgation wherein the soul is purified and detached in the spirit, and which subdues and disposes it for union with God in love. The night of sense is common, and the lot of many: these are the beginners, of whom I shall first speak. The spiritual night is the portion of very few (pp. 33–34).

"Recollected persons enter the dark night sooner than others, after they have begun their spiritual course; because they are kept at a greater distance from the occasions of falling away, and because they correct more quickly their worldly desires, which is necessary in order to begin to enter the blessed night of sense. In general, there elapses no great length of time after they have begun before they enter the night of sense, and most of them do enter it, for they generally suffer aridities. The holy Scriptures throughout, but especially the psalms and the prophetical books, furnish many illustrations of the night of sense, for it is so common (p. 36).

"But as these aridities frequently proceed, not from this night and purgation of the sensitive appetite, but from sins or imperfections, from weakness or lukewarmness, from some physical derangement or bodily indisposition, we shall here propose certain tests by which we may ascertain whether a particular aridity proceeds from the purgation of sense or from any one of the vices I have just enumerated. There are three chief tests for this purpose:

"The first is this: when we find no comfort in the things of God, and none also in created things. For when God brings the soul into the dark night in order to wean it from sweetness and to purge the desire of sense, He does not allow it to find sweetness or comfort anywhere. It is then probable, in such a case, that this dryness is not the result of sins or of imperfections recently committed; for if it were, we should feel some inclination or desire for other things than those of God. Whenever we give the reins to our desires in the way of any imperfection, our desires are instantly attracted to it, much or little, in proportion to the affection for it. But still, inasmuch as this absence of pleasure in the things of heaven and of earth may proceed from bodily indisposition or a melancholy temperament, which frequently cause dissatisfaction with all things, the second test and condition become necessary.

"The second test and condition of this purgation are that the memory dwells ordinarily upon God with a painful anxiety and carefulness, the soul thinks it is not serving God, but going backwards, because it is no longer conscious of any sweetness in the things of God. In that case it is clear that this weariness of spirit and aridity are not the results of weakness and lukewarmness; for the peculiarity of lukewarmness is the want of earnestness in, and of interior solicitude for, the things of God (pp. 37–38).

"The third sign we have for ascertaining whether this dryness be the purgation of sense is inability to meditate and make reflections, and to excite the imagination, as before, notwithstanding all the efforts we may make; for God begins now to communicate Himself, no longer through the channel of sense, as formerly, in consecutive reflections, by which we arranged and divided our knowledge, but in pure spirit, which admits not of successive reflections, and in the act of pure contemplation, to which neither the interior nor the exterior senses of our lower nature can ascend (p. 42).

"This night and purgation of the appetite is full of happiness to the soul, involving grand benefits, though, as I have said, it seems to it as if all were lost. As Abraham made a great feast on the day of Isaac's weaning, so there is joy in heaven when God takes a soul out of its swaddling clothes; when He takes His arms from under it, and makes it walk alone; when He denies it the sweet milk of the breast and the delicate food of children, and gives it bread with the crust to eat; when it begins to taste the bread of the strong, which, in the aridities and darkness of sense, is given to the spirit emptied and dried of all sensible sweetness; namely, the bread of infused contemplation, of which I have spoken. This is the first and chief benefit which the soul gains here, and from which almost all the others flow" (p. 53; translation from: *The Dark Night of the Soul* by St. John of the Cross, publ. by Thomas Baker, London).

November 25

ST. CATHERINE, Virgin and Martyr

May we reach the mountain that is Christ

1. **St. Catherine.** *Day of death*: Greeks and Latins keep November 25 as our saint's day of death. *Grave*: in the convent of St. Catherine at Mt. Sinai. *Picture*: with wheel, sword, and book. *Life*. Catherine (*etym.*, "the pure one") is venerated by the Greeks as a martyr of highest rank. The account of her martyrdom, however, is legendary and defies every attempt to cull out the historical kernel. Old Oriental sources make no mention of her. In the West her cult does not appear before the eleventh century, when the crusaders made it popular. She became the patroness of philosophical faculties, is one of the Fourteen Holy Helpers. The breviary offers the following.

Catherine, virgin of Alexandria, devoted herself to the pursuit of knowledge; at the age of eighteen, she surpassed all her contemporaries in science. Upon seeing how the Christians were being tortured, she went before Emperor Maximin (311–313), upbraided him for his cruelty, and with convincing reasons demonstrated the need of Christian faith in order to be saved. Astounded by her wisdom, the Emperor ordered her to be kept confined, and having summoned the most learned philosophers, promised them magnificent rewards if they could confound the virgin and turn her from belief in Christ. Far from being successful, a considerable number of the philosophers were inflamed by the sound reasons and persuasiveness of Catherine's speech with such a love for Jesus Christ that they declared themselves willing to offer their lives for the Gospel.

Then the Emperor attempted to win her by flattery and by promises, but his efforts proved equally fruitless. He ordered her whipped with rods, scourged with leaden nodules, and then left to languish eleven days without food in prison. The Emperor's wife and Porphyrius, general of the army, visited Catherine in prison; her words brought both to Christ and later they too proved their love in blood. Catherine's next torture consisted of being placed upon a wheel with sharp and pointed knives;

from her lacerated body prayers ascended to heaven and the infernal machine fell to pieces. Many who witnessed the miracle embraced the faith. Finally, on November 25 Christ's servant was beheaded (307 or 312). By the hands of angels (see the Collect) her body was carried to Mt. Sinai, where it was interred in the convent which bears her name.

2. Holy Mass (Loquebar). The Mass is from the Common of Virgin-Martyrs, see p. 424. Note again the parousia theme. The parable of the wise and foolish virgins (*Gosp.*), taken from Christ's great eschatological discourse, admonishes us to be vigilant and to await our Lord's Second Coming. In the *Collect* we ask that "we may reach the mountain that is Christ."

November 26

ST. SYLVESTER, Abbot

I am what this man was, I will be what this man is

1. St. Sylvester. *Day of death*: November 26, 1267. *Grave*: in his monastery at Monte Fano near Fabriano, Italy. *Life*. Abbot Sylvester founded the Sylvestrine Order, a reform congregation of the Order of St. Benedict, in 1231. Upon seeing the corpse of an aristocrat relative, who had been very handsome, in the coffin, he cried out, "I am what this man was, I will be what this man is!" After the funeral services the words of our Lord kept ringing in his ears, "If anyone wishes to come after Me, let him deny himself, and take up his cross and follow Me" (Matt. 16:24). He betook himself to a hermitage, led a life of perfection, died at the age of ninety in 1267.

The members of his Order wear a Benedictine habit, Turkish blue in color. Today there remain seven Sylvestrine monasteries in Italy and several mission houses in Ceylon and in the United States. — The Mass is from the Common of Abbots (*Os justi*), see p. 421. The *Collect* recalls how St. Sylvester, by meditating at an open coffin, saw the vanity of this world and began a life of solitude. How appropriate the thought of death is at the end of the Church year. Glance back over the year and see how vain the world appears with its TV standard of living.

2. **St. Peter, Bishop of Alexandria.** While in prison some priests pleaded for him with Arius, whom he had condemned. The action was reported to Peter; he replied that Jesus had appeared to him that very night with a torn garment, and when he sought an explanation, the Lord answered, "Arius has torn asunder My garment which is My Church." Peter's foremost virtue was perseverance; once he had made a decision he never vacillated. He is known as "the last martyr" of the Diocletian persecution (d. 311). *Application.* We may apply Christ's words to St. Peter to ourselves. The Church is the garment of Jesus and I form part of that garment. The heretic tears, the sinner soils that garment. By a virtuous life I can adorn it with pearls and precious stones.

November 29

ST. SATURNINUS, Martyr

God is wonderful in His saints

St. Saturninus. *Day of death*: November 29, about 300. *Grave*: at first in the cemetery of Thrason on the Via Salaria, then on the Coelian Hill. *Life.* The Martyrology gives these details: "At Rome on the Via Salaria the death of the holy matryr, the aged Saturninus, and of the deacon Sisinius. Under the emperor Maximianus they suffered long in prison. The prefect of Rome ordered them placed on the rack till their joints were torn loose, then beaten with knotted whips, and burnt with torches; at last removed from the rack, they were beheaded." According to the inscription on his tomb by Pope St. Damasus, Saturninus hailed from Carthage. The Acts of Marcellus say he was condemned as a frail old man to carry sand for the construction of the Baths of Diocletian; but when by his patience and prayer and encouragement he led many to the faith, he was beheaded. *Application.* "God is wonderful in His saints" — so the Church exclaims when contemplating the heroism of her martyrs. Yes, the virtues of the saints are a reflection of God's greatness and beauty. If the splendor of nature moves us to admiration of God, how much more the virtues of His chosen ones.

November 30

ST. ANDREW, Apostle

Hail, precious Cross, receive a disciple!

1. **St. Andrew.** *Day of death*: November 30 (year unknown). *Grave*: at first in Patras; on March 3, 357, his relics were transferred to Constantinople; since 1208 the apostle's burial church is at Amalfi, his head in St. Peter's. *Picture*: with an oblique cross, known as St. Andrew's cross. *Life*. Andrew, Peter's brother, and John were the first disciples to follow the Lord. With tender delicacy the Gospel (John 1:35–42) describes their first meeting with Jesus. Andrew did not belong to the inner circle of the apostles, Peter, James and John, and the evangelists narrate nothing extraordinary about him (John 6:8); but tradition (resting on apocrpyhal Acts) extols his great love of the Cross and of the Savior; and the Church distinguishes him both in the Mass (his name occurs in the Canon and in the *Libera* since the time of Pope St. Gregory I who had a special devotion to him) and in the Breviary.

The story of his martyrdom rests on the apocryphal Acts which lack historical foundation. The pagan judge exhorted him to sacrifice to the gods. Andrew replied: "I sacrifice daily to almighty God, the one and true God. Not the flesh of oxen and the blood of goats do I offer, but the unspotted Lamb upon the altar. All the faithful partake of His flesh, yet the Lamb remains unharmed and living." Angered by the reply, Aegeas commanded him to be thrown into prison. With little difficulty the people would have freed him, but Andrew personally calmed the mob and earnestly entreated them to desist, as he was hastening toward an ardently desired crown of martyrdom.

When Andrew was led to the place of martyrdom, on beholding the cross from a distance he cried out: "O good Cross, so long desired and now set up for my longing soul! Confident and rejoicing I come to you; exultingly receive me, a disciple of Him who hung on you." Forthwith he was nailed to the cross. For two days he hung there alive, unceasingly proclaiming the doctrine of Christ until he passed on to Him whose likeness in death he had so vehemently desired. — The legendary account of our saint's martyrdom has this value: it presents to us the mysticism of the Cross of later times. May Andrew, apostle and teacher of the Church, bestow on us the grace to see and imitate the Crucified in whatever crosses we encounter.

2. Divine Office. Many of the antiphons and responsories employ material found in the apocryphal Acts. The Cross is the ever recurring theme. "Hail, beloved Cross, consecrated by the body of Christ, adorned by His members as with precious gems!" "Blessed Andrew prayed saying: O Lord, King of eternal glory, accept me hanging on the cross." While the Divine Office is of later origin and rests on the apocryphal Acts, the Mass text follows ancient classic form.

3. Holy Mass (Mihi autem). Central in the formulary stands the second and final call of the apostle at Lake Gennesareth (*Gospel*); this too marks the action of the mystery, as the *Communion* so beautifully proves: "Follow Me!" The Lord is inviting us, and we leave all and follow Him to His sacred banquet, "I will make you fishers of men." Jesus' word applies first of all to ordained priests, as they are the divinely commissioned fishers of the *pisciculi*, the little fishes in the Church's net; they are the preachers of the faith. With this in mind the *Epistle* becomes easier to interpret; faith is necessary for all, whether Jew or Gentile; but faith presupposes divinely sent messengers to declare it. Of these the apostle Andrew was one of the most illustrious. The other parts of the Mass are taken from the Common. — If you are not ordained, it would certainly be in harmony with liturgical spirit to apply the Lord's words to yourself; lay persons too must be "fishers of men" — by example, by charity, by the fulfillment of duties and by speech!

the
commons
of the saints

THE COMMONS OF THE SAINTS

Both the missal and the breviary contain a section entitled *Commune Sanctorum*, "Common of the Saints," apart from the *Proprium de Tempore*, "The Temporal Cycle of Seasons and Feasts," and the *Proprium Sanctorum*, "The Proper of the Saints." The "Common of the Saints" classifies saints according to some illustrious act or a characteristic of office or sex, viz., Common of Apostles, of Martyrs (in which there are three subdivisions — that of One Martyr, of Several Martyrs, of Martyrs during Eastertime), of Confessor-Bishops or Abbots, of Doctors of the Church, of Virgins, of Holy Women. Then, to complete the series, there is a given a Common of the Blessed Virgin Mary, and, finally, that of the Dedication of a Church. Because most of the feasts of saints during the course of the year use Masses from the Common, it is very important to have a good understanding of the general purpose of the Common, as well as of the content of the various formularies.

Classification of saints into groups according to function, office, or merit is as old as the liturgy itself. As an example, in the *Te Deum*, the first part of which is very old, we find the following triple division: "the glorious choir of *apostles* praise You, the admirable company of the *prophets* praise You, the white-robed army of *martyrs* praise You" (confessors are not mentioned because at that early date they were not yet honored). On the feast of All Saints a classification is made that stems from the Middle Ages: "Angels, archangels (and seven other choirs of angels are listed), patriarchs, and prophets, the holy doctors of the Law, the apostles, all the martyrs of Christ, the holy confessors, virgins of the Lord, hermits and all saints" (*Magn. Ant.* at First Vespers). The Litany of All Saints arranges the saints in various groups, similar to those of the Commons. The responsories at

Matins on the feast of All Saints reflect the various groupings, using psalm texts usually associated with each specific class.

But what lies at the basis of such classification, what justification is there for the division? History helps us here, especially early history. At first no feasts in honor of saints were observed. The liturgical cult of saints began with memorials made at the graves of martyrs. Each year on the anniversary of the day of death, the Eucharistic sacrifice was offered where they lay buried. Such celebration at a martyr's grave was the Christian parallel to the pagan funeral banquets. At the tombs of their deceased the pagans would eat a meal, under the impression that the act brought them into communion with the departed. Now in a very true sense Christians could and did unite themselves with the saints through the holy Eucharist, patricularly when the Sacrifice was offered at their very grave; it then became a genuine *communio*, an actual coming-together.

The memorials to the martyrs were followed by observances in honor of the apostles. As witnessed by the *Te Deum*, these two groups were the only ones so honored for centuries. In those early times martyrs were "the holy ones," or "the just" (*justus*); only martyrs were esteemed as saints. A long time passed before the Church found it possible to regard someone publicly as a saint who had not died for the faith (the first confessor-saints were Sts. Sylvester and Martin of Tours).

The development of specific groups or classes of saints was aided and guided by the Church's spiritual ideals. What was the norm of sanctity in the ancient Church? Martyrdom and virginity. Or better, virginity wreathed with the crown of martyrdom. Here we could well have the reason for the three feasts immediately following Christmas. Go to meet your King as martyrs, as virgins, as virgin-martrys! These, then, constituted two very definitely marked classes of saints for the Common.

Persons aspiring to sanctity would have no other ideal but Christ and the Church. Every Christian indeed was obliged to be a reflection of Christ — *alter Christus*, another Christ. He also was the personal embodiment of the Church; the Church and the individual soul must form a single entity. Christ is the King of martyrs "from whom all martyrdom is derived." In his own flesh the martyr completes what is lacking to the suffering of the (mystical) Christ, the Church (Col. 1:24). Hence the martyr is the most perfect exemplification of Christ.

The Church is Christ's Virgin-Bride. The Church is pictured as the virgin or the widow who for the sake of Christ refrains from a second marriage. The most perfect example of the Church as Virgin-Mother is, of course, the Blessed Virgin.

When the persecutions ceased during the course of the fourth century and the Church no longer produced martyrs, the ideal of sainthood was necessarily somewhat modified. There arose the class of saints known as confessors. The word *confessor* had a history of its own. At an earlier date it was practically synonymous with the word *martyr*, one who "professed the admirable Name of the Only-begotten before kings and potentates with a loud voice" (preface for the blessing of palms in the old Holy Week liturgy). Those who suffered for Christ in the persecutions but were not put to death were called "confessors." With this precedent it was but a small step to the notion of unbloody martyrdom, the Christian who renounced the joys of the world and dedicated himself perfectly to Christ. The best Biblical example was that of the vigilant servant who "with loins girt and with burning lamp awaits his Lord's return." In the texts of the Common of Confessors the parousia spirituality of the primitive Church as expressed in the Gospel is normative. Christ had taught that spirituality in a series of parables that form part of His great eschatological discourse (Matt. 24–25).

From the Common of Confessors various other groups broke off in the course of time, viz., bishops, doctors, abbots. The High Priesthood of Christ is best exemplified in the office of a bishop, while our Savior's mission of teaching is continued by the doctors of the Church. Thus the reason for various classes of saints is anchored in the very nature of Christianity; given the needed time and circumstances, the development was inevitable.

Exactly because the liturgy in her most important categories of saints relies on basic types and does not become lost in a maze of individual, personal traits, do the various Commons enjoy high religious importance. Every Christian is able to aspire to the ideal, in his own manner, of course. One's gaze is directed to that which is essential, to the whole. There is masterful pedagogical wisdom concealed in the texts of the various Commons. To counter the seeming standardization of personalities in the missal, there are the biographical sketches in the breviary. Thus one complements the other, details are set against the broad, solid background of principle, and the saint stands vividly before us. We see how a given ideal was achieved by a particular person.

Now a word on the origin of the formularies in the Common. It would not be correct to imagine that the Church composed these texts according to some preconceived pattern; they have their source in special Masses for specific saints. A particular formulary, because of its propriety, would be used for other saints of the same category until it became universalized as a "Common." For certain formularies the process has been scientifically traced; scholarly research is seeking the answers to details on others.

The various Commons in the breviary offer many useful points for understanding the Mass formularies; we should, therefore, not overlook the advantages derived from a comparative study of texts.

One further observation. New approaches and helpful insights into the spiritual message of the Common Masses can be derived if studied in context with the liturgical season at which they are used. During the Christmas season the texts assume a coloring and meaning that is quite different from that during Eastertime. Easter too and the first weeks of autumn inject overtones quite distinctive of the season and the current mystery. At Christmas, to point out one detail, the saints form the retinue of the heavenly King as He makes His first appearance in the holy City Jerusalem, while during the Easter season the martyrs are the prime exhibits in the Redeemer's triumph over death and hell.

Quite easily do the Common Masses fit into the symbolism of the Church's Harvest Time with its stress on awaiting the return of the divine King. It is a characteristic of the Common Masses —

a proof, too, of their antiquity — that they contain many passages readily related to the parousia. This quality betrays the inherent *mysterium*, for through his death the saint goes to meet the returning Lord. Now the Mass re-actualizes the saint's death, and united with him we prepare ourselves for Christ's Coming. These ideas are proper to the Church's Harvest Time, and therefore the Masses in the Common are peculiarly apropos at that season. Moreover, it is during the Pentecostal season that greater attention is given to the cult of the saints, and therefore the Common Masses are used more frequently. Here too we have the reason why the saints receive much greater space in the last two volumes of this work.

1.   COMMON OF THE BLESSED VIRGIN MARY

You are blessed, O Virgin Mother of God,
  for you have believed the Lord.
The things that were told you
  have been fulfilled in you.
Behold, you are exalted above the choirs of angels.
Intercede for us with the Lord our God.
  Hail, Mary, full of grace,
  the Lord is with thee.
          — *Responsory on All Saints' Day*

In the celestial choirs of saints, Mary takes a first and unique position. Therefore there can be no question of a Common of Marian Masses in the same sense that the term applies to a group of saints. Mary's role is singular, she admits of no classification. Rather, she stands superior to all categories as Queen — Queen of apostles, Queen of martyrs, Queen of confessors, Queen of virgins, as we pray in her litany. Missal and breviary contain a Common only in the sense that Marian texts are brought together for common use, while her separate feasts emphasize one or the other specific grace or privilege. It is easily seen how

important the Common becomes for the full appreciation of the
different Marian Offices; we will gain a better understanding of
the individual feasts if we assimilate the great underlying
theology proper to the Common.

What are the ideas fundamental to the Marian Common? We
could select the Invitatory at Matins as the briefest summary:
"Holy Mary, Virgin, Mother of God, plead our cause." These
few words proclaim all Mary's greatness. (a) *Holy Mary* — her
personal sanctity. (b) *Virgin* — it is with special predilection that
the liturgy calls Mary Virgin; it is her unique title shared with
no other, she who is both Virgin and Mother. (c) *Mother of
God* — this prerogative is her most sublime privilege, the basic
reason for all her other graces. (d) *Intercessor* — from this stems
the boundless trust Christianity places in the "Help of Christians." These four truths are the fundamental points in the
Marian Common; each separate prayer text can be related ultimately to one or the other.

The Common Office of the Blessed Virgin Mary in the breviary
as well as the formularies for the separate Marian feasts are rich
in metaphor; with colorful pictures and parables the liturgy
brings our beloved Mother before us. Three of these figures
deserve our special attention, viz., Bride, Wisdom, the holy City
Jerusalem.

1. *The Bride of God*. Numerous passages from the Canticle
of Canticles are found in the breviary's Marian Common. The
Canticle of Canticles is one of the three Old Testament books
ascribed to King Solomon; on first reading it might seem that its
contents consisted simply of love poems between Solomon and
a shepherdess. Topic headings would include: the longing of
the two lovers for nuptial union; attempts to attain that objective; ditties and dialog betraying their inclinations and feelings;
the obstacles preventing marriage. Actually, however, the message of the text when properly analyzed is God's love toward
His people, a love that in turn prefigured the intimate bond
between Christ and His Church, between Christ and the soul
endowed with divine grace. The Bridegroom-Bride relationship
is a very common one in the sacred books of the Old and New

Testaments. God is "wedded" to the Chosen People; He calls Himself a "jealous" God; idol worship is equivalent to "adultery."

Christ, and later St. Paul, deepened the spiritual implications of the comparison; to his followers John the Baptist introduced Christ as the Bridegroom, and Jesus referred to Himself as the Church's Spouse (John 3:29; Matt. 9:15). Christianity's chiefest blessings are indicated by the nuptial analogy — our oneness with God, the union of the soul with Christ, a union that attains its most perfect intimacy in the saints. This is why the Canticle of Canticles is used so often in the Marian Common; for with Mary the bond of divine love found the most intense expression imaginable; the holy Virgin was not only the most immaculate and most perfect of God's creatures, she was granted a most singular physical union with divinity in that for nine months she carried the Son of God in her womb.

2. *Wisdom.* Mary is meant when the term *wisdom* is used in her Offices. In the Old Testament Wisdom books God's attribute of wisdom is at times personified; a celebrated passage speaks of divine wisdom as a child that at the beginning played in Yahweh's presence and at His side during the work of creation; in another text wisdom is an instructress of God who teaches mankind wisdom and virtue, true religion. By wisdom the sacred writers often meant the divine attribute, the wisdom by which God created and arranged everything in the world, or the eternal divine ideas that God gives expression to more or less perfectly in creatures. The Fathers of the Church at times see the Son of God "through whom God created the world" in personified wisdom.

In the sacred books the word *wisdom* is also used of a type of created wisdom, the virtue of wisdom which God gave to His people through revealed religion. The concept of wisdom here becomes much more embracive than in modern languages; it is used to express morality, virtue, holiness, prudence. Somewhat similarly foolishness and sinfulness are correlative terms.

Wisdom texts are applied to Mary in the liturgy. Why? Creatures are reflections of God's wisdom; the more beautiful and perfect they are, the more do they mirror God's beauty, wisdom, holiness. Mary, God's most perfect creation, may then be equated with wisdom itself. Moreover, it was part of God's eternal plan and providence that His Son should become incarnate through her; with all the perfection of her beauty Mary stood in the divine presence from all eternity. And lastly, she possessed created wisdom, i.e., sanctity, the virtues, in the highest degree possible, another sense in which the term *wisdom* may rightly be used of her.

3. *Jerusalem.* In a goodly number of liturgical passages Mary is meant when the words *holy City Jerusalem* (or *Sion*) occur. Here is the reason. Among all the cities of the world, Jerusalem was unique. Jerusalem was the city where Yahweh set His throne. Jerusalem was His chosen city, His beloved city. Surely the application to Mary is not strained! In Jerusalem stood the temple, the dwelling — place of the Most High — Mary provided a living temple for God! Jerusalem was the "chosen city" of the great King — Mary, "blessed among women," Jerusalem, mother of nations, "whither all the tribes go up," Gentiles included — Mary, the Mother of Christendom. Jerusalem, besieged and smitten — Mary, Mother of sorrows. Jerusalem, prized and beloved by every Jew — Mary, most dear to every Christian.

MASS OF OUR LADY ON SATURDAY

Since ancient times the Roman Church has dedicated Saturday to the Blessed Virgin. A special Office and Mass in her honor is provided for all Saturdays on which no feast of some rank occurs. The psalms of the Office are those of the feria, Saturday; the remaining prayers are Marian from some aspect. Following the major divisions of the ecclesiastical year, five different formularies are given for the Mass of our Lady on Saturday, viz., (1) during Advent, the *Rorate* Mass; (2) during Christmastide; (3) from February 3 to Lent; (4) during Paschaltide; (5) after Pentecost. The formulary for the Pentecost season best reflects the spirit and tenor of the Marian Common; the following comment will help to understand its message.

The Mass *Salve Sancta Parens* is an ancient composition, profound in its simplicity. Two trends of thought are nicely interwoven: (a) the "Mother of God" theme runs like a golden thread through the formulary. Mary's greatest privilege and the reason for all her graces was her divine motherhood. (b) We Christians may and should take part in her dignity, through the medium of holy Mass. We may and should become "God's mother" — to use Christ's own words — in two ways: (1) by taking the "Word of God" into ourselves in a docile and obedient manner (the Foremass); (2) by receiving the living "Word of God" in the Eucharist and thus becoming in a still higher sense "mothers unto God." If we use this approach, a Marian feast with its Mass will always be a thrilling experience.

Upon entering the church we greet the "Holy Mother" who bore the King of heaven and earth in the words of an ancient Christian poet, Sedulius (ca. 450); our salutation continues with the bridal-psalm, 44, which applies so perfectly to Mary. The two Readings proclaim the dignity of divine motherhood. In the *Lesson* divine Wisdom, i.e, Christ, comes to live in the holy City Sion and there takes root in the Chosen People, i.e., Christ enters the womb of the Virgin Mary, becomes man, and founds the Church, the new Sion.

Thus in the Lesson the physical and spiritual motherhood of Mary, of the Church, and of individual souls is expressed mystically. "My abode is in the full assembly of the saints" — how these words ring true now at Mass! For the assembled congregation represents the Church in minature; to it divine Wisdom, Christ, descends full of grace in the holy Sacrifice; here the divine Vine "takes root." In the *Gospel* our Lord Himself reveals the beautiful doctrine of spiritual, divine motherhood. Alongside praise of His own Mother, He places praise for "all who hear the word of God and keep it." According to the spirit of the liturgy, the "word of God" in this passage is the Son of God.

Because of the Eucharistic banquet, the *Communion* text is easily applied to the Church and to souls: "Blessed the womb of

the Virgin Mary that bore the Son of the eternal Father." Thus
Mary is the model *par excellence* of holy Church and of our souls.
The *Offertory*, culled from the *Rorate* Mass of Advent, repeats
the "eternal greeting" of the angel Gabriel, the *Ave Maria* (the
source of our "Hail, Mary"). The angel's greeting is directed to
Mary and to all who now at Mass share her privilege of bearing
Christ.

2.   THE COMMON OF THE APOSTLES

Now we meet those who during their earthly lives
    planted the Church with their own blood.
They drank the chalice of the Lord and became
    God's friends.
Their voice resounds through all the world,
    their words to the very ends of the earth.

One can readily recognize a text from the Common of Apostles — its tone and character are so sharply defined. There are
two major thought areas, viz., the apostles are *friends of Christ*,
and they are *princes*, the Church's royal sons. Typical is the oft-
repeated verse: "Your friends, O God, are very honorable to
me; their rule is well established" (*Ps. 138*). Here is the reason
why Psalm 138 is used at the Introit and for second Vespers (the
psalm itself has little bearing on the office of the apostles; and
even this very verse is a faulty translation of the original text).
The antiphons of first Vespers give fine expression to the
"friendship with Christ" theme; they are taken from the Gospel
of what once was the vigil Mass: "You are My friends, if you
do what I command you, says the Lord."

Beside the high dignity of the apostolic office, the Common
reminds us of the call and the sufferings of the apostles. Their
mission was to establish and spread Christ's kingdom on earth.
They were, therefore, the first missionaries. To express this
there is the text from Psalm 18, "Their voice resounds through

all the world, their words to the very ends of the earth." In ancient times Psalm 18 was entitled "The Apostle," because the whole composition was commonly sung on feasts of the chosen Twelve. In one of his homilies St. Augustine tells how "the apostles declared God's glory as other heavens" ("The heavens declare the glory of God" — the opening verse of Psalm 18).

Typical too is the so-called chapter at Vespers and Lauds: "Brethren, you are now no longer guests and strangers; you are citizens with the saints, members of God's household; you are built upon the foundation of the apostles and the prophets, with Christ Jesus Himself as the chief cornerstone." In the lofty edifice of the Church, Christ is the cornerstone; the apostles form the foundation, the members are the stones resting upon that foundation. Therefore the feasts of the apostles are not feasts of mere individual saints, rather they are redemption feasts, feasts of holy Church. During the Middle Ages churches often had twelve special pillars to represent the twelve apostles.

Union with Christ in love presupposes union with Christ in suffering. The apostles "drank the chalice of the Lord," and willingly embraced the pain of martyrdom. An apostle-feast should be a genuine religious solemnity.

3. THE COMMON OF SOVEREIGN PONTIFFS

On January 9, 1952, Pope Pius XII introduced a new Common, that of "One or Several Sovereign Pontiffs." The official bull gave the following reasons for the innovation:

"At all times holy Church has accorded a very special honor to those Roman Pontiffs who zealously defended the rights of the Apostolic See, who spread the truths of the Gospel through the world, and who by the holiness of their lives and by witnessing unto death were a glowing example to the faithful flock entrusted to them. In every age the gates of hell have struck out at the immovable rock of Peter through vain but ever more gruesome and bloody persecution, while at the present time the enemies of the Church endeavor to overwhelm the Popes with their venom and to disgrace them with diabolical calumnies. Now to counter these attacks and to increase the honor of the papacy — an office conferred by God Himself — and also to celebrate with greater solemnity those Popes who were distinguished for holiness, Pope Pius XII introduced the new Common."

In the breviary this new Common consists merely of an Oration and a homily for the third nocturn; all the remaining prayers and texts are from the Common of a Martyr or the Common of a Confessor. The Mass, however, is a completely new formulary; from the opening words of the Introit it is referred to by the name *Si diligis me*. The dominant theme of this new Mass is our Savior's promise to Peter as it continues to be fulfilled and realized in the Apostle's successors, the Roman Pontiffs. Two of Christ's pronouncements to Peter dominate the text; the words, "If you love Me, Simon Peter, feed My sheep, feed My lambs," ring out in the Introit and continue to resound during the first part of the Mass as the "shepherd motif"; while the words, "You are Peter, and upon this rock I will build My Church," occur repeatedly from the Alleluia verse to the end of the sacred service.

The *Introit* departs from classical models by using a New Testament text as an antiphon. Enclosed in its frame, Psalm 29 comes from the lips of the day's pope-saint as an expression of gratitude for the call to shepherd the flock of Christ and for the protection from enemies accorded him in the task. We think of Christ's words, "The gates of hell shall not prevail." (There is no indication that the remaining verses of the psalm are alluded to.)

Reference to the Mass's double theme is easily seen in the two *Collects*. In the first God is addressed as "the eternal Shepherd" who should look mercifully upon His flock and protect it through the intercession of the day's saint and sovereign pontiff whom He appointed as shepherd over the whole Church. The second Oration, which is used very rarely, bases its petition upon the promise, "The gates of hell. . . ."

Appropriately the *Epistle*, a new selection, comes from the pen of Peter himself. The first supreme shepherd is admonishing his successors: "I exhort the presbyters among you — I, your fellow presbyter and witness to the sufferings of Christ (Peter was present on Olivet during Christ's agony and seizure), the partaker also of the glory that is to be revealed in time to come — tend the flock of God which is among you, governing not by constraint, but willingly, according to God; nor yet as lording it over your charges, but becoming from the heart a pattern to the flock. And when the Prince of shepherds appears, you will receive the unfading crown of glory. . . . The God of all grace, who has called us unto His eternal glory in Christ Jesus, will Himself, after we have suffered a little while, perfect, strengthen and establish us. To Him is the dominion forever and ever. Amen." There is no need to labor the point that this selection significantly enriches the treasury of missal readings.

The *Gradual*, which by nature should echo the Epistle, associates the words *seniores* and *consenior* with a verse from Psalm 106 and points to the elevation of the day's saint to the Chair of Peter. The *Alleluia* verse anticipates the Gospel, putting into relief its principal message: "You are Peter (the Rock), and upon this rock I will build My Church." Christ's words have been fulfilled in the papacy; for through the ages the popes have proven to be the immovable rock-foundation of holy Church. The *Gospel* presents Biblical proof that the primacy of Peter and of his successors was divinely willed and instituted. Through the centuries the popes have guided the Church with a sure and steady hand; they have held the keys to God's kingdom in heaven and on earth; and in them we see realized repeatedly our blessed Savior's prophecy that hell with all its powers will not triumph.

Today's *Offertory*, a passage from Jeremias, is usually applied to the Savior's precursor in the liturgy: "See, I am putting My words in your mouth. I am placing you over nations and kingdoms that you may destroy and tear down, that you may build and plant" (Jer. 1:9–10). The divine Shepherd is addressing Peter and his successors; to them He entrusts the work of teaching infallibly; upon them He places the threefold crown (tiara), and leaves with them the power to bind and to loose.

The *Secret* again touches upon the Introit motif: may God's pleasure rest upon flock and shepherd. While the faithful approach the Lord's table, we hear the familiar passage, "You are Peter, and upon this rock I will build My Church." It is a message that applies not only to the day's sainted pontiff, but to every one present before the altar. For each Christian must be a rock in faith and in grace and in love — a rock upon which Christ can build a spiritual Church. Holy Communion is part of His construction work.

Classic in form and content, the first *Postcommunion* is pointed less toward individual Christians than toward the Church now "nourished with holy refreshment" through the Eucharist; it petitions guidance, freedom, and purity of faith for the papacy. In the second Postcommunion the shepherd motif is met for the last time; note in particular the phrase parallelism: "The shepherd will not lack obedience from his flock, nor the flock lack the shepherd's protecting care." — All considered, a beautiful and instructive Mass formulary. One might, however, remark that its frequent occurrence (more than twenty-four times a year) could lessen devotion, while the previous arrangement did offer greater variety.

4.   THE COMMON OF MARTYRS

You, My holy ones, bitter conflict was your lot
    in the days of your mortal life.
Now will I grant you reward for your sufferings.
Come, blessed of My Father,
    take possession of the kingdom.

How highly the Church esteems martyrs is indicated by the great number of Commons proper to them. Three series are distinguished: the Common of One Martyr, the Common of Several Martyrs, and a special Common of Martyrs during Paschaltide.

A. THE COMMON OF ONE MARTYR

This Common has four distinct formularies, two for martyr-bishops, two for martyrs who were not bishops.

1. Mass *Statuit*

This formulary blends together reflections on the priesthood as the extension of Christ's High Priesthood (*Allel.*) with martyrdom. In the priest ascending the altar we see represented the day's martyr-bishop; in him our saint is present before us. Of him the *Introit* says: "The Lord has confided to him the covenant of peace," i.e., the treasures of the Church. He is a prince in the kingdom of God; his priesthood is eternal because it is the priesthood of Jesus Christ. Psalm 131 follows. The reason for the choice lies in the psalm as such. David was chosen by a special act of God and therefore typified the call and consecration of our saint to the office of bishop. The psalm records a reciprocal oath; David swore to erect a temple for God, while God promised under oath to keep David's descendants upon the throne forever. David represents our sainted bishop who zealously safeguarded the interests of the Church, even to the point of shedding his blood. With his merits in mind we make our appeal: "Lord, think of David, and of his many services." *Collect*: our weakness crushes us down to the very ground, may our holy martyr-bishop come to our assistance by his intercession.

Ordinarily in the *Epistle* or *Lectio* the day's saint addresses us, or Mother Church speaks of him. Today it is the latter. The apostle James the Younger, himself an illustrious bishop (Jerusalem's first) and martyr, provides the script. Blessed is the martyr, he who stood the test. Martyrdom is God's norm for testing, His proving grounds. The prize for perseverance is the "(victor's) crown of eternal life, which God has promised to those who love Him." Eternal beatitude! Today, the anniversary of his death, our martyr received this crown from the hands of his divine King; and through the Eucharist we are enabled to share that glory. The remaining portion of the Epistle would have no relation to the feast, apart from the conclusion perhaps: eternal beatitude is that "best gift, that perfect gift coming from above, from the Father of lights." Thus does God love His children, the first fruits of His creatures; we hope we are numbered among them.

In the *Gradual* God (or Christ) says: "I have found Myself a servant in David." Again David typifies God's chosen ones! Just as David, so too our bishop was anointed with holy oil; God's hand aided him, God's arm supported him in his every project (it may help to think of the scene on Lake Gennesareth, Christ and Peter walking hand in hand toward the little ship). Against such an alliance for defense and offense Satan can make no inroads. Upon these words of divine assurance do we rest our trust in our holy bishop.

The *Alleluia* signals the King's approach. Today He appears in priestly vestments; we greet Him with a verse from Psalm 109: "A priest You are forever, after the manner of Melchisedech!" Christ is our Eucharistic Priest forever; His priestly dignity finds an extension in our holy bishop and in the celebrant at the altar. It is the *Gospel*, and the divine High Priest stands in our midst. Next to Him is the day's saint, to whom He refers constantly. With serious and decisive words He says: You can be My followers on one condition, if you detach yourselves from "father, mother, wife, children, brothers, sisters — yes, and hate even your own life!"

All that pleases the natural man must be sacrificed, if God so asks; and even more, the cross of life with all its thorns must be borne patiently, perseveringly, after our cross-laden Savior. It is martyrdom by blood that He is alluding to. Christ, the King of martyrs, has a perfect right to enjoin so high an ideal, for He Himself set the example in every detail; and today's martyr imitated it perfectly. If we find it difficult to understand the Gospel's injunction about "hating" and "cross-carrying," relate it to the lives of Christ and His martyr; its implications will then be quickly seen. A tower is to be built — God's kingdom in my soul. A war is to be fought — Satan's hordes are ever lurking.

Neither operation will be finished before death. Our bishop-saint
has completed his.

The *Offertory* affords God (or Christ) another opportunity
to speak of the day's martyr. Two "angel guardians" accompanied him through life, fidelity and mercy. Fidelity prompted
him to meet all obligations, mercy poured redemption's graces
lavishly into his soul; and thus came the day of death for him
who "exalted his horn in God's Name." A last time God speaks
of His beloved in the *Communion* refrain, again in terms of
David. God swore to David that his descendants would occupy
the throne forever, that his throne would continue glorious, like
the sun and moon. In Christ Yahweh's solemn promise was fulfilled; and all His followers, the holy martyrs in particular, share
in that eternal kingship. The holy Eucharist is the pledge and
guarantee of its final, full realization.

2. Mass *Sacerdotes*

In this Mass more emphasis is placed on the eternal reward
the holy martyrs receive than in the preceding one; it is also
more joyous in tone and triumphant. The *Entrance Chant* chal-
lenges priest and people, the two great divisions of Christendom,
to praise God (the laity are called the "holy and humble of
heart"). Furthermore, all creation should praise God. By way
of exception, a psalm is not used here, but the familiar "Canticle
of the Three Youths." The reason for the joyous outburst of
divine praise is the exaltation of our bishop-martyr whose anniversary we are celebrating (*Coll.*). In the *Epistle* the holy martyr
uses words from St. Paul as he speaks to us. It is an exceptionally
beautiful passage, and puts our celebration in a new light, viz.,
as a communion in suffering and consolation with the saint, and
with Christ. We imagine the saint saying in our presence:
Christ's "sufferings" abounded in me; therefore my "consolation" too is incomparably great in heaven; in both, you too may
share, for "you ought be partakers in the passion and in the
consolation, in Christ Jesus our Lord."

This is realized through the holy Sacrifice; for at the *Offer-*

tory our martyr places his palm of martyrdom upon the altar and we follow his lead; by our oblation we merge ourselves into Christ's saving passion. Thus do the sufferings of Christ and those of the day's martyr become ours. In the sacrificial Banquet we share in his "consolation"; for the fruit of the Sacrifice is participation in his exaltation. So we sing at *Communion* time: "Lord, You have placed upon his head a crown of precious stones." Such is true of the martyr, it also holds true for us who are mystically one with him. The *Gradual* too crowns the day's saint "with glory and honor," while the *Alleluia* casts him in the role of a royal priest.

Presently Christ, the first among martyrs, appears (*Gosp.*). He repeats His homily on the necessity of shouldering the Cross. There is no other road leading to eternal good save the Way of Calvary. "He who wishes to follow Me must deny himself, embrace his cross, and walk in My footsteps." All through our earthly lives we must be "partakers in the suffering" of Christ and of His holy martyrs. For the sake of Christ we must "lose our earthly life." Our Lord closes His homiliy with a reference to the Last Day when He will return "with the angels in the glory of His Father," the day when we are destined to become partners and sharers of His consolation. This is typical of ancient Mass formularies — there must always be some allusion to the Second Coming. At the death of today's saint the Lord did return "to render him reward according to his works." In the Mass we experience this return of the glorified Savior with His angels and His martyr when at the consecration He appears under the veil of the sacred species. In the Offertory God says: "I have found Myself a servant in David." David represents the elect. Like David, our bishop was anointed with sacred oil; as a martyr he was anointed to fight; God's powerful hand assisted him in the mortal combat.

To sum up. The basic theme of this formulary is communion in suffering and communion in consolation. In the Foremass, communion in suffering dominates, in the Mass proper communion in consolation. It is a theme underlying most Mass formularies in honor of saints.

3. Mass *In virtue*

This, the first Mass of a martyr-not-a-bishop, likewise features the joy and glory at the triumph over suffering. The day's saint (*justus*) enters at the *Introit* (in the person of the celebrant) resplendent with glory; he rejoices in the power of God and exults in the salvation accorded him; his heart's desire has been granted, he stands in our presence, the winner! (All of Psalm 20 would be appropriate here; wherever the word *king* occurs, simply substitute the name of the day's saint.) The psalm was a thanksgiving prayer of one of Israel's kings after a telling victory.

The *Collect* affords occasion to voice our plea that this martyr-feast "make us strong in love toward God." A very special fervor should mark our observance of ancient martyr-feasts, for these fill us with the spirit of the early Church. In the *Reading* the Church shows how our saint lived; how "the Lord conducted him on the proper road and showed him the kingdom of God"; how He accompanied him in every struggle; how He did not abandon him in time of distress but went down with him into the pit of prison, in chains; then He favored him with the "sceptre of the kingdom" and "everlasting glory" (in its original context the passage describes the lot of Joseph in Egypt; it would add depth to our use of the text if we placed it against the background of Joseph's experience, his suffering and exaltation in the land of pharaoh). True to its nature the *Gradual* echoes our reflections on the Lesson. Blessed is the person who fears God! His children will be influential on earth. We are "his children," we who now associate ourselves with him at Mass.

Standing alongside Christ, we see our martyr wearing his heavenly crown as the *Alleluia* is chanted. Then the Lord tells how necessary it is to follow in the way of the Cross (as in the two preceding formularies). His words help us realize the implications of martyrdom, and how to make it part of our own lives. His message is no soft soap: "I have not come to bring peace but the sword!" Christianity is not a dollard's dream, no asylum for idlers — Christianity means struggle. Above all it is a struggle against flesh and blood; it presumes a willingness to take the cross upon oneself and to follow Christ. (Note that our Lord throws out the same challenge in all three Masses!) Jesus keeps His finger pointed at the martyr, he actually fulfilled His words most perfectly. We too, although an identical crisis may not confront us, may share with him the honor of "witnessing" to Christ by showing testimony in smaller ways, e.g., a cup of water handed to His poor.

Again in the *Offertory* we see our saint wearing the crown of victory, advancing toward the altar. During the Eucharistic Banquet we do not, as otherwise, sing a text reflecting the saint's (and our) transfiguration; rather, today's is a sobering message: "If you wish to follow Me, embrace your cross. . . ." Why these words at so sacred a meal? Perhaps Mother Church is reminding you that after Mass your "Way of the Cross" begins; and your source of strength is this holy Meal.

4.   Mass *Laetabitur*

The second Mass for a martyr-not-a-bishop! We see the holy martyr (*justus*) in heavenly glory, and are very happy — such is the general content of today's text (*Intr.*). Read Psalm 63 as a description of the saint's martyrdom, listen to the *Epistle* as a sermon coming from the prison of our holy martyr who "for the Gospel of the Lord's resurrection labored even unto chains, as if he were an evildoer." He assures us that he suffers also for us, God's "elect," so that we "might attain salvation." He continues, exhorting us to a similar patience in trials and persecution. "All who live piously in Christ Jesus should be prepared for persecution." Yes, we are determined to walk in the footsteps of the martyrs, witnesses unto Christ.

The *Gradual*, a community meditation upon our saint, points out how the Lord sustained him when he fell, the victim of enemy hate; but now he stands erect, transfigured in glory. During life he dedicated himself to good deeds, therefore he now is blessed.

In the *Alleluia* Jesus speaks — through darkness to light. Such was the martyr's lot, such is ours. In the *Gospel* He urges us to a fearless profession of our faith. Now in the sacred precincts of church His holy words gladden us, but soon we must leave to "confess" Him before men fearlessly, for they can kill only the body. While our blessed Lord speaks He points to the day's martyr who puts His counsels into perfect practice. As an answer to His concluding exhortation comes the *Offertory* hymn; our saint stands "confessed" before the heavenly Father, "crowned with the crown of life." Again at the *Communion* Jesus whispers into our ear: Now you are with Me at a banquet, later be with Me through the cross and suffering.

B.   COMMON OF SEVERAL MARTYRS

Because of the dramatic and mystery element in the liturgy, the saints commemorated on a given day are to be regarded as personally present. It is important therefore to note whether the prayer texts employed use the singular or plural, whether one or several of the blessed are in our midst. Here too we have the reason why distinct formularies are had for one or several martyrs. Three different Masses are found in the missal; there is no distinction between martyrs who were bishops and those who were not.

1.   Mass *Intret*

There is a marked difference between this formulary and other martyr Masses, for in the present text it is not glory and triumph that receive attention, but torment, pain, and suffering. The Mass begins with a wrenching cry as Mother Church sees her children languishing in prison chains. Picture yourself at the scene of martyrdom. (At the night vigil the acts of the martyrs are read.) Our first reaction is spontaneous and natural, the sentiments voiced in the *Entrance Chant*. For we hear the "cries of the martyrs in chains," we see their blood flowing under torture. Our sense of justice is roused, and we call out for justice (*Intr.*).

Now Mother Church seeks to raise our sights (*Epistle*). It is as if a consoling voice sounded from the heavens as we hear: "The souls of the just are in God's hand. In the opinion of fools they seemed to die, but they are in peace (i.e., transfigured by glory). God tried them and found them worthy of His presence. He accepted their sacrifice; now they shine and reign. The Lord is their King forever." How beautifully the Church can spiritualize and idealize suffering! And our own attitude begins to change as we turn from lamentation to praise. At the Introit we may not have understood God's seeming complacence, but now we praise His majesty and His strong arm in our saint's heroic passion. How differently the same act is viewed by nature and by grace! The mystery of martyrdom is becoming intelligible: "The bodies of the saints are buried in peace while their names continue to live" (*Allel.*).

The *Gospel*: from the lips of Christ we hear the signs presaging His Second Advent; among them are the trials of the martyrs: "They will lay hands on you and persecute you . . . dragging you before kings and civil officials on My account . . . you will be hated by all." In the case of our saints these predictions were fulfilled to the letter. United to them through the bond of Christ's Mystical Body, we too must be witnesses unto Christ. "By your perseverance you will save your souls." Today we will take to the altar the little martyrdoms of life as our *Offertory* gift. The Communion Banquet provides strength for the conflict.

Do not fail to note the contrast between the opening and closing chants. The Introit approached martyrdom from the human viewpoint; in the course of the Mass nobler insights are presented; at the end the *Communion* antiphon enables us to see in a fully supernatural perspective — it is God who tries the martyrs. They are gold, and any slag must be removed; this is possible only through the fire of suffering. Martyrdom is an acceptable holocaust, which when united to Christ's, possesses an infinite value. This contrast between the initial and final chants is typical of the spirit of the entire formulary. Man comes to the sanctuary with all his natural bents and inclinations, unredeemed, one might say; by means of the sacred Sacrifice he is sanctified, his work and suffering are consecrated. Oppressed he goes to Mass, relieved and consoled he returns home. God did not take away the cross from him, but He did transform and glorify it.

2. Mass *Sapientiam*

Originally this Mass was proper to the physician saints, Cosmas and Damian. Therefore it was quite fitting for the Gospel to begin with a reference to the Lord's work of healing; the Introit too praises the "wisdom" of these saints. At a later date the formulary was appropriated by the Common.

At the *Introit* "Christ's faithful" and the "nations" from afar (viz., ourselves) enter the burial church of our martyr-saints and admire their "wisdom." At the same time we invite them to "exult in the Lord." In the Readings it is the Church who sounds their praises: "The just will live forever and their reward is with the Lord . . . therefore will they receive a beauteous diadem and a splendid crown from the hand of the Lord." In the battle of spirit hosts that will rage about God's kingdom until the very end, the saints are well-equipped soldiers; they will provide protection for us too. In the *Gradual* we hear the martyrs say: we were like birds that a bird-catcher entices into his snare; now the snare is broken, God has freed us (so they represent their martyrdom).

The *Alleluia* chant gives a different view; we see the just above in the heavens, happy and merry at the celestial nuptial banquet. The *Gospel* is more easily understood if we recall the ancient practice of bringing the sick to the graves of the holy martyrs or of placing upon the sick linens that touched their tombs or relics. Christians were convinced that "a healing strength went out from them." The Gospel proposes a beautiful mystery-action, i.e., the episode recounted repeats itself spiritually in the holy Sacrifice; "much people," i.e., we the faithful about the altar, have come together to be healed of our spiritual ills. Jesus "descends from the (heavenly) mountain into the plain" (to us). And "all the people sought to touch Him (in ancient times the consecrated Host was placed in the hands of the communicants) for strength went out from Him (present in the holy Eucharist)." Immediately the good Lord pronounces our martyrs blessed, for in their lives they actualized His beatitudes, especially the fourth in St. Luke's series, "Blessed are you when men hate and persecute and calumniate you, and despoil you of your good name for the sake of the Son of Man; rejoice and be glad because your reward is great in heaven."

The *Offertory* affords us a glimpse into the heavens where we see Christ's promise fulfilled. There the saints are in their heavenly homes, in glory and peace, ever praising God. During the *Communion* banquet the Lord speaks to us. He calls us His friends: "Do not fear your persecutors." Implicitly He gives two reasons for His statement; look at today's martyrs; they did not fear, and now they are in glory; keep in mind, too, that I am with you; the Eucharist is your strength and power. The Communion chant should, of course, be sung during the distribution of the holy Eucharist.

3. Mass *Salus autem*

In this third Mass formulary the theology of our Savior's Second Advent is again strikingly prominent. For a summarizing picture imagine Christ appearing at the head of His "white-robed army of martyrs" in preview for the return on the last day (*Epist.* and *Gosp.*). The *Introit* directs our thoughts to the life of today's martyrs (the remaining verses of the psalm give further detail); evil persons were strong and fortunate, they oppressed the good, yes, tortured and put them to death, but God, the "salvation of the just," did not forsake them.

In the *Epistle* the martyrs speak to us. They recall the "former days" when Christians, after "being enlightened (baptized), endured great suffering." They languished in prisons, sustaining the loss of all earthly goods with joy. Will you join them? "You have need of patience that, doing the will of God, you may receive the promise: For yet a very little while, and He who is to come, will come" (Heb. 10:32–38). (Now at Mass we are witnessing a dress rehearsal of the parousia.)

The *Gradual* reflects the sentiments of the Epistle. The martyrs cried out in their need and God heard them. It will not be otherwise with us, "For the Lord is close to the broken-hearted; and those who are crushed in spirit He saves." In the *Gospel* Christ appears as the rewarder of martyrs (*Tract*), and seeks to instill the spirit of martyrdom in His followers; what we hear during the silent hour of worship must be preached aloud to the whole world.

We must not fear those who can "kill the body"; in fact, apart from everlasting death, we need not fear anything. Rather our efforts will be directed toward developing a lively sense of God's good providence, realizing that not even a hair goes lost without His knowledge. This attitude will aid us in becoming Christ's heralds upon earth, so that He "will confess us before the angels of God" at the Second Coming. Both Readings instill the spirit of martyrdom. In the first the martyrs speak to us, in the second, Christ Himself. Both have the same purpose, both come to a climax in the parousia theme.

In the *Offertory* hymn it is martyrdom again, but from a higher plane: "The souls of the just are in the hand of God . . . in the opinion of the unwise they seemed to die, but they are in peace" (Wis. 3:1–3), i.e., they are enjoying the beatific vision. The *Communion* reminds us of the dark catacombs from which these witnesses unto blood came forth. What the Lord in the nightly stillness whispered into their ears, they "preached from the housetops." This is our duty too. In the morning Mass Christ comes to us softly and, as it were, whispers in the darkness. Then we return to a hostile world as His confessors. In what does the secret of our strength lie? In an abiding love of Christ. May such love come to us through receiving His Body and imitating the example of the saints.

C. THE COMMON OF MARTYRS IN PASCHALTIDE

The high honor accorded martyrs by Mother Church finds its culmination in the special Common granted them during Easter time. This is to show that martyrdom is most intimately associated with Christ's own passion and triumph. The "white-robed company of martyrs" form the retinue for the Conqueror over death and hell. In celebrating the feasts of martyrs the liturgy seeks to dramatize in mystery St. Paul's dictum: "As you are partakers of His sufferings, so will you also be of the comfort." The two formularies, Common of One Martyr and Common of Several Martyrs, are classic in form and content, and breathe the triumphant martyr spirit of the ancient Church.

1. Mass for One Martyr *Protexisti*

The dramatic directness and freshness of the text, indications of its antiquity, impress us immediately. Without much ado the liturgy introduces the saint, has him speak, and projects a series of pictures descriptive of his life. In the *Introit* the martyr himself sings a hymn of thanksgiving; persecution merely heightened his triumph. On Good Friday and Holy Saturday, Psalm 63 (the whole composition must be considered) described the passion of Christ; today our martyr uses it to voice his own sufferings. We hear his cries and lamentations. We see his enemies whet "their tongues like a sword . . . and bend their bow to shoot down the righteous." We observe them devising their diabolical plans. Yet they never win, for their weapons "wound no more than children's arrows!" Enraged and humbled, they are forced to acknowledge God's good providence. But "the just man rejoices in the Lord, in Him glory all the upright of heart."

Equally dramatic is the *Lesson*. In spirit we are present at the last judgment and see both the martyrs and their persecutors. The latter now behold their victims in heavenly glory and cry out in agony and fear: "These are they whom we once derided. . . . Fools, we thought their life madness. . . . See, now they are numbered among the children of God."

The *Alleluia* song voices the reflections of the congregation; heaven and earth, i.e., the heavenly and earthly *ecclesia*, praise and confess God's wondrous designs as manifested in the martyrdom of the saints and in their heavenly reward. In Christian antiquity the word *confessio* or *confiteri* applied in a very special way to martyrs. The martyr was a "confessor" in the highest sense; he had "confessed" the Lord before men, and now the Lord and all the heavenly court "confess him crowned with glory."

At first glance the *Gospel* may disappoint us. As in other martyr Masses, we might have expected Christ's exhortation to take up our cross and follow Him; instead we find the allegory of the vine and the branches. But for what reason? It may be simply an historical coincidence. In ancient times the last part of St. John's Gospel was used as the *lectio continua* in paschal time. Today's Mass formulary undoubtedly dates to that period (see the Gospels for the Sundays after Easter and the feast of Sts. Philip and James).

A sensitive soul, however, will detect certain delicate relationships between martyrdom and this figure of the vine. Christ, the King of martyrs, is the Vine that entwined itself around a Cross; the martyrs are the ripe grapes hanging thereon. The Eucharistic wine, flowing from the wine-press of our Savior's passion, becomes the martyr's inebriating drink. In ancient Christian thinking the three concepts, Cross, Eucharist, and martyrdom, were so intimately related that one explained the other. In the Canon of the Mass, for instance, there are two lists of martyrs. Our Gospel provides pictorial explanation. Christ, the divine Vine clinging to the Cross, is likewise the Tree of life in the new paradise. The martyrs are the grapes hanging from the Vine; they have proven the Gospel true, for by remaining attached to Christ they have "brought forth much fruit," even the fruit of martyrdom.

We too are branches on the Vine, Christ. Now at Mass the life-giving sap of the Eucharist flows from the stem into the branches, so that we may "bring forth much fruit." The Vine unites us to the martyrs. And it is precisely in the Mass that this union is operative, for the Communion of Saints is a communion both of suffering and of consolation. See how the liturgy and patristics have made us understand the Gospel allegory.

At the *Offertory* God's great kingdom in heaven and on earth again praises, "confesses," and marvels at the wondrous work of the divine Vine. In the *Communion* we see our saint rejoicing at the heavenly banquet, while we, partaking of the Eucharistic Banquet, share his joy on earth. (Psalm 63 begins and concludes the Mass.) Note that most chants refer to the saint in the singular.

2. Mass for Several Martyrs *Sancti tui*

This second Mass is equally beautiful and edifying. With the *Introit* there rises a shout of praise from the "saints," (i.e., the martyrs, and we in union with them). This double choir proclaims the "glory of the kingdom" of Christ. Psalm 144 praises God (or Christ) for His goodness, greatness, fidelity. It is one of the finer psalms, although unfortunately it rarely occurs in the liturgy. What a beautiful picture the Introit sketches — Christ, the risen King, receiving the praises of His "confessors."

The theme continues in the *Epistle*. Through His resurrection Christ has procured for us an "incorruptible and unfading inheritance" in heaven. Toward this we are moving, even though it be through the dark valley of earthly trials and temptations; *modicum*, only a "little while," however, will these sorrows last. The gold must be purified by fire in preparation for the great day of "the revelation of Jesus Christ," a preview of which we experience with the martyrs at today's holy Mass. Again we see the holy martyrs in their lily-white garments; they are sweet like the odor of balsam, and their martyrdom precious in the sight of the Lord (*Allel.*).

The first three verses of the *Gospel* are identical with the final three verses of the preceding formulary. But taken as a whole, the emphasis is somewhat different. Christ is the divine Vine, and we the branches. It is a figure that touches the liturgy's very soul; there exists no consideration more profound. Both the saints and we enjoy organic union with Christ; from Him we draw the sap of divine life, the wine of the blessed Eucharist. From Him, the Vine, we receive strength to obey the commandments, and "to bring forth much fruit." (See comment on the previous Mass's Gospel.) Filled with Easter's joy, we proceed twice to the altar with the martyrs; once to die with Christ (*Off.*), and once to rise glorified with Him (*Comm.*).

In the Divine Office, too, martyrs receive special attention during Easter time; some of the shorter texts are particularly beautiful.

> His elect are gleaming white, alleluia;
>> upon them shines God's glory, alleluia.
> They are white as milk, alleluia, alleluia.
> They are purer than snow, whiter than milk;
>> they are more shimmering than old ivory,
>> more beautiful than sapphire. (*Resp.*).

"Come forth, daughters of Jerusalem, and behold the martyrs and the crowns with which the Lord crowned them on this solemn, joyous day, alleluia, alleluia (*Ben. Ant.*).

5. THE COMMON OF CONFESSORS

> Your loins should be girt,
>> your hands should be holding lighted lamps.
> You should resemble servants
>> who are awaiting their master
>> as he returns from a wedding feast.
> Be vigilant, for you do not know the hour
>> at which the Lord will return.

According to the Gospel ideal, a Christian is a confessor if during the night of earthly life he "awaits the returning Lord with girt loins and burning lamp in hand." This ideal is one after which we are bound to strive.

The liturgy allows confessors four Commons, viz., the Common of Bishops, of Doctors of the Church, of Abbots, of other Confessors.

A. THE COMMON OF CONFESSOR-BISHOPS

There are two formularies in this Common. The first stresses the gratuitous, divine election of the saint; the second emphasizes his priesthood.

1. Mass *Statuit*

The bishop is the faithful "steward" of the divine fountain of life in the Church, of God's revealed word, and of the sacraments. In him Christ's priesthood finds its fullest extension. The celebrant of the Mass typifies or represents the bishop-saint commemorated. There is a mystic oneness between him, Christ, and the priest at the altar. Repeatedly the Mass text correlates the priest's actions and movements with the saint, and the saint with the divine High Priest.

As the priest approaches the altar, it is our holy bishop whom we see. The Church sings the praise of his divine election: "The Lord entrusted to him the covenant of peace" (i.e., the treasures of the Church); he is a prince in God's kingdom, a priest forever (*Intr.*). Psalm 131 follows, a reciprocal oath. David swears to build a temple unto God, God swears to grant David the throne forever. Of course, David here represents our saint-bishop who zealously cared for the Church, and therefore receives an eternal reward for himself and graces for the Church.

The *Lectio* praises the divinely wonderful selection of our sainted bishop. "See, before you there stands (in the person of the celebrant) the great high priest (our saint, and Christ too) who was pleasing to God during his life." He was the instrument of redemption unto many; his call is proclaimed in ringing words: "He gave him the crown of glory, He entered into an eternal covenant with him . . . that he should be His priest and praise His Name and present Him with a worthy incense offering, an agreeable and sweet-smelling odor." The message is re-echoed in the *Gradual*; in awesome wonder no new ideas are added, the text of the *Lectio* being simply repeated.

With the *Gospel* the divine High Priest stands before us, He who will consummate the offering "after the manner of Melchis-

edech." Typical of the *mysterium* character of ancient Mass formularies, the returning Lord calls for an accounting of talents
entrusted to His followers. These talents are the graces of the
priesthood; today, the day of his death, our bishop "enters into
the joys of his Lord." We who have not received as many talents
must still make good use of the two entrusted to us.

The Sacrifice proper now begins. At the altar table our sainted
confessor is standing; as "David anointed with holy oil" he of-
ficiates in the Name of Christ; the "arm" of the divine High
Priest supports him (*Off.*). Upon the altar we place all the hard-
gained talents of our own efforts; then during the sacred offering "the Lord comes to His servants to demand an accounting as
well as to confer the great reward." The pledge and earnest of
that reward is the Eucharist; today our good bishop extends it
to us during the Sacrifice-Banquet, for he is "the faithful steward
whom the Lord placed over all His possessions and who now
gives us our due measure of the divine wheat" (*Comm.*). Do not
overlook the final Communion prayer. First we express our
gratitude for the gifts received (rarely does the Postcommunion
express thanksgiving) and then we ask for "greater blessings."
Is there anything greater than the Eucharist? Only heavenly
beatitude, the vision of God face to face!

2. Mass *Sacerdotes*

This formulary, which is used less frequently than the preceding one, shows more clearly how the priesthood is the extension of
Christ's priestly dignity. Again today we see the saint commemorated approaching the altar in the person of the celebrant and
offering the holy Sacrifice. There is an equation between the
priest at the altar, the saint of the day, and our High Priest Christ.
The Foremass is devoted to a consideration of the dignity of
the priesthood. Our saint-bishop enters, clothed in the "garment
of justice," the vestments of holy Mass. At his appearance we,
"the saints," rejoice, for it is on his account that Christ Himself
will now show His countenance. The oath in Psalm 131 involves
mutual obligations; David, typifying our holy bishop, faithfully
seeks the Church's welfare.

The *Epistle* teaches us the reason for a priest's high dignity: in him Christ, the eternal High Priest, manifests Himself. Through the priesthood "Christ lives on as a mediator for mankind." His sacrifice offered once — Himself as priest and sacrificial lamb — is reactualized in the Church through the priesthood. In a few words the Epistle tells the high significance of holy Mass and of the priestly office; also the strict duty of the priest to be "holy, innocent, undefiled, separated from sinners." Today's bishop-saint satisfactorily fulfilled this requirement; his salvation is indicated by the priestly vestments in which he is robed and over which we, "the saints," rejoice (*Grad.*)

In the *Gospel* the eternal High Priest appears; His entrance is greeted with a triple *Alleluia*. Again the Gospel sets the stage well for the Mass-mystery; our bishop is the "faithful and wise servant whom the Lord appoints over His family." "Until He comes" He gives us in type or proxy, i.e., through the priest who celebrates, the "meat" (doctrine and Eucharist) "in due season" (the present time). Today's holy bishop was found faithful at the Lord's advent, i.e., at his death; that advent we now commemorate by the anniversary Mass. Through participation we too become "watchful servants whom the Lord sets over all His possessions." The Eucharist is the pledge of these eternal possessions. Do not overlook how the *Communion* antiphon becomes intelligible only in context with the distribution of the holy Eucharist.

B. THE COMMON OF DOCTORS

The formulary (*In medio*) from the Common of Doctors applies easily to the various types of saints who have been declared doctors of the Church. In the person of the celebrant the Church sees the particular saint-doctor commemorated today. As the priest (formerly the bishop) approaches the altar clothed in priestly vestments, we all sing: "In the midst of the Church God opens his mouth; the Lord fills him with wisdom and understanding; He clothes him with the garment of glory" (*Intr.*). Yes, today in our church a doctor of the Church speaks to us; he speaks to us through the voice of the celebrant. The priestly vestments symbolize the *stola gloriae*, the garment of his heavenly transfiguration. Using the words of Psalm 91 we praise God in His saint.

The *Collect* reminds us of the fact that our doctor-saint is a *doctor vitae* for us here upon earth — a teacher of life (i.e., how to live according to true wisdom, hence a physician of divine life), and at the same time an intercessor in heaven. In the *Epistle* we see the saint walking in the footsteps of St. Paul, a fearless, tireless soldier and herald of God's kingdom "in season and out of season." Today, the day of his death, is the Lord's parousia for him; today he might well say: "I have fought the good fight, I have finished my course . . . there is laid up for me a crown of justice which the Lord, the just Judge, will render to me in that day." With our saint we now relive "that day" in the holy Sacrifice. *Gospel*: the holy doctor is the salt of the earth, the city upon a mountain (we may think of the bishop enthroned in his cathedral), the lamp upon a candlestick in the Lord's house. Our little lamps must be lit from his. He is called "great" in the kingdom of heaven because he "does and teaches."

When we approach the altar carrying our gifts, our saint multiplies himself in us; he is the palm or cedar which is reproduced when we imitate him (*Off.*). While the *Communion* antiphon and psalm are sung, it is the doctor of the Church rather than the celebrant who distributes the Eucharist. With the eyes of the ancient Church we see the bishop performing his liturgical duties of preacher and priest; in the Foremass we hear him teaching; at the sacrificial Banquet he presides over the sacred meal; both, doctrine and Eucharist, are the divine wheat which the steward of God's family "wisely and faithfully" administers. This very day from the hands of the priest at the altar we receive that wheat according to the special spirit exemplified by the doctor-saint commemorated.

C. THE COMMON OF ABBOTS

The Mass for the Common of Abbots (*Os justi*) borrows part from the Common of Bishops, part from the Common of Confessors; for abbots take a place midway between bishops and confessors. Among his own brethren the abbot is head and father, still he does not possess the full powers of jurisdiction and orders as bishops do. This is found expressed in the Mass; we see the abbot-saint as the faithful and wise steward who in due season administers the measure of wheat to his community (*Comm.*; the same verse occurs in the Common of Bishops and Doctors). The religious "leaves all things — home, brothers, sisters, father and mother and fields for the Lord's sake" and thereby complies most exactly with that evangelical counsel; he will accordingly share to a greater degree in the transfiguration at Christ's Second Coming (*Gosp.*). Today, the day of his death, he entered into glory; today he obtained "his heart's desire" upon receiving the "crown of precious stones" (*Grad., Off.*); it is a transfiguration in which we may share through the holy Sacrifice. The *Lesson* tells of our saint's elevation to the abbatial dignity in a mystery-enshrouded dialog between himself and God. The passage in the Bible refers to Moses; the comparison between Moses and an abbot has much to commend it.

D. THE COMMON OF CONFESSORS

This Common has two Mass formularies. The first seems to be more typical. Called the Mass of the "Vigilant Servant," it is more positive in content than the second, in which the ascetical aspect of Christian life, mortification, receives greater stress.

1. Mass *Os justi*

The Mass of the "Vigilant Servant" quite closely resembles the "Bridal Mass" in the Common of Virgins; both emphasize awaiting the Lord's return as essential to the Christian way of

life. "The just man finds true wisdom in meditation" is the
theme of the *Os justi* Mass (*Intr.*). The mysterium is that of the
vigilant servant who "with girt loins and with burning lamp in
hand awaits the Lord." Such was the life of the confessor-saint
now honored; during the night of earthly life he was ever
prepared for the journey home, the light of divine love always
glowed brightly within him, his life was one long desire for
the parousia. At death the Lord "knocked" and our saint "opened
to Him immediately." "The Lord found him watching" and
transported him to the heavenly banquet, there to "wait upon
him" personally. Today at Mass we recall not only the day of
the Lord's advent for our saint, but in the Eucharist his transfiguration assumes new glory, and we, united with him, meet
the returning Lord. Thus we constitute the *dramatis personae* for
the *Gospel*.

At the banquet table we witness the mystery unfolding itself
further; the Lord knocks, we open to Him. He invites us to
the wedding feast; *transiens ministrabit*, "passing by He ministers" to us. These words well describe the holy Eucharist —
passing by, in contrast to the "eternal enjoyment of His divinity"
in heaven. It is our task to "watch" as did our saint, with girt
loins and burning lamp. Such response would be our guarantee
to "stewardship over all His possessions." Here too one can see
how expressive the *Communion* antiphon becomes when prayed
in the perspective of the "Lord's Eucharistic coming."

The remaining texts of the Mass need no special explanation.
Note, however, that the *Introit* text, "Do not envy evildoers,"
simply marks the beginning of the psalm (the passage itself has
no connection with the feast). The *Lesson* describes the "Good
Man" untouched by the lure of bribes or the enticement of
money; now the *ecclesia sanctorum*, i.e., ourselves, praises his
good works. The saint "flourishes like the palm" and "multiplies
like the cedar of Lebanon" among those mystically united with
him in the holy Sacrifice (*Grad.*). He was not spared the cross
of suffering during life, and therefore at death and now again
in the sacrifice of Calvary he receives the "crown of life" (*Allel.*).

2. Mass *Justus ut palma*

The two Masses in the Common of Confessors complement each other; the first emphasizes the positive, the second the negative requirements in professing the faith. The major theme in *Os justi* is that of the servant who with loins girt and burning lamp in hand awaits the returning Lord, i.e., preparation and longing for the parousia. In the second the primary notion is mortification and self-denial. The confessor commemorated detached himself from all the enticements of the world; he "left all to follow the Lord," a phrase from the Communion antiphon which could perhaps serve as title to the whole formulary. Text analysis is easy. Perhaps the walls of your church are decorated with palm trees; according to the *Introit* they would today represent our saint. In the *Epistle* he rises in our midst to speak; he makes a comparison between himself and us; it is a sad picture indeed, for we are yet so earthly-minded, ambitious, covetous, vain; while he, scorned as a fool, goes hungry, thirsty, the outcast of men. Yet the saint fears being too severe and exacting with us; he excuses himself, saying he only wanted to admonish us, his beloved children.

In the *Gospel* Christ says: "Fear not, My little flock. . . ." What consolation for us! They who want to follow the steep and narrow way after Christ will walk alone, because the great masses follow the broad highways of this world. The Gospel also counsels us: give up earthly goods; your treasure must be located in heaven. "Where your treasure is, there your heart will also be." While the faithful receive the Bread from heaven, Christ reveals the hundredfold reward reserved for those who have abandoned all to follow Him (*Comm.*). He is distributing to each the pledge and earnest of that reward.

E.   THE COMMON OF VIRGINS

At midnight a cry was made:
   See, the bridegroom comes!

Go out to meet him!
Wise virgins, trim your lamps.

This Common has four formularies, two for virgin-martyrs and two for virgins who were not martyrs.

1. Mass *Loquebar*

The first formulary tenders to the saint commemorated the double crown of martyrdom and virginity. Standing before us in the *Introit* our saint recounts her profession of faith: "Before kings I acknowledged Your testimony, I was not ashamed." Allusion is made also to the virgin's purity of heart: "I meditated upon Your commands, which I loved exceedingly," while the psalm verse praises her "immaculate way" of life. The *Lesson* is the martyr's prayer of thanks for her supreme victory over suffering: "I will glorify You, O Lord, O King; I will praise You, O God, my Savior . . . for You were my helper and protector. You preserved my body from destruction . . . from those who roared, ready to devour . . . from annihilation by the flames that surrounded me . . . therefore my soul will praise the Lord even unto death." It would seem that we were present in Rome's Colosseum watching the virgin consummate her martyrdom.

The *Gradual* and *Offertory* chants and the Gospel between them (on the wise virgins) feature the "bride theme." The Church's bridal song, Psalm 44, tells the glories of Christ the Bridegroom and the Church His Bride; today's virgin-saint is one of the maidens in the royal retinue. The picture is embellished by the *Gospel*; here she becomes one of the five wise virgins who, having filled their lamps with the oil of virginal love, wait till the Bridegroom comes. He did come at her death; and at Mass we go to meet Him with lamps well filled under our virgin's leadership. At the *Offertory* we are the virgins who with today's saint (*post eam* . . . after her) are presented and offered (the old texts do not have *afferentur* but *offerentur*, hence a true offertory). With the *Communion* antiphon the liturgy again takes us to the scene of the martyrdom; again the saint speaks, giving testimony to God and professing her fidelity. In union with her and supported by Eucharistic strength, we try to make the same profession.

2. Mass *Me exspectaverunt*

The second formulary for a virgin-martyr differs from the first by giving greater prominence to the theme of martyrdom. In the *Introit* the day's martyr stands before us and we hear her pray: "The wicked waited for me . . . but I kept Your precepts in my heart." The *Lesson* is the saint's thanksgiving prayer upon triumphing over the ordeal: "O Lord, my God, You have exalted me to a dwelling high above the earth. I prayed that death should pass me by. I begged the Lord not to abandon me in my day of agony . . . I will praise Your Name forever . . . for You have snatched me from destruction."

In the *Gradual* the saint is compared to the city of Jerusalem besieged by enemies but still invincible: "The rush of the river means nought but joy to the city of God; for the Most High has sanctified His tabernacle." God who is in her soul will not permit her to waver. The "rush of the river" is her martyrdom, stirred up by hell. In the *Gospel* we follow the virgin as she seeks and finds the "hidden treasure" and the "pearl of great price." See, in exchange she gives all that earth can offer, even life itself. The bride-motif rings through the *Offertory*; we watch the holy virgin as she advances toward her Spouse in shining splendor (the altar is Christ; to it the faithful go with their offertory gifts). The *Communion* antiphon affords the martyr a final opportunity to give witness to Christ; under her guidance and strengthened by the Eucharist, we too proclaim: "I hate all wicked ways."

3. Mass *Dilexisti*

No other formulary in the Common betrays a prayer structure that so well develops a single theme. It is a genuine "bridal Mass." The Church, as the Lord's stainless Bride, appears in the person of the holy virgin whose feast we celebrate, who today stands in our midst in the *mysterium*. Moreover, she is a model for us, and more than a model — we enter into wondrous union with her, we become mystically one with her. This rapport may be detected in the various texts of today's Mass. The Gospel etches it in fine relief as it indicates the mystery; the saint (and we with her) are the virgin-spouses who during the night of this life remain ready with brightly burning lamps to meet the Bridegroom whenever He should come to the eternal wedding. The final reality takes place at the parousia (and at our death); but today at Mass it takes place by anticipation. Such are the implications of the text.

The route to church today is marked by a wedding procession; the saint leads, the faithful follow. Picture the festal march: the bishop, fully vested, proceeds to the altar; meanwhile Psalm 44, the Church's bridal song, is sung. Christ is the royal Bridegroom; the Church, the holy Virgin, myself, the royal bride. Yes, regard yourself as Christ's bride.

The *Epistle* continues the thought; we are again spoken of as brides of Christ. The divine Bridegroom is jealous of His bride. He will share His beloved treasure with no one; as an inviolate virgin must she be presented to her divine Spouse. Verses from Psalm 44 are to be found in all the chanted portions of the formulary. As the deacon in festal vestments proceeds with the Gospel book (i.e., Christ) to the ambo, we are again witnessing a wedding procession. There follows the *Gospel* with the beautiful parable of the five wise virgins (the five foolish ones do not form a part of the liturgical picture). It is we who are the virgins (the acolytes, holding lights while the Gospel is read, help us visualize this).

During the Sacrifice proper the Gospel becomes a reality; for at the *Offertory* procession we, virgin-brides, approach Christ (the altar is Christ). Our offertory gifts are our oil-filled lamps, gifts to the Spouse. The bridal song is meanwhile chanted, occasioning new slants upon the familiar words; about the Queen richly appurtenanced we, the virgin-brides, are standing. At the consecration the Spouse makes His appearance; and at the Banquet we approach Him, *obviam Christo Domino* — Behold, the Bridegroom cometh! Open your hearts to Him! (Note the new turn in meaning the text receives after the consecration.) For the fourth time the bridal song is sung during the *Communion* procession.

4. Mass *Vultum tuum*

There is no essential difference between this formulary and the preceding ones. Here too the Church's bridal song, Psalm 44, is thematic. In the *Epistle* St. Paul shows the value of virginity in relation to the Second Advent: "The time is short." It will be virgins who will find it easier to give themselves wholly to the Lord. The *Gospel* may be either that of the wise virgins or the pearl of great price.

F.   THE COMMON OF HOLY WOMEN

Holy women, too, viz., those who embraced the state of matrimony, particularly holy widows, have a special Common with two formularies, one for martyrs, another for non-martyrs.

1. Mass *Me exspectaverunt*

There is little difference between this formulary and those for virgin-martyrs; practically no text is wholly proper to it. The martyr leads us to the altar; we hear her pray: "The wicked have waited for me in order to destroy me . . . in my heart I have kept Your precepts." The *Lesson* is a beautiful prayer of gratitude sung by the martyr after her triumph over suffering: "I will glorify You, O Lord, O King . . . for You were my helper and protector. You preserved my body from destruction . . . from those who roared, ready to devour . . . from annihilation by the flames that surrounded me . . . therefore my soul will praise the Lord even unto death." Hearing these words we feel ourselves witnesses to the martyrdom.

The two following chants (*Grad.* and *Off.*) are culled from the Church's bridal song. In both we see the saint in the full attire of a bride worthy of God. The *Gospel* shows us how the martyr sought after and found the "hidden treasure," the "pearl of great price," i.e., the kingdom of God. To acquire this heavenly treasure she divested herself of all earthly belongings, including life itself. Thus she paid the supreme price for it. In the *Communion* antiphon the saint again speaks. She tells how her enemies pursued her, while she feared God alone. Yes, she rejoiced over the kingdom of God as though she had found a great treasure. We too must feel these sentiments. The Eucharist gives us strength against the enemies of salvation; for us it is the one great treasure.

2. Mass *Cognovi*

This formulary for holy women expresses well two aspects of woman's nature, maidenly fervor and motherly foresight; virginal love for Christ and courageous resolve; regard for material needs, yet ever rising above earthly attachments; carefree like Mary, yet careful about many things like Martha. The Mass begins, as is frequently the case, with a monolog by the day's saint. She glances back over her life; God had visited upon her many a sorrow, many a humiliation (widowhood, lack of appreciation for many sacrifices); now she acknowledges that all this was to her good and asks for an unbloody martyrdom.

The two Readings seem to stand in opposition to each other. In the *Lesson* an ideal woman and wife is described, one who is wholly occupied with her manifold duties, one who provides for her husband, children, servants, and who has a kindly heart for the poor — a woman with both feet on the ground. The two parables of the *Gospel* (the hidden treasure and the pearl) show the woman whose heart is with Christ, the woman who surrenders all earthly things for the precious pearl of God's kingdom. It is our saint who understands how to combine harmoniously these seemingly contrary ideals, action and contemplation. The Lesson could serve as a good mirror for any woman. "A virtuous woman, where may she be found?" We have found her in today's saint. "Favor is deceitful, and beauty is vain; the woman who fears the Lord, she shall be praised."

The Gospel points out the reason for her greatness and her

spiritual beauty; it is the "hidden treasure," i.e., her love for Christ. To us also does the Eucharist give direction and aid, both to find the treasure and zealously to perform our round of duties. The Eucharist keeps the fire of love for Christ aglow and it strengthens us to carry this fire abroad in the world. The Church's wedding hymn (Ps. 44) forms part of the three following chants; its theme, as we know, is the espousal of Christ to the Church. Does not our saint typify the Church, who is both Mother and Virgin? Do not the two Lessons reveal the nature of our Mother? Children should reflect their Mother's features.

THE DEDICATION OF A CHURCH

Annually the Church celebrates in a solemn manner the day commemorating the dedication of her churches in order to recall to the minds of the faithful the high dignity and sanctity and also the deep symbolism of the material edifice. She celebrates the dedication of the parish church, the cathedral church, and the four principal churches of Rome, the mother churches, we may call them, of Christendom.

Every parish church, then, celebrates two feastdays of its own each year, a namesday feast (patron saint) and a baptism feast (dedication). These two days should again be solemnized, using the means and inspiration provided in the liturgy. The house of God, the parish church, is dear to Christians for many reasons:

a) It is *the* house of prayer and *the* place of sacrifice for the whole congregation. Here the Triune God has set up His tent of grace and blessing. The altar signifies Christ and is to be considered the holiest spot in the structure. During the Sacrifice of Mass Christ personally enters this house and through His visitation our "salvation is again effected."

b) The parish church is the visible symbol of God's kingdom upon earth. Here Mother Church holds her official services; here her heart beast fastest for her Bridegroom Christ, as also for her children. The Church of Christ stands upon the foundation stones of the twelve apostles; of this fact the twelve crosses on the walls (the twelve places where the walls were anointed) are reminders. The parish priest should know the location of these holy crosses and have them marked by burning candles on the anniversary of the day of the dedication. The dignity and beauty of the material edifice should be a sign of the excellence and supreme importance of holy Mother Church.

c) The parish church is for us the gate of heaven, a fore-taste of heaven, a preview of our heavenly home. The liturgy performed in the parish church continues the symbolism — much of its drama has its setting in heaven. The same holds true of the Office of Dedication, of many Masses during the ecclesiastical year, especially of the last Sundays after Pentecost. The entrance procession of priest and ministers to the altar is a figure of our journey heavenward (*Intr.* 18th, 23rd, 24th Sundays).

d) Lastly, the parish church symbolizes the individual Christian. This comparison was frequently used by the early Church Fathers to teach the sanctity of Christian life: "Do you not know that your body is the temple of the Holy Spirit, who lives in you?" Such symbolism is given beautiful expression in the dedication ceremonies of a church, for these rites in a very tangible way are modeled after the liturgy of baptism (exorcism, water specially consecrated, baptismal robes) and confirmation (anointing, invocation of the Holy Spirit, Mass with distribution of holy Communion). Here we find the reason for the imposition of a name and the celebration of the saint's day (titular); for if individual Christians celebrate their patronal feast, why not the parish body?

For understanding the Mass of Dedication two things must be kept in mind: (1) the liturgy identifies the anniversary and the actual day of consecration; (2) the material edifice as such represents the bride of Christ. Whenever we commemorate the consecration of a church, it is actually a feast *par excellence* of the Church that we are observing. The Dedication Mass is one of gratitude for all the favors and blessings that have come to us through the instrumentality of the Church. The text also stresses the rich symbolism of the house of God. Considered in itself, the edifice is most worthy of honor (*Grad.*) because (1) it has become the residence of God; and God has chosen it as the place for the distribution of His special graces (*Intr.*), as the place of sacrifice by the High Priest Jesus Christ (*Gosp.* and *Coll.*), and as the divinely appointed place of prayer (*Coll., Allel., Comm.*); (2) it represents the Catholic Church upon earth, Christ's immaculate Bride; (3) it is a symbol of the soul sanctified through baptism and the Eucharist (*Postc.*).

We enter the sacred edifice remembering that it has been solemnly consecrated by the bishop. Two seemingly contrary emotions well up within us, fear and joy. "How awe-inspiring is this place!" If we but realized that God had made this building the abode of His august presence! "Take off your shoes, for the place upon which you stand is holy ground," echoes in our ears, as from the burning bush. Psalm 83 in its entirety is most appropriate: "How lovely is Thy tabernacle, O Lord of hosts." What the temple was to the Jews, that and far more the church must be to us Christians (*Intr.*). Mother Church knows that here is the place for official, liturgical prayer; here God has promised to answer our petitions (*Coll., Comm.*).

Presently another picture unfolds before our eyes; we see Christ's bride magnificently adorned — the New Jerusalem — descending from heaven (*Epist.*). Do not overlook the *mysterium* identity between the earthly and the heavenly. "*Today* has salvation come to this house!" This *today* must be taken literally. Not only on the occasion when the bishop first consecrated the church, *today* at the holy Sacrifice the Lord enters His tabernacle on earth, and we, poor publicans, are privileged to receive Him as guest. Remember that in spirit the Church repeats the day of consecration; that day's graces are reactivated today through the Mass mystery.

The awesome revelation of the Epistle echoes in the *Gradual*: This place is truly an unutterable mystery! The heart of Mother Church beats here! It is a temple peopled with choirs of angels! With them the faithful vie in the praise of the Lord their God (*Sanctus*).

With the *Alleluia* antiphon we turn and imagine the approach of Christ our King. Him we worship, Him we praise. The *Gospel* carries us back near the tax-gatherer's sycamore tree. With such joy, with such humility, with such a spirit of sacrifice as Zachaeus had, we too want to gaze upon the Lord. "See, half of all my goods do I give to the poor." In a like spirit let us come to the *Offertory*, and its antiphon will put our oblation into words. It is a prayer that David composed when he dedicated to God the funds and the materials he had gathered for the construction of the temple.

The *Secret* implies a "perfect oblation of body and soul." In the holy Sacrifice Christ comes into this building, the parish church, into this temple which is my soul, and says: "This day is salvation come to this house." In the *Communion* antiphon the Lord promises to answer all petitions made in "His house," while Mother Church straightway fulfills that promise and gives us the holy Eucharist as the guarantee of every needed gift and grace. The *Postcommunion* regards the material structure as a symbol of the spiritual edifice constructed from "living and predestined stones"; we petition that the excellence of the visible edifice may be signal of an ever-increasing invisible magnificence.

TE DEUM LAUDAMUS!